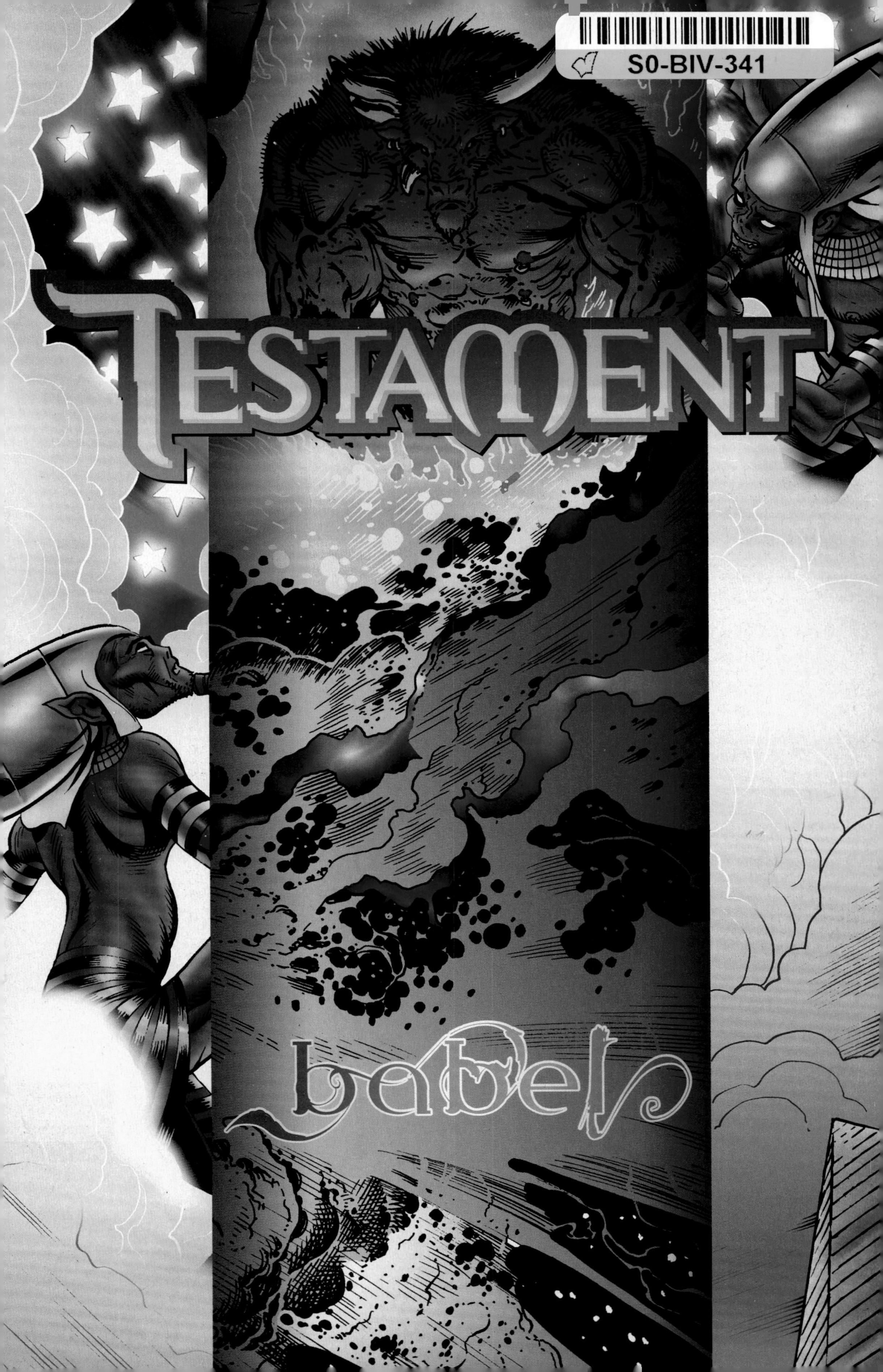
TESTAMENT
babel

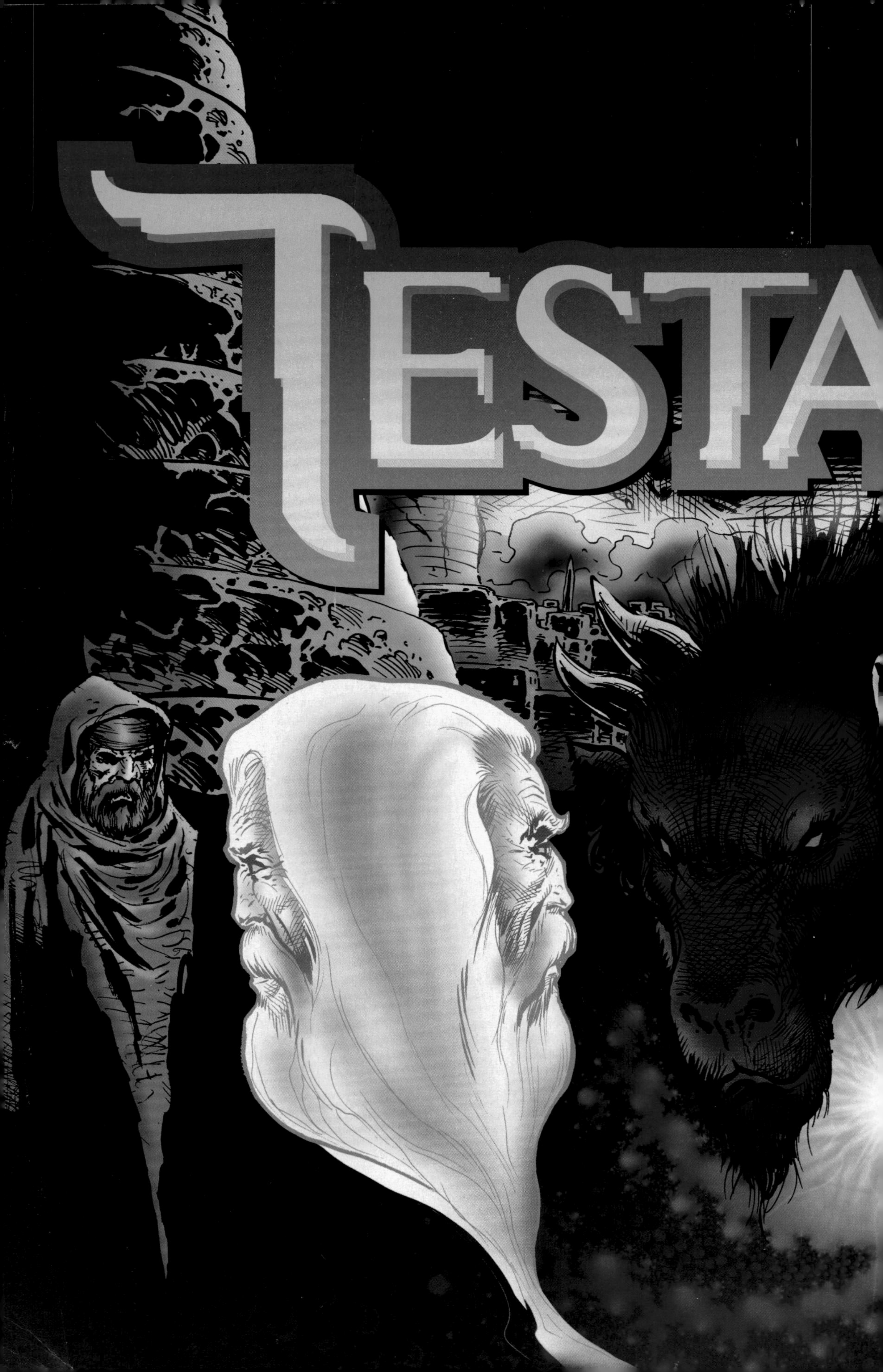
TESTA

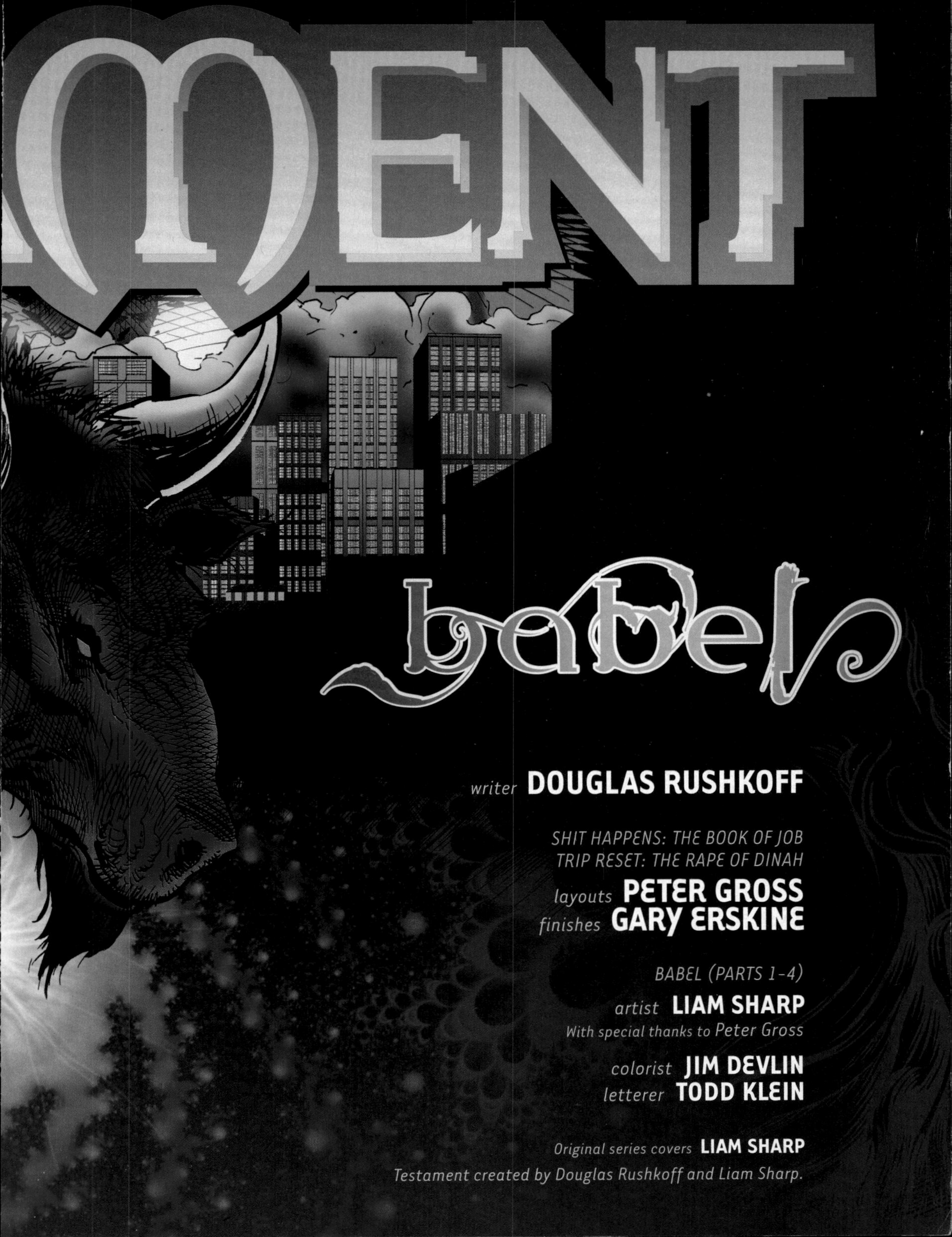
MENT

babel

writer **DOUGLAS RUSHKOFF**

SHIT HAPPENS: THE BOOK OF JOB
TRIP RESET: THE RAPE OF DINAH

layouts **PETER GROSS**
finishes **GARY ERSKINE**

BABEL (PARTS 1-4)

artist **LIAM SHARP**
With special thanks to Peter Gross

colorist **JIM DEVLIN**
letterer **TODD KLEIN**

Original series covers **LIAM SHARP**
Testament created by Douglas Rushkoff and Liam Sharp.

Karen Berger *Senior VP-Executive Editor* • **Jonathan Vankin** *Editor-original series*
Pornsak Pichetshote *Associate Editor-original series* • **Bob Harras** *Editor-collected edition*
Robbin Brosterman *Senior Art Director* • **Paul Levitz** *President & Publisher*
Georg Brewer *VP-Design & DC Direct Creative* • **Richard Bruning** *Senior VP-Creative Director*
Patrick Caldon *Executive VP-Finance & Operations* • **Chris Caramalis** *VP-Finance*
John Cunningham *VP-Marketing* • **Terri Cunningham** *VP-Managing Editor* • **Alison Gill** *VP-Manufacturing*
David Hyde *VP-Publicity* • **Hank Kanalz** *VP-General Manager, WildStorm* • **Jim Lee** *Editorial Director-WildStorm*
Paula Lowitt *Senior VP-Business & Legal Affairs* • **MaryEllen McLaughlin** *VP-Advertising & Custom Publishing*
John Nee *Senior VP-Business Development* • **Gregory Noveck** *Senior VP-Creative Affairs*
Sue Pohja *VP-Book Trade Sales* • **Steve Rotterdam** *Senior VP-Sales & Marketing*
Cheryl Rubin *Senior VP-Brand Management* • **Jeff Trojan** *VP-Business Development, DC Direct*
Bob Wayne *VP-Sales*

Cover illustration by Liam Sharp
Logo and publication design by Brainchild Studios/NYC

TESTAMENT: BABEL

Published by DC Comics. Cover, afterword and compilation copyright © 2007 DC Comics. All Rights Reserved.

Originally published in single magazine form as TESTAMENT 11-16. Copyright © 2006, 2007 Douglas Rushkoff and Liam Sharp. All Rights Reserved. All characters, their distinctive likenesses and related elements featured in this publication are trademarks of Douglas Rushkoff and Liam Sharp. The stories, characters and incidents featured in this publication are entirely fictional. DC Comics does not read or accept unsolicited submissions of ideas, stories or artwork.

DC Comics, 1700 Broadway, New York, NY 10019
A Warner Bros. Entertainment Company.
Printed in Canada. First Printing.
ISBN: 1-4012-1496-7
ISBN 13: 978-1-4012-1496-8

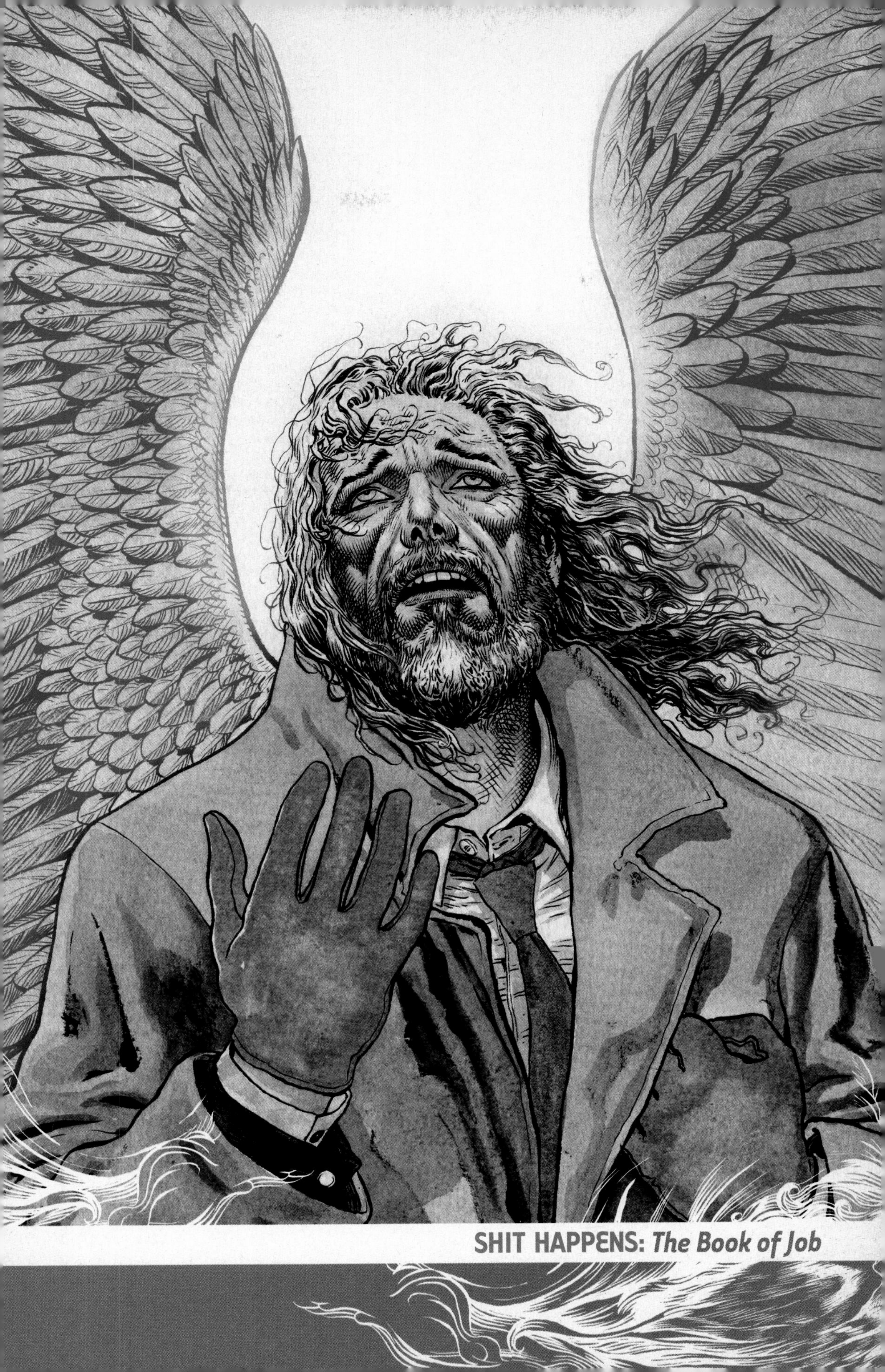

SHIT HAPPENS: *The Book of Job*

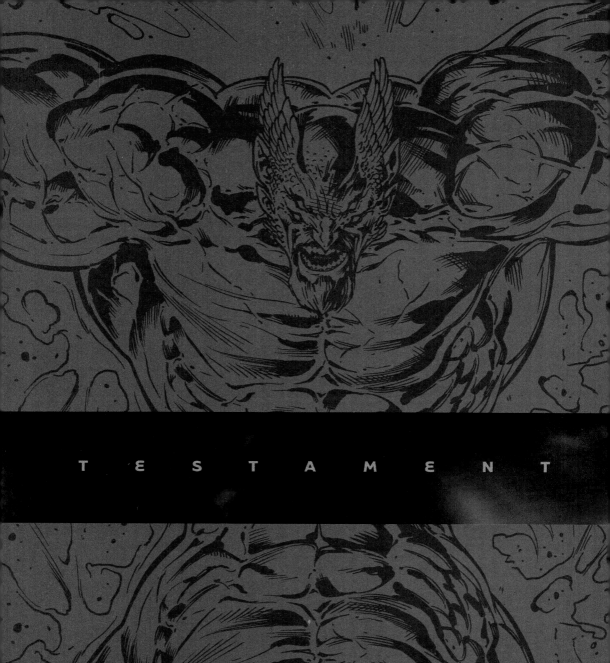

TESTAMENT

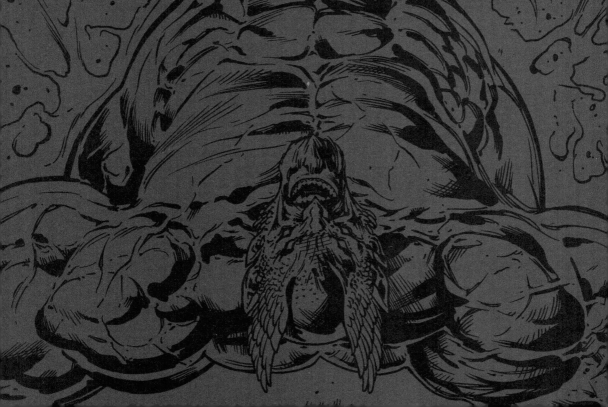

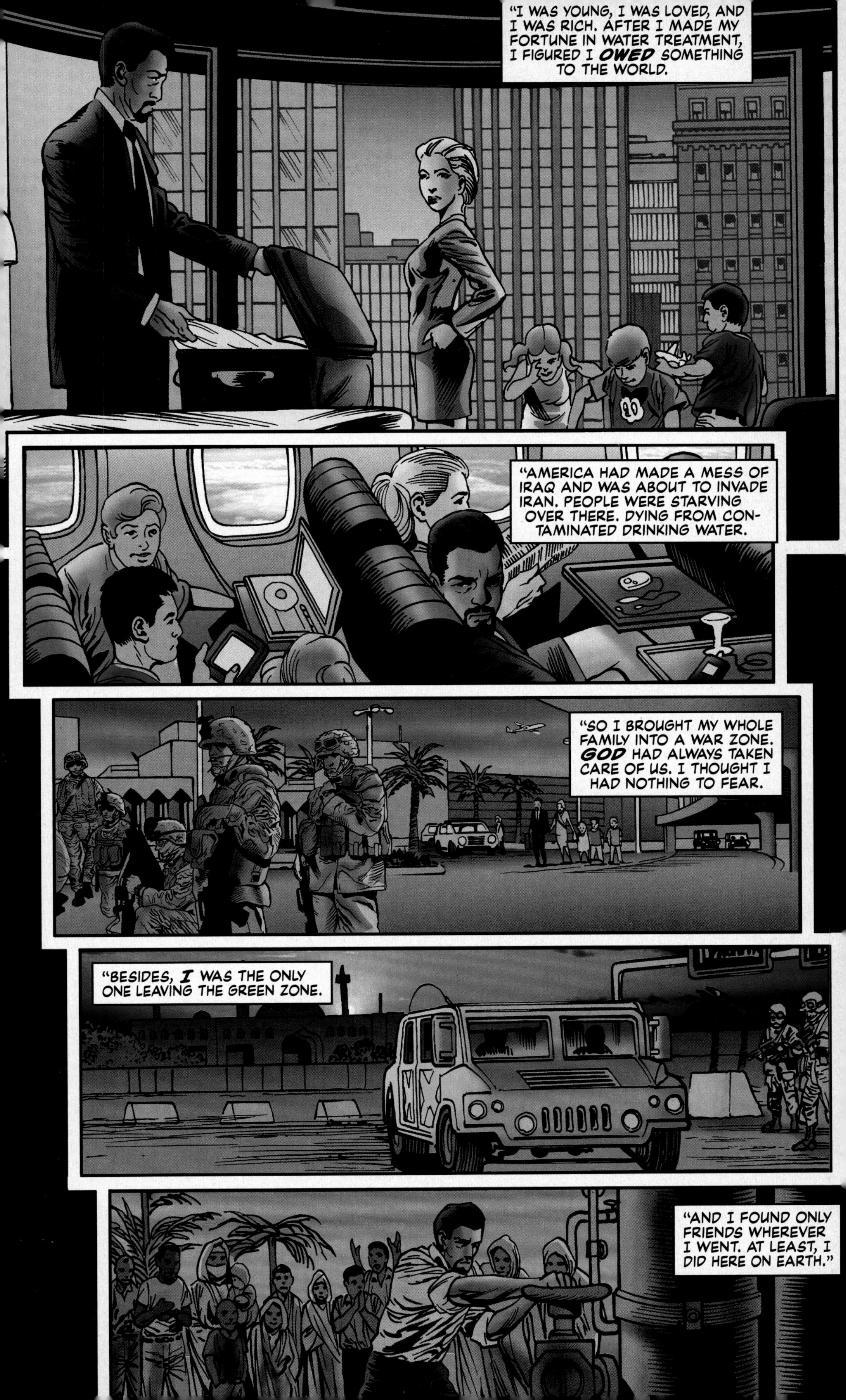
"I WAS YOUNG, I WAS LOVED, AND I WAS RICH. AFTER I MADE MY FORTUNE IN WATER TREATMENT, I FIGURED I OWED SOMETHING TO THE WORLD.
"AMERICA HAD MADE A MESS OF IRAQ AND WAS ABOUT TO INVADE IRAN. PEOPLE WERE STARVING OVER THERE. DYING FROM CONTAMINATED DRINKING WATER.
"SO I BROUGHT MY WHOLE FAMILY INTO A WAR ZONE. GOD HAD ALWAYS TAKEN CARE OF US. I THOUGHT I HAD NOTHING TO FEAR.
"BESIDES, I WAS THE ONLY ONE LEAVING THE GREEN ZONE.
"AND I FOUND ONLY FRIENDS WHEREVER I WENT. AT LEAST, I DID HERE ON EARTH."

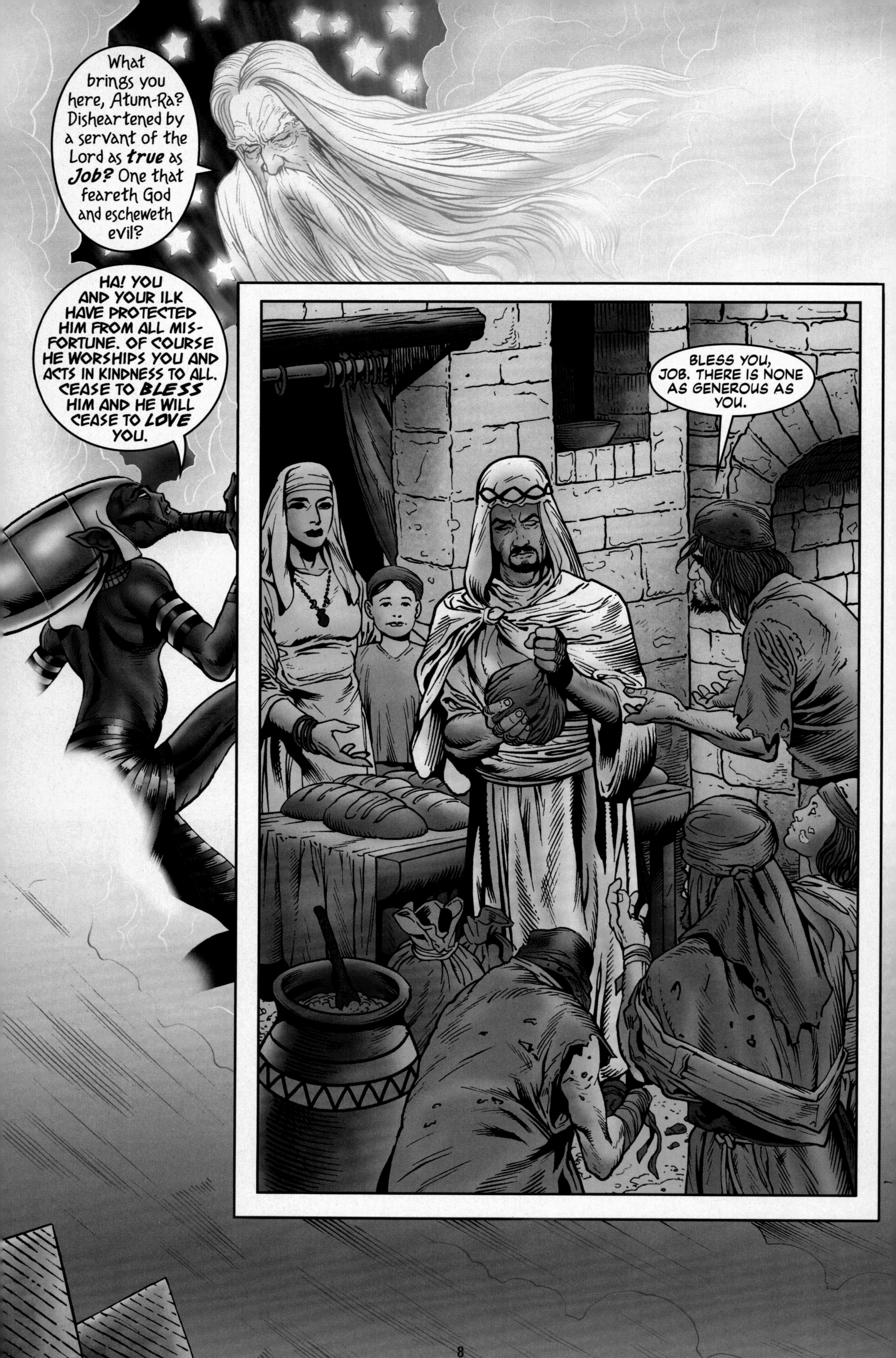
What brings you here, Atum-Ra? Disheartened by a servant of the Lord as *true* as *Job?* One that feareth God and escheweth evil?
HA! YOU AND YOUR ILK HAVE PROTECTED HIM FROM ALL MIS-FORTUNE. OF COURSE HE WORSHIPS YOU AND ACTS IN KINDNESS TO ALL. CEASE TO *BLESS* HIM AND HE WILL CEASE TO *LOVE* YOU.
BLESS YOU, JOB. THERE IS NONE AS GENEROUS AS YOU.

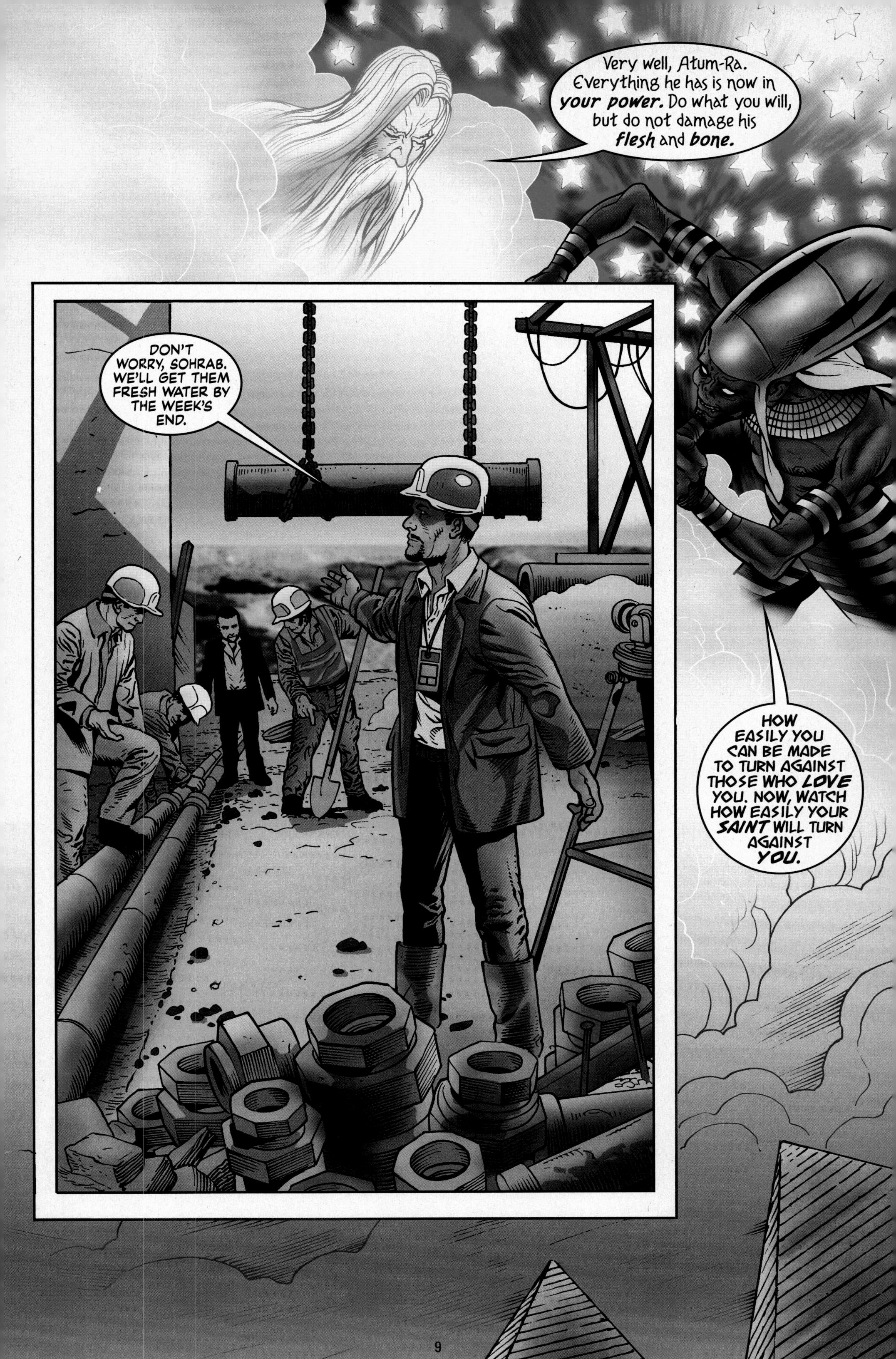

Very well, Atum-Ra. Everything he has is now in your power. Do what you will, but do not damage his flesh and bone.
DON'T WORRY, SOHRAB. WE'LL GET THEM FRESH WATER BY THE WEEK'S END.
HOW EASILY YOU CAN BE MADE TO TURN AGAINST THOSE WHO LOVE YOU. NOW, WATCH HOW EASILY YOUR SAINT WILL TURN AGAINST YOU.

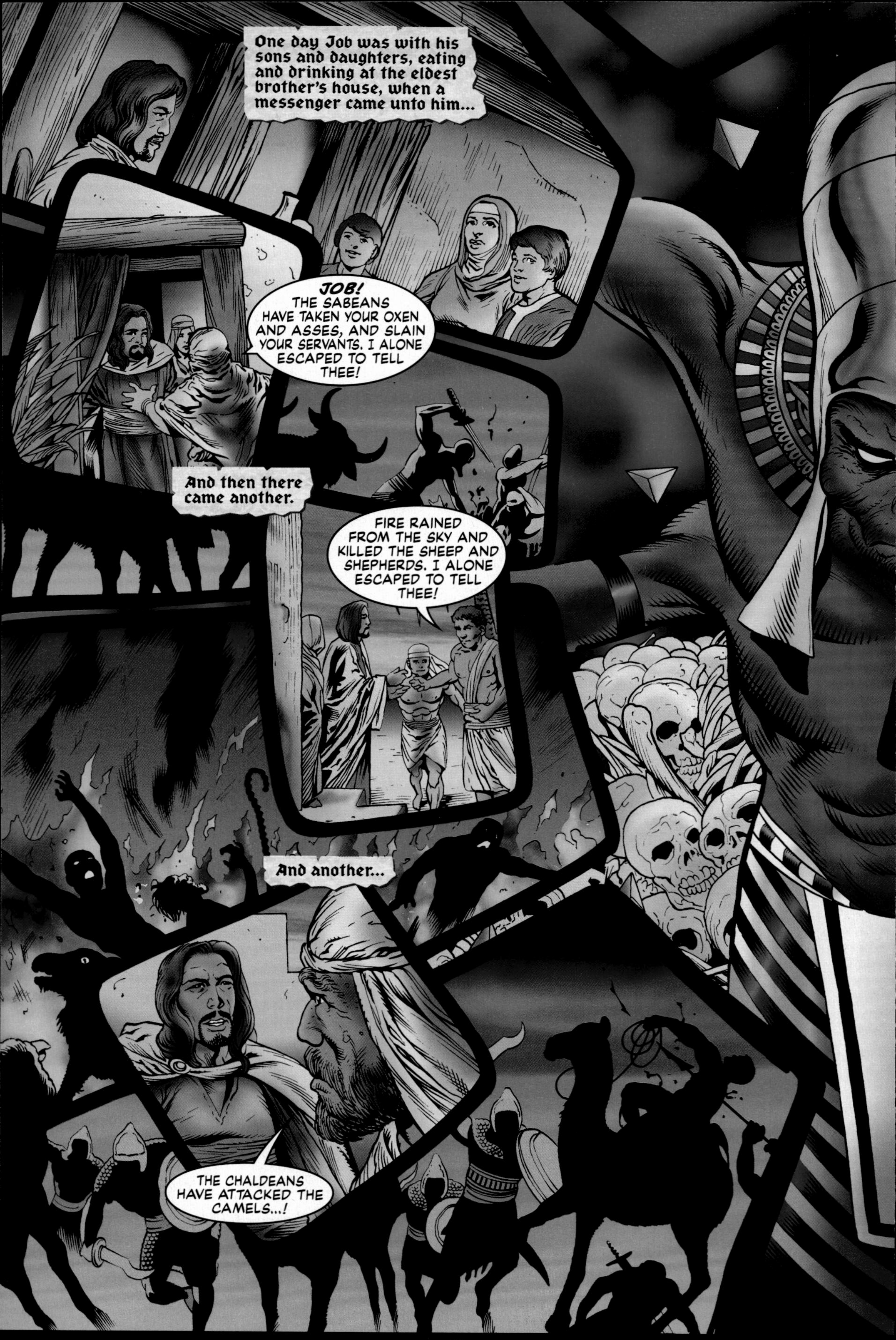

One day Job was with his sons and daughters, eating and drinking at the eldest brother's house, when a messenger came unto him...
JOB! THE SABEANS HAVE TAKEN YOUR OXEN AND ASSES, AND SLAIN YOUR SERVANTS. I ALONE ESCAPED TO TELL THEE!
And then there came another.
FIRE RAINED FROM THE SKY AND KILLED THE SHEEP AND SHEPHERDS. I ALONE ESCAPED TO TELL THEE!
And another...
THE CHALDEANS HAVE ATTACKED THE CAMELS...!

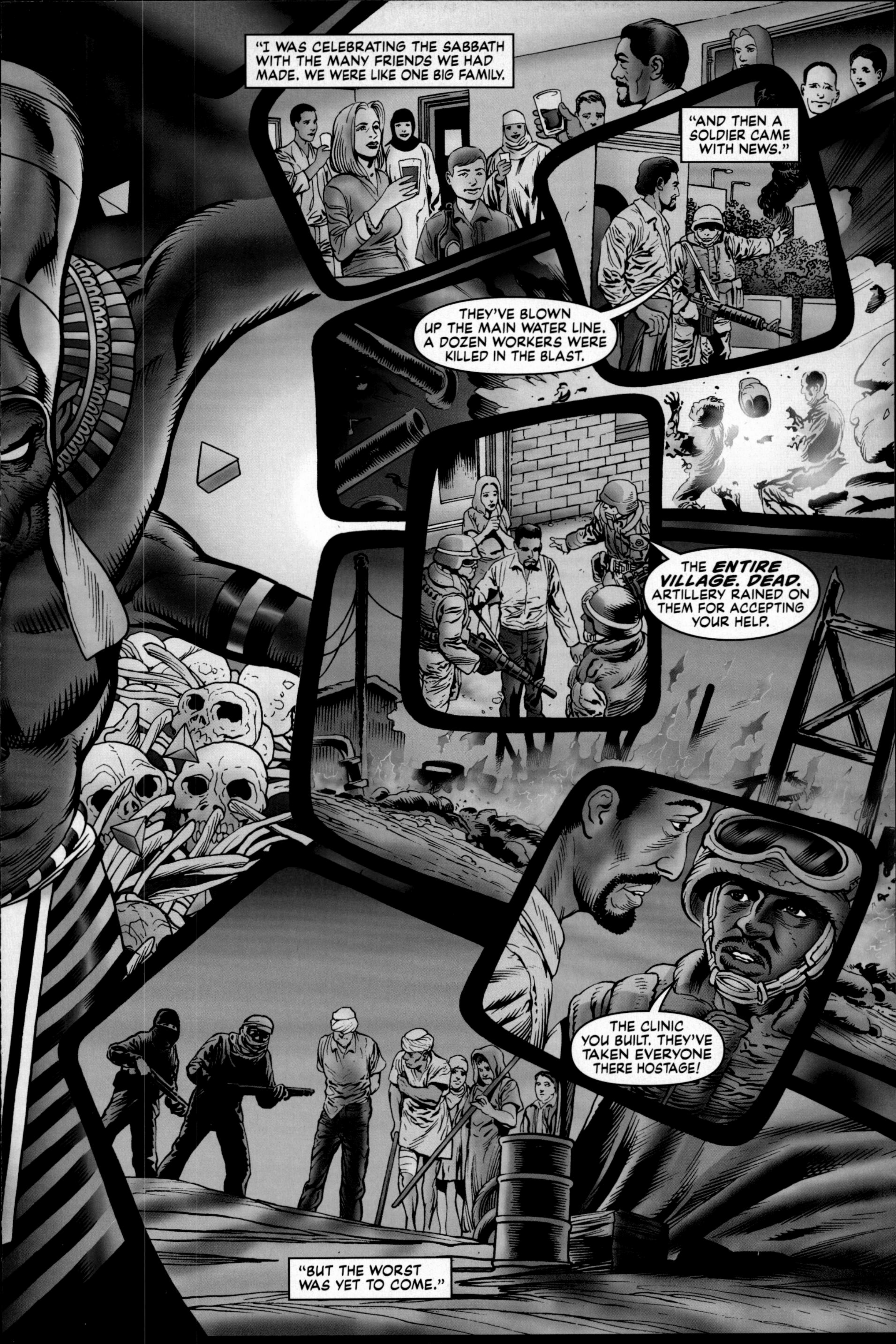
"I WAS CELEBRATING THE SABBATH WITH THE MANY FRIENDS WE HAD MADE. WE WERE LIKE ONE BIG FAMILY.
"AND THEN A SOLDIER CAME WITH NEWS."
THEY'VE BLOWN UP THE MAIN WATER LINE. A DOZEN WORKERS WERE KILLED IN THE BLAST.
THE ENTIRE VILLAGE. DEAD. ARTILLERY RAINED ON THEM FOR ACCEPTING YOUR HELP.
THE CLINIC YOU BUILT. THEY'VE TAKEN EVERYONE THERE HOSTAGE!
"BUT THE WORST WAS YET TO COME."

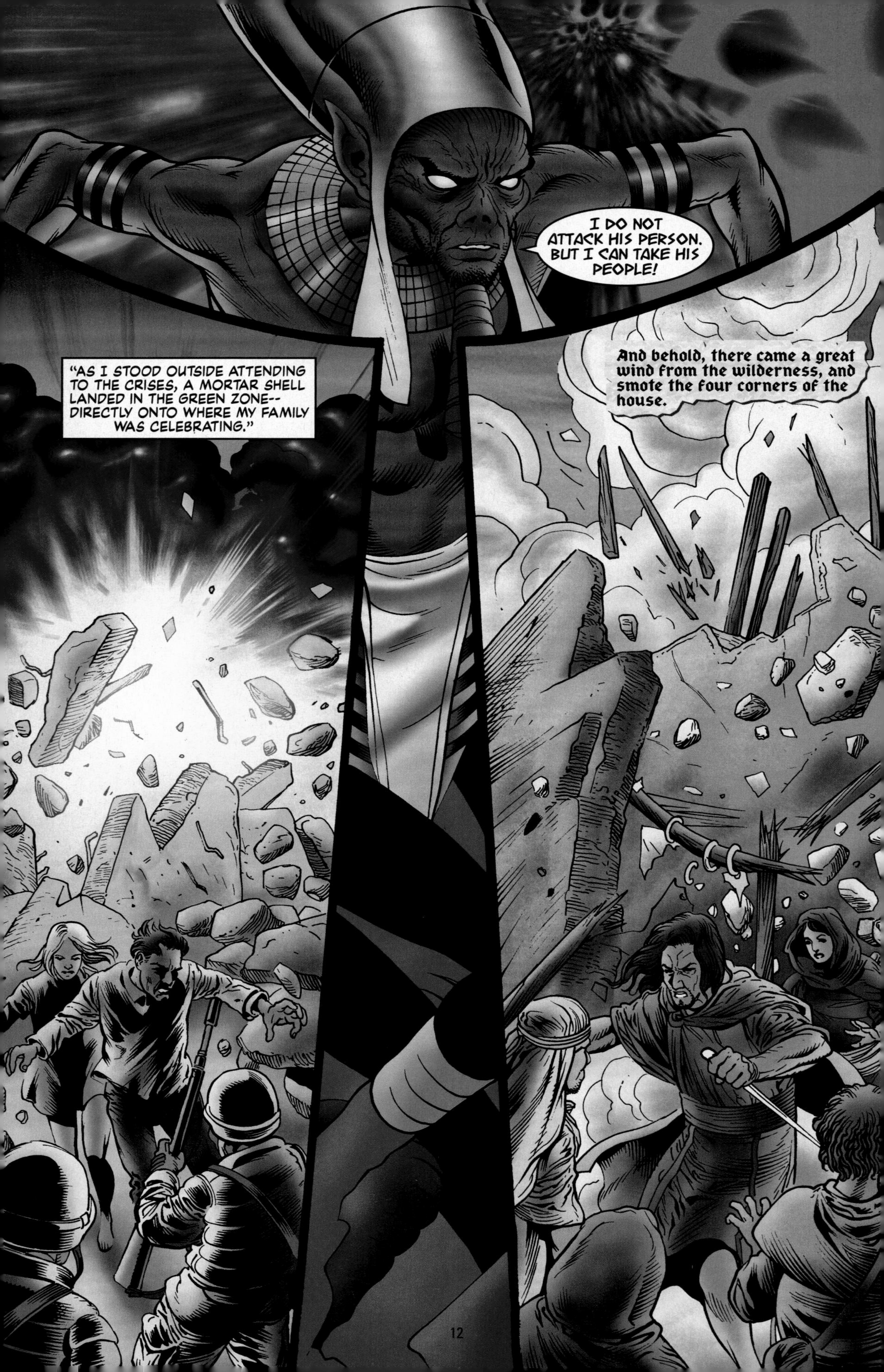
I DO NOT ATTACK HIS PERSON. BUT I CAN TAKE HIS PEOPLE!
"AS I STOOD OUTSIDE ATTENDING TO THE CRISES, A MORTAR SHELL LANDED IN THE GREEN ZONE-- DIRECTLY ONTO WHERE MY FAMILY WAS CELEBRATING."
And behold, there came a great wind from the wilderness, and smote the four corners of the house.

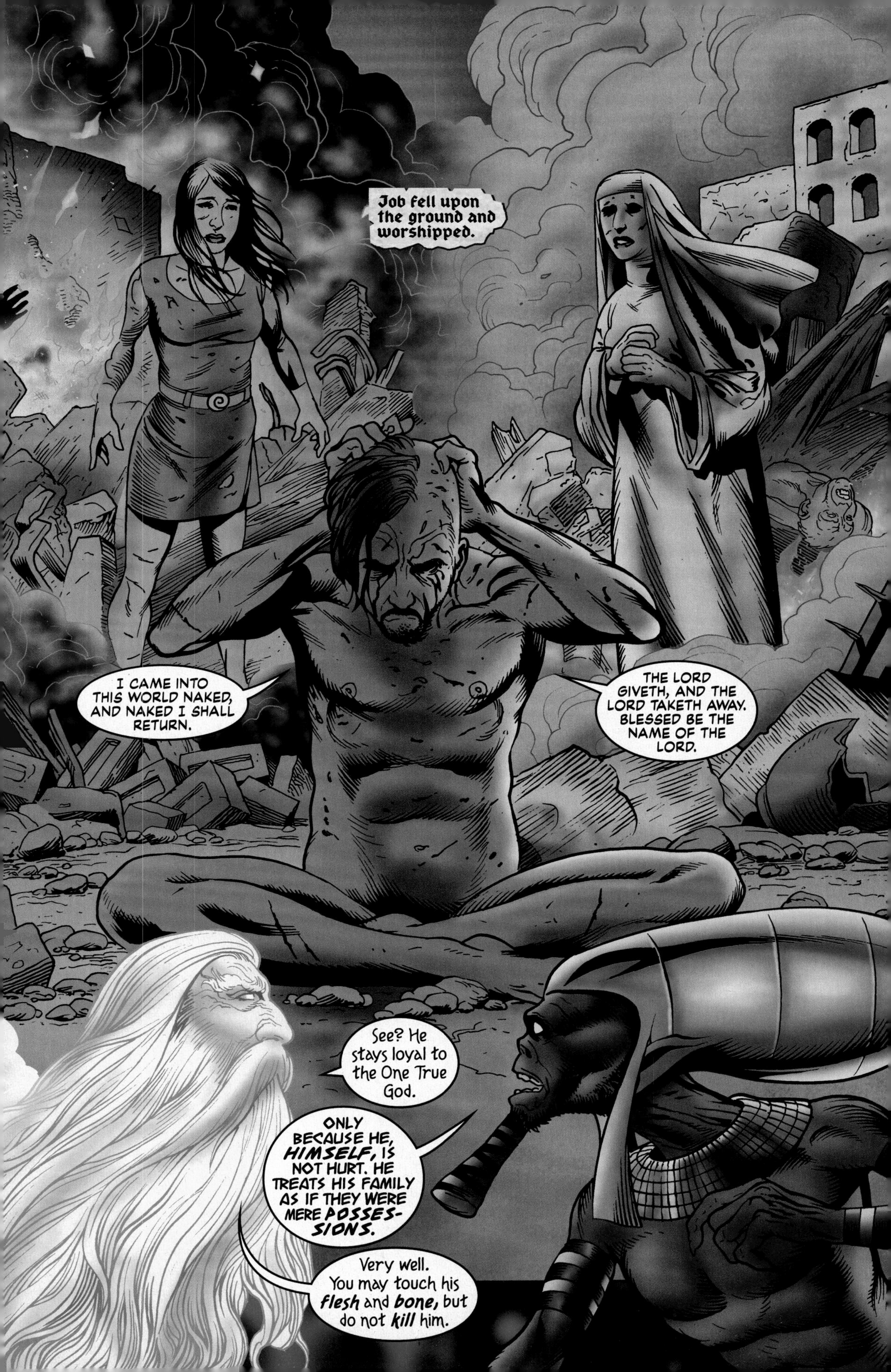
Job fell upon the ground and worshipped.
I CAME INTO THIS WORLD NAKED, AND NAKED I SHALL RETURN.
THE LORD GIVETH, AND THE LORD TAKETH AWAY. BLESSED BE THE NAME OF THE LORD.
See? He stays loyal to the One True God.
ONLY BECAUSE HE, HIMSELF, IS NOT HURT. HE TREATS HIS FAMILY AS IF THEY WERE MERE POSSES-SIONS.
Very well. You may touch his flesh and bone, but do not kill him.

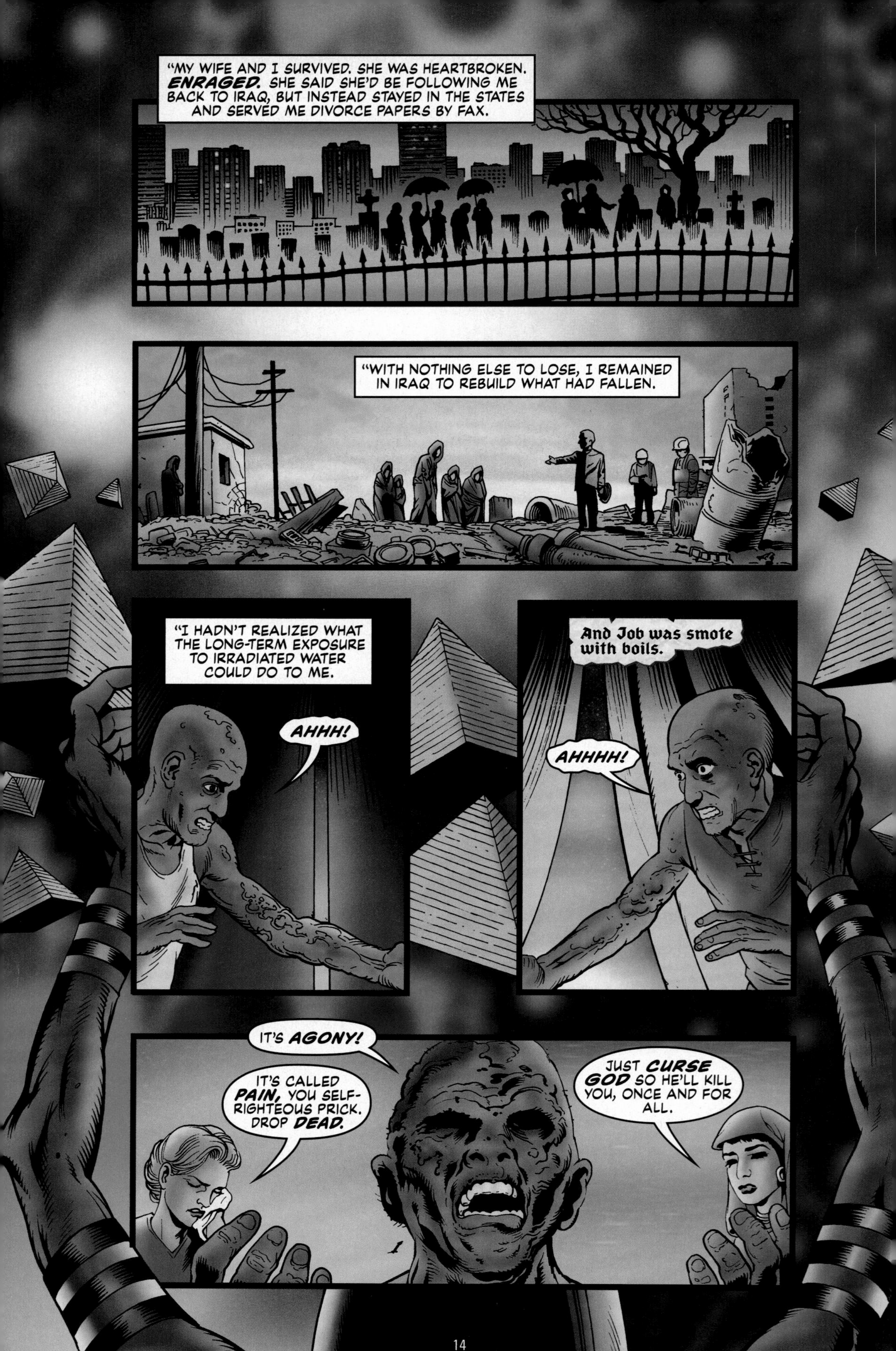
"MY WIFE AND I SURVIVED. SHE WAS HEARTBROKEN. ENRAGED. SHE SAID SHE'D BE FOLLOWING ME BACK TO IRAQ, BUT INSTEAD STAYED IN THE STATES AND SERVED ME DIVORCE PAPERS BY FAX.
"WITH NOTHING ELSE TO LOSE, I REMAINED IN IRAQ TO REBUILD WHAT HAD FALLEN.
"I HADN'T REALIZED WHAT THE LONG-TERM EXPOSURE TO IRRADIATED WATER COULD DO TO ME.
AHHH!
And Job was smote with boils.
AHHHH!
IT'S AGONY!
IT'S CALLED PAIN, YOU SELF-RIGHTEOUS PRICK. DROP DEAD.
JUST CURSE GOD SO HE'LL KILL YOU, ONCE AND FOR ALL.

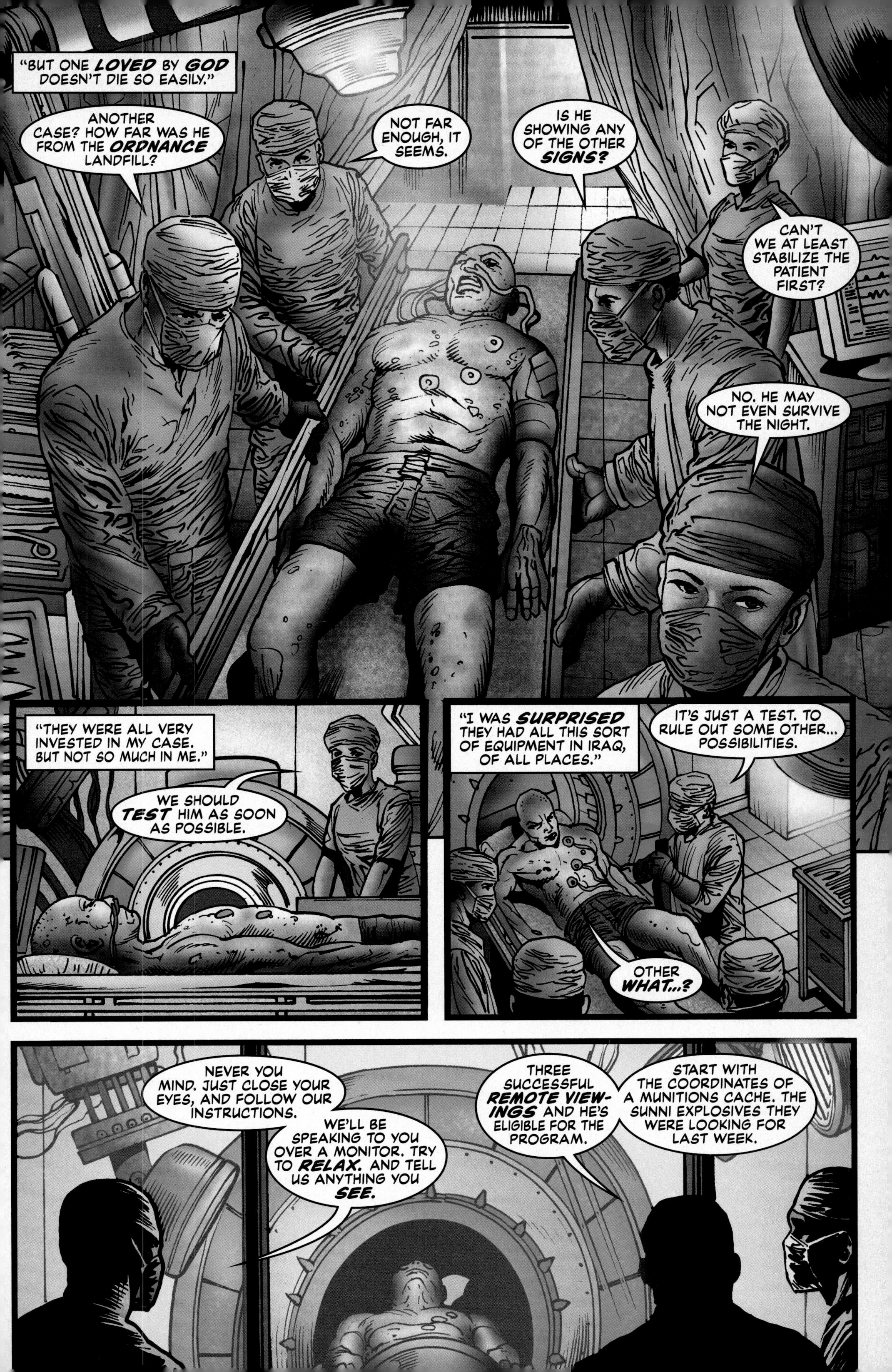
"BUT ONE LOVED BY GOD DOESN'T DIE SO EASILY."
ANOTHER CASE? HOW FAR WAS HE FROM THE ORDNANCE LANDFILL?
NOT FAR ENOUGH, IT SEEMS.
IS HE SHOWING ANY OF THE OTHER SIGNS?
CAN'T WE AT LEAST STABILIZE THE PATIENT FIRST?
NO. HE MAY NOT EVEN SURVIVE THE NIGHT.
"THEY WERE ALL VERY INVESTED IN MY CASE. BUT NOT SO MUCH IN ME."
WE SHOULD TEST HIM AS SOON AS POSSIBLE.
"I WAS SURPRISED THEY HAD ALL THIS SORT OF EQUIPMENT IN IRAQ, OF ALL PLACES."
IT'S JUST A TEST. TO RULE OUT SOME OTHER... POSSIBILITIES.
OTHER WHAT...?
NEVER YOU MIND. JUST CLOSE YOUR EYES, AND FOLLOW OUR INSTRUCTIONS.
WE'LL BE SPEAKING TO YOU OVER A MONITOR. TRY TO RELAX. AND TELL US ANYTHING YOU SEE.
THREE SUCCESSFUL REMOTE VIEWINGS AND HE'S ELIGIBLE FOR THE PROGRAM.
START WITH THE COORDINATES OF A MUNITIONS CACHE. THE SUNNI EXPLOSIVES THEY WERE LOOKING FOR LAST WEEK.

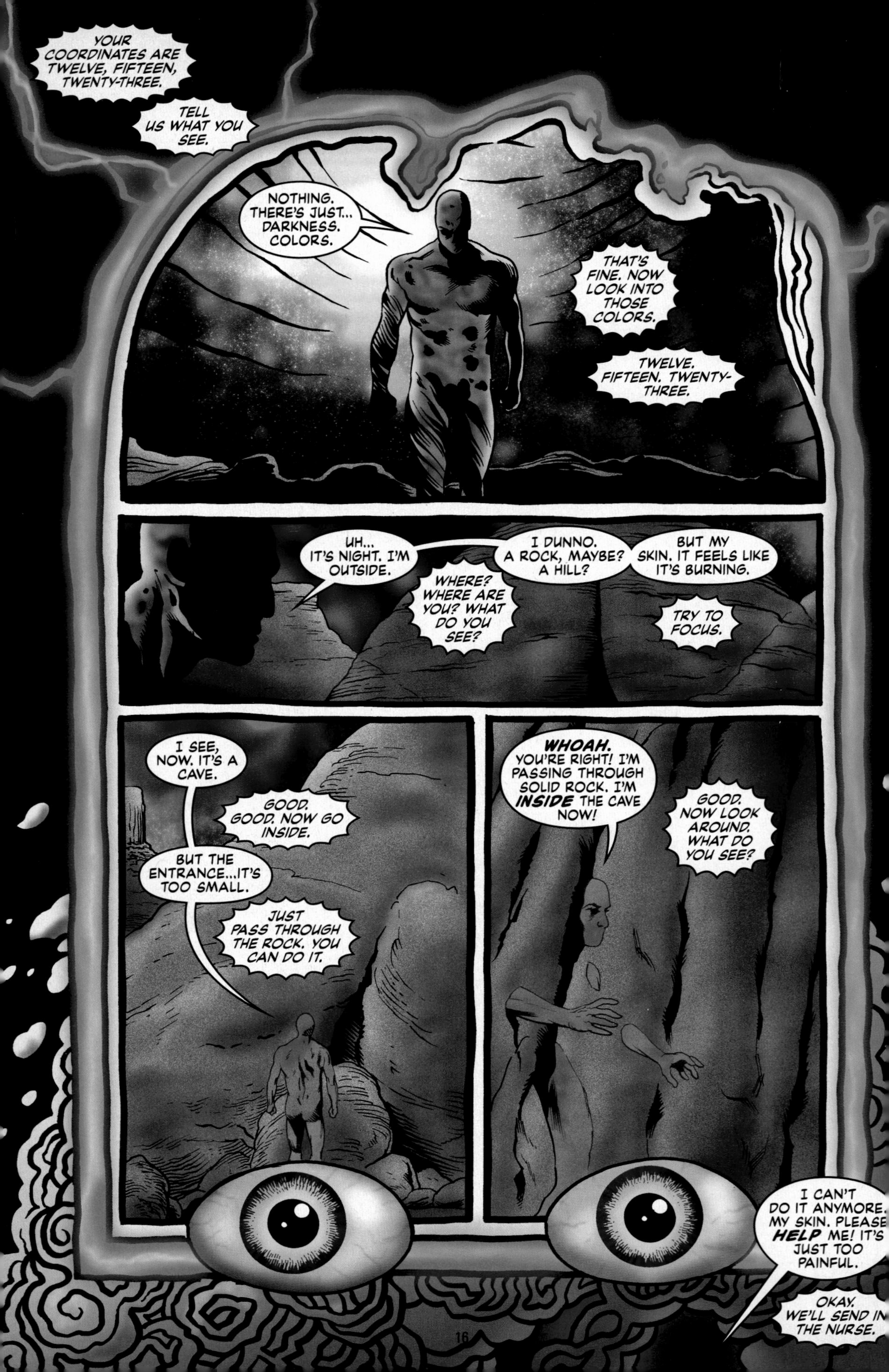
YOUR COORDINATES ARE TWELVE, FIFTEEN, TWENTY-THREE.
TELL US WHAT YOU SEE.
NOTHING. THERE'S JUST... DARKNESS. COLORS.
THAT'S FINE. NOW LOOK INTO THOSE COLORS.
TWELVE. FIFTEEN. TWENTY-THREE.
UH... IT'S NIGHT. I'M OUTSIDE.
WHERE? WHERE ARE YOU? WHAT DO YOU SEE?
I DUNNO. A ROCK, MAYBE? A HILL?
BUT MY SKIN. IT FEELS LIKE IT'S BURNING.
TRY TO FOCUS.
I SEE, NOW. IT'S A CAVE.
GOOD. GOOD. NOW GO INSIDE.
BUT THE ENTRANCE...IT'S TOO SMALL.
JUST PASS THROUGH THE ROCK. YOU CAN DO IT.
WHOAH. YOU'RE RIGHT! I'M PASSING THROUGH SOLID ROCK. I'M INSIDE THE CAVE NOW!
GOOD. NOW LOOK AROUND. WHAT DO YOU SEE?
I CAN'T DO IT ANYMORE. MY SKIN. PLEASE HELP ME! IT'S JUST TOO PAINFUL.
OKAY. WE'LL SEND IN THE NURSE.

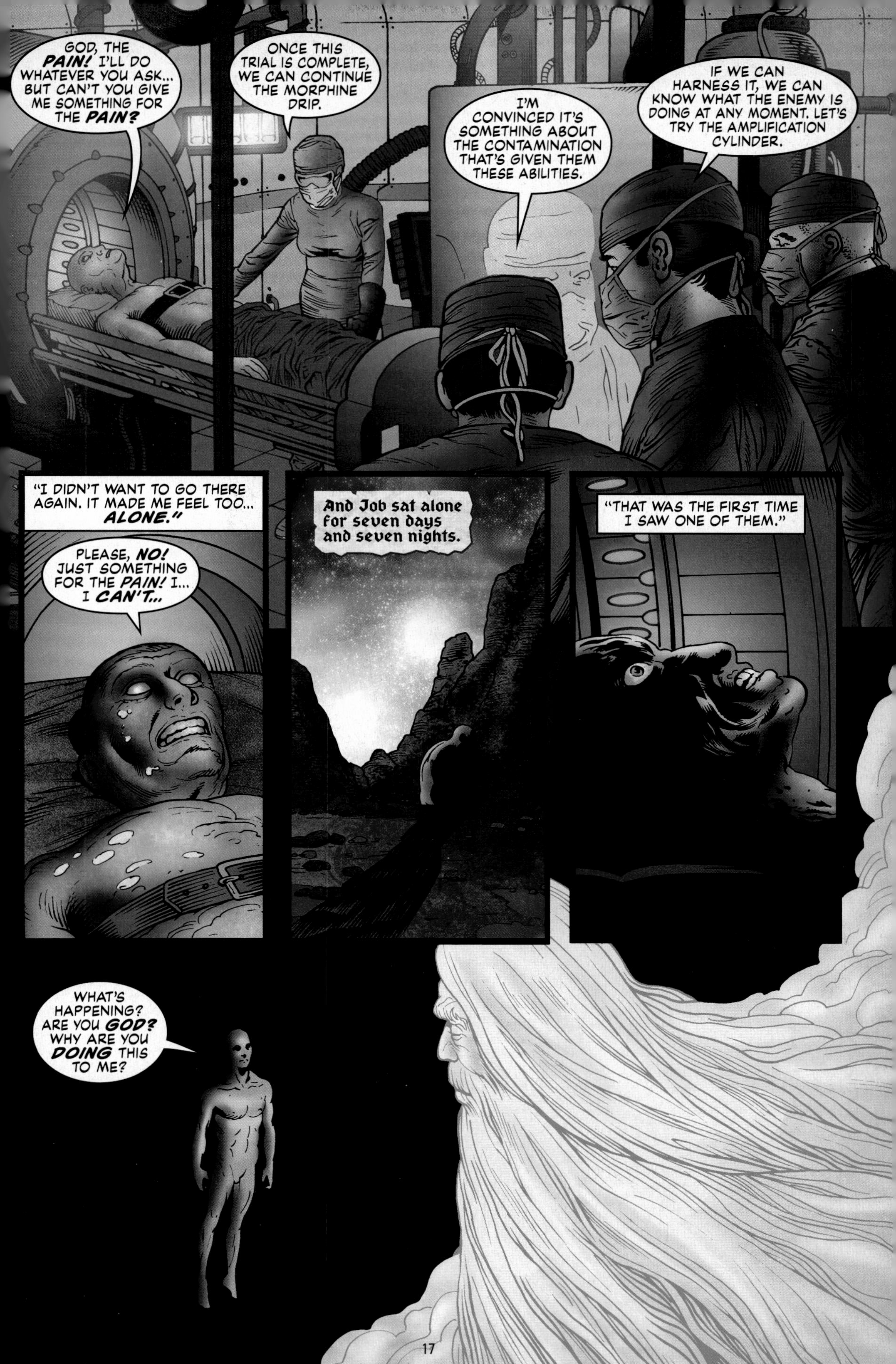
GOD, THE PAIN! I'LL DO WHATEVER YOU ASK... BUT CAN'T YOU GIVE ME SOMETHING FOR THE PAIN?
ONCE THIS TRIAL IS COMPLETE, WE CAN CONTINUE THE MORPHINE DRIP.
I'M CONVINCED IT'S SOMETHING ABOUT THE CONTAMINATION THAT'S GIVEN THEM THESE ABILITIES.
IF WE CAN HARNESS IT, WE CAN KNOW WHAT THE ENEMY IS DOING AT ANY MOMENT. LET'S TRY THE AMPLIFICATION CYLINDER.
"I DIDN'T WANT TO GO THERE AGAIN. IT MADE ME FEEL TOO... ALONE."
PLEASE, NO! JUST SOMETHING FOR THE PAIN! I... I CAN'T...
And Job sat alone for seven days and seven nights.
"THAT WAS THE FIRST TIME I SAW ONE OF THEM."
WHAT'S HAPPENING? ARE YOU GOD? WHY ARE YOU DOING THIS TO ME?

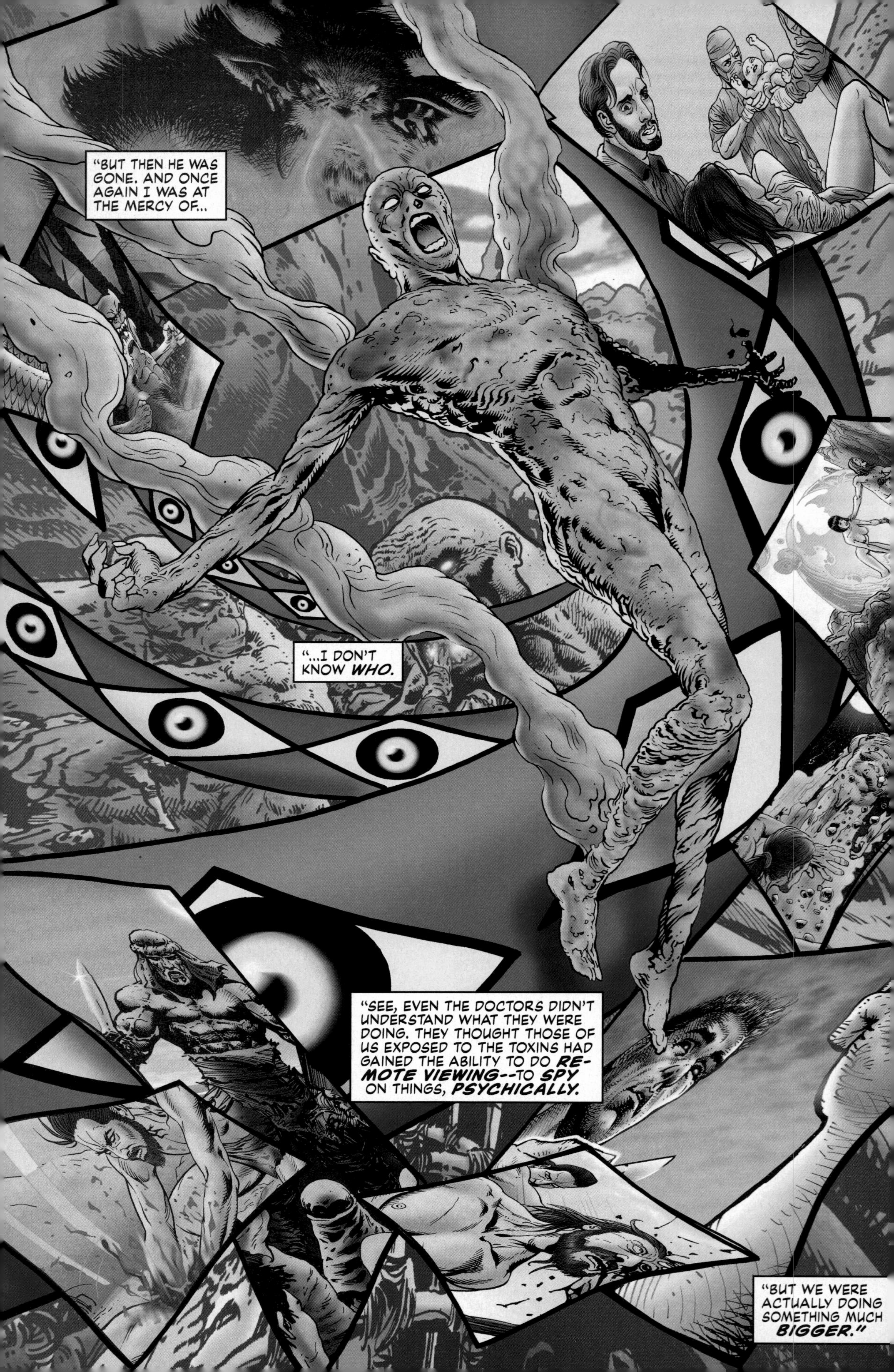
"BUT THEN HE WAS GONE. AND ONCE AGAIN I WAS AT THE MERCY OF...
"...I DON'T KNOW WHO.
"SEE, EVEN THE DOCTORS DIDN'T UNDERSTAND WHAT THEY WERE DOING. THEY THOUGHT THOSE OF US EXPOSED TO THE TOXINS HAD GAINED THE ABILITY TO DO RE-MOTE VIEWING--TO SPY ON THINGS, PSYCHICALLY.
"BUT WE WERE ACTUALLY DOING SOMETHING MUCH BIGGER."

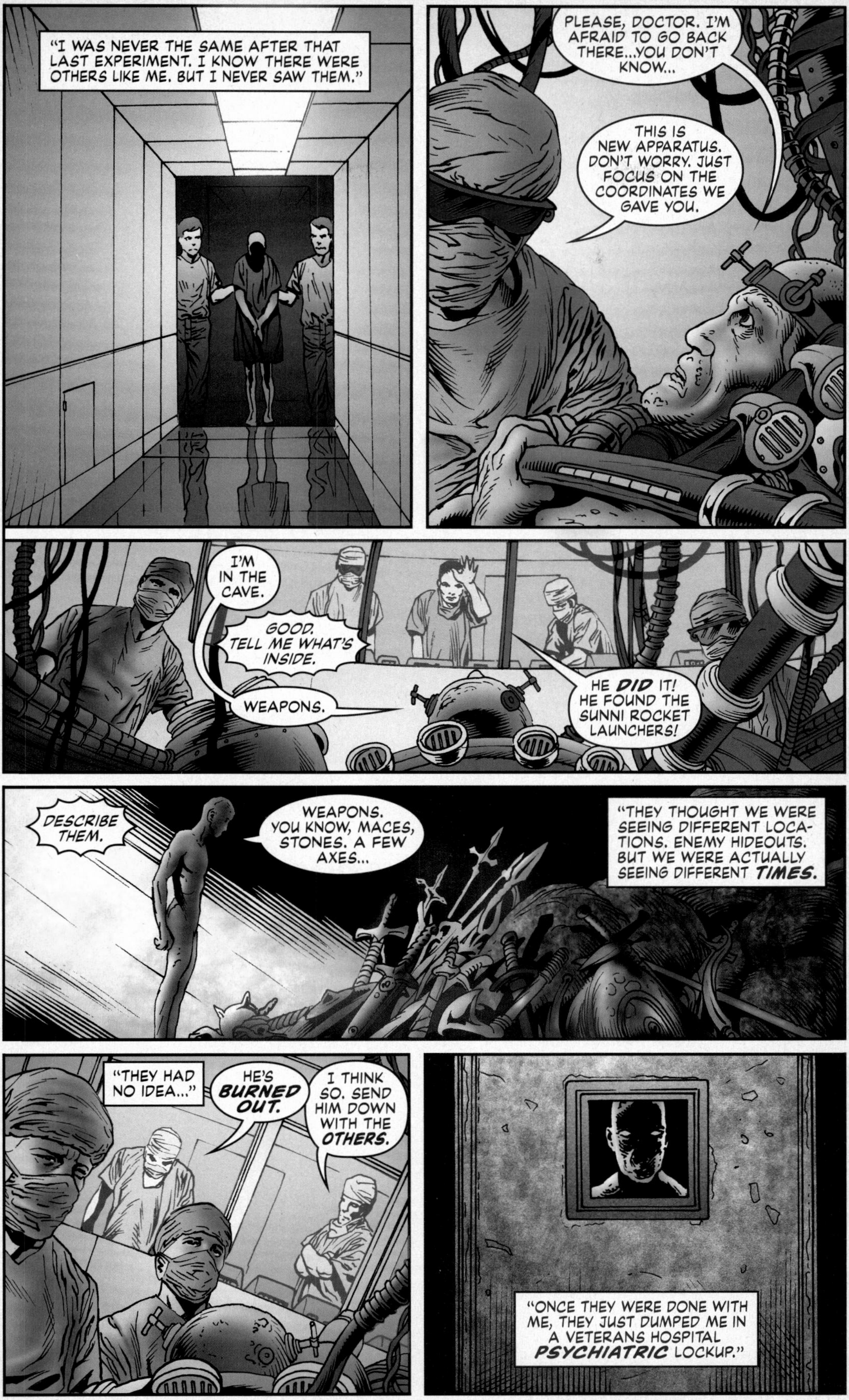
"I WAS NEVER THE SAME AFTER THAT LAST EXPERIMENT. I KNOW THERE WERE OTHERS LIKE ME. BUT I NEVER SAW THEM."
PLEASE, DOCTOR. I'M AFRAID TO GO BACK THERE...YOU DON'T KNOW...
THIS IS NEW APPARATUS. DON'T WORRY. JUST FOCUS ON THE COORDINATES WE GAVE YOU.
I'M IN THE CAVE.
GOOD. TELL ME WHAT'S INSIDE.
WEAPONS.
HE DID IT! HE FOUND THE SUNNI ROCKET LAUNCHERS!
DESCRIBE THEM.
WEAPONS. YOU KNOW, MACES, STONES. A FEW AXES...
"THEY THOUGHT WE WERE SEEING DIFFERENT LOCATIONS. ENEMY HIDEOUTS. BUT WE WERE ACTUALLY SEEING DIFFERENT TIMES.
"THEY HAD NO IDEA..."
HE'S BURNED OUT.
I THINK SO. SEND HIM DOWN WITH THE OTHERS.
"ONCE THEY WERE DONE WITH ME, THEY JUST DUMPED ME IN A VETERANS HOSPITAL PSYCHIATRIC LOCKUP."

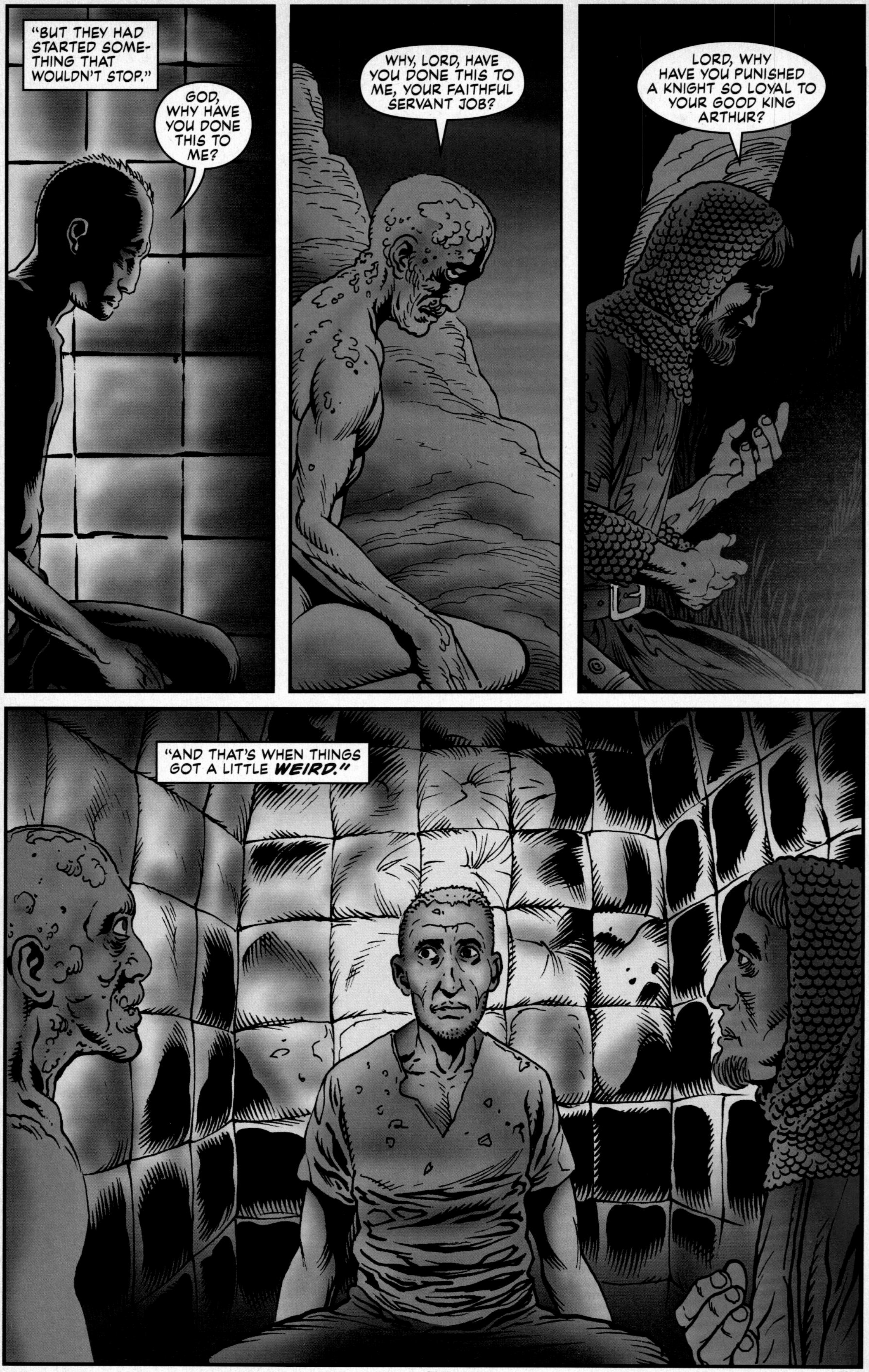
"BUT THEY HAD STARTED SOMETHING THAT WOULDN'T STOP."
GOD, WHY HAVE YOU DONE THIS TO ME?
WHY, LORD, HAVE YOU DONE THIS TO ME, YOUR FAITHFUL SERVANT JOB?
LORD, WHY HAVE YOU PUNISHED A KNIGHT SO LOYAL TO YOUR GOOD KING ARTHUR?
"AND THAT'S WHEN THINGS GOT A LITTLE *WEIRD.*"

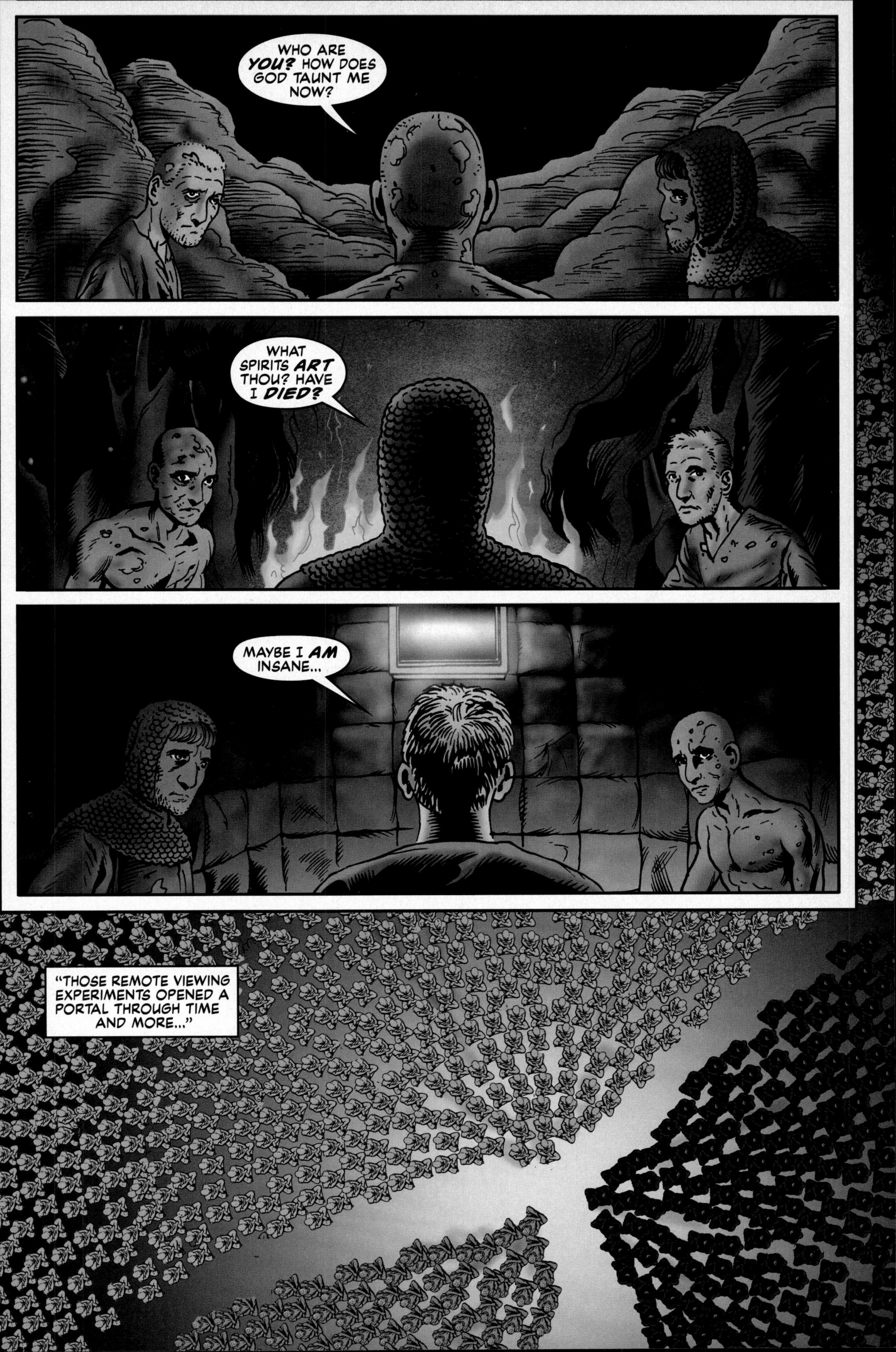
WHO ARE YOU? HOW DOES GOD TAUNT ME NOW?
WHAT SPIRITS ART THOU? HAVE I DIED?
MAYBE I AM INSANE...
"THOSE REMOTE VIEWING EXPERIMENTS OPENED A PORTAL THROUGH TIME AND MORE..."

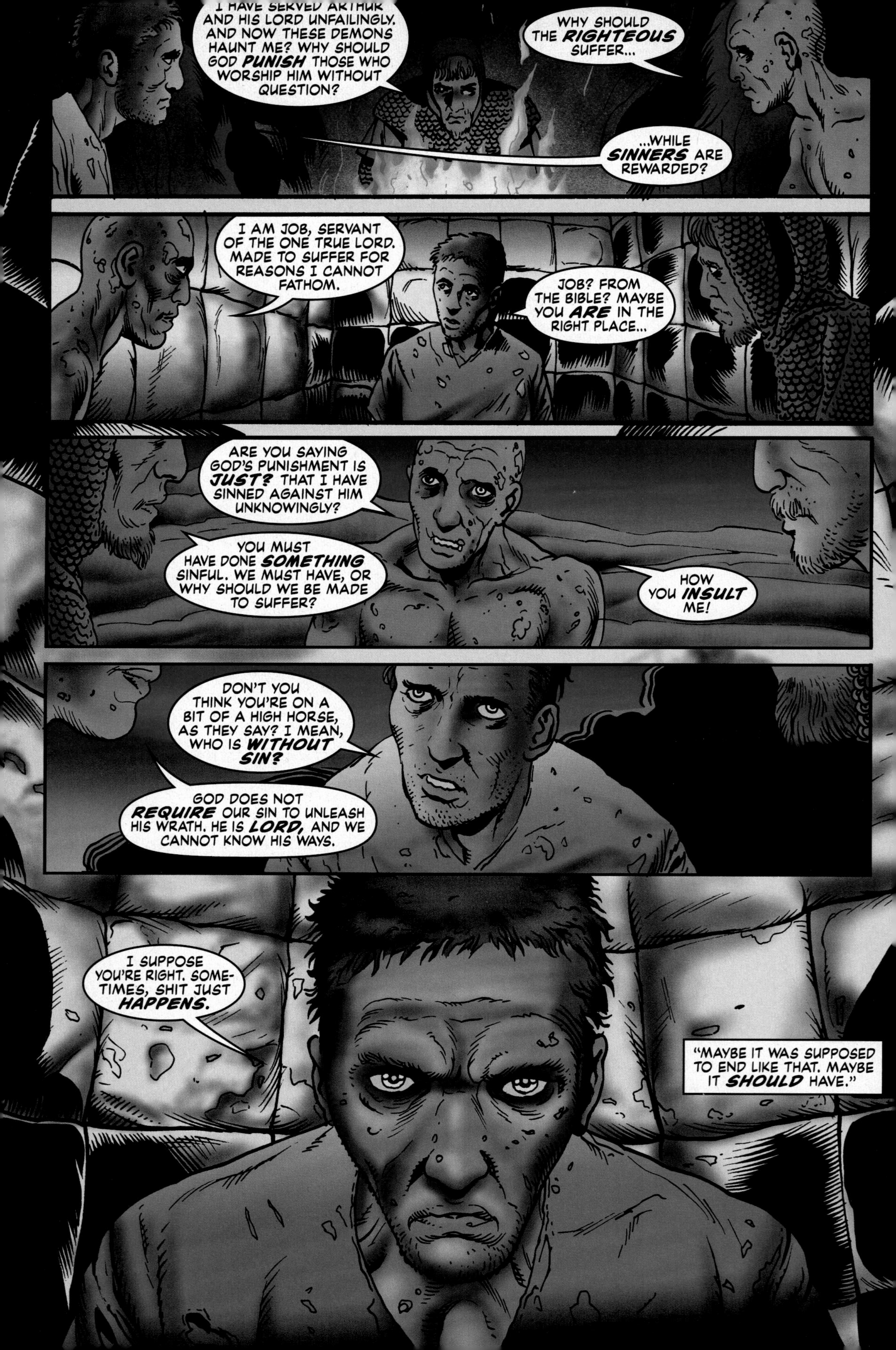
I HAVE SERVED ARTHUR AND HIS LORD UNFAILINGLY. AND NOW THESE DEMONS HAUNT ME? WHY SHOULD GOD PUNISH THOSE WHO WORSHIP HIM WITHOUT QUESTION?
WHY SHOULD THE RIGHTEOUS SUFFER...
...WHILE SINNERS ARE REWARDED?
I AM JOB, SERVANT OF THE ONE TRUE LORD. MADE TO SUFFER FOR REASONS I CANNOT FATHOM.
JOB? FROM THE BIBLE? MAYBE YOU ARE IN THE RIGHT PLACE...
ARE YOU SAYING GOD'S PUNISHMENT IS JUST? THAT I HAVE SINNED AGAINST HIM UNKNOWINGLY?
YOU MUST HAVE DONE SOMETHING SINFUL. WE MUST HAVE, OR WHY SHOULD WE BE MADE TO SUFFER?
HOW YOU INSULT ME!
DON'T YOU THINK YOU'RE ON A BIT OF A HIGH HORSE, AS THEY SAY? I MEAN, WHO IS WITHOUT SIN?
GOD DOES NOT REQUIRE OUR SIN TO UNLEASH HIS WRATH. HE IS LORD, AND WE CANNOT KNOW HIS WAYS.
I SUPPOSE YOU'RE RIGHT. SOME-TIMES, SHIT JUST HAPPENS.
"MAYBE IT WAS SUPPOSED TO END LIKE THAT. MAYBE IT SHOULD HAVE."

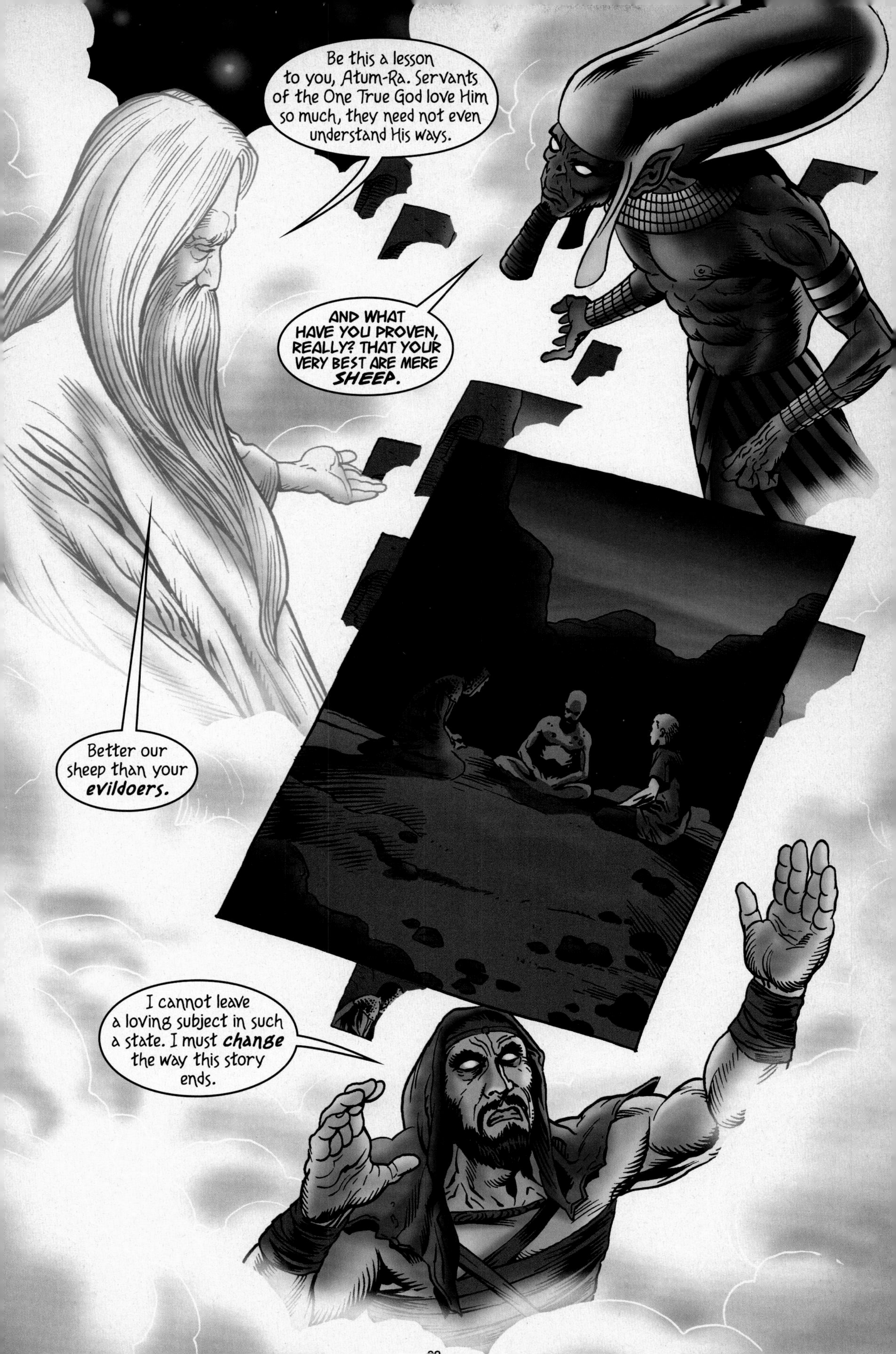

Be this a lesson to you, Atum-Ra. Servants of the One True God love Him so much, they need not even understand His ways.
AND WHAT HAVE YOU PROVEN, REALLY? THAT YOUR VERY BEST ARE MERE SHEEP.
Better our sheep than your evildoers.
I cannot leave a loving subject in such a state. I must change the way this story ends.

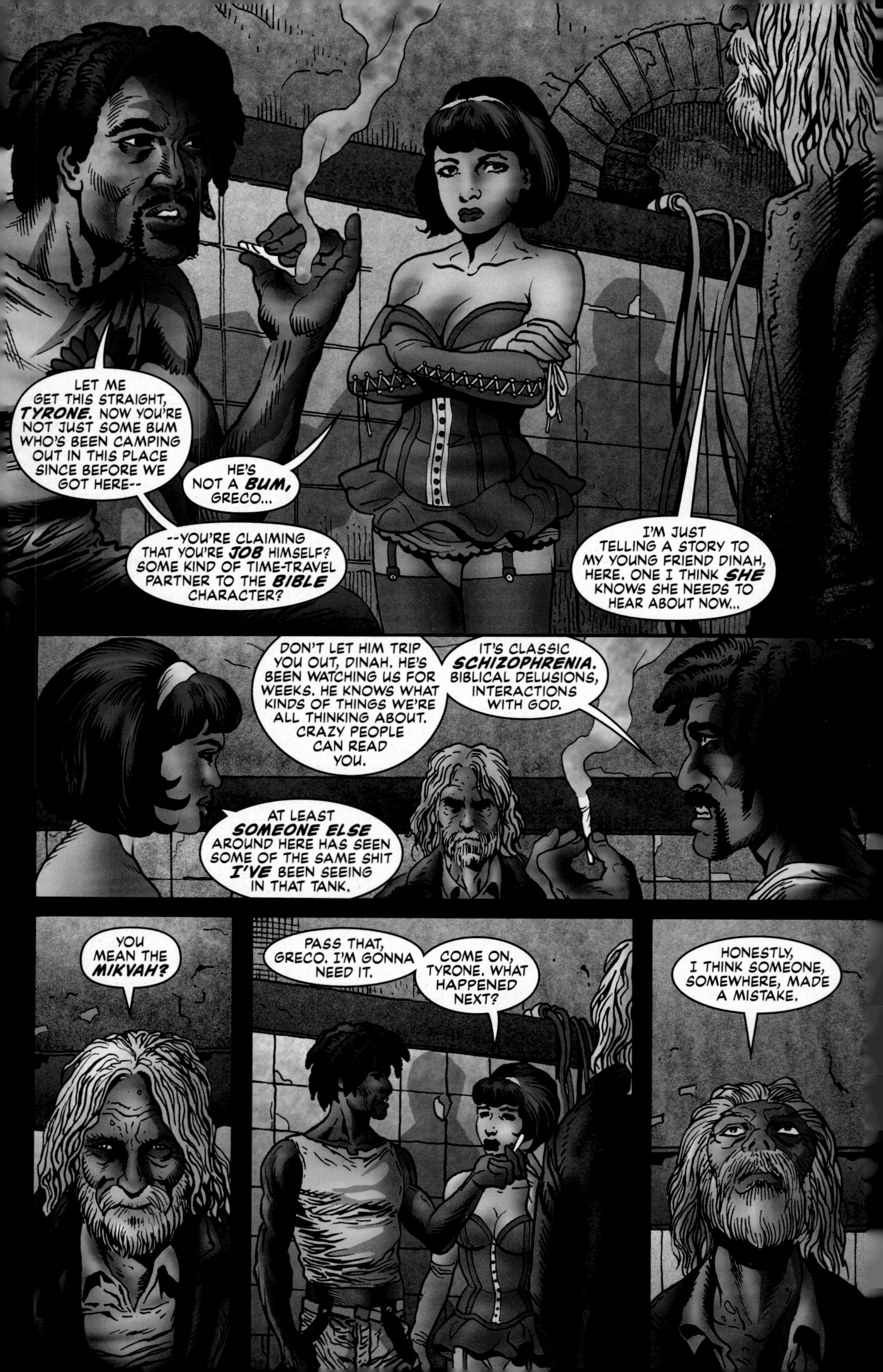
LET ME GET THIS STRAIGHT, TYRONE. NOW YOU'RE NOT JUST SOME BUM WHO'S BEEN CAMPING OUT IN THIS PLACE SINCE BEFORE WE GOT HERE--
HE'S NOT A BUM, GRECO...
--YOU'RE CLAIMING THAT YOU'RE JOB HIMSELF? SOME KIND OF TIME-TRAVEL PARTNER TO THE BIBLE CHARACTER?
I'M JUST TELLING A STORY TO MY YOUNG FRIEND DINAH, HERE. ONE I THINK SHE KNOWS SHE NEEDS TO HEAR ABOUT NOW...
DON'T LET HIM TRIP YOU OUT, DINAH. HE'S BEEN WATCHING US FOR WEEKS. HE KNOWS WHAT KINDS OF THINGS WE'RE ALL THINKING ABOUT. CRAZY PEOPLE CAN READ YOU.
IT'S CLASSIC SCHIZOPHRENIA. BIBLICAL DELUSIONS, INTERACTIONS WITH GOD.
AT LEAST SOMEONE ELSE AROUND HERE HAS SEEN SOME OF THE SAME SHIT I'VE BEEN SEEING IN THAT TANK.
YOU MEAN THE MIKVAH?
PASS THAT, GRECO. I'M GONNA NEED IT.
COME ON, TYRONE. WHAT HAPPENED NEXT?
HONESTLY, I THINK SOMEONE, SOMEWHERE, MADE A MISTAKE.

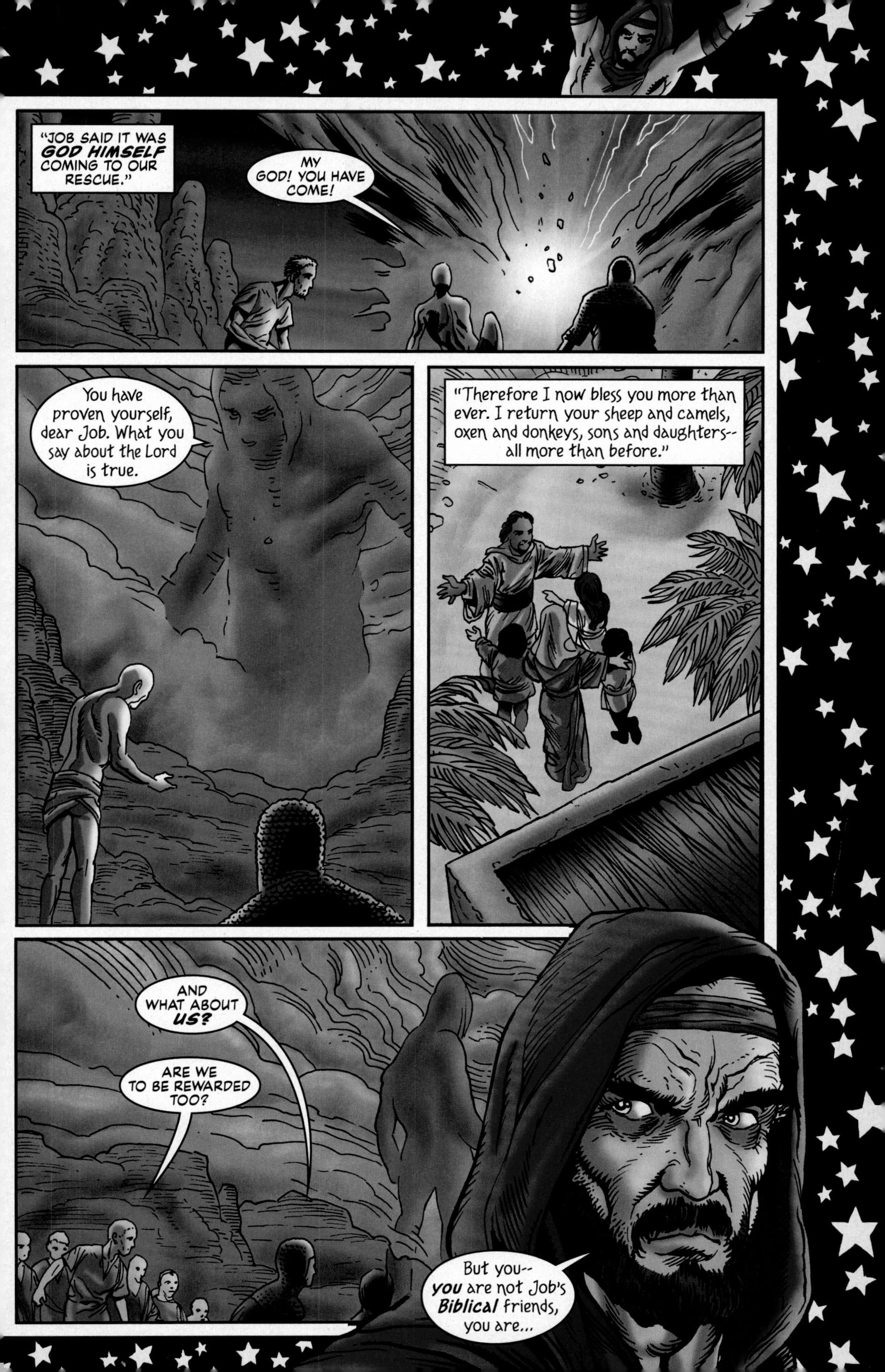
"JOB SAID IT WAS GOD HIMSELF COMING TO OUR RESCUE."
MY GOD! YOU HAVE COME!
You have proven yourself, dear Job. What you say about the Lord is true.
"Therefore I now bless you more than ever. I return your sheep and camels, oxen and donkeys, sons and daughters--all more than before."
AND WHAT ABOUT US?
ARE WE TO BE REWARDED TOO?
But you--you are not Job's Biblical friends, you are...

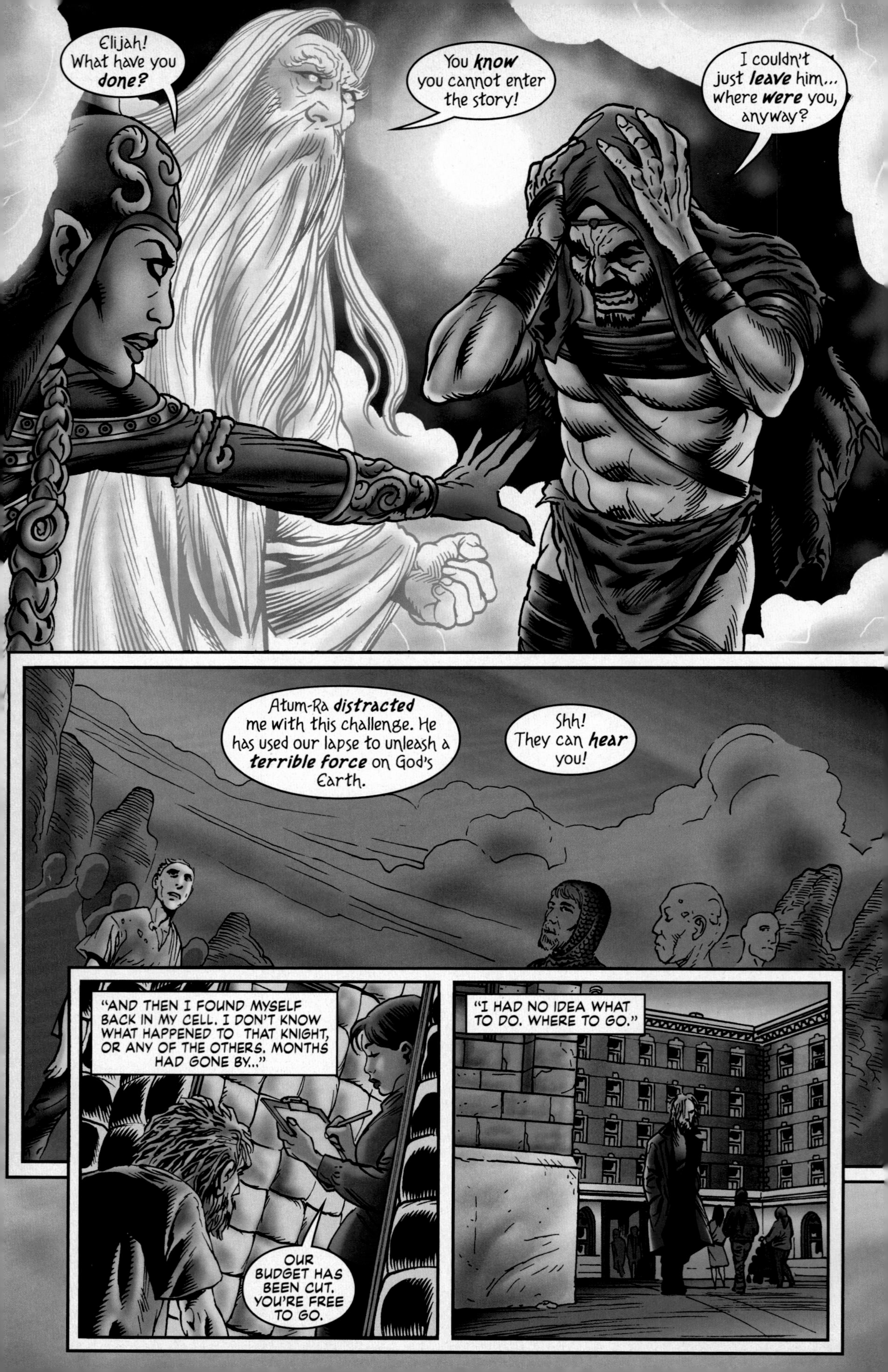
Elijah! What have you done?
You know you cannot enter the story!
I couldn't just leave him... where were you, anyway?
Atum-Ra distracted me with this challenge. He has used our lapse to unleash a terrible force on God's Earth.
Shh! They can hear you!
"AND THEN I FOUND MYSELF BACK IN MY CELL. I DON'T KNOW WHAT HAPPENED TO THAT KNIGHT, OR ANY OF THE OTHERS. MONTHS HAD GONE BY..."
OUR BUDGET HAS BEEN CUT. YOU'RE FREE TO GO.
"I HAD NO IDEA WHAT TO DO. WHERE TO GO."

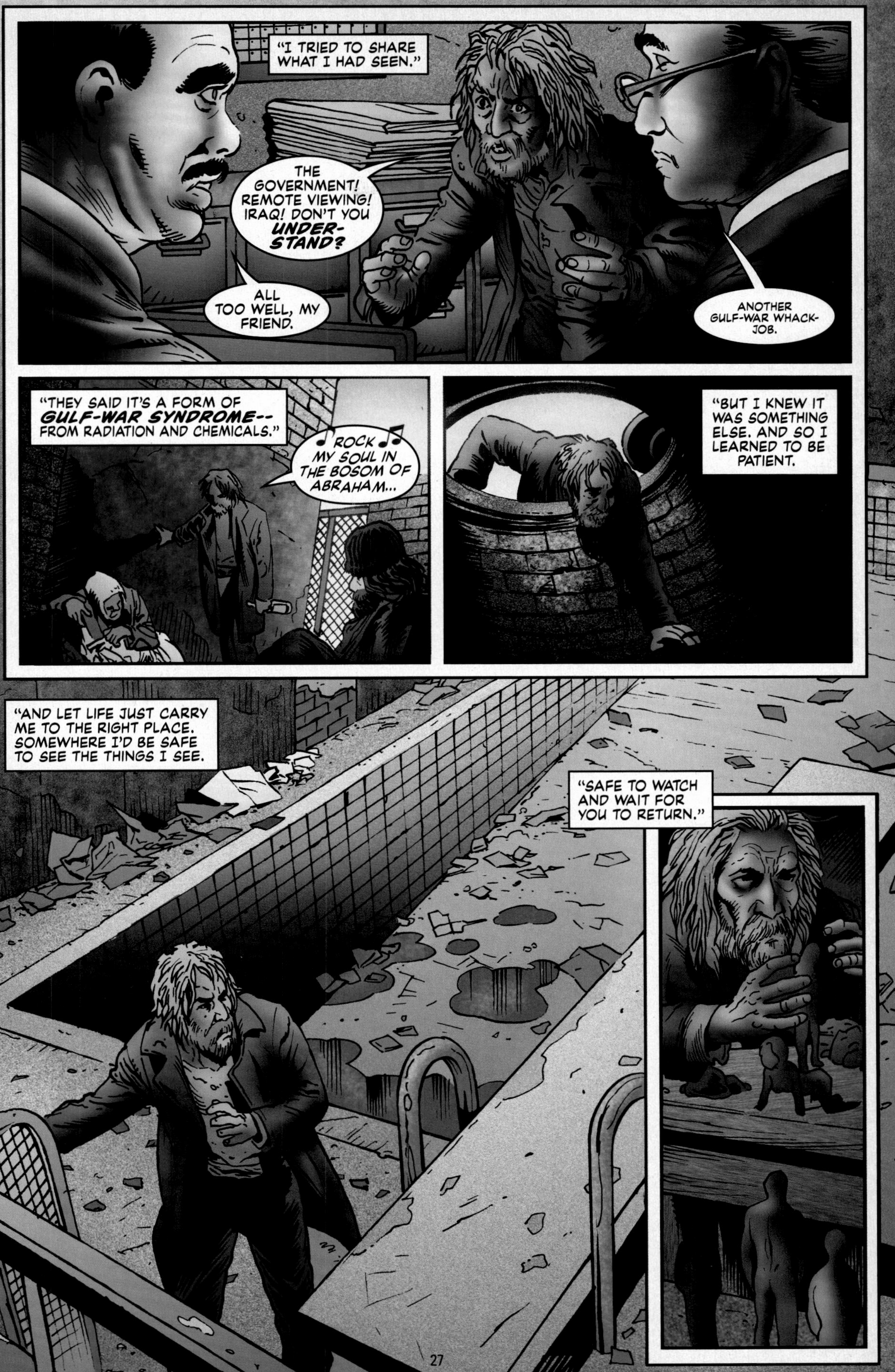
"I TRIED TO SHARE WHAT I HAD SEEN."
THE GOVERNMENT! REMOTE VIEWING! IRAQ! DON'T YOU UNDER-STAND?
ALL TOO WELL, MY FRIEND.
ANOTHER GULF-WAR WHACK-JOB.
"THEY SAID IT'S A FORM OF GULF-WAR SYNDROME-- FROM RADIATION AND CHEMICALS."
ROCK MY SOUL IN THE BOSOM OF ABRAHAM...
"BUT I KNEW IT WAS SOMETHING ELSE. AND SO I LEARNED TO BE PATIENT.
"AND LET LIFE JUST CARRY ME TO THE RIGHT PLACE. SOMEWHERE I'D BE SAFE TO SEE THE THINGS I SEE.
"SAFE TO WATCH AND WAIT FOR YOU TO RETURN."

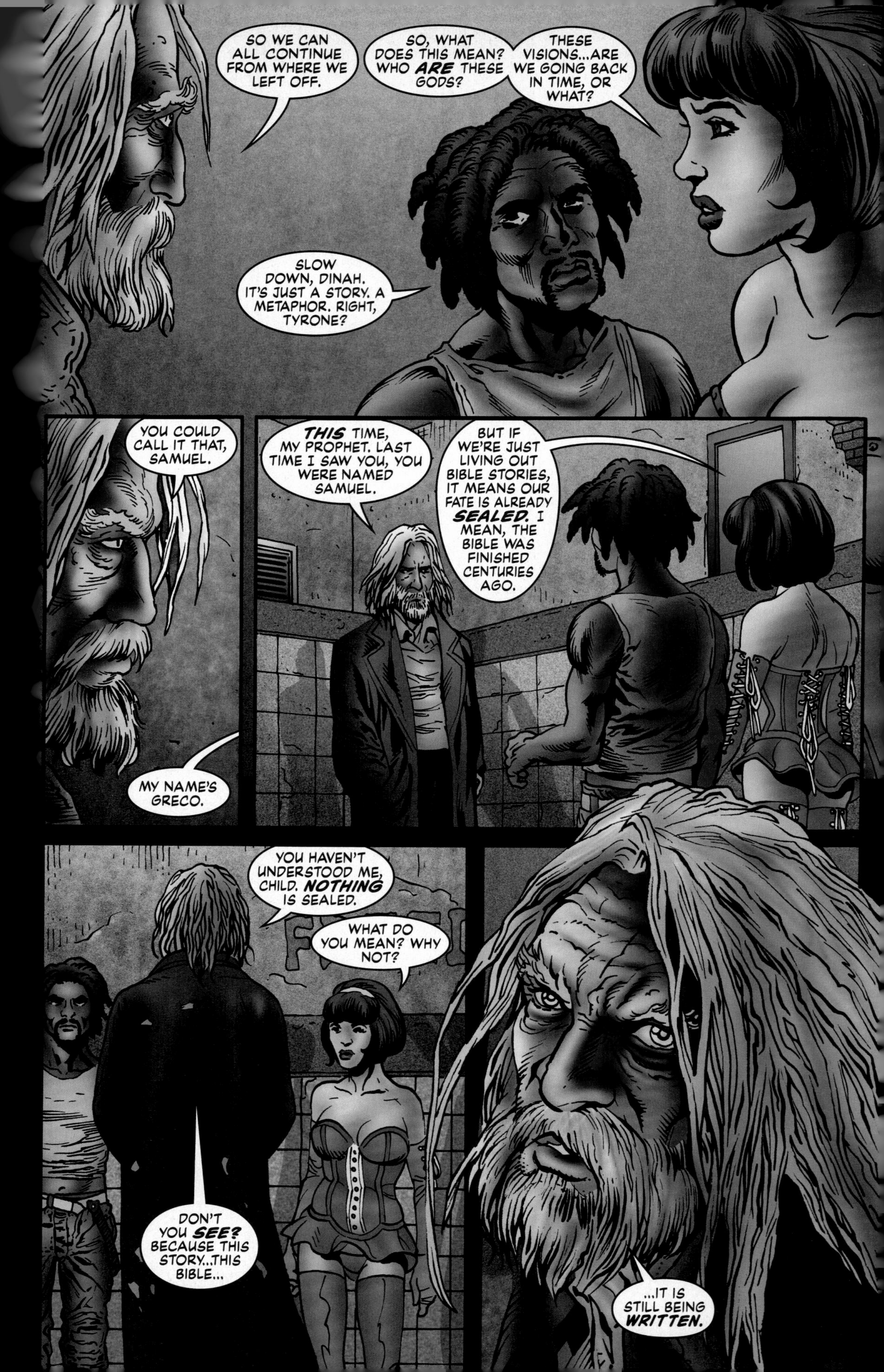
SO WE CAN ALL CONTINUE FROM WHERE WE LEFT OFF.
SO, WHAT DOES THIS MEAN? WHO ARE THESE GODS?
THESE VISIONS...ARE WE GOING BACK IN TIME, OR WHAT?
SLOW DOWN, DINAH. IT'S JUST A STORY. A METAPHOR. RIGHT, TYRONE?
YOU COULD CALL IT THAT, SAMUEL.
MY NAME'S GRECO.
THIS TIME, MY PROPHET. LAST TIME I SAW YOU, YOU WERE NAMED SAMUEL.
BUT IF WE'RE JUST LIVING OUT BIBLE STORIES, IT MEANS OUR FATE IS ALREADY SEALED. I MEAN, THE BIBLE WAS FINISHED CENTURIES AGO.
YOU HAVEN'T UNDERSTOOD ME, CHILD. NOTHING IS SEALED.
WHAT DO YOU MEAN? WHY NOT?
DON'T YOU SEE? BECAUSE THIS STORY...THIS BIBLE...
...IT IS STILL BEING WRITTEN.

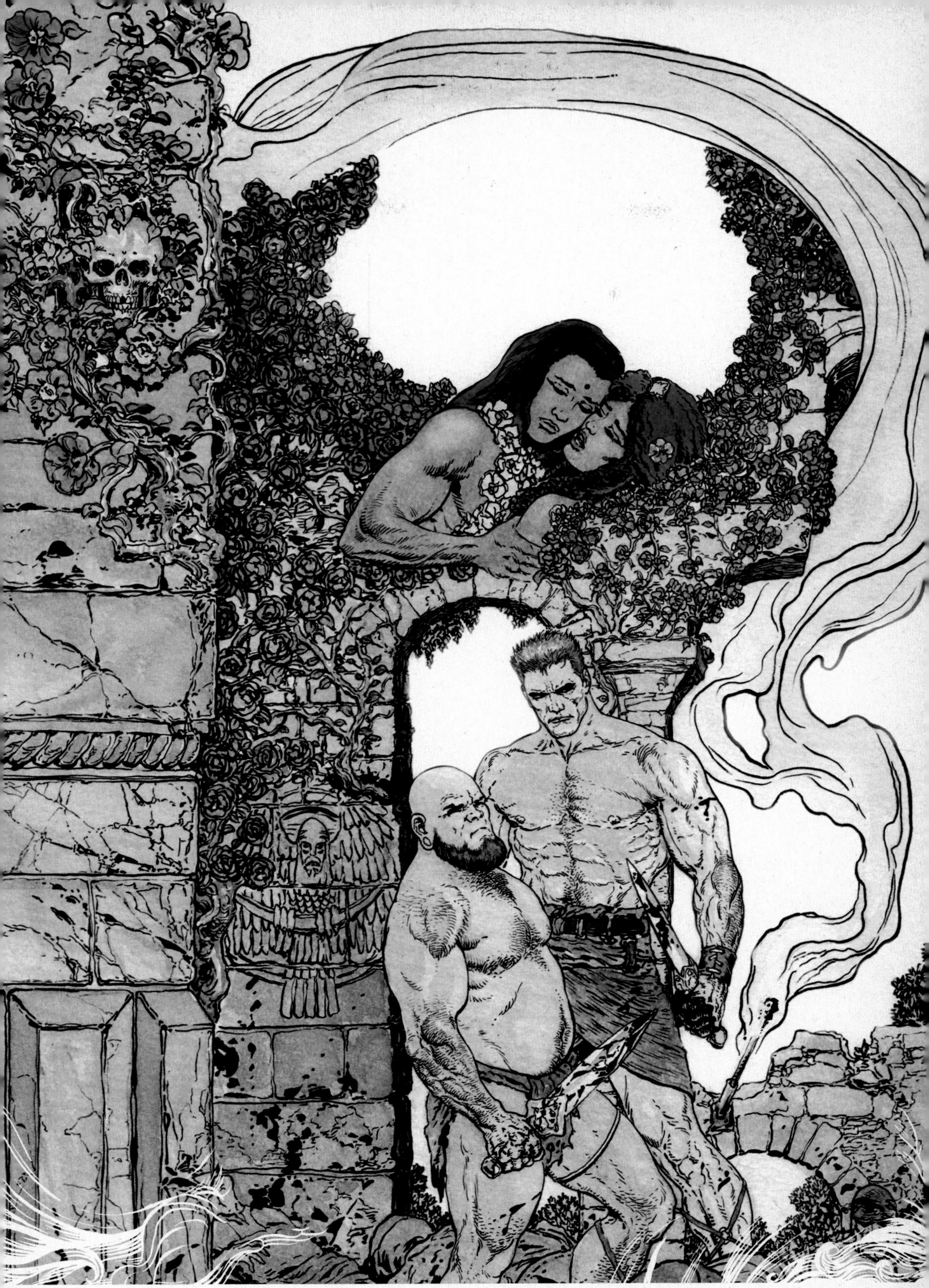

TRIP RESET: *The Rape of Dinah*

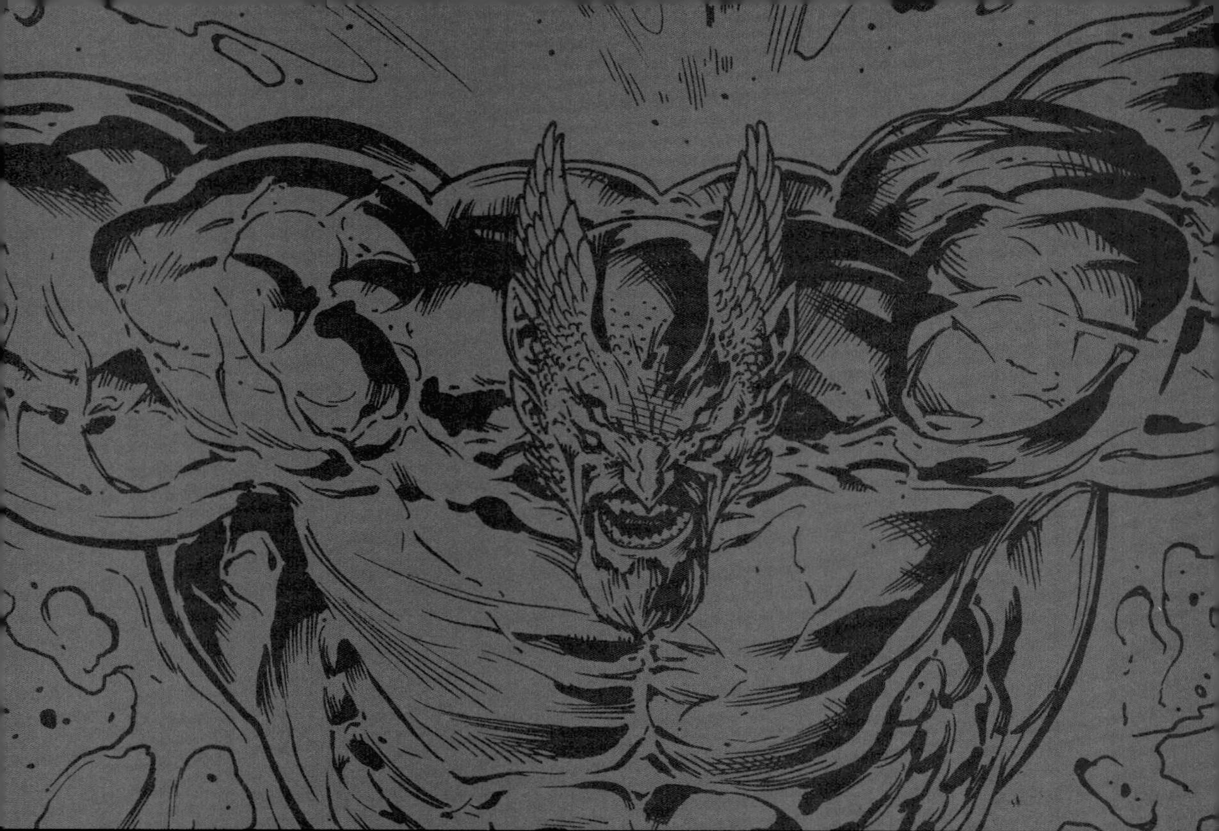

TESTAMENT

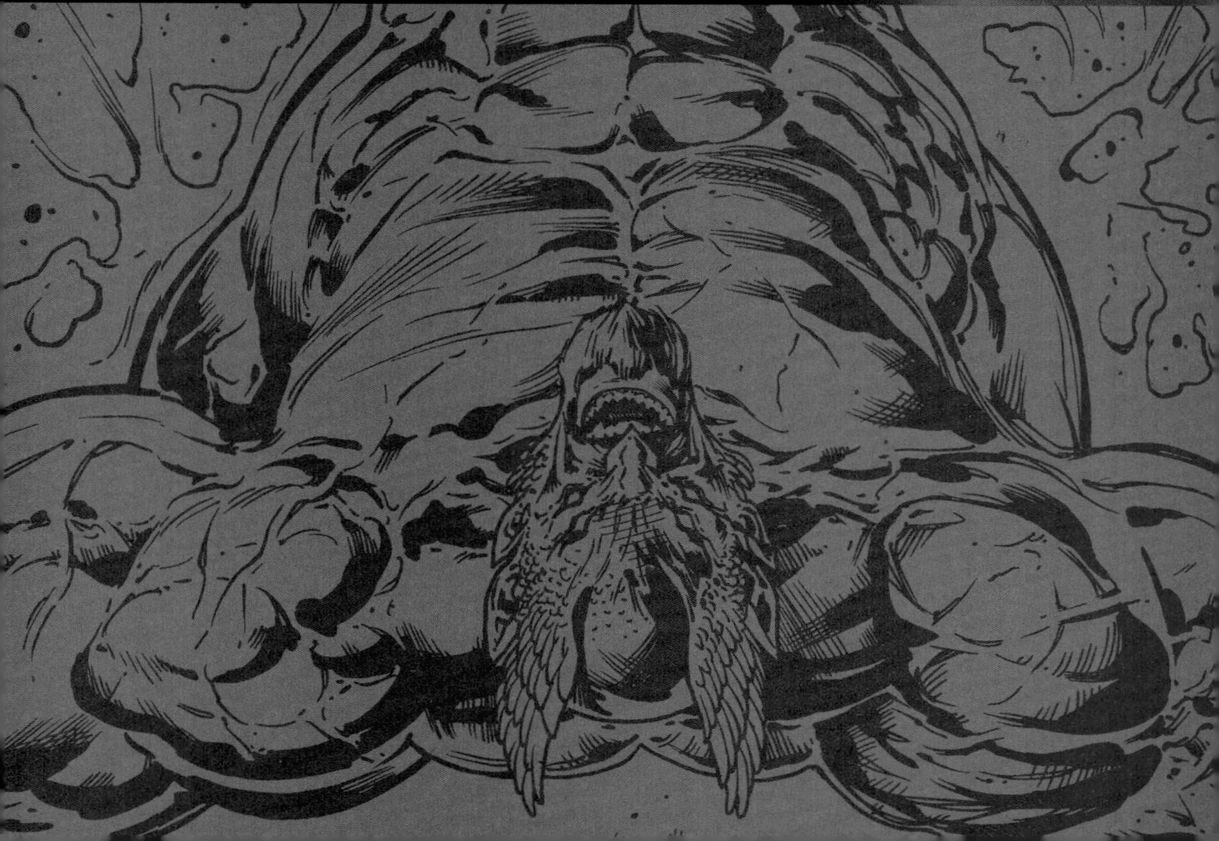

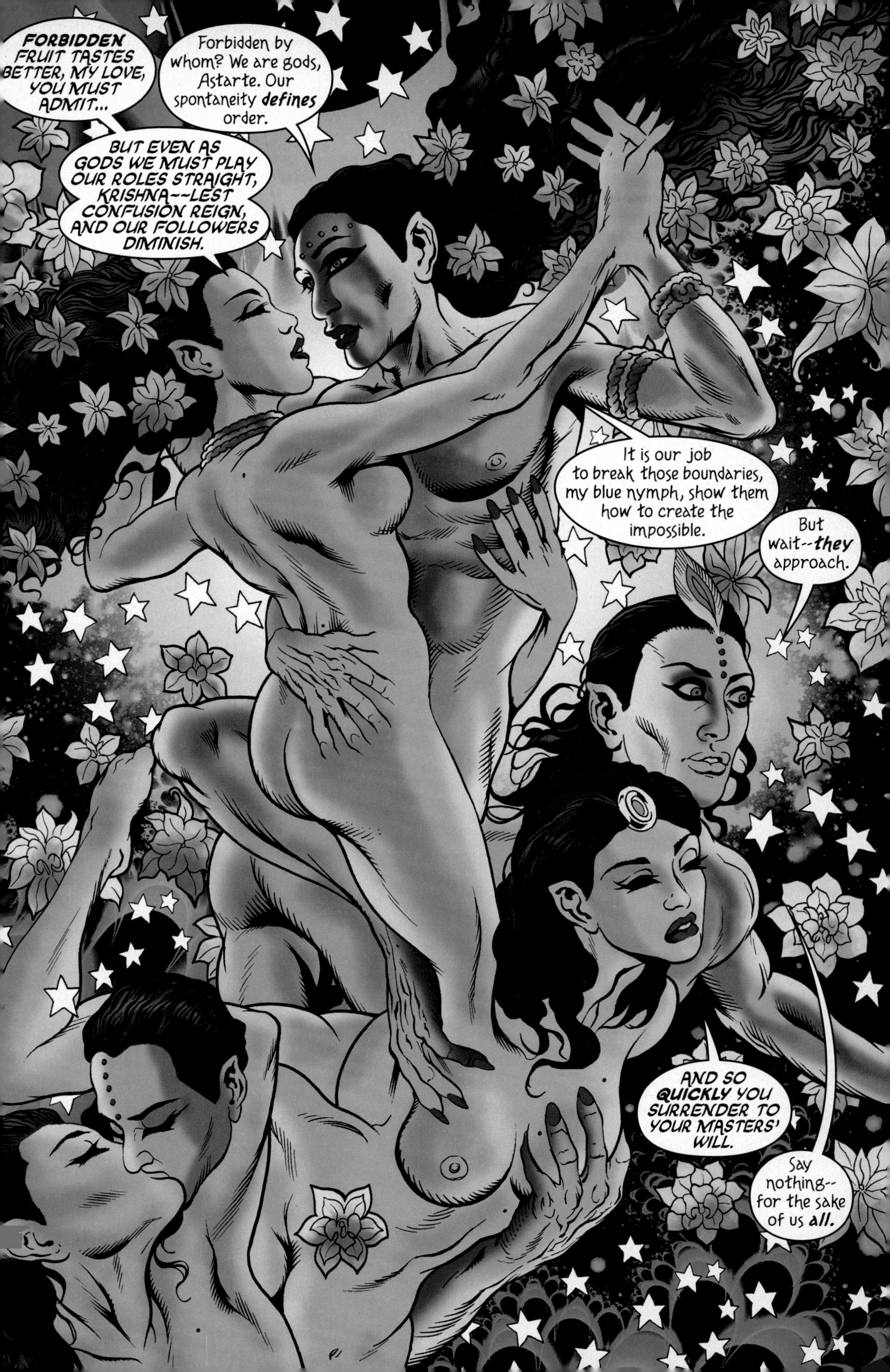
FORBIDDEN FRUIT TASTES BETTER, MY LOVE, YOU MUST ADMIT...
Forbidden by whom? We are gods, Astarte. Our spontaneity defines order.
BUT EVEN AS GODS WE MUST PLAY OUR ROLES STRAIGHT, KRISHNA--LEST CONFUSION REIGN, AND OUR FOLLOWERS DIMINISH.
It is our job to break those boundaries, my blue nymph, show them how to create the impossible.
But wait--they approach.
AND SO QUICKLY YOU SURRENDER TO YOUR MASTERS' WILL.
Say nothing--for the sake of us all.

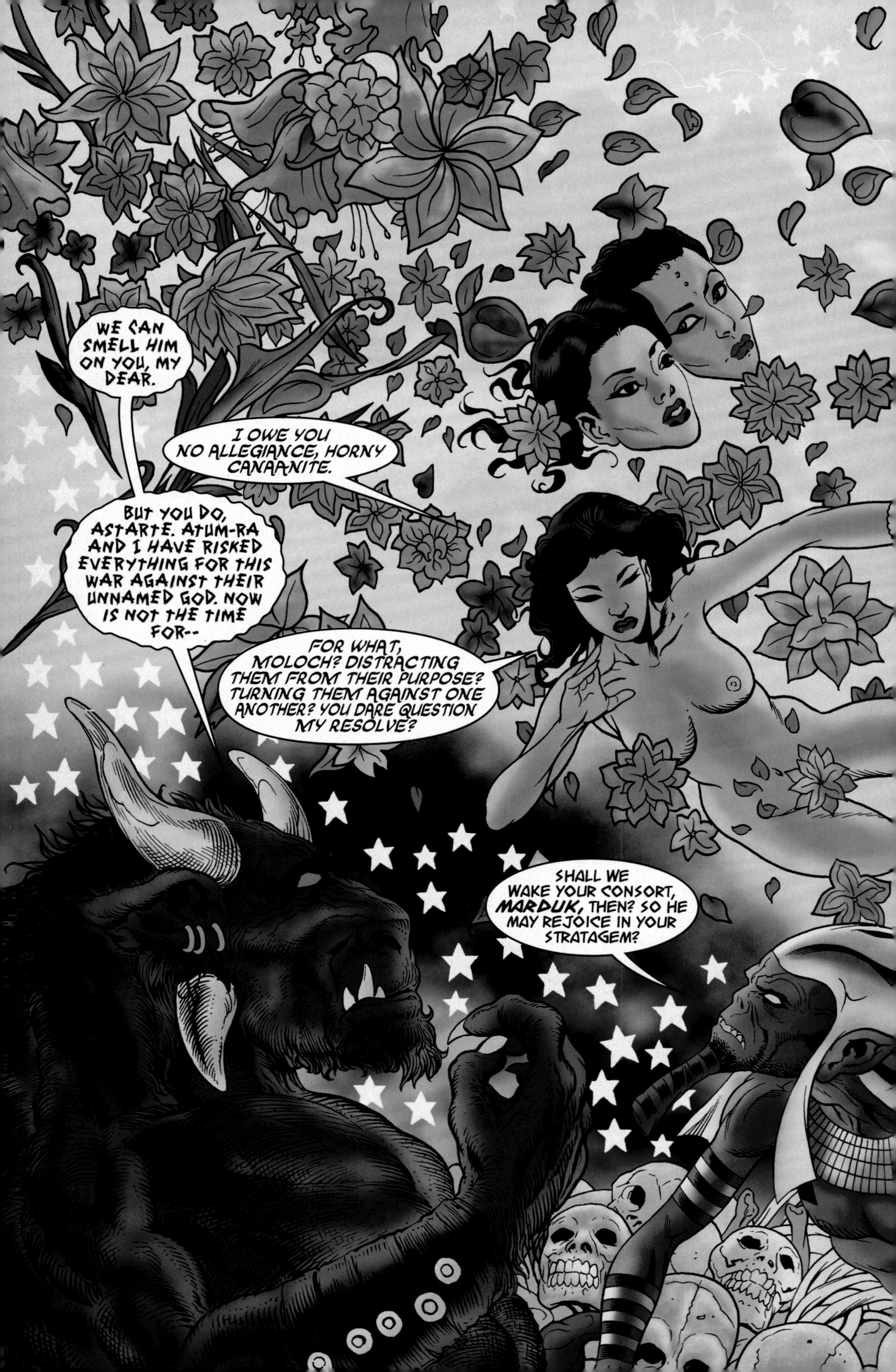
WE CAN SMELL HIM ON YOU, MY DEAR.
I OWE YOU NO ALLEGIANCE, HORNY CANAANITE.
BUT YOU DO, ASTARTE. ATUM-RA AND I HAVE RISKED EVERYTHING FOR THIS WAR AGAINST THEIR UNNAMED GOD. NOW IS NOT THE TIME FOR--
FOR WHAT, MOLOCH? DISTRACTING THEM FROM THEIR PURPOSE? TURNING THEM AGAINST ONE ANOTHER? YOU DARE QUESTION MY RESOLVE?
SHALL WE WAKE YOUR CONSORT, MARDUK, THEN? SO HE MAY REJOICE IN YOUR STRATAGEM?

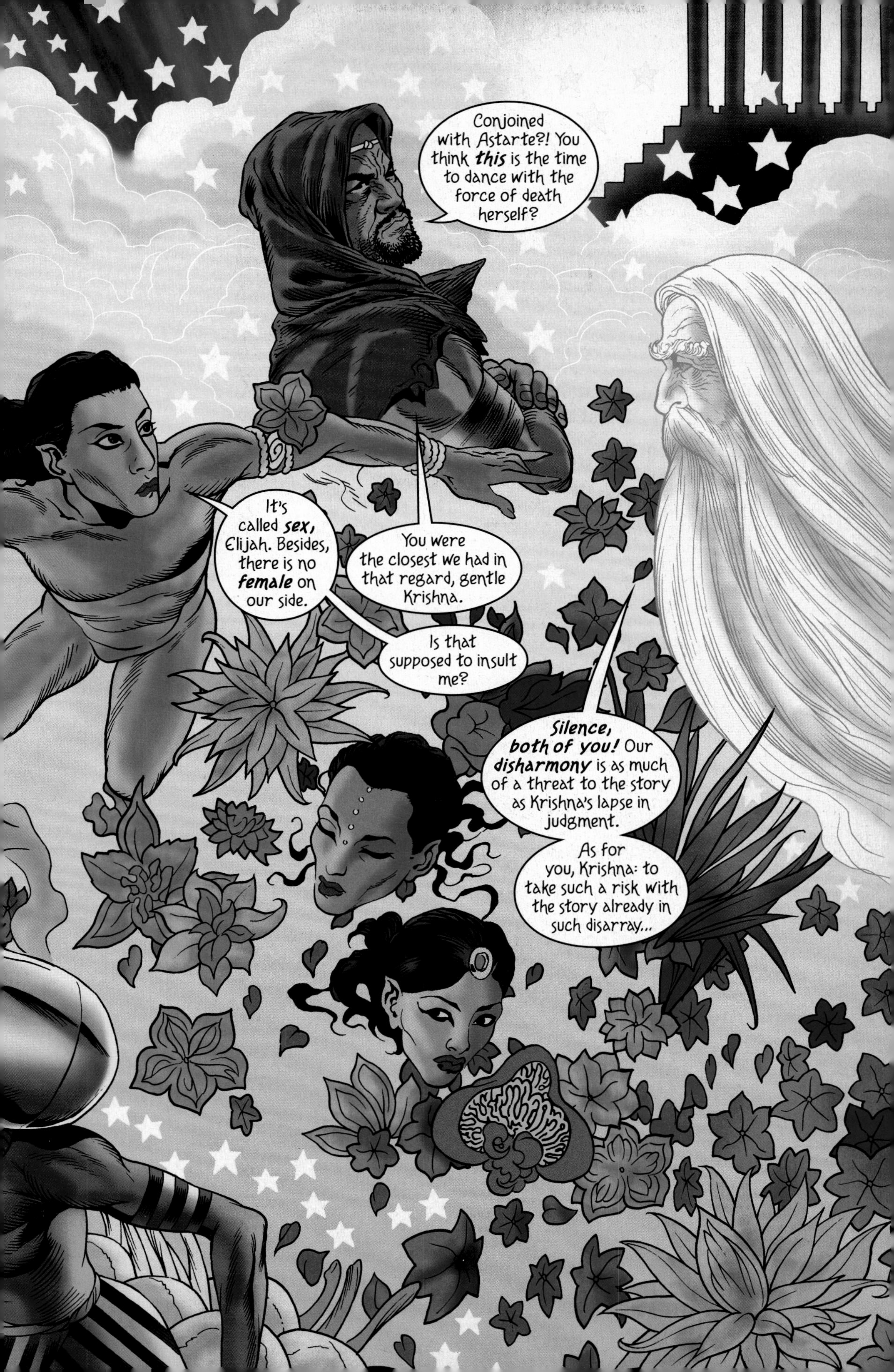
Conjoined with Astarte?! You think this is the time to dance with the force of death herself?
It's called sex, Elijah. Besides, there is no female on our side.
You were the closest we had in that regard, gentle Krishna.
Is that supposed to insult me?
Silence, both of you! Our disharmony is as much of a threat to the story as Krishna's lapse in judgment.
As for you, Krishna: to take such a risk with the story already in such disarray...

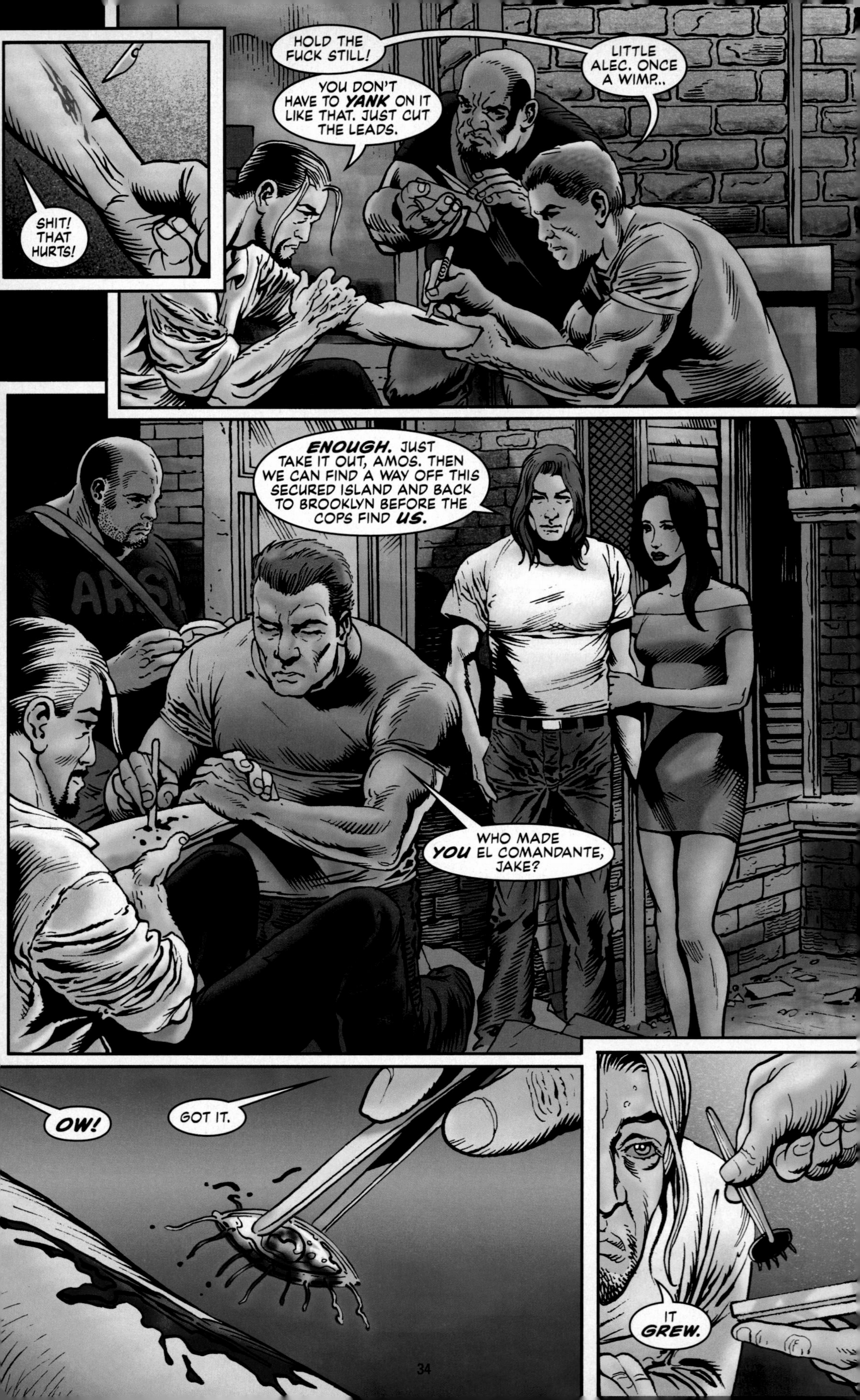
SHIT! THAT HURTS!
HOLD THE FUCK STILL!
YOU DON'T HAVE TO YANK ON IT LIKE THAT. JUST CUT THE LEADS.
LITTLE ALEC. ONCE A WIMP...
ENOUGH. JUST TAKE IT OUT, AMOS. THEN WE CAN FIND A WAY OFF THIS SECURED ISLAND AND BACK TO BROOKLYN BEFORE THE COPS FIND US.
WHO MADE YOU EL COMANDANTE, JAKE?
OW!
GOT IT.
IT GREW.

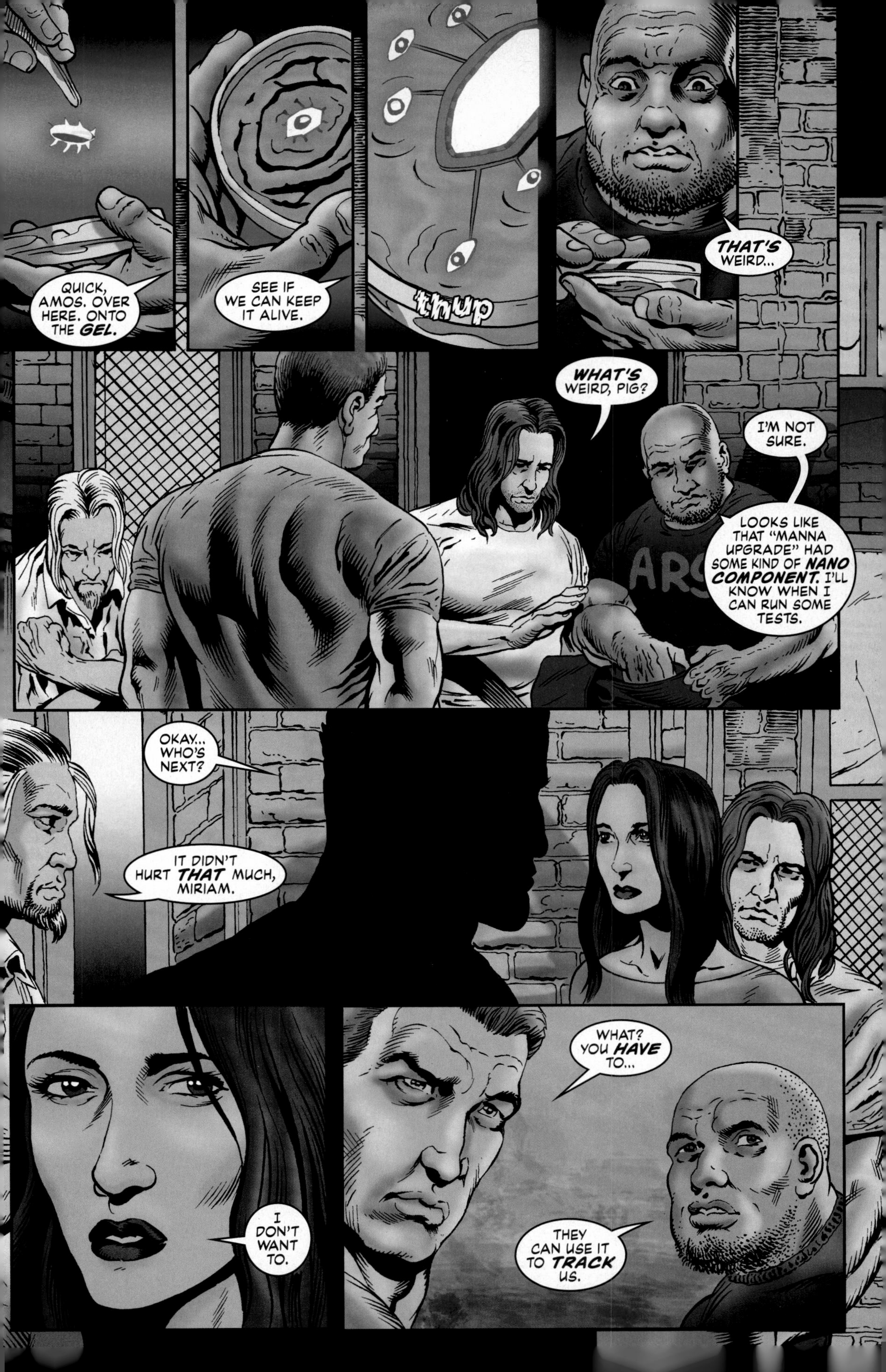

QUICK, AMOS. OVER HERE. ONTO THE GEL.
SEE IF WE CAN KEEP IT ALIVE.
thup
THAT'S WEIRD...
WHAT'S WEIRD, PIG?
I'M NOT SURE.
LOOKS LIKE THAT "MANNA UPGRADE" HAD SOME KIND OF NANO COMPONENT. I'LL KNOW WHEN I CAN RUN SOME TESTS.
ARS
OKAY... WHO'S NEXT?
IT DIDN'T HURT THAT MUCH, MIRIAM.
I DON'T WANT TO.
WHAT? YOU HAVE TO...
THEY CAN USE IT TO TRACK US.

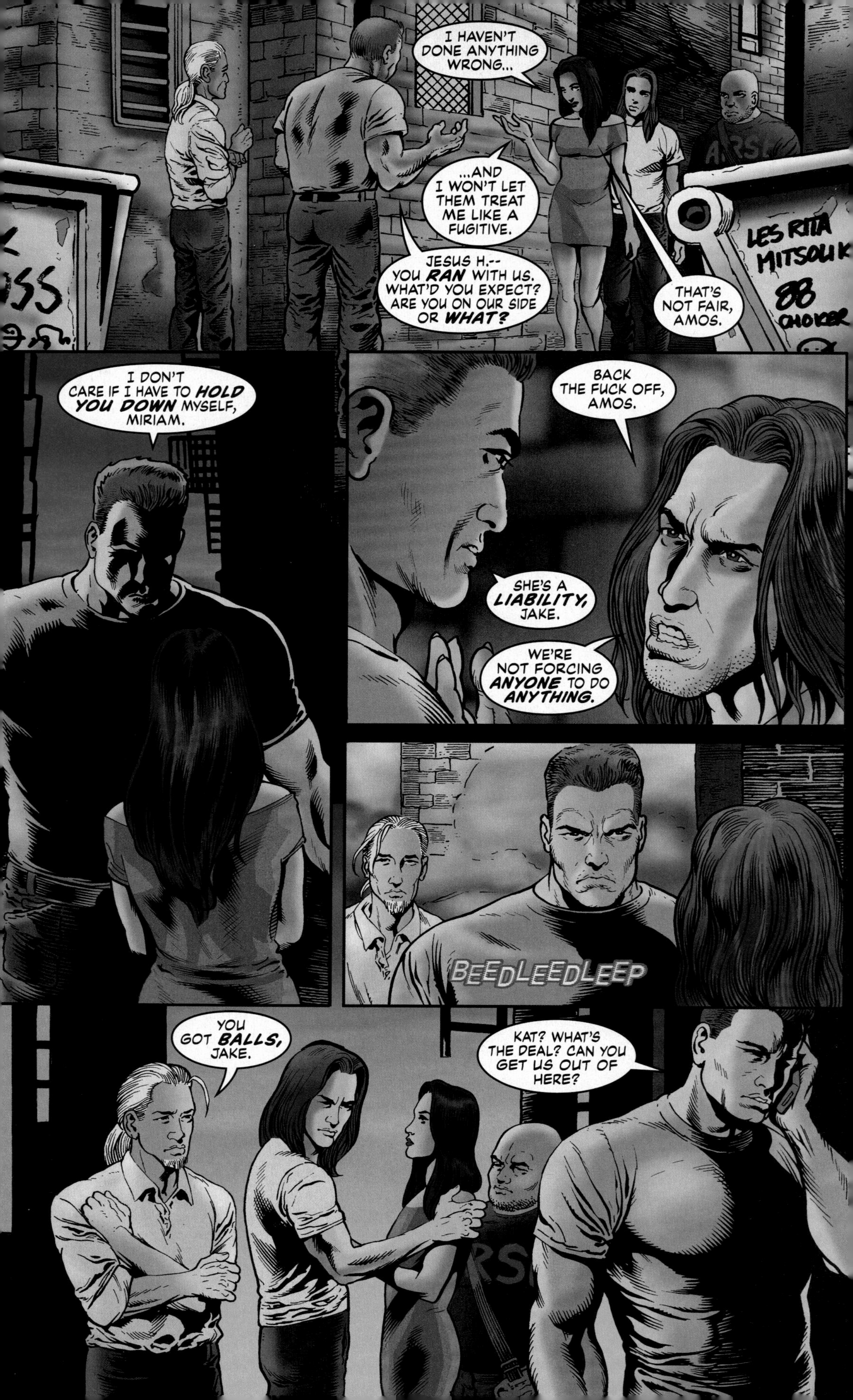
I HAVEN'T DONE ANYTHING WRONG...
...AND I WON'T LET THEM TREAT ME LIKE A FUGITIVE.
JESUS H.-- YOU RAN WITH US. WHAT'D YOU EXPECT? ARE YOU ON OUR SIDE OR WHAT?
THAT'S NOT FAIR, AMOS.
LES RITA MITSOUKO
88 CHOKER
I DON'T CARE IF I HAVE TO HOLD YOU DOWN MYSELF, MIRIAM.
BACK THE FUCK OFF, AMOS.
SHE'S A LIABILITY, JAKE.
WE'RE NOT FORCING ANYONE TO DO ANYTHING.
BEEDLEEDLEEP
YOU GOT BALLS, JAKE.
KAT? WHAT'S THE DEAL? CAN YOU GET US OUT OF HERE?

SO THIS IS YOUR NEW ORDER?

YOU CAN'T BLAME AMOS FOR WANTING TO BE CAREFUL, MIRIAM.

I DON'T. I BLAME *YOU* FOR STOOPING TO *HIS* LEVEL.

I'M STOOPING? YOU DO A PROTEST ALONG WITH THE *NATS* OF ALL PEOPLE, GET CAUGHT AND BRAINWASHED, AND THEN *WE* COME AND RESCUE YOU. *THAT'S* WHY WE'RE FUGITIVES.

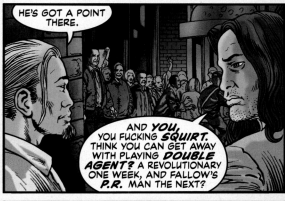

HE'S GOT A POINT THERE.

AND *YOU*, YOU FUCKING *SQUIRT*. THINK YOU CAN GET AWAY WITH PLAYING *DOUBLE AGENT?* A REVOLUTIONARY ONE WEEK, AND FALLOW'S *P.R.* MAN THE NEXT?

ALEC MEANT WELL, JAKE...

AND I'M SURE *YOU* DID, *TOO*, MIRIAM, WHEN YOU *SET US UP* TO BE ARRESTED.

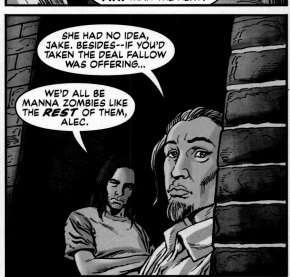

SHE HAD NO IDEA, JAKE. BESIDES--IF YOU'D TAKEN THE DEAL FALLOW WAS OFFERING...

WE'D ALL BE MANNA ZOMBIES LIKE THE *REST* OF THEM, ALEC.

I'M SORRY, JAKE. YOU GOTTA BELIEVE ME. I HAD NO IDEA.

I KNOW, ALEC. BUT THE *DAMAGE* HAS ALREADY BEEN DONE.

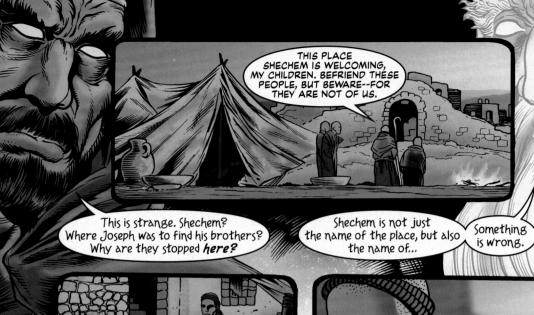

THIS PLACE SHECHEM IS WELCOMING, MY CHILDREN. BEFRIEND THESE PEOPLE, BUT BEWARE--FOR THEY ARE NOT OF US.

This is strange. Shechem? Where Joseph was to find his brothers? Why are they stopped *here?*

Shechem is not just the name of the place, but also the name of...

Something is wrong.

I AM *SHECHEM.* YOU WILL BE *MINE.*

IS THAT SO?

FASCINATING. DINAH IS JUST WALKING INTO THIS. IT WAS SUPPOSED TO BE A *RAPE.*

WAIT YET, HIS LUST IS STRONG.

NO... STOP!

STRUGGLE FOR YOUR FATHER'S *NAME,* IF YOU MUST. I KNOW THIS IS WHAT YOU REALLY *WANT.*

THERE HE GOES...

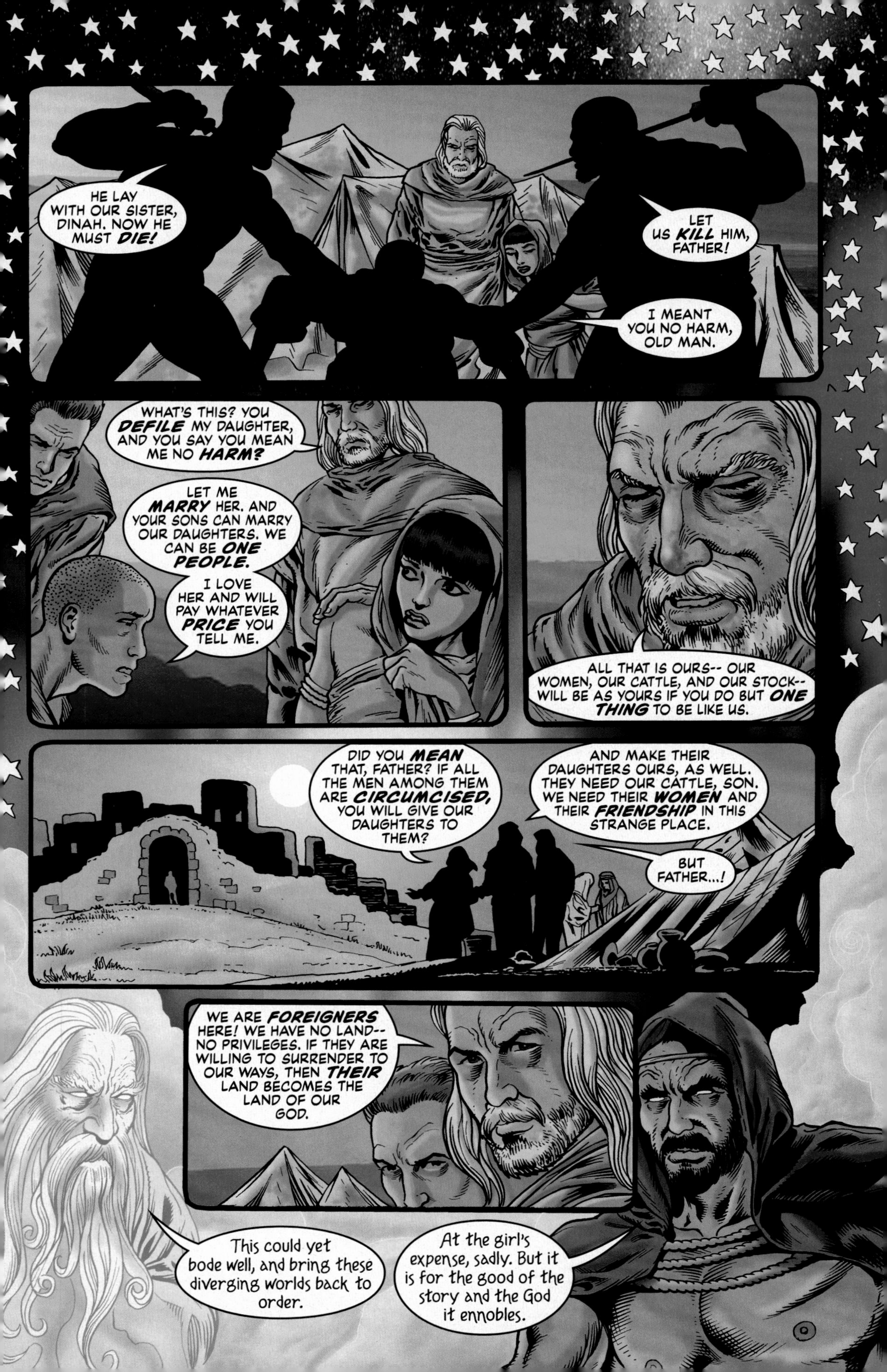

HE LAY WITH OUR SISTER, DINAH. NOW HE MUST DIE!
LET US KILL HIM, FATHER!
I MEANT YOU NO HARM, OLD MAN.
WHAT'S THIS? YOU DEFILE MY DAUGHTER, AND YOU SAY YOU MEAN ME NO HARM?
LET ME MARRY HER. AND YOUR SONS CAN MARRY OUR DAUGHTERS. WE CAN BE ONE PEOPLE.
I LOVE HER AND WILL PAY WHATEVER PRICE YOU TELL ME.
ALL THAT IS OURS-- OUR WOMEN, OUR CATTLE, AND OUR STOCK-- WILL BE AS YOURS IF YOU DO BUT ONE THING TO BE LIKE US.
DID YOU MEAN THAT, FATHER? IF ALL THE MEN AMONG THEM ARE CIRCUMCISED, YOU WILL GIVE OUR DAUGHTERS TO THEM?
AND MAKE THEIR DAUGHTERS OURS, AS WELL. THEY NEED OUR CATTLE, SON. WE NEED THEIR WOMEN AND THEIR FRIENDSHIP IN THIS STRANGE PLACE.
BUT FATHER...!
WE ARE FOREIGNERS HERE! WE HAVE NO LAND-- NO PRIVILEGES. IF THEY ARE WILLING TO SURRENDER TO OUR WAYS, THEN THEIR LAND BECOMES THE LAND OF OUR GOD.
This could yet bode well, and bring these diverging worlds back to order.
At the girl's expense, sadly. But it is for the good of the story and the God it ennobles.

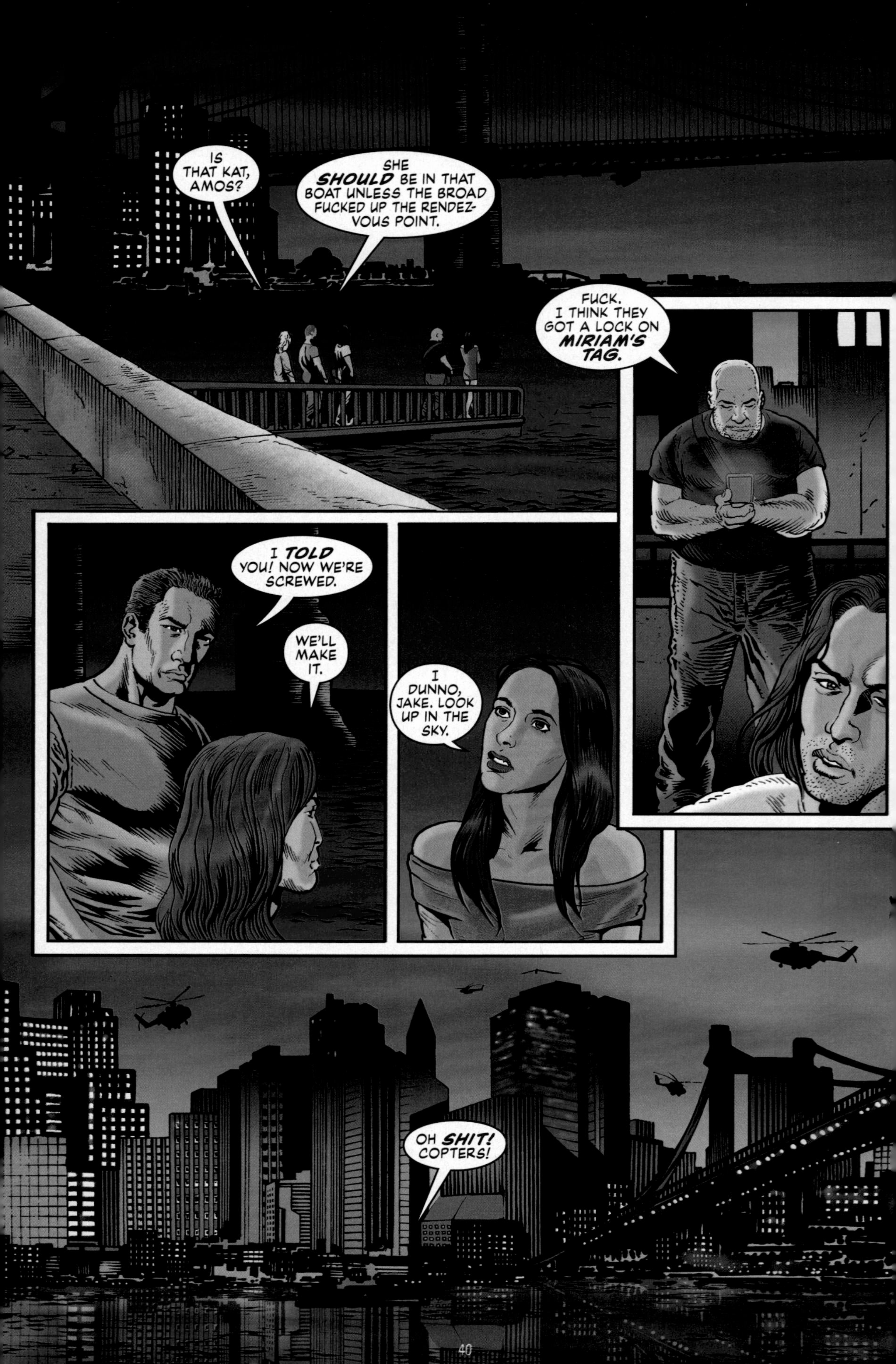

IS THAT KAT, AMOS?
SHE SHOULD BE IN THAT BOAT UNLESS THE BROAD FUCKED UP THE RENDEZ-VOUS POINT.
FUCK. I THINK THEY GOT A LOCK ON MIRIAM'S TAG.
I TOLD YOU! NOW WE'RE SCREWED.
WE'LL MAKE IT.
I DUNNO, JAKE. LOOK UP IN THE SKY.
OH SHIT! COPTERS!

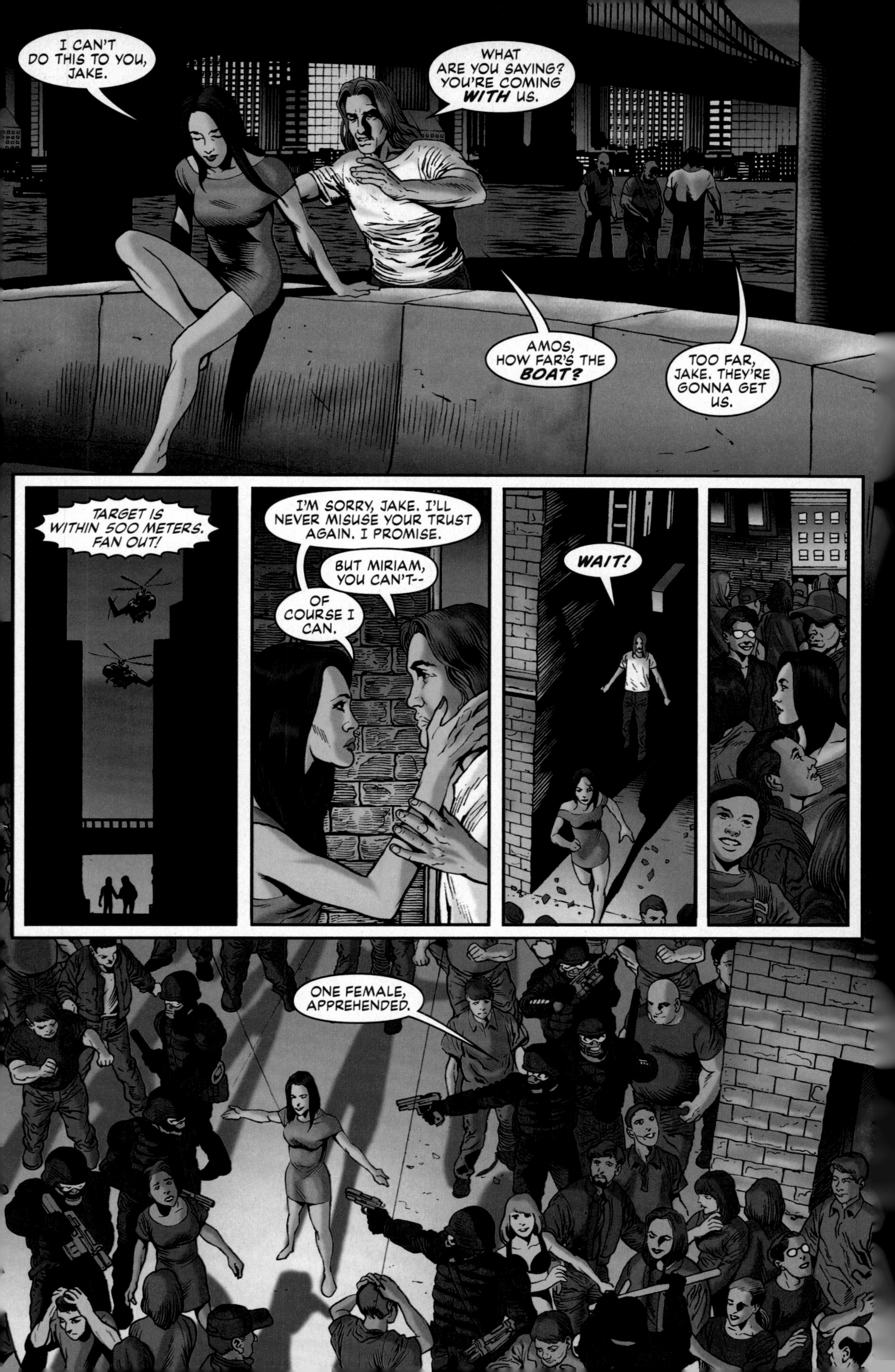
I CAN'T DO THIS TO YOU, JAKE.
WHAT ARE YOU SAYING? YOU'RE COMING WITH US.
AMOS, HOW FAR'S THE BOAT?
TOO FAR, JAKE. THEY'RE GONNA GET US.
TARGET IS WITHIN 500 METERS. FAN OUT!
I'M SORRY, JAKE. I'LL NEVER MISUSE YOUR TRUST AGAIN. I PROMISE.
BUT MIRIAM, YOU CAN'T--
OF COURSE I CAN.
WAIT!
ONE FEMALE, APPREHENDED.

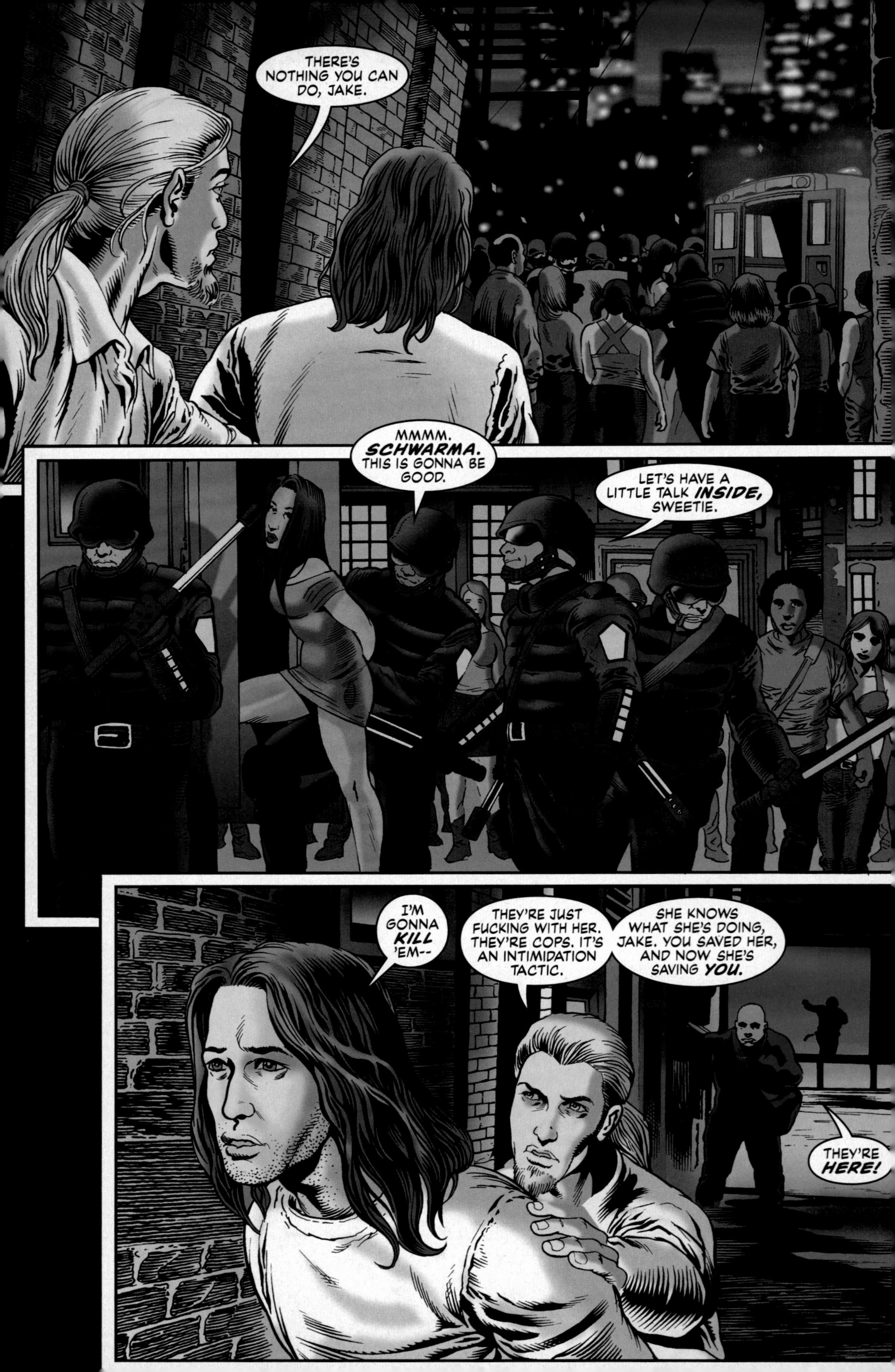
THERE'S NOTHING YOU CAN DO, JAKE.
MMMM. SCHWARMA. THIS IS GONNA BE GOOD.
LET'S HAVE A LITTLE TALK INSIDE, SWEETIE.
I'M GONNA KILL 'EM--
THEY'RE JUST FUCKING WITH HER. THEY'RE COPS. IT'S AN INTIMIDATION TACTIC.
SHE KNOWS WHAT SHE'S DOING, JAKE. YOU SAVED HER, AND NOW SHE'S SAVING YOU.
THEY'RE HERE!

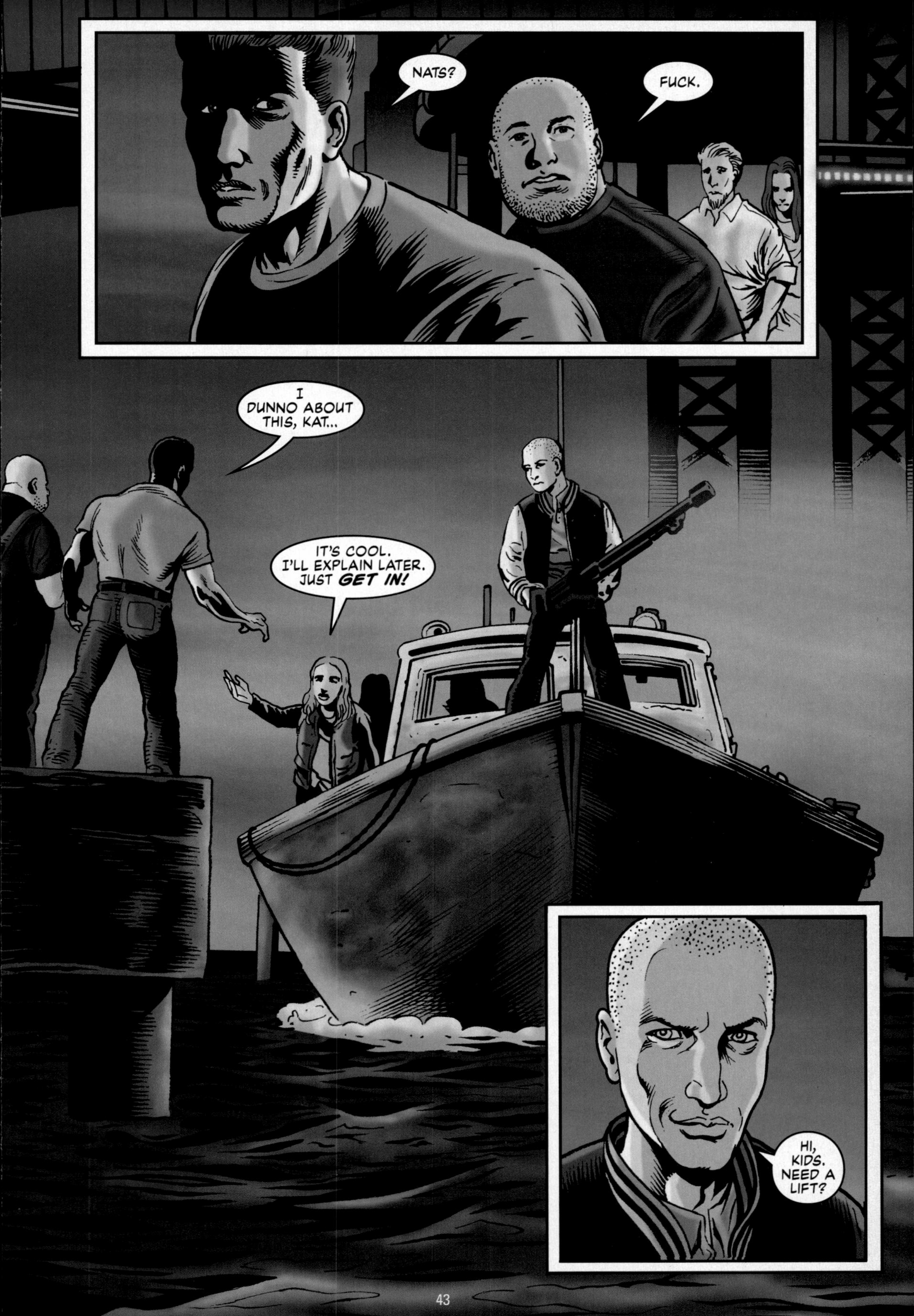
NATS?
FUCK.
I DUNNO ABOUT THIS, KAT...
IT'S COOL. I'LL EXPLAIN LATER. JUST **GET IN!**
HI, KIDS. NEED A LIFT?

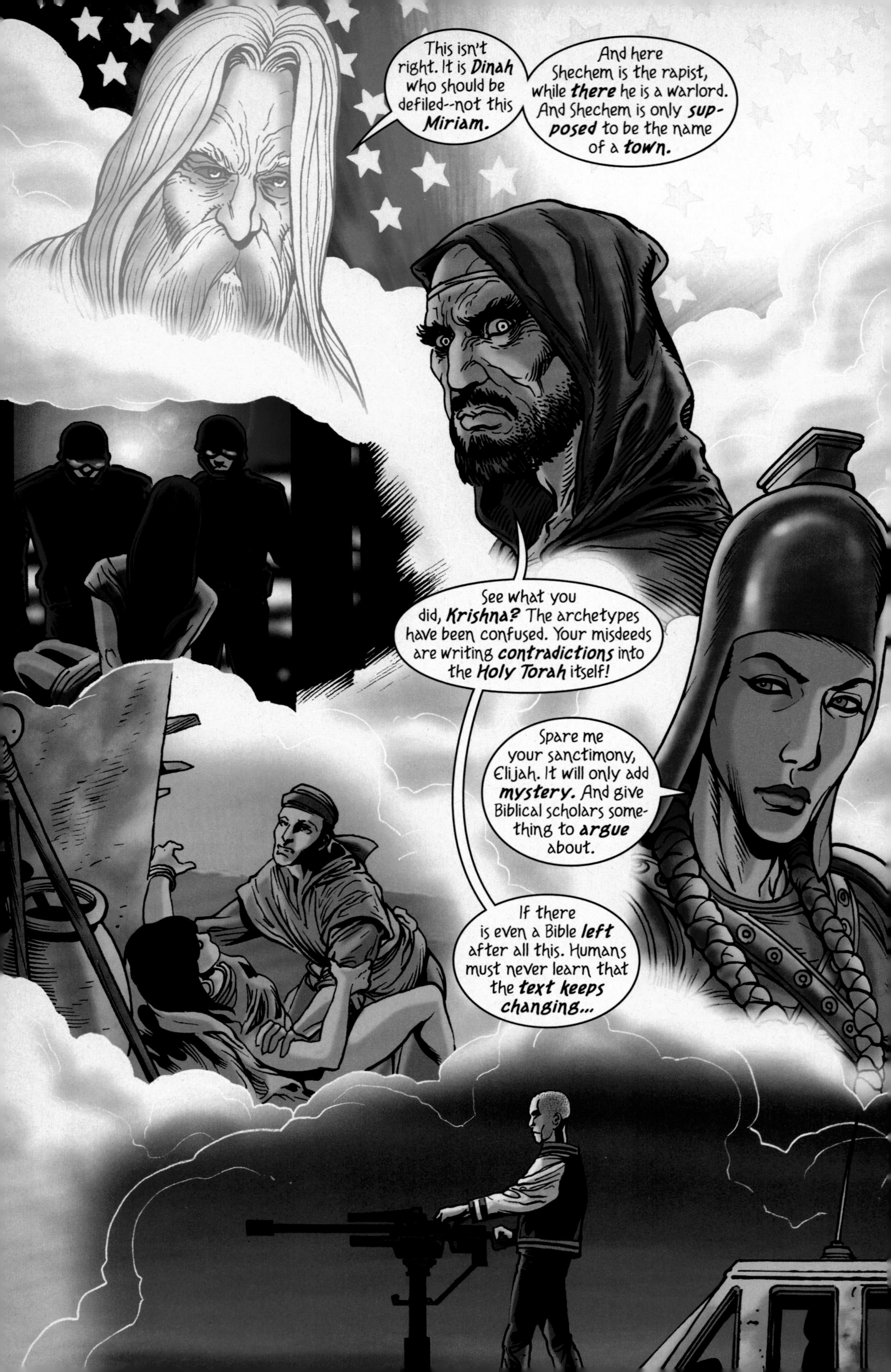
This isn't right. It is Dinah who should be defiled--not this Miriam.
And here Shechem is the rapist, while there he is a warlord. And Shechem is only supposed to be the name of a town.
See what you did, Krishna? The archetypes have been confused. Your misdeeds are writing contradictions into the Holy Torah itself!
Spare me your sanctimony, Elijah. It will only add mystery. And give Biblical scholars something to argue about.
If there is even a Bible left after all this. Humans must never learn that the text keeps changing...

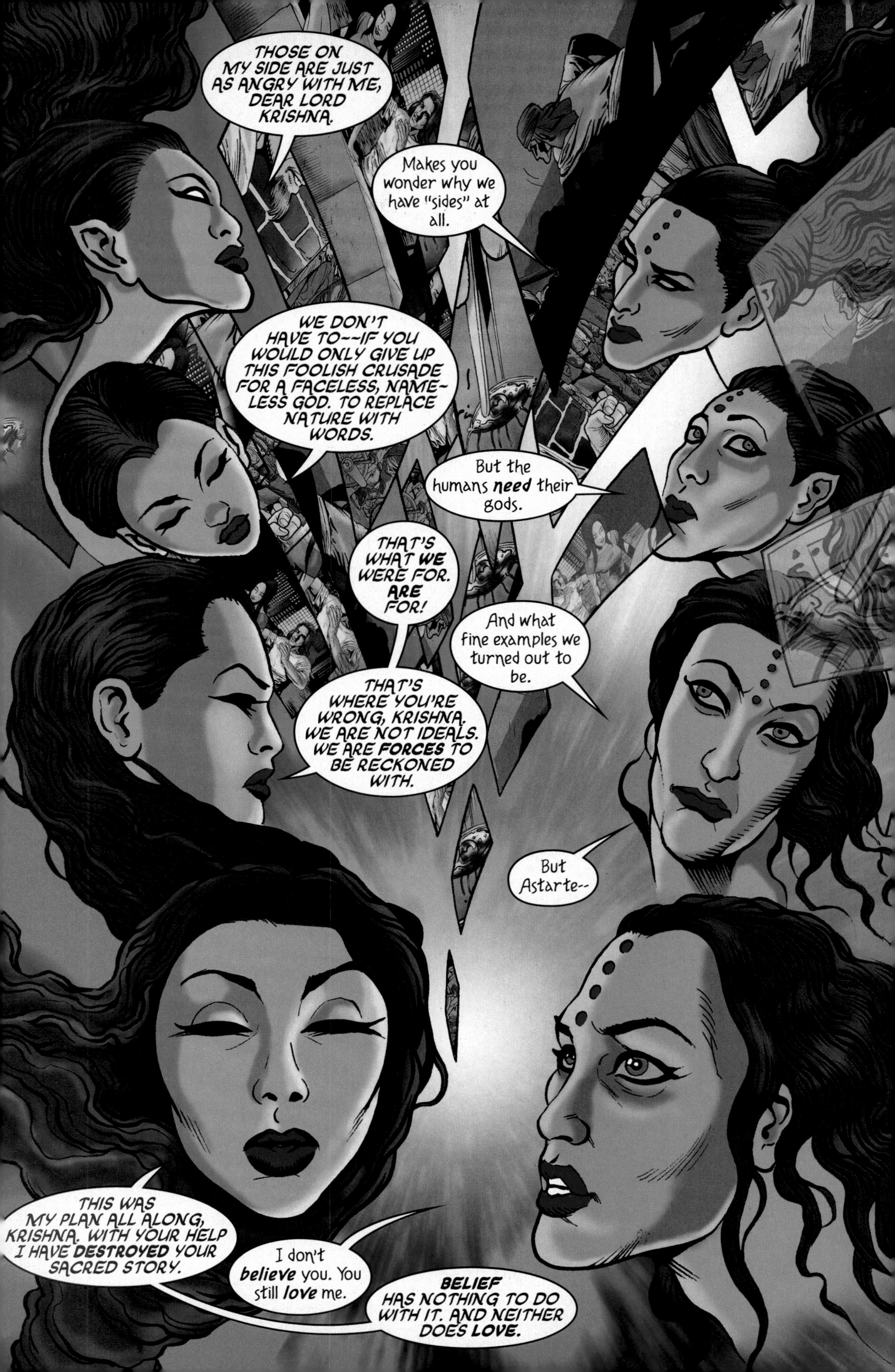
THOSE ON MY SIDE ARE JUST AS ANGRY WITH ME, DEAR LORD KRISHNA.
Makes you wonder why we have "sides" at all.
WE DON'T HAVE TO--IF YOU WOULD ONLY GIVE UP THIS FOOLISH CRUSADE FOR A FACELESS, NAME-LESS GOD. TO REPLACE NATURE WITH WORDS.
But the humans **need** their gods.
THAT'S WHAT **WE** WERE FOR. **ARE** FOR!
And what fine examples we turned out to be.
THAT'S WHERE YOU'RE WRONG, KRISHNA. WE ARE NOT IDEALS. WE ARE **FORCES** TO BE RECKONED WITH.
But Astarte--
THIS WAS MY PLAN ALL ALONG, KRISHNA. WITH YOUR HELP I HAVE **DESTROYED** YOUR SACRED STORY.
I don't **believe** you. You still **love** me.
BELIEF HAS NOTHING TO DO WITH IT. AND NEITHER DOES **LOVE.**

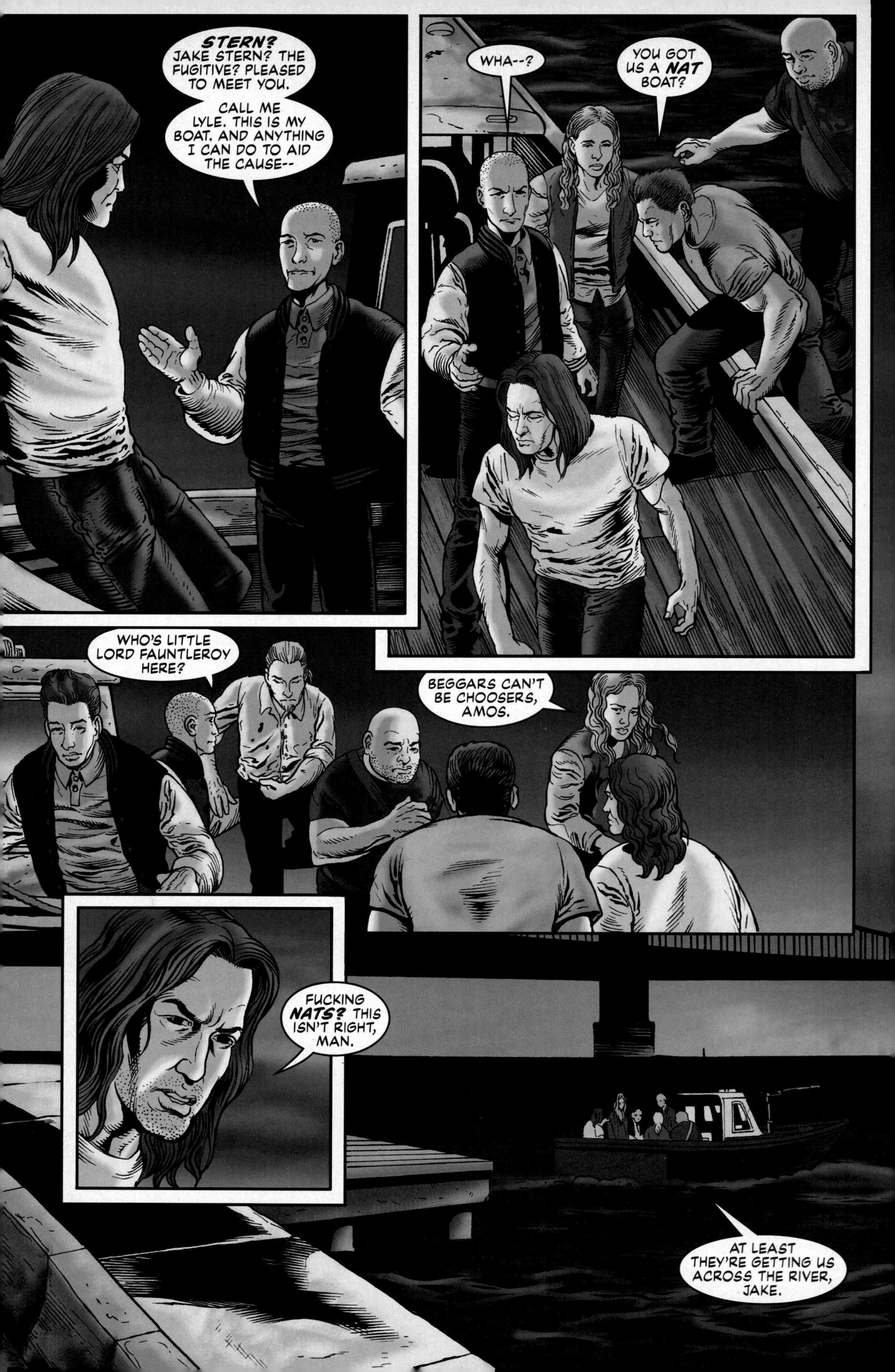
STERN? JAKE STERN? THE FUGITIVE? PLEASED TO MEET YOU.
CALL ME LYLE. THIS IS MY BOAT. AND ANYTHING I CAN DO TO AID THE CAUSE--
WHA--?
YOU GOT US A NAT BOAT?
WHO'S LITTLE LORD FAUNTLEROY HERE?
BEGGARS CAN'T BE CHOOSERS, AMOS.
FUCKING NATS? THIS ISN'T RIGHT, MAN.
AT LEAST THEY'RE GETTING US ACROSS THE RIVER, JAKE.

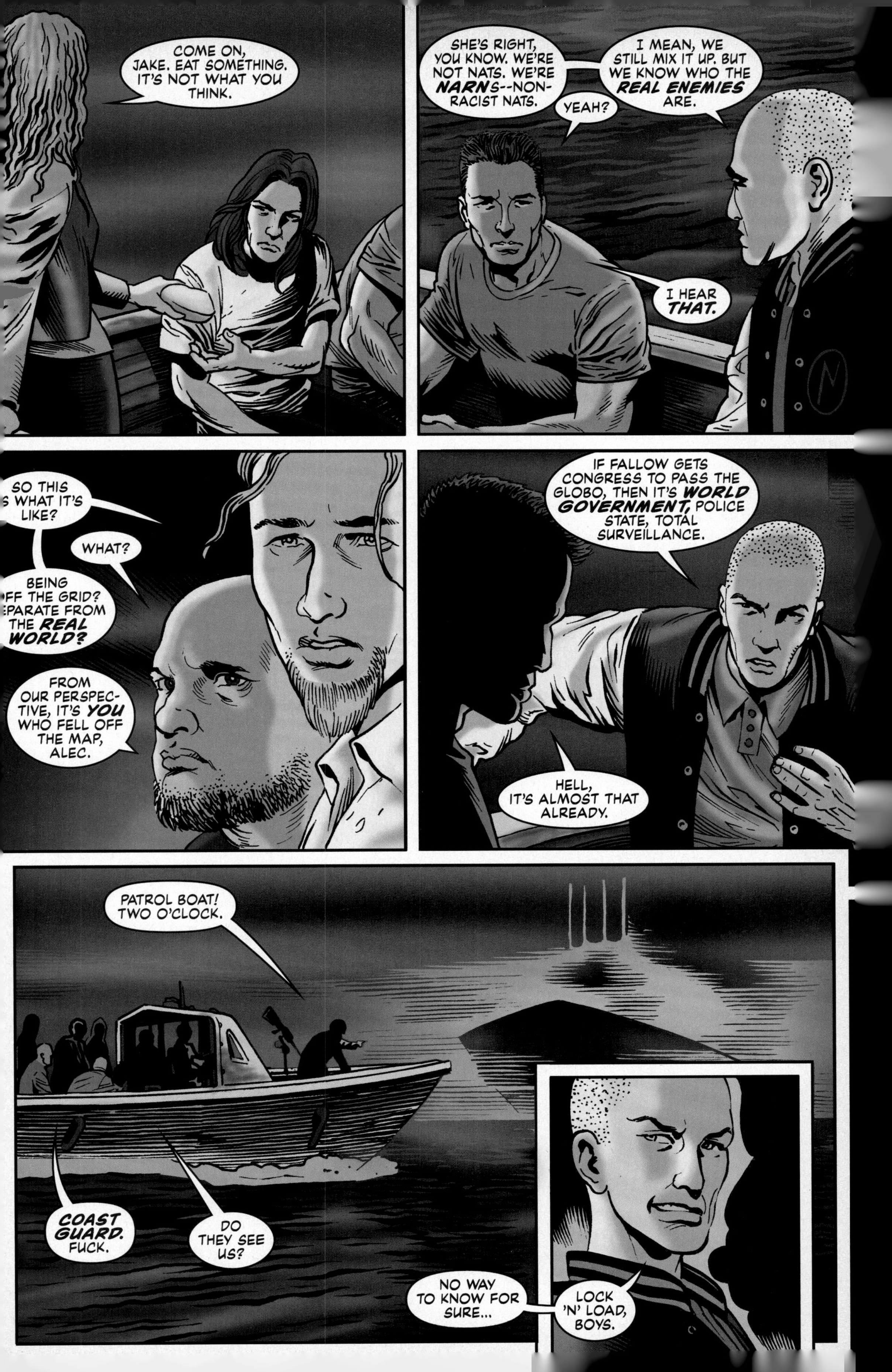
COME ON, JAKE. EAT SOMETHING. IT'S NOT WHAT YOU THINK.
SHE'S RIGHT, YOU KNOW. WE'RE NOT NATS. WE'RE NARNS--NON-RACIST NATS.
I MEAN, WE STILL MIX IT UP. BUT WE KNOW WHO THE REAL ENEMIES ARE.
YEAH?
I HEAR THAT.
SO THIS S WHAT IT'S LIKE?
WHAT?
BEING FF THE GRID? EPARATE FROM THE REAL WORLD?
FROM OUR PERSPECTIVE, IT'S YOU WHO FELL OFF THE MAP, ALEC.
IF FALLOW GETS CONGRESS TO PASS THE GLOBO, THEN IT'S WORLD GOVERNMENT, POLICE STATE, TOTAL SURVEILLANCE.
HELL, IT'S ALMOST THAT ALREADY.
PATROL BOAT! TWO O'CLOCK.
COAST GUARD. FUCK.
DO THEY SEE US?
NO WAY TO KNOW FOR SURE...
LOCK 'N' LOAD, BOYS.

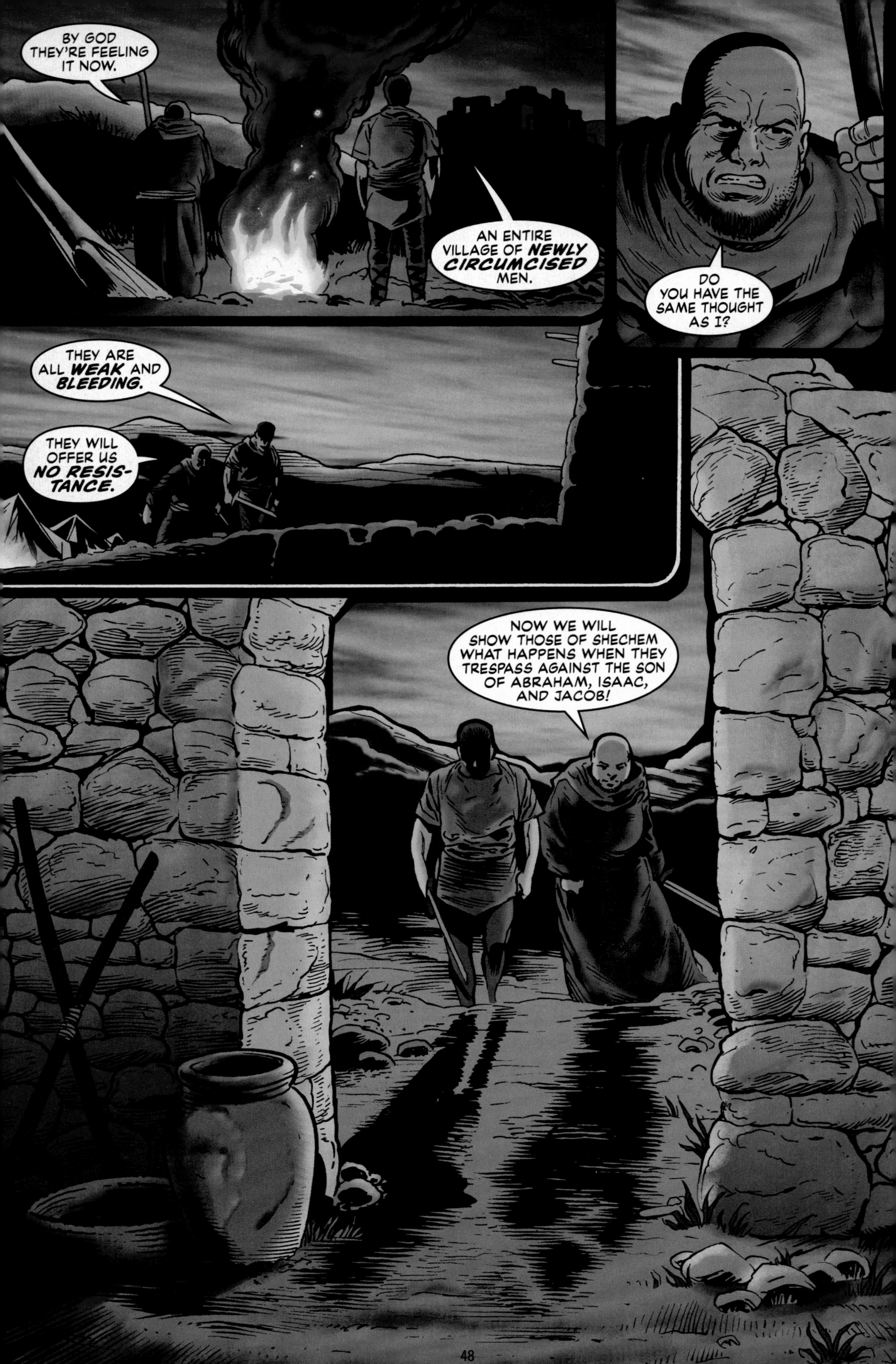
BY GOD THEY'RE FEELING IT NOW.
AN ENTIRE VILLAGE OF NEWLY CIRCUMCISED MEN.
DO YOU HAVE THE SAME THOUGHT AS I?
THEY ARE ALL WEAK AND BLEEDING.
THEY WILL OFFER US NO RESIS-TANCE.
NOW WE WILL SHOW THOSE OF SHECHEM WHAT HAPPENS WHEN THEY TRESPASS AGAINST THE SON OF ABRAHAM, ISAAC, AND JACOB!

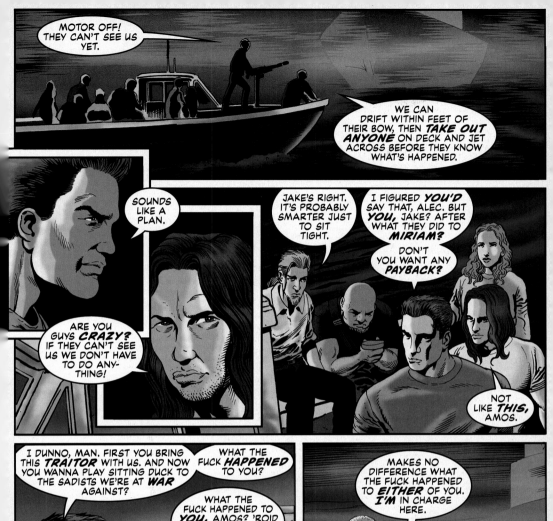

MOTOR OFF! THEY CAN'T SEE US YET.

WE CAN DRIFT WITHIN FEET OF THEIR BOW, THEN *TAKE OUT ANYONE* ON DECK AND JET ACROSS BEFORE THEY KNOW WHAT'S HAPPENED.

SOUNDS LIKE A PLAN.

JAKE'S RIGHT. IT'S PROBABLY SMARTER JUST TO SIT TIGHT.

I FIGURED *YOU'D* SAY THAT, ALEC. BUT *YOU*, JAKE? AFTER WHAT THEY DID TO *MIRIAM?*

DON'T YOU WANT ANY *PAYBACK?*

ARE YOU GUYS *CRAZY?* IF THEY CAN'T SEE US WE DON'T HAVE TO DO ANY-THING!

NOT LIKE *THIS*, AMOS.

I DUNNO, MAN. FIRST YOU BRING THIS *TRAITOR* WITH US. AND NOW YOU WANNA PLAY SITTING DUCK TO THE SADISTS WE'RE AT *WAR* AGAINST?

WHAT THE FUCK *HAPPENED* TO YOU?

WHAT THE FUCK HAPPENED TO *YOU*, AMOS? 'ROID RAGE? YOU REALLY WANNA *SHOOT* PEOPLE?

MAKES NO DIFFERENCE WHAT THE FUCK HAPPENED TO *EITHER* OF YOU. *I'M* IN CHARGE HERE.

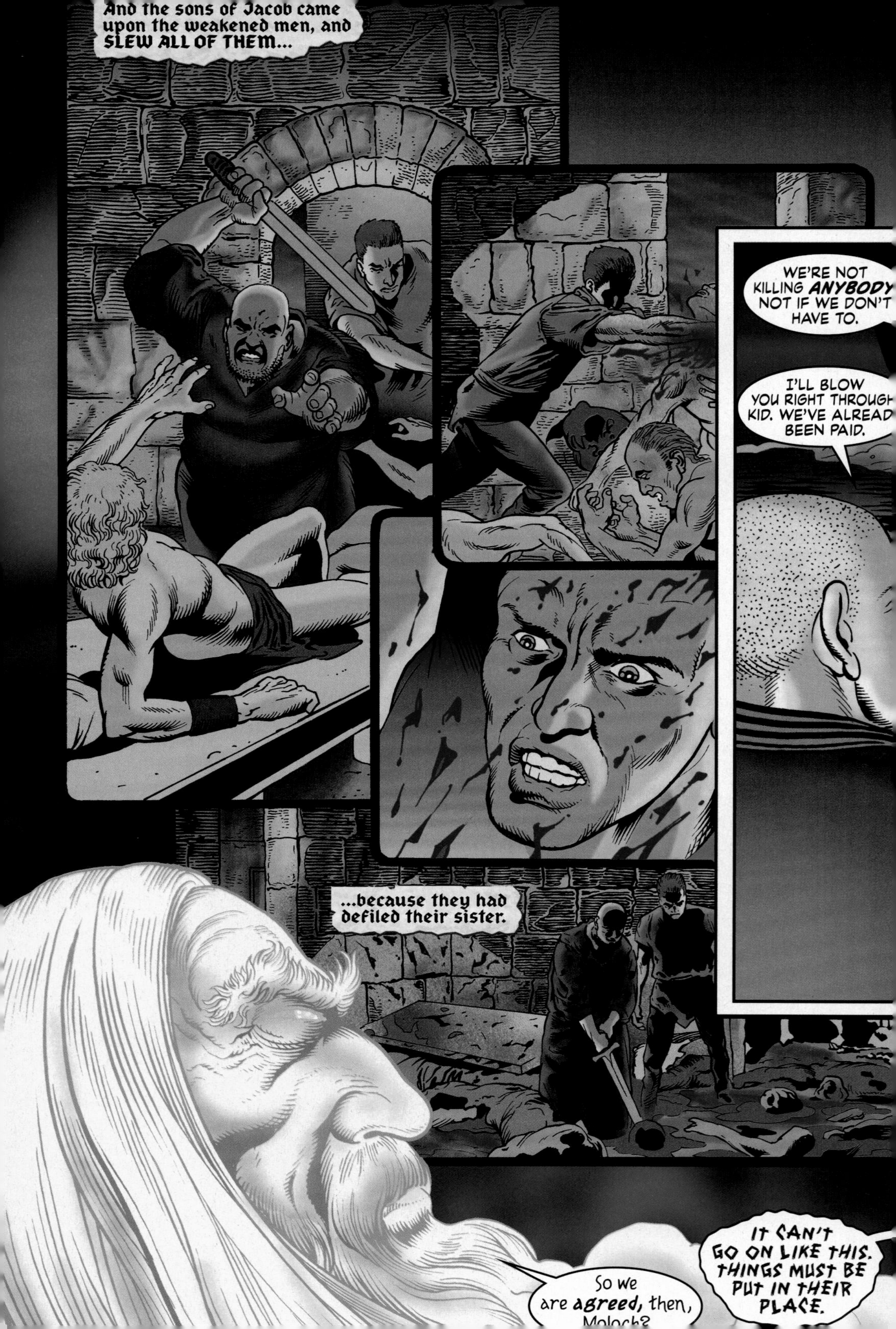
And the sons of Jacob came upon the weakened men, and SLEW ALL OF THEM...
WE'RE NOT KILLING ANYBODY NOT IF WE DON'T HAVE TO.
I'LL BLOW YOU RIGHT THROUGH KID. WE'VE ALREAD BEEN PAID.
...because they had defiled their sister.
So we are agreed, then,
IT CAN'T GO ON LIKE THIS. THINGS MUST BE PUT IN THEIR PLACE.

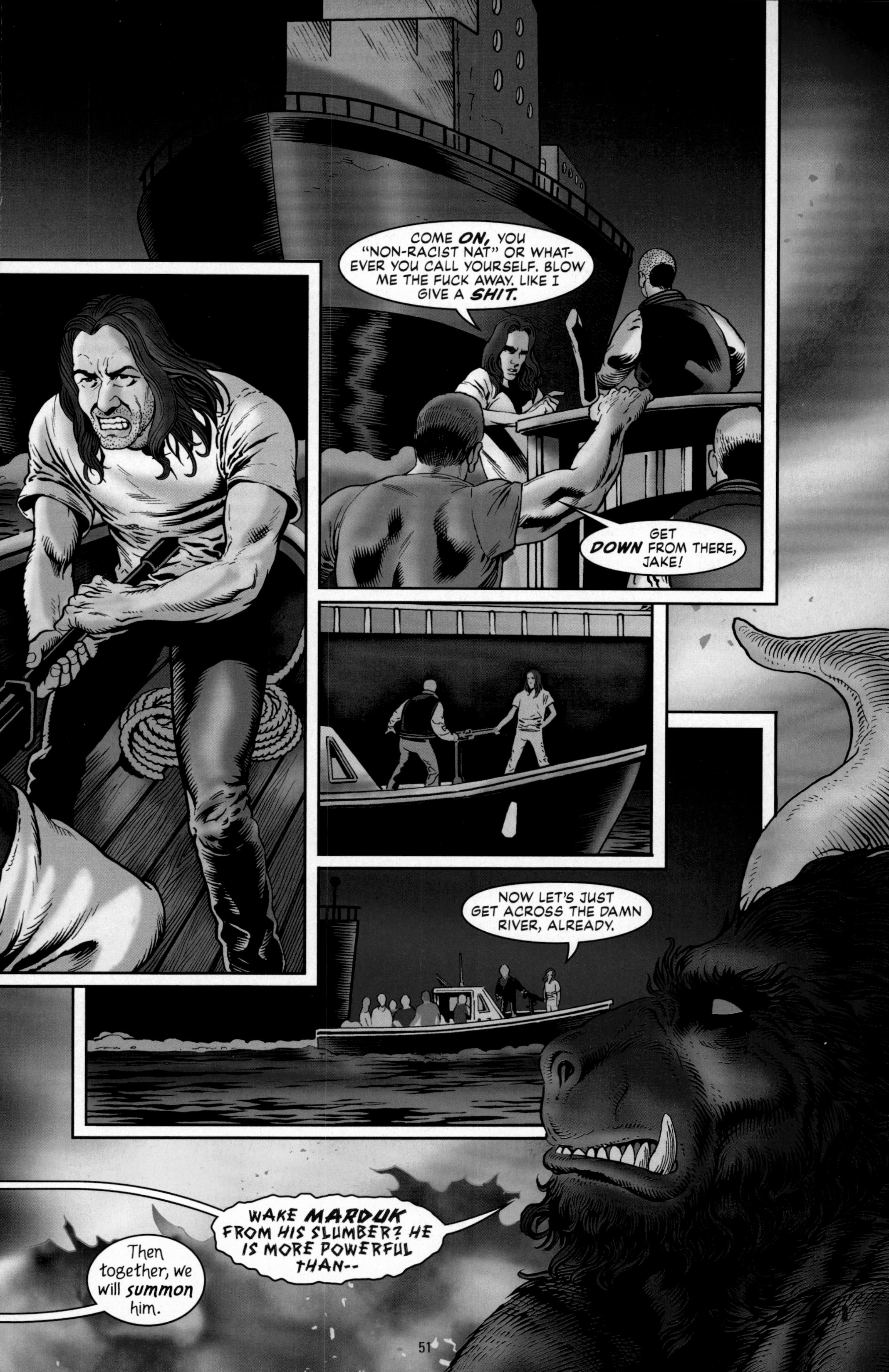

COME ON, YOU "NON-RACIST NAT" OR WHAT-EVER YOU CALL YOURSELF. BLOW ME THE FUCK AWAY. LIKE I GIVE A SHIT.
GET DOWN FROM THERE, JAKE!
NOW LET'S JUST GET ACROSS THE DAMN RIVER, ALREADY.
WAKE MARDUK FROM HIS SLUMBER? HE IS MORE POWERFUL THAN--
Then together, we will summon him.

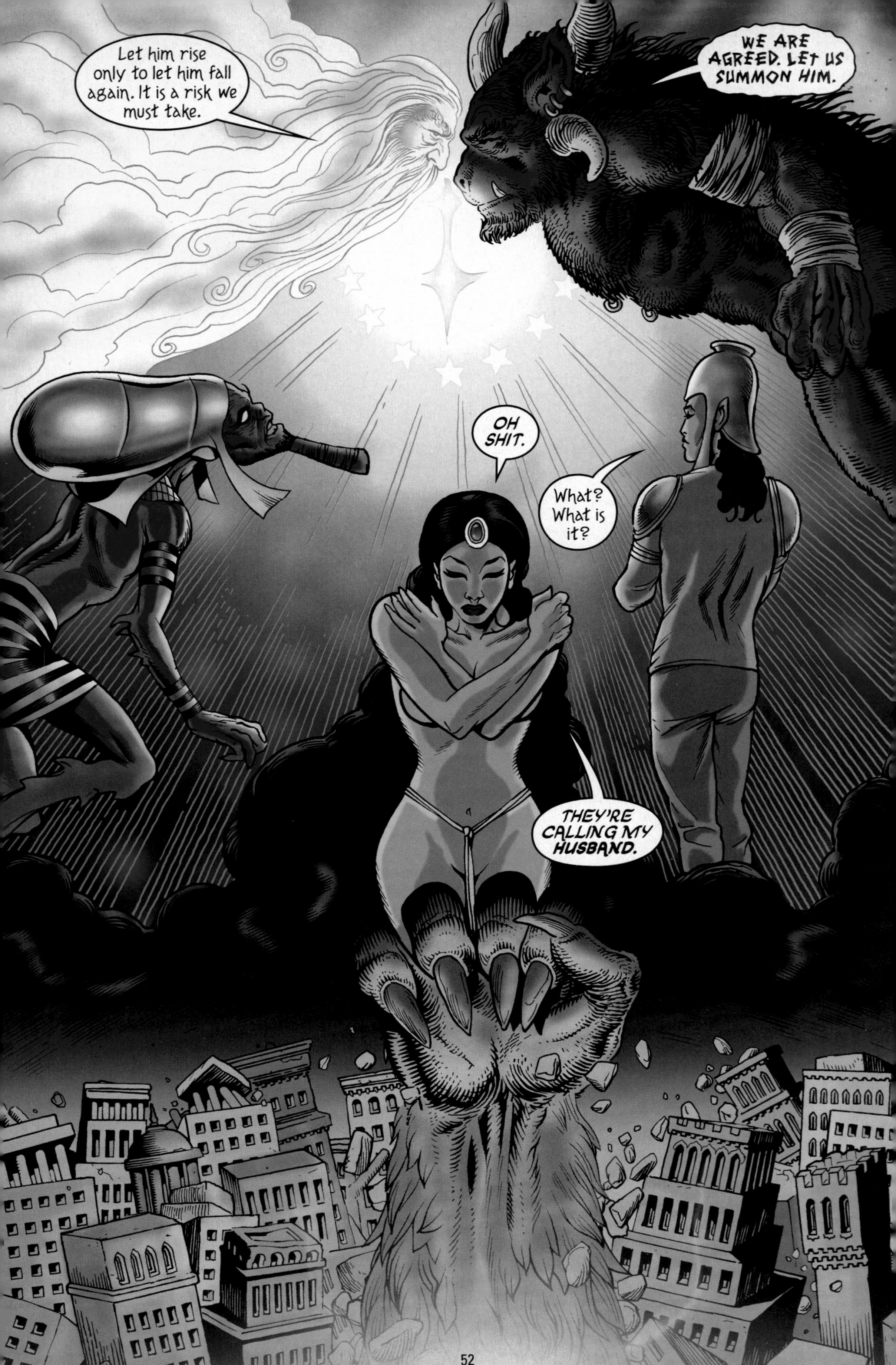
Let him rise only to let him fall again. It is a risk we must take.
WE ARE AGREED. LET US SUMMON HIM.
OH SHIT.
What? What is it?
THEY'RE CALLING MY HUSBAND.

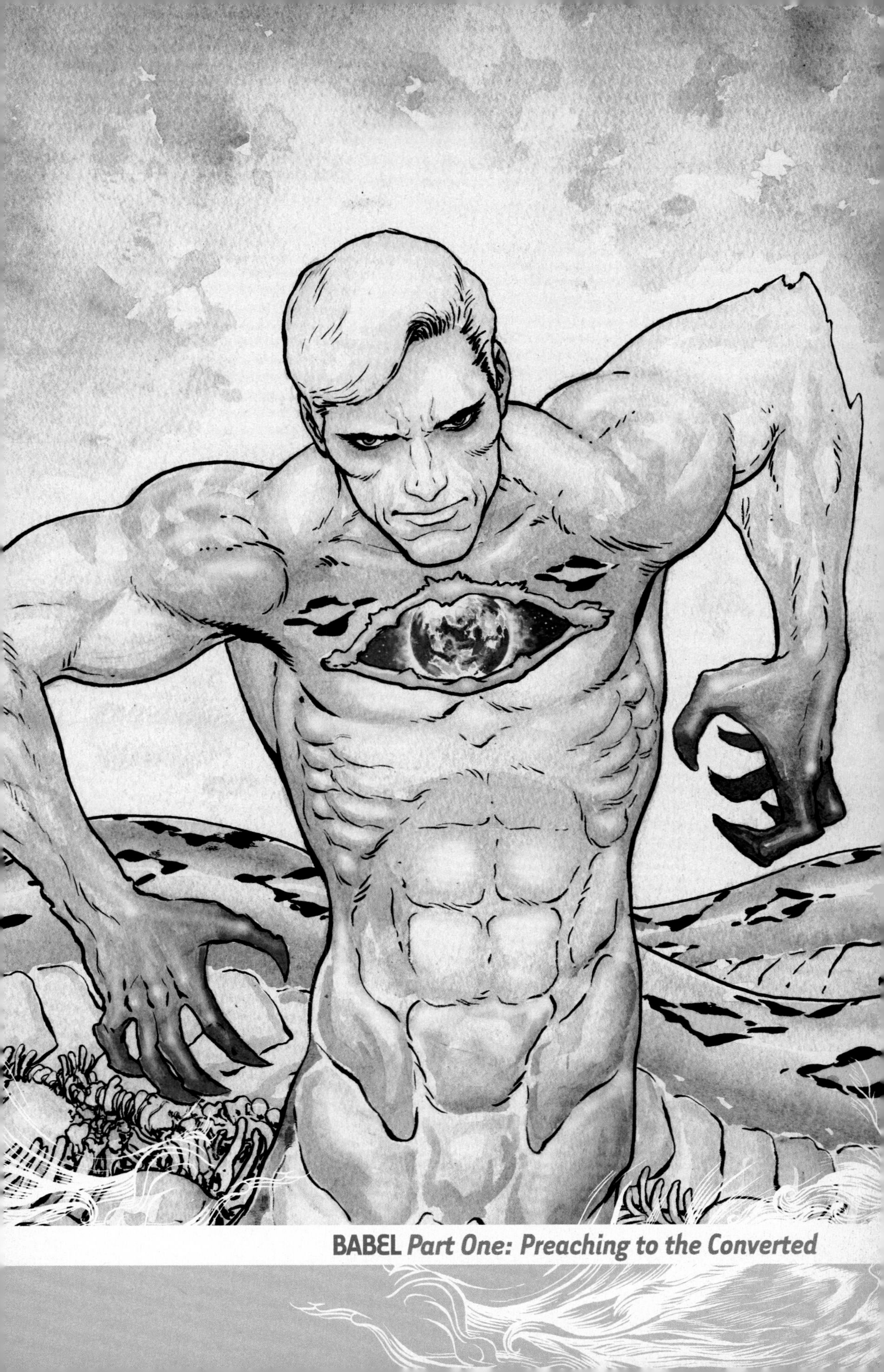

BABEL ***Part One: Preaching to the Converted***

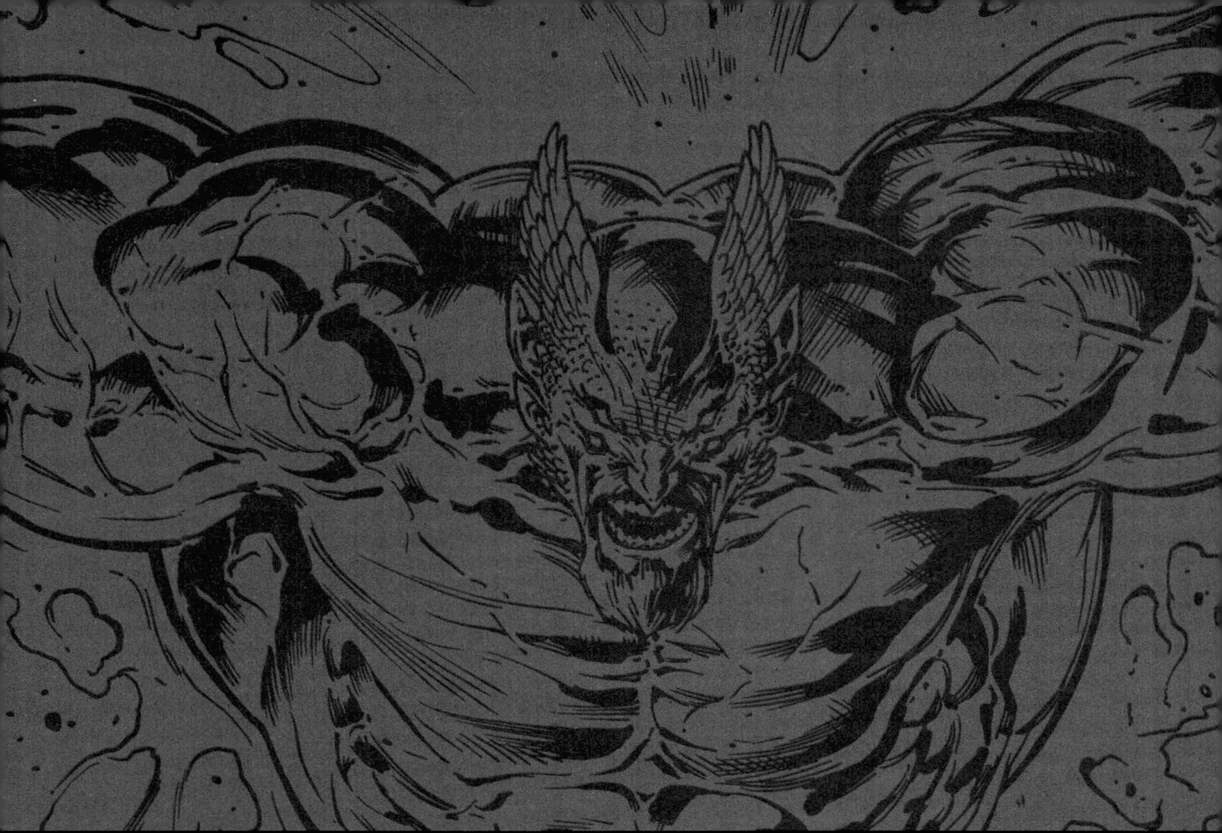

TESTAMENT

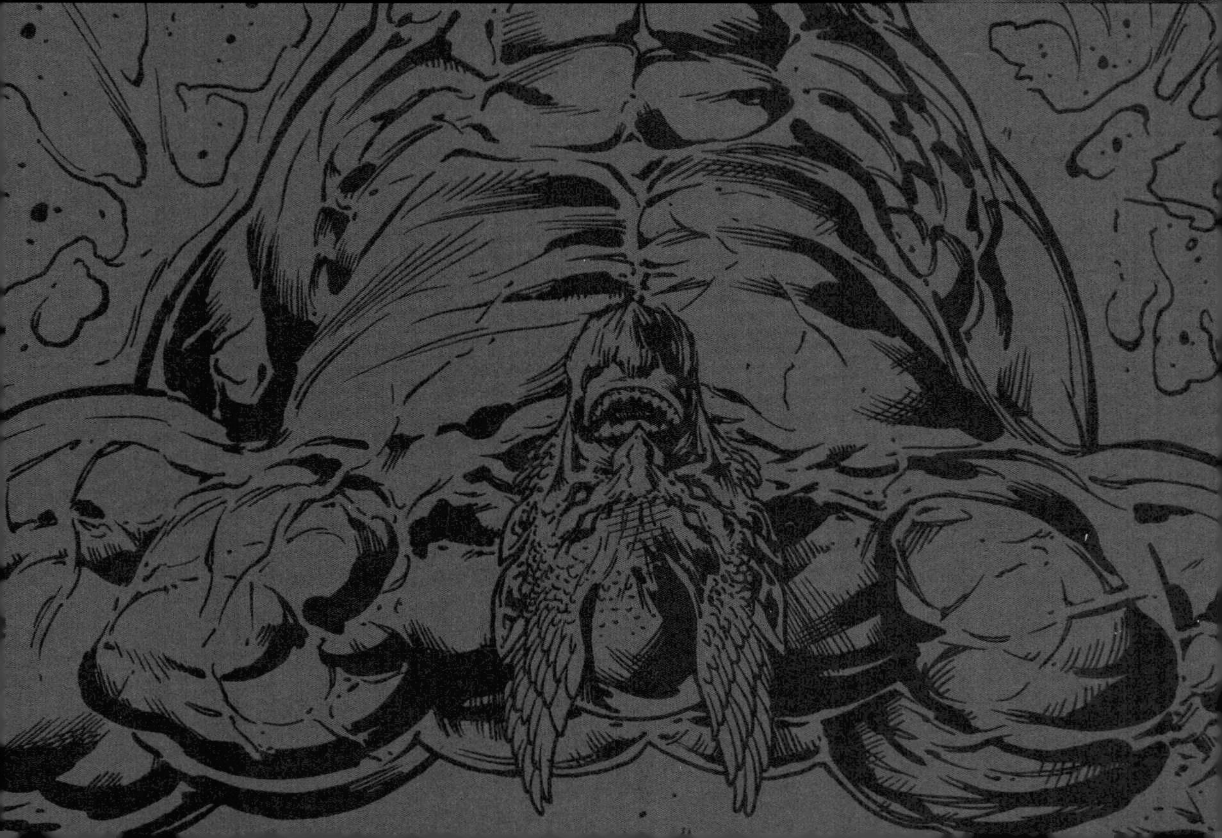

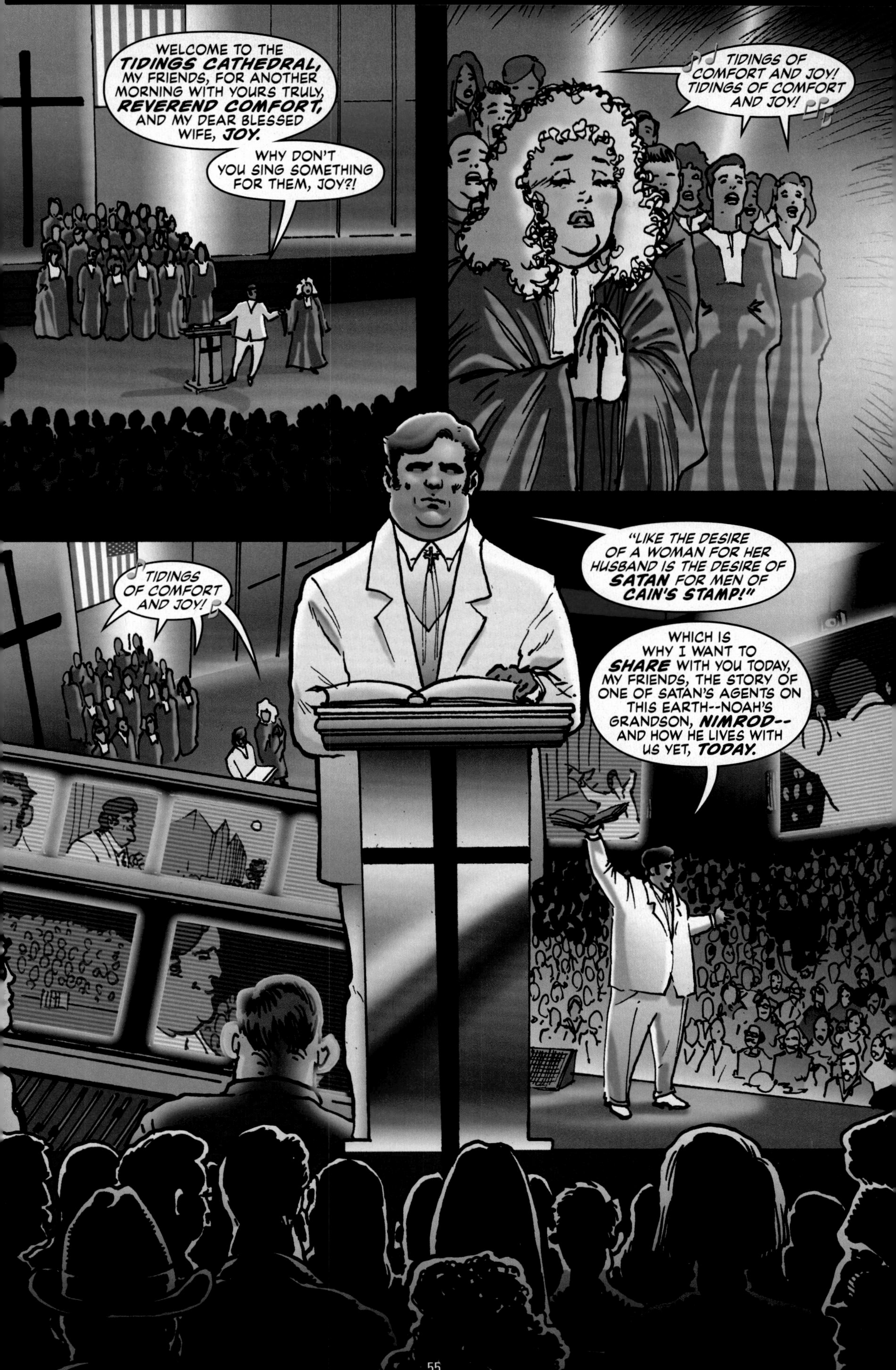
WELCOME TO THE TIDINGS CATHEDRAL, MY FRIENDS, FOR ANOTHER MORNING WITH YOURS TRULY, REVEREND COMFORT, AND MY DEAR BLESSED WIFE, JOY.
WHY DON'T YOU SING SOMETHING FOR THEM, JOY?!
TIDINGS OF COMFORT AND JOY! TIDINGS OF COMFORT AND JOY!
TIDINGS OF COMFORT AND JOY!
"LIKE THE DESIRE OF A WOMAN FOR HER HUSBAND IS THE DESIRE OF SATAN FOR MEN OF CAIN'S STAMP!"
WHICH IS WHY I WANT TO SHARE WITH YOU TODAY, MY FRIENDS, THE STORY OF ONE OF SATAN'S AGENTS ON THIS EARTH--NOAH'S GRANDSON, NIMROD--AND HOW HE LIVES WITH US YET, TODAY.

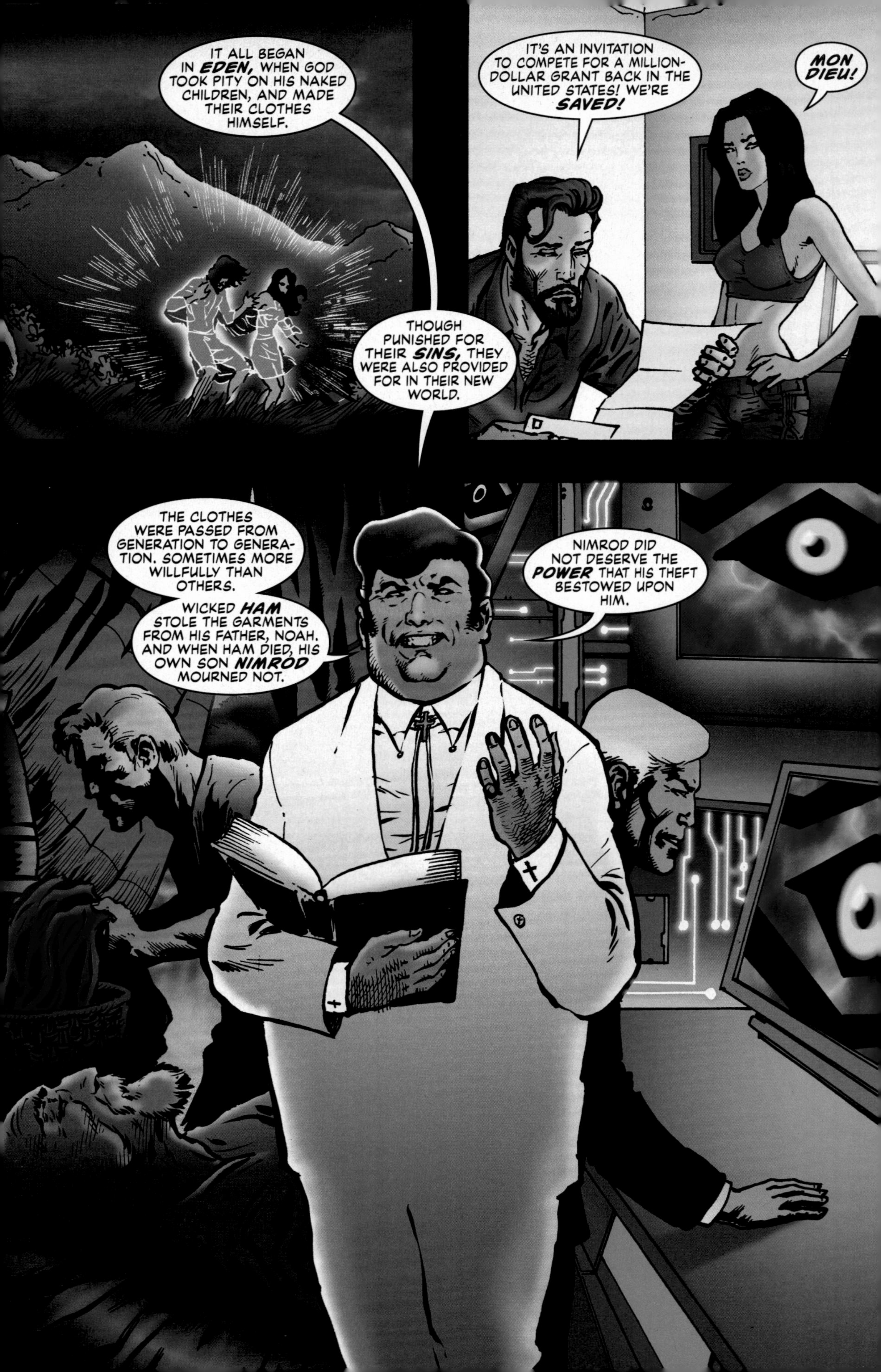
IT ALL BEGAN IN EDEN, WHEN GOD TOOK PITY ON HIS NAKED CHILDREN, AND MADE THEIR CLOTHES HIMSELF.
THOUGH PUNISHED FOR THEIR SINS, THEY WERE ALSO PROVIDED FOR IN THEIR NEW WORLD.
IT'S AN INVITATION TO COMPETE FOR A MILLION-DOLLAR GRANT BACK IN THE UNITED STATES! WE'RE SAVED!
MON DIEU!
THE CLOTHES WERE PASSED FROM GENERATION TO GENERATION. SOMETIMES MORE WILLFULLY THAN OTHERS.
WICKED HAM STOLE THE GARMENTS FROM HIS FATHER, NOAH. AND WHEN HAM DIED, HIS OWN SON NIMROD MOURNED NOT.
NIMROD DID NOT DESERVE THE POWER THAT HIS THEFT BESTOWED UPON HIM.

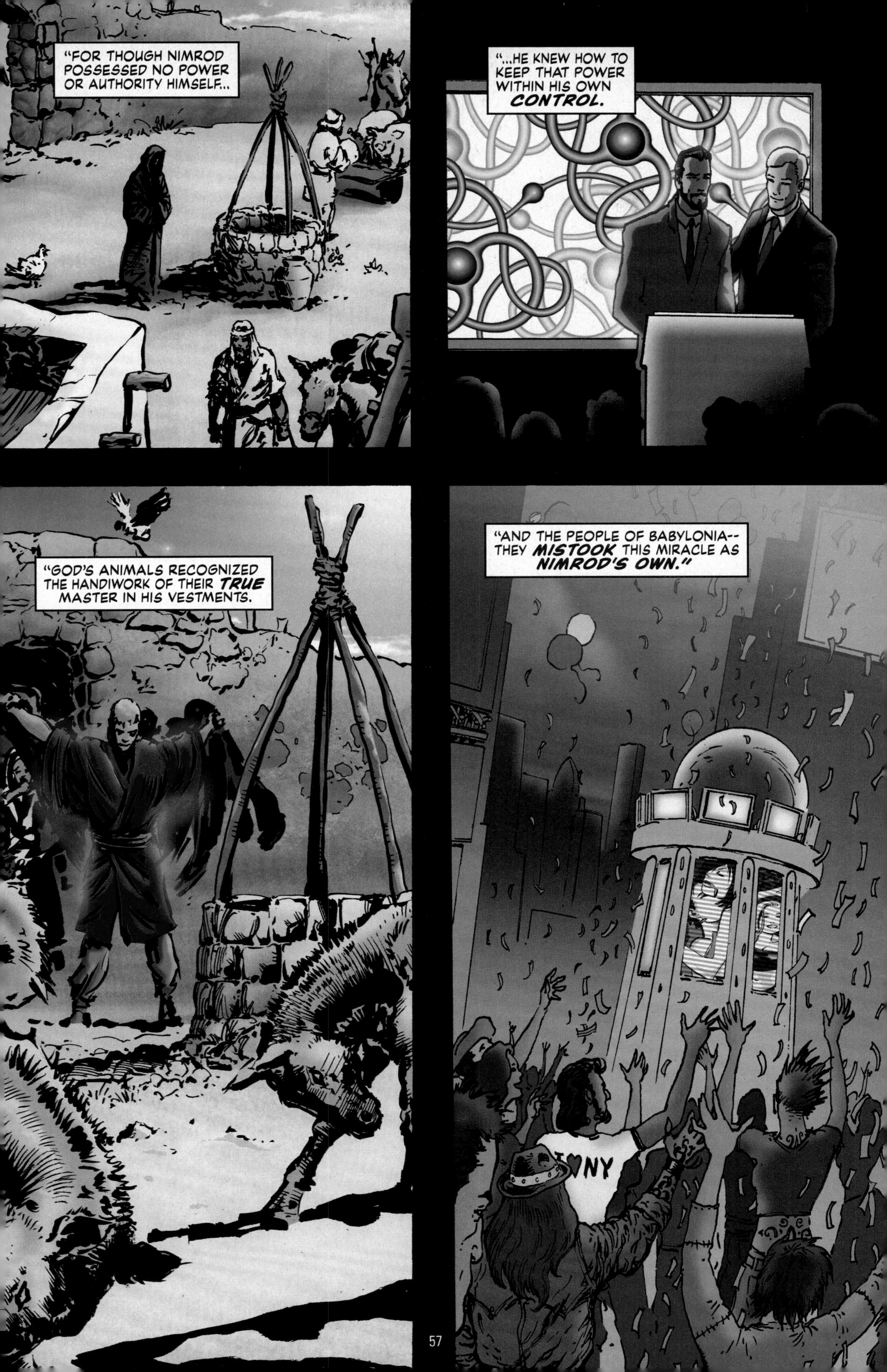
"FOR THOUGH NIMROD POSSESSED NO POWER OR AUTHORITY HIMSELF...
"...HE KNEW HOW TO KEEP THAT POWER WITHIN HIS OWN CONTROL.
"GOD'S ANIMALS RECOGNIZED THE HANDIWORK OF THEIR TRUE MASTER IN HIS VESTMENTS.
"AND THE PEOPLE OF BABYLONIA-- THEY MISTOOK THIS MIRACLE AS NIMROD'S OWN."
I♥NY

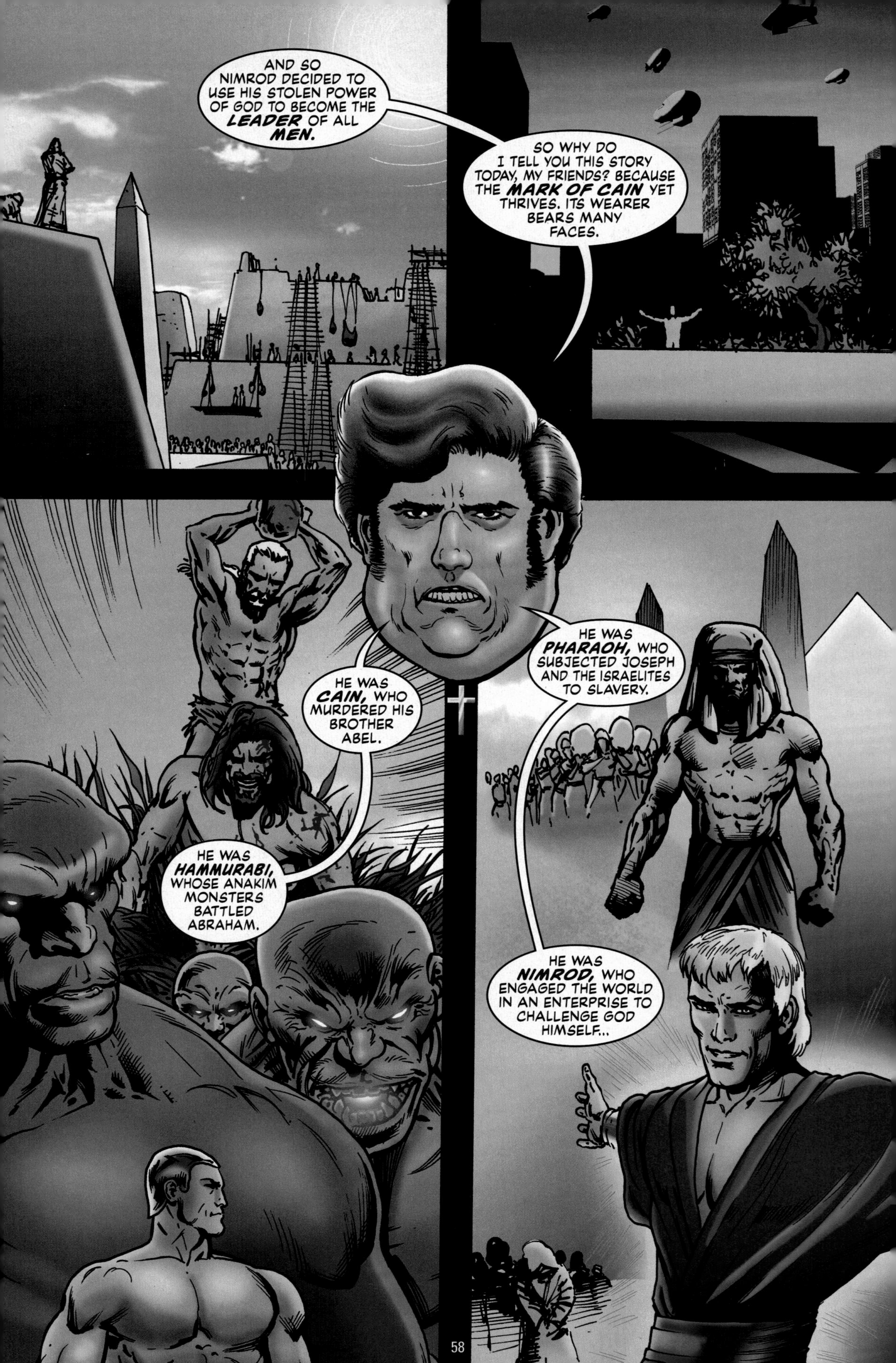
AND SO NIMROD DECIDED TO USE HIS STOLEN POWER OF GOD TO BECOME THE LEADER OF ALL MEN.
SO WHY DO I TELL YOU THIS STORY TODAY, MY FRIENDS? BECAUSE THE MARK OF CAIN YET THRIVES. ITS WEARER BEARS MANY FACES.
HE WAS CAIN, WHO MURDERED HIS BROTHER ABEL.
HE WAS HAMMURABI, WHOSE ANAKIM MONSTERS BATTLED ABRAHAM.
HE WAS PHARAOH, WHO SUBJECTED JOSEPH AND THE ISRAELITES TO SLAVERY.
HE WAS NIMROD, WHO ENGAGED THE WORLD IN AN ENTERPRISE TO CHALLENGE GOD HIMSELF...

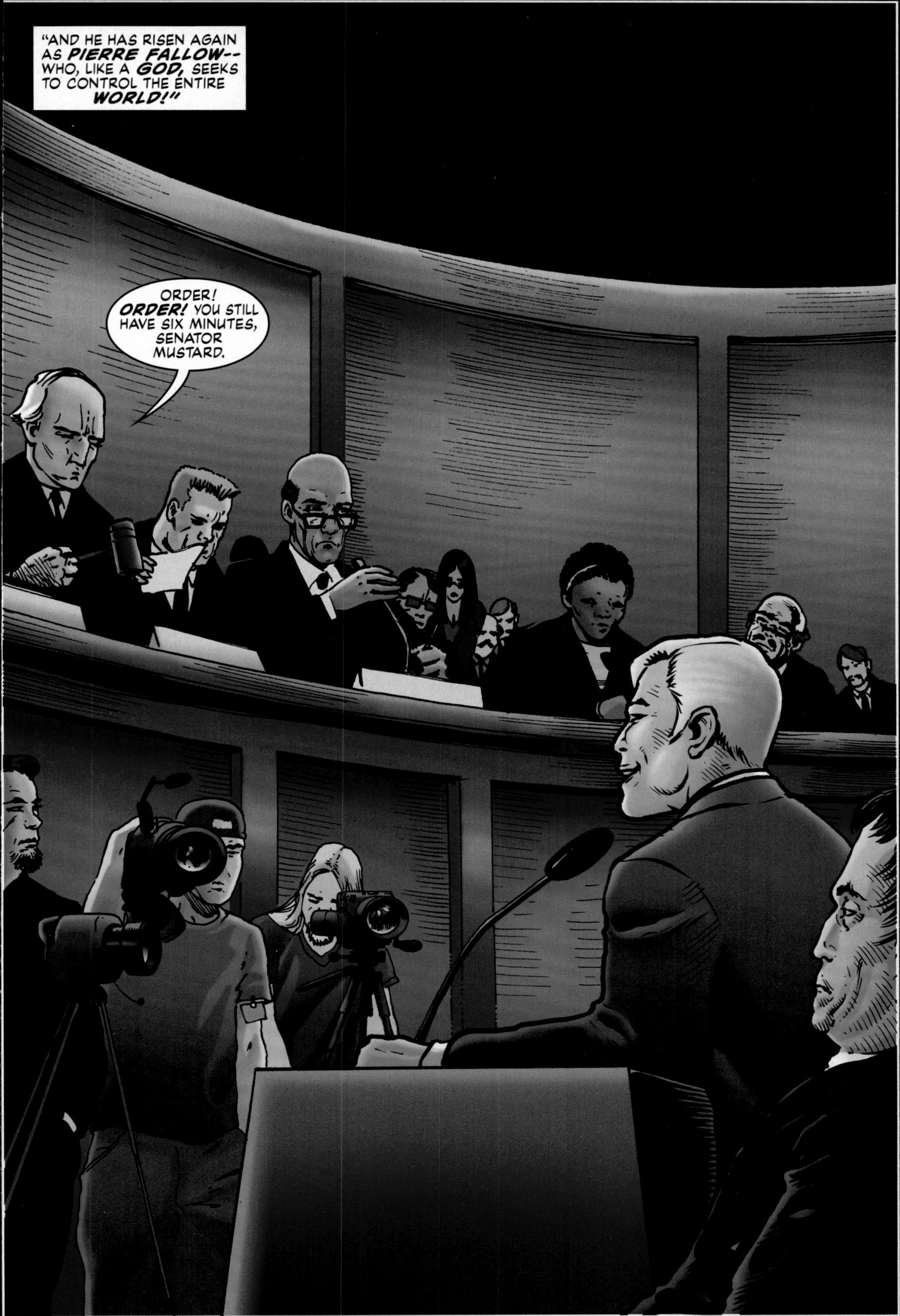
"AND HE HAS RISEN AGAIN AS PIERRE FALLOW-- WHO, LIKE A GOD, SEEKS TO CONTROL THE ENTIRE WORLD!"
ORDER! ORDER! YOU STILL HAVE SIX MINUTES, SENATOR MUSTARD.

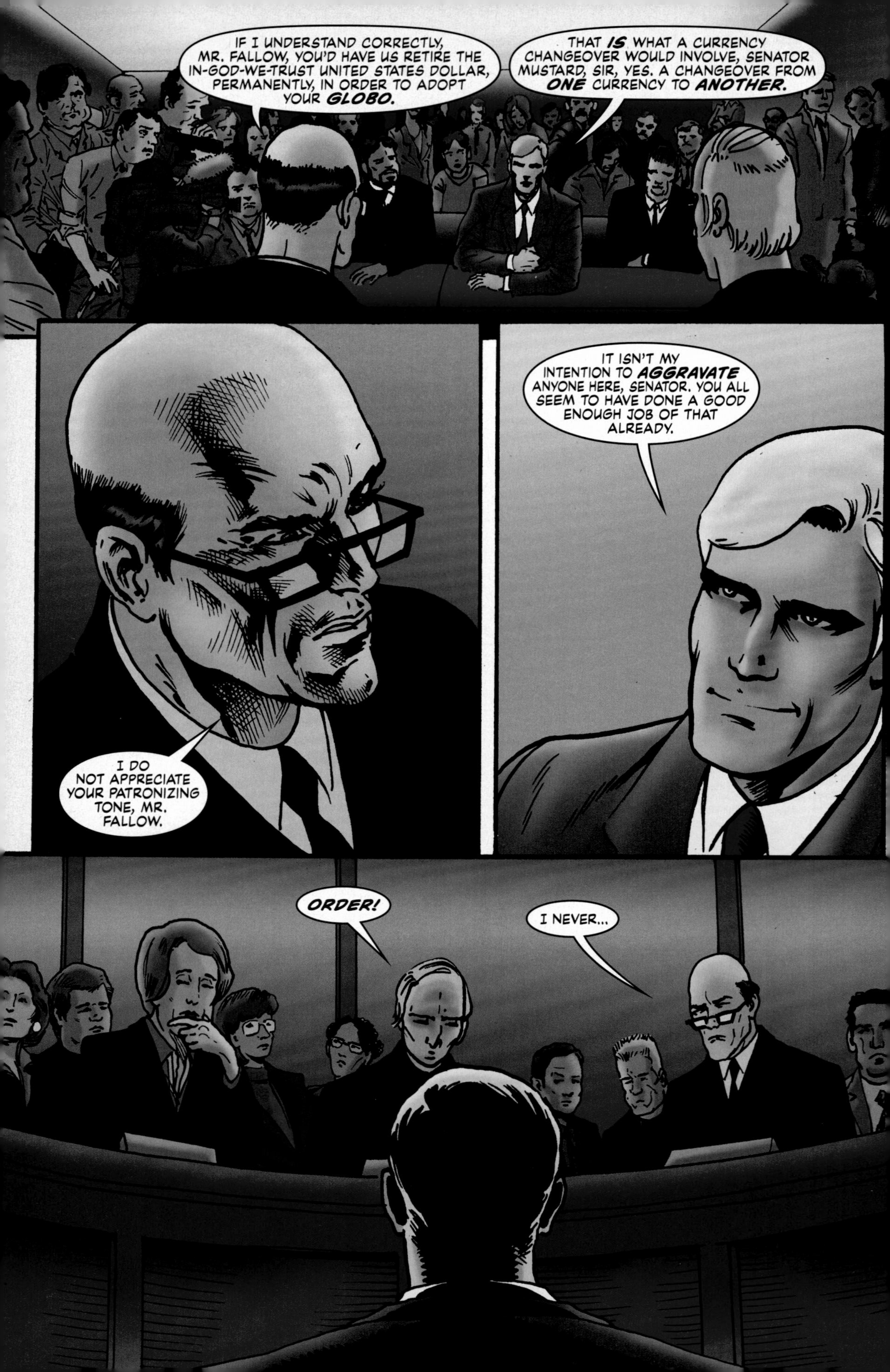
IF I UNDERSTAND CORRECTLY, MR. FALLOW, YOU'D HAVE US RETIRE THE IN-GOD-WE-TRUST UNITED STATES DOLLAR, PERMANENTLY, IN ORDER TO ADOPT YOUR *GLOBO*.
THAT *IS* WHAT A CURRENCY CHANGEOVER WOULD INVOLVE, SENATOR MUSTARD, SIR, YES. A CHANGEOVER FROM *ONE* CURRENCY TO *ANOTHER*.
I DO NOT APPRECIATE YOUR PATRONIZING TONE, MR. FALLOW.
IT ISN'T MY INTENTION TO *AGGRAVATE* ANYONE HERE, SENATOR. YOU ALL SEEM TO HAVE DONE A GOOD ENOUGH JOB OF THAT ALREADY.
ORDER!
I NEVER...

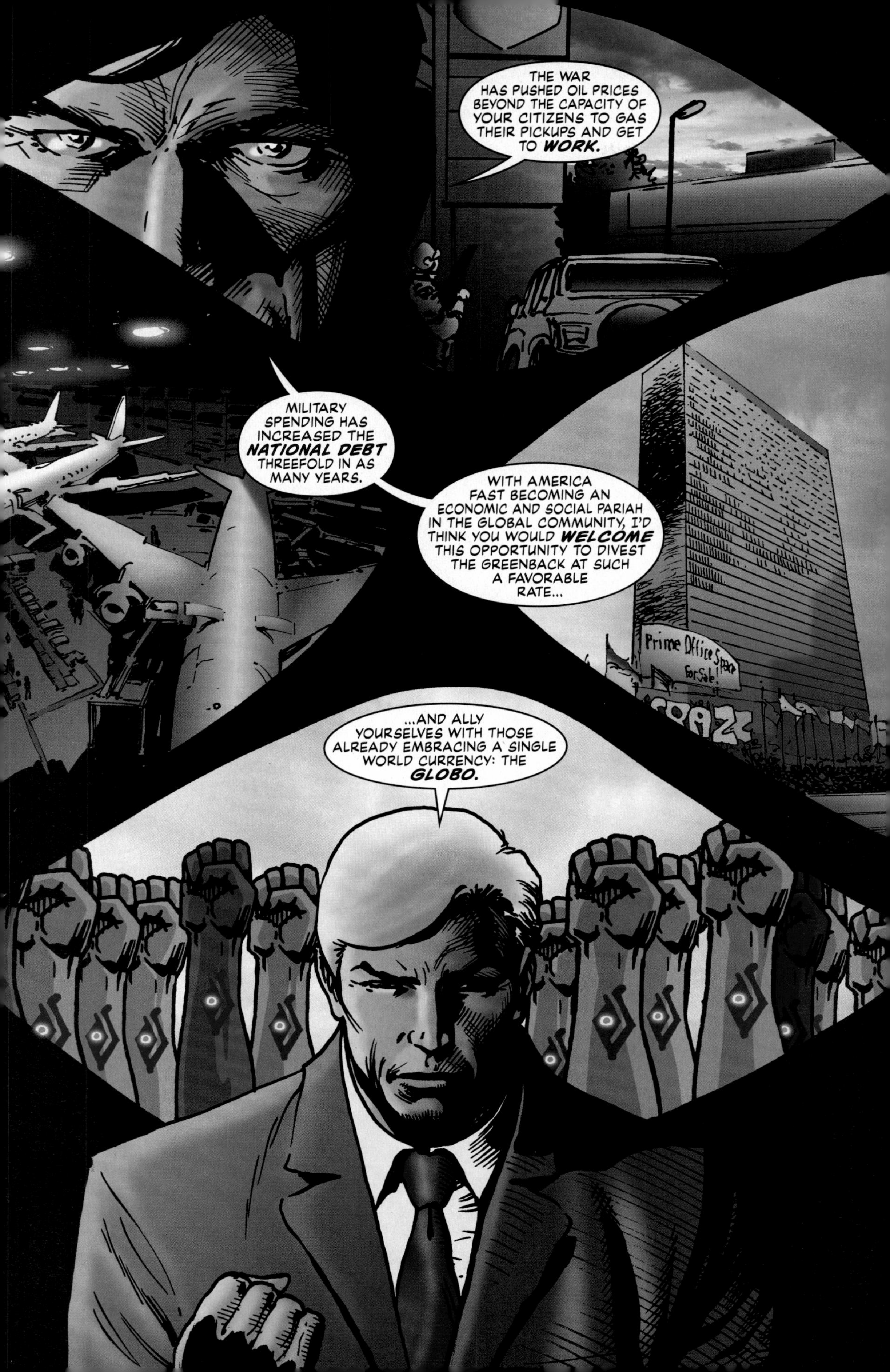
THE WAR HAS PUSHED OIL PRICES BEYOND THE CAPACITY OF YOUR CITIZENS TO GAS THEIR PICKUPS AND GET TO WORK.
MILITARY SPENDING HAS INCREASED THE NATIONAL DEBT THREEFOLD IN AS MANY YEARS.
WITH AMERICA FAST BECOMING AN ECONOMIC AND SOCIAL PARIAH IN THE GLOBAL COMMUNITY, I'D THINK YOU WOULD WELCOME THIS OPPORTUNITY TO DIVEST THE GREENBACK AT SUCH A FAVORABLE RATE...
Prime Office Space For Sale!
...AND ALLY YOURSELVES WITH THOSE ALREADY EMBRACING A SINGLE WORLD CURRENCY: THE GLOBO.

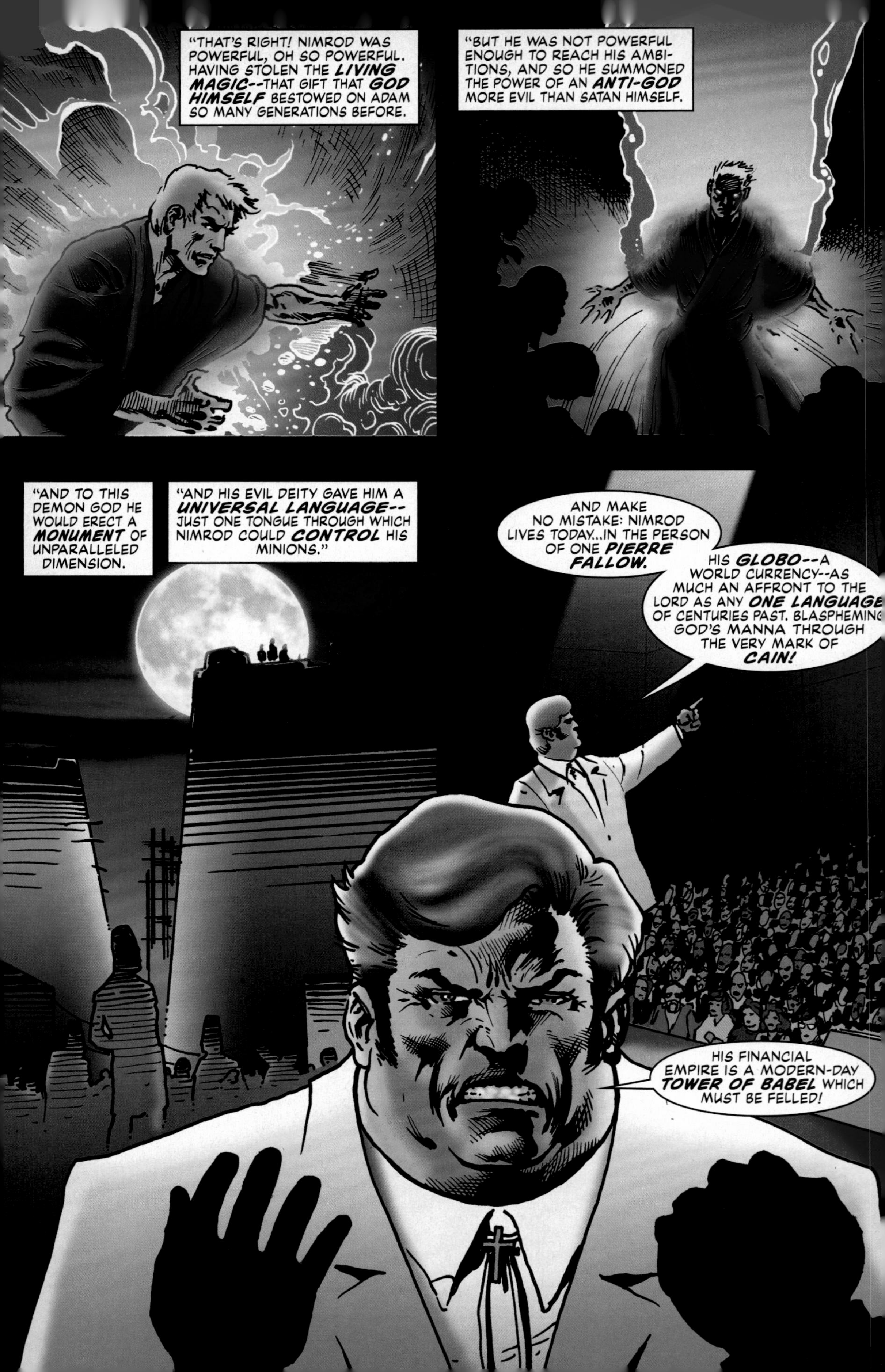
"THAT'S RIGHT! NIMROD WAS POWERFUL, OH SO POWERFUL. HAVING STOLEN THE LIVING MAGIC--THAT GIFT THAT GOD HIMSELF BESTOWED ON ADAM SO MANY GENERATIONS BEFORE.
"BUT HE WAS NOT POWERFUL ENOUGH TO REACH HIS AMBITIONS, AND SO HE SUMMONED THE POWER OF AN ANTI-GOD MORE EVIL THAN SATAN HIMSELF.
"AND TO THIS DEMON GOD HE WOULD ERECT A MONUMENT OF UNPARALLELED DIMENSION.
"AND HIS EVIL DEITY GAVE HIM A UNIVERSAL LANGUAGE-- JUST ONE TONGUE THROUGH WHICH NIMROD COULD CONTROL HIS MINIONS."
AND MAKE NO MISTAKE: NIMROD LIVES TODAY...IN THE PERSON OF ONE PIERRE FALLOW.
HIS GLOBO--A WORLD CURRENCY--AS MUCH AN AFFRONT TO THE LORD AS ANY ONE LANGUAGE OF CENTURIES PAST. BLASPHEMING GOD'S MANNA THROUGH THE VERY MARK OF CAIN!
HIS FINANCIAL EMPIRE IS A MODERN-DAY TOWER OF BABEL WHICH MUST BE FELLED!

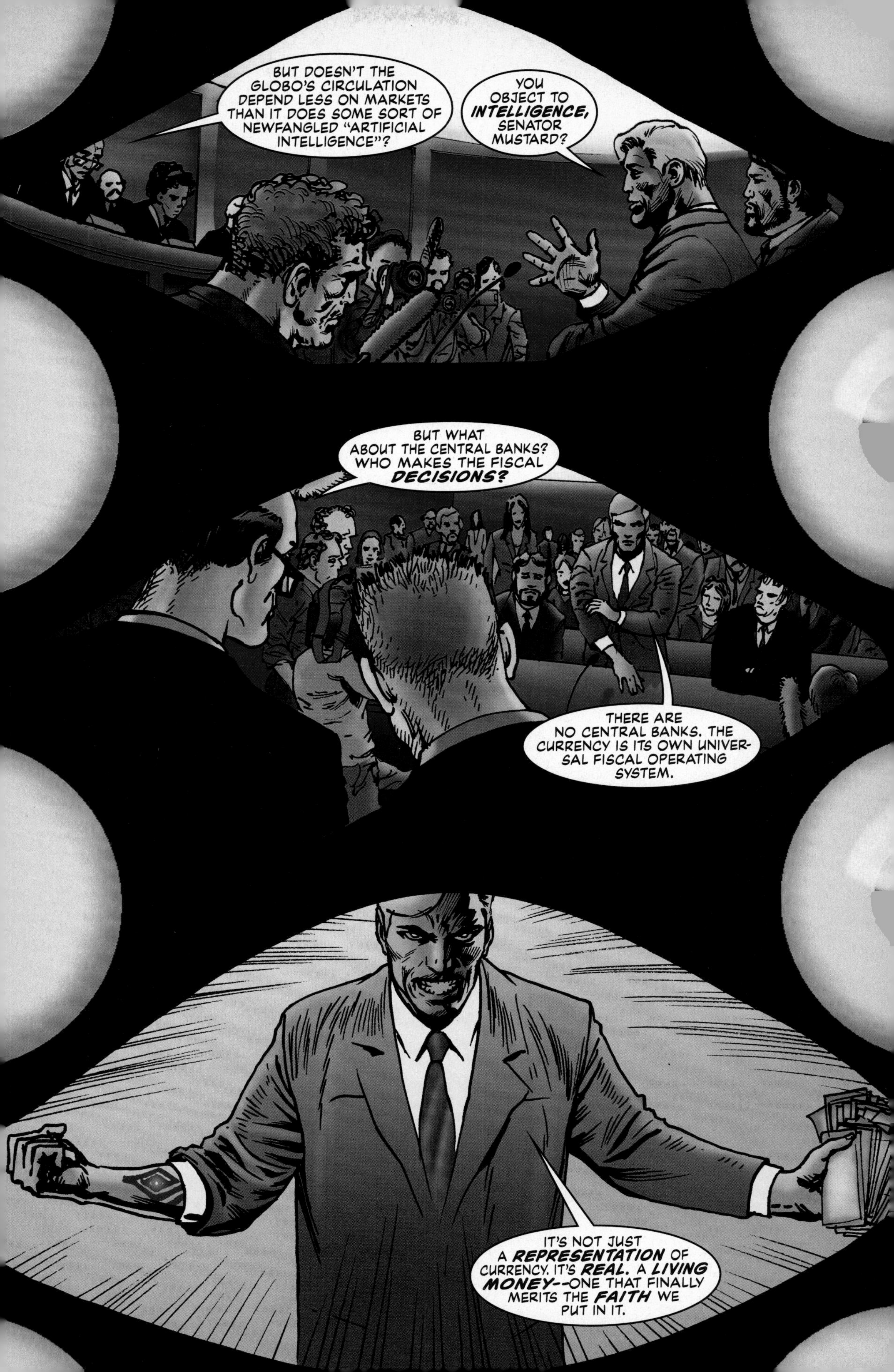
BUT DOESN'T THE GLOBO'S CIRCULATION DEPEND LESS ON MARKETS THAN IT DOES SOME SORT OF NEWFANGLED "ARTIFICIAL INTELLIGENCE"?
YOU OBJECT TO *INTELLIGENCE,* SENATOR MUSTARD?
BUT WHAT ABOUT THE CENTRAL BANKS? WHO MAKES THE FISCAL *DECISIONS?*
THERE ARE NO CENTRAL BANKS. THE CURRENCY IS ITS OWN UNIVERSAL FISCAL OPERATING SYSTEM.
IT'S NOT JUST A *REPRESENTATION* OF CURRENCY. IT'S *REAL.* A *LIVING MONEY*--ONE THAT FINALLY MERITS THE *FAITH* WE PUT IN IT.

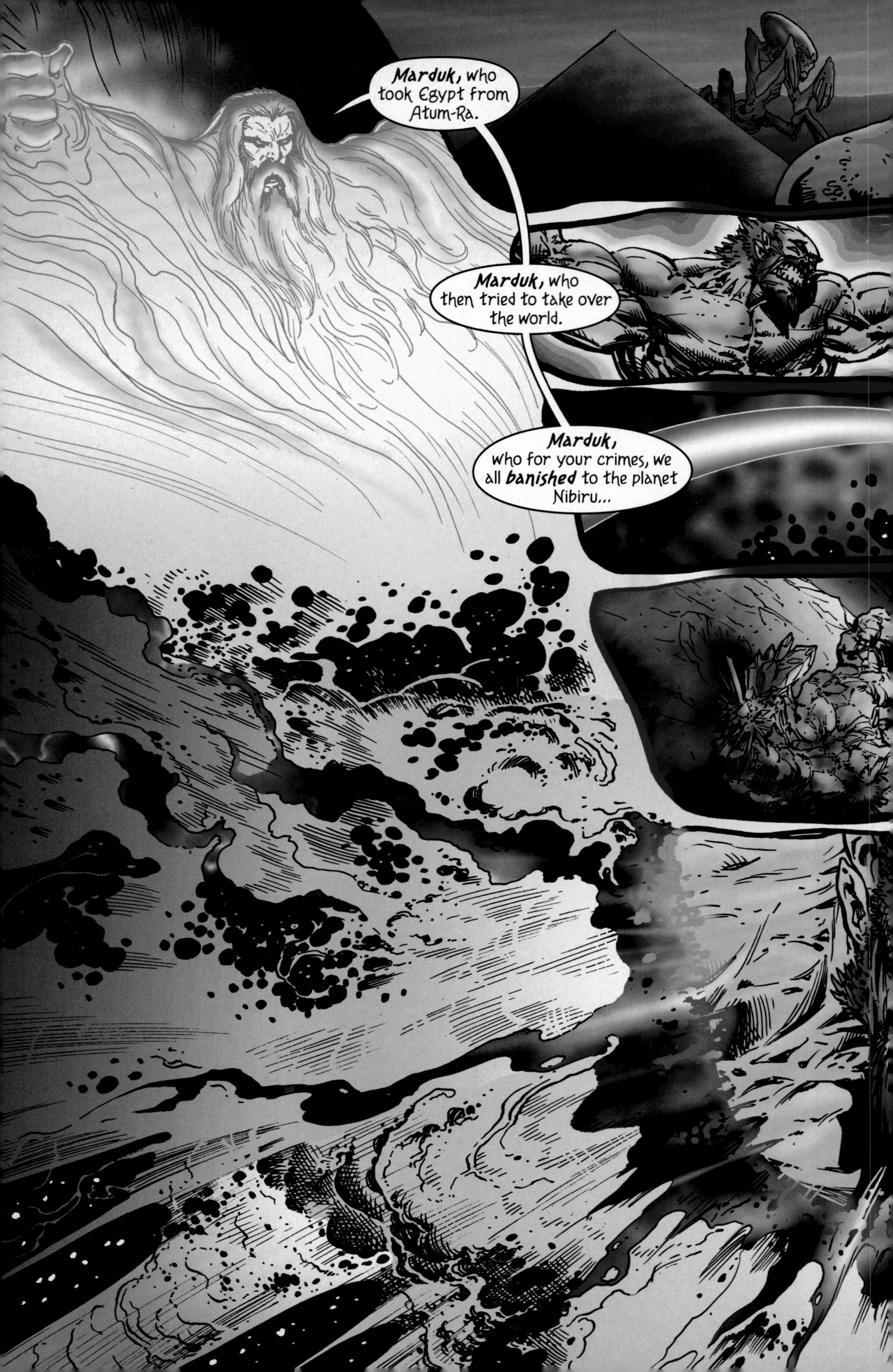

Marduk, who took Egypt from Atum-Ra.
Marduk, who then tried to take over the world.
Marduk, who for your crimes, we all banished to the planet Nibiru...

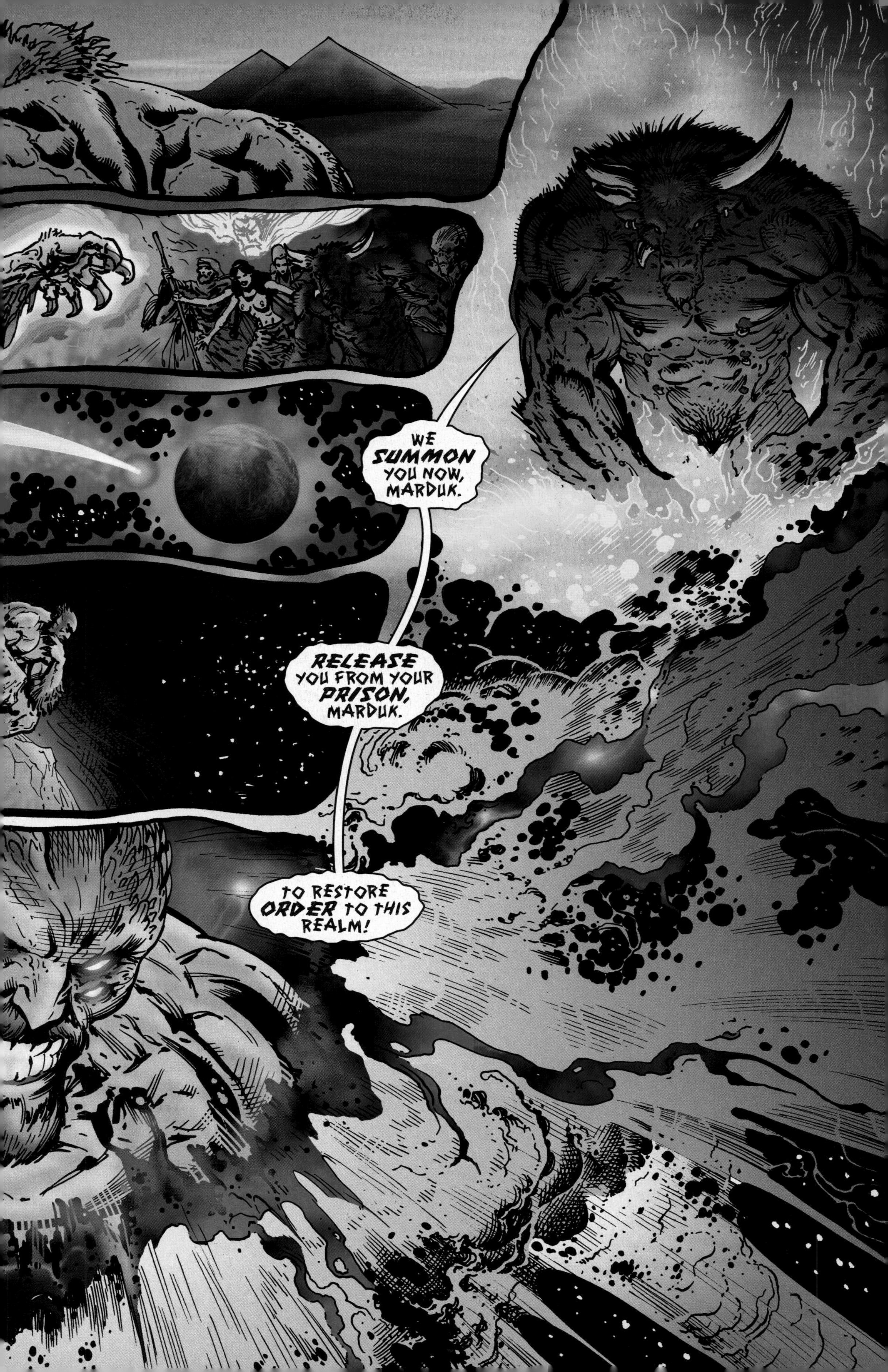
WE SUMMON YOU NOW, MARDUK.
RELEASE YOU FROM YOUR PRISON, MARDUK.
TO RESTORE ORDER TO THIS REALM!

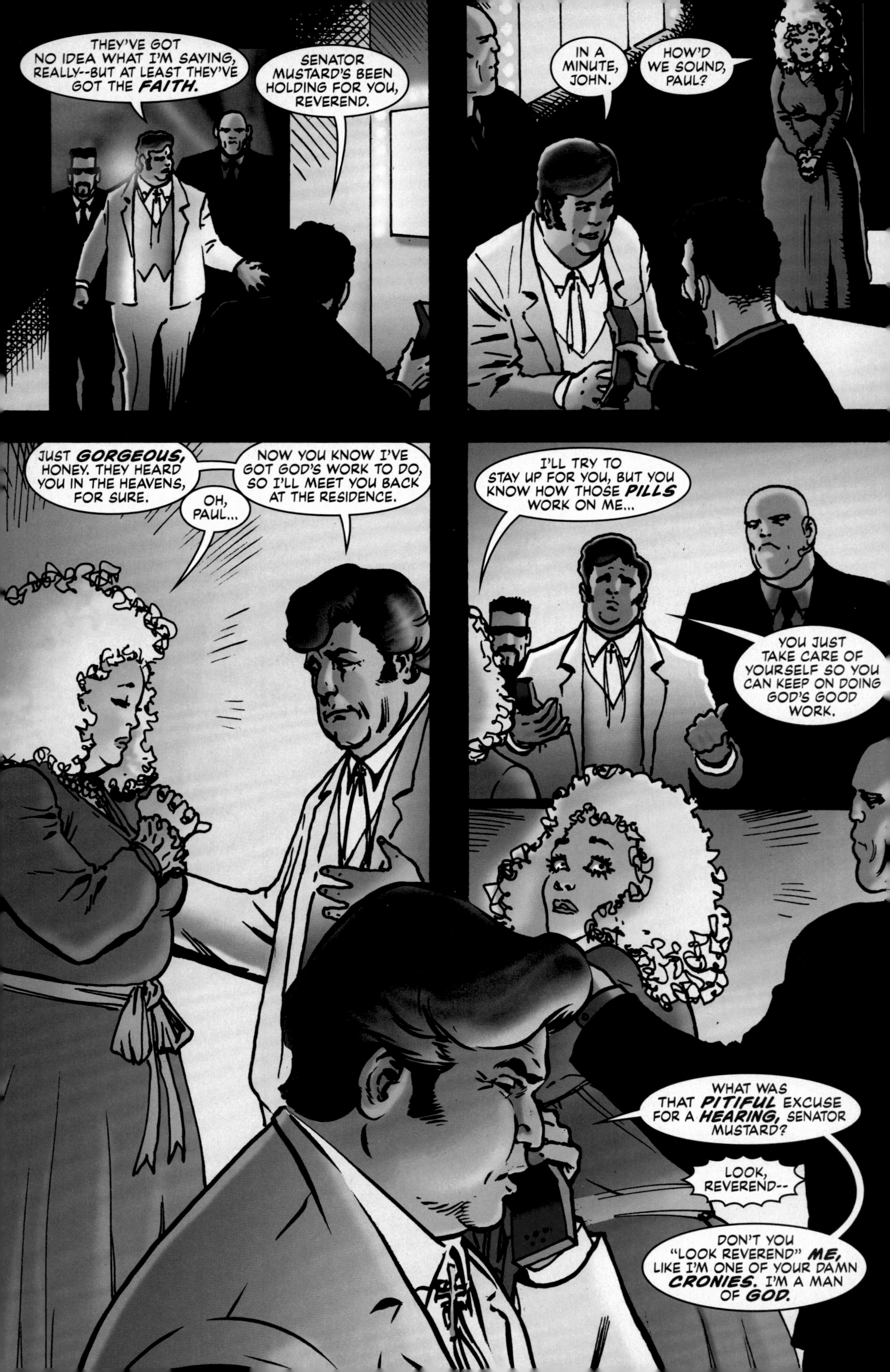
THEY'VE GOT NO IDEA WHAT I'M SAYING, REALLY--BUT AT LEAST THEY'VE GOT THE *FAITH.*
SENATOR MUSTARD'S BEEN HOLDING FOR YOU, REVEREND.
IN A MINUTE, JOHN.
HOW'D WE SOUND, PAUL?
JUST *GORGEOUS,* HONEY. THEY HEARD YOU IN THE HEAVENS, FOR SURE.
OH, PAUL...
NOW YOU KNOW I'VE GOT GOD'S WORK TO DO, SO I'LL MEET YOU BACK AT THE RESIDENCE.
I'LL TRY TO STAY UP FOR YOU, BUT YOU KNOW HOW THOSE *PILLS* WORK ON ME...
YOU JUST TAKE CARE OF YOURSELF SO YOU CAN KEEP ON DOING GOD'S GOOD WORK.
WHAT WAS THAT *PITIFUL* EXCUSE FOR A *HEARING,* SENATOR MUSTARD?
LOOK, REVEREND--
DON'T YOU "LOOK REVEREND" *ME,* LIKE I'M ONE OF YOUR DAMN *CRONIES.* I'M A MAN OF *GOD.*

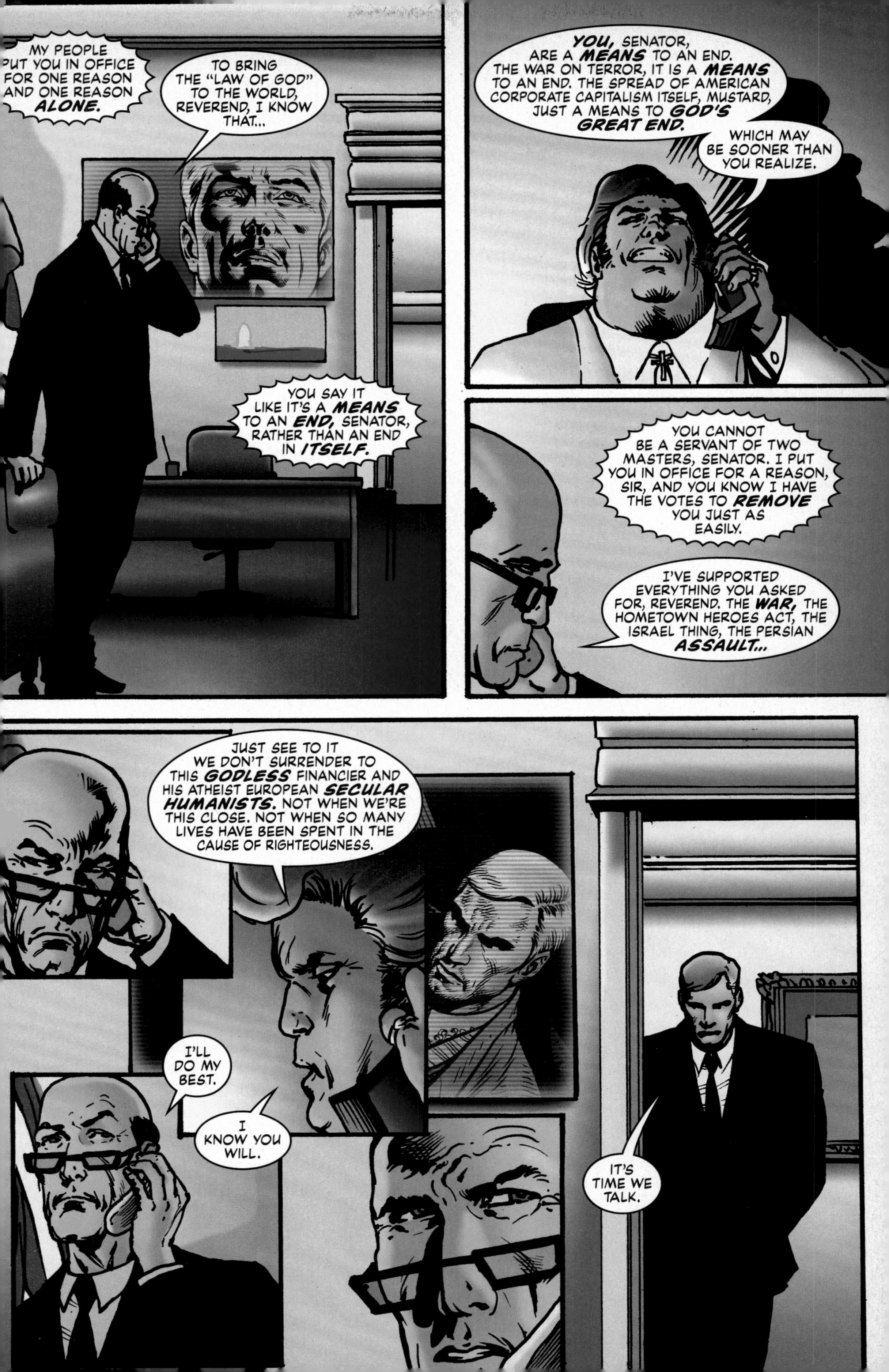
MY PEOPLE PUT YOU IN OFFICE FOR ONE REASON AND ONE REASON ALONE.
TO BRING THE "LAW OF GOD" TO THE WORLD, REVEREND, I KNOW THAT...
YOU SAY IT LIKE IT'S A MEANS TO AN END, SENATOR, RATHER THAN AN END IN ITSELF.
YOU, SENATOR, ARE A MEANS TO AN END. THE WAR ON TERROR, IT IS A MEANS TO AN END. THE SPREAD OF AMERICAN CORPORATE CAPITALISM ITSELF, MUSTARD, JUST A MEANS TO GOD'S GREAT END.
WHICH MAY BE SOONER THAN YOU REALIZE.
YOU CANNOT BE A SERVANT OF TWO MASTERS, SENATOR. I PUT YOU IN OFFICE FOR A REASON, SIR, AND YOU KNOW I HAVE THE VOTES TO REMOVE YOU JUST AS EASILY.
I'VE SUPPORTED EVERYTHING YOU ASKED FOR, REVEREND. THE WAR, THE HOMETOWN HEROES ACT, THE ISRAEL THING, THE PERSIAN ASSAULT...
JUST SEE TO IT WE DON'T SURRENDER TO THIS GODLESS FINANCIER AND HIS ATHEIST EUROPEAN SECULAR HUMANISTS. NOT WHEN WE'RE THIS CLOSE. NOT WHEN SO MANY LIVES HAVE BEEN SPENT IN THE CAUSE OF RIGHTEOUSNESS.
I'LL DO MY BEST.
I KNOW YOU WILL.
IT'S TIME WE TALK.

FALLOW? HOW DID YOU--?

I HAVE MANY *FRIENDS* HERE ON THE HILL, SENATOR MUSTARD. AND I'VE ALWAYS HOPED TO COUNT YOU AMONG THEM.

I REPRESENT MY CONSTITUENTS' INTERESTS, MR. FALLOW.

WHAT A QUAINT PERSPECTIVE ON THE *PROPAGANDA MACHINE* YOU AMERICANS LIKE TO CALL *DEMOCRACY.* ALL THOSE INTELLIGENT DECISIONS MADE BY YOUR *INFORMED* VOTERS.

NOBODY SAID IT WAS PERFECT, BUT--

WHICH IS WHY THE AUGUST BODY OF INCUMBENTS OF WHICH YOU ARE A PART CHOSE TO REPLACE THAT ARCANE PROCESS WITH A MORE, SHALL WE SAY--*PREDICTABLE* COMPUTERIZED SYSTEM.

I RESENT THE IMPLICATIONS OF THAT REMARK, MR. FALLOW.

BUT IT WAS A SHORT-SIGHTED MOVE, SENATOR.

BECAUSE NOW YOUR "CONSTITUENCY" IS AN INTEGRATED CIRCUIT BOARD RUN BY PROPRIETARY CODE AND OWNED BY A PRIVATE CORPORATION.

ONE OF *MINE.*

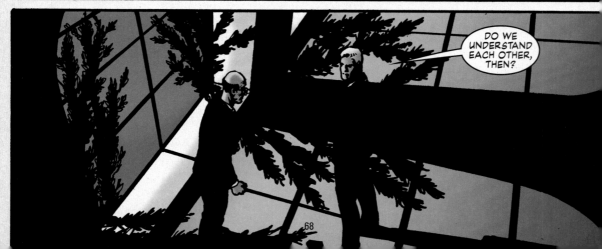

DO WE UNDERSTAND EACH OTHER, THEN?

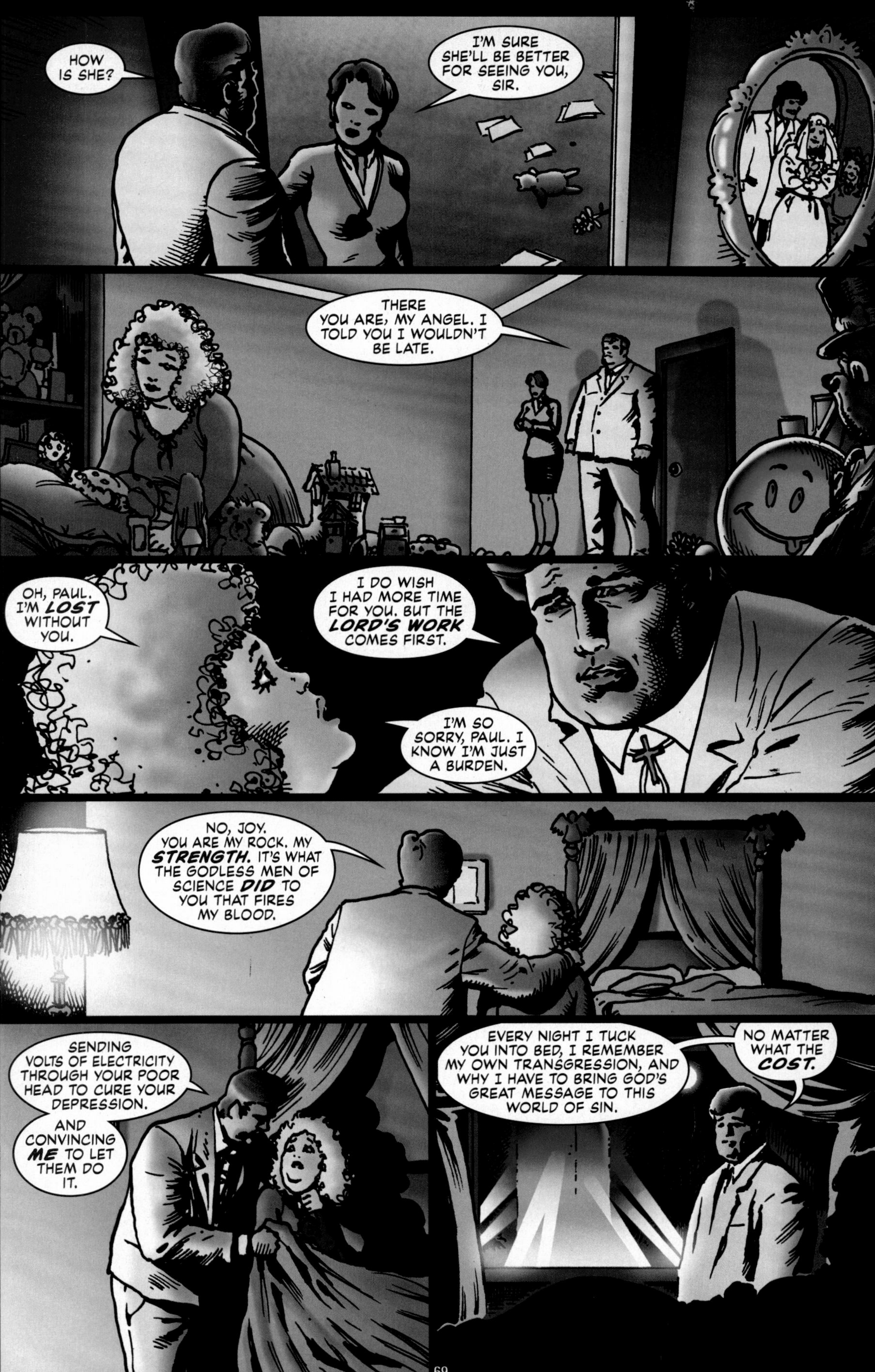
HOW IS SHE?
I'M SURE SHE'LL BE BETTER FOR SEEING YOU, SIR.
THERE YOU ARE, MY ANGEL. I TOLD YOU I WOULDN'T BE LATE.
OH, PAUL. I'M LOST WITHOUT YOU.
I DO WISH I HAD MORE TIME FOR YOU. BUT THE LORD'S WORK COMES FIRST.
I'M SO SORRY, PAUL. I KNOW I'M JUST A BURDEN.
NO, JOY. YOU ARE MY ROCK. MY STRENGTH. IT'S WHAT THE GODLESS MEN OF SCIENCE DID TO YOU THAT FIRES MY BLOOD.
SENDING VOLTS OF ELECTRICITY THROUGH YOUR POOR HEAD TO CURE YOUR DEPRESSION.
AND CONVINCING ME TO LET THEM DO IT.
EVERY NIGHT I TUCK YOU INTO BED, I REMEMBER MY OWN TRANSGRESSION, AND WHY I HAVE TO BRING GOD'S GREAT MESSAGE TO THIS WORLD OF SIN.
NO MATTER WHAT THE COST.

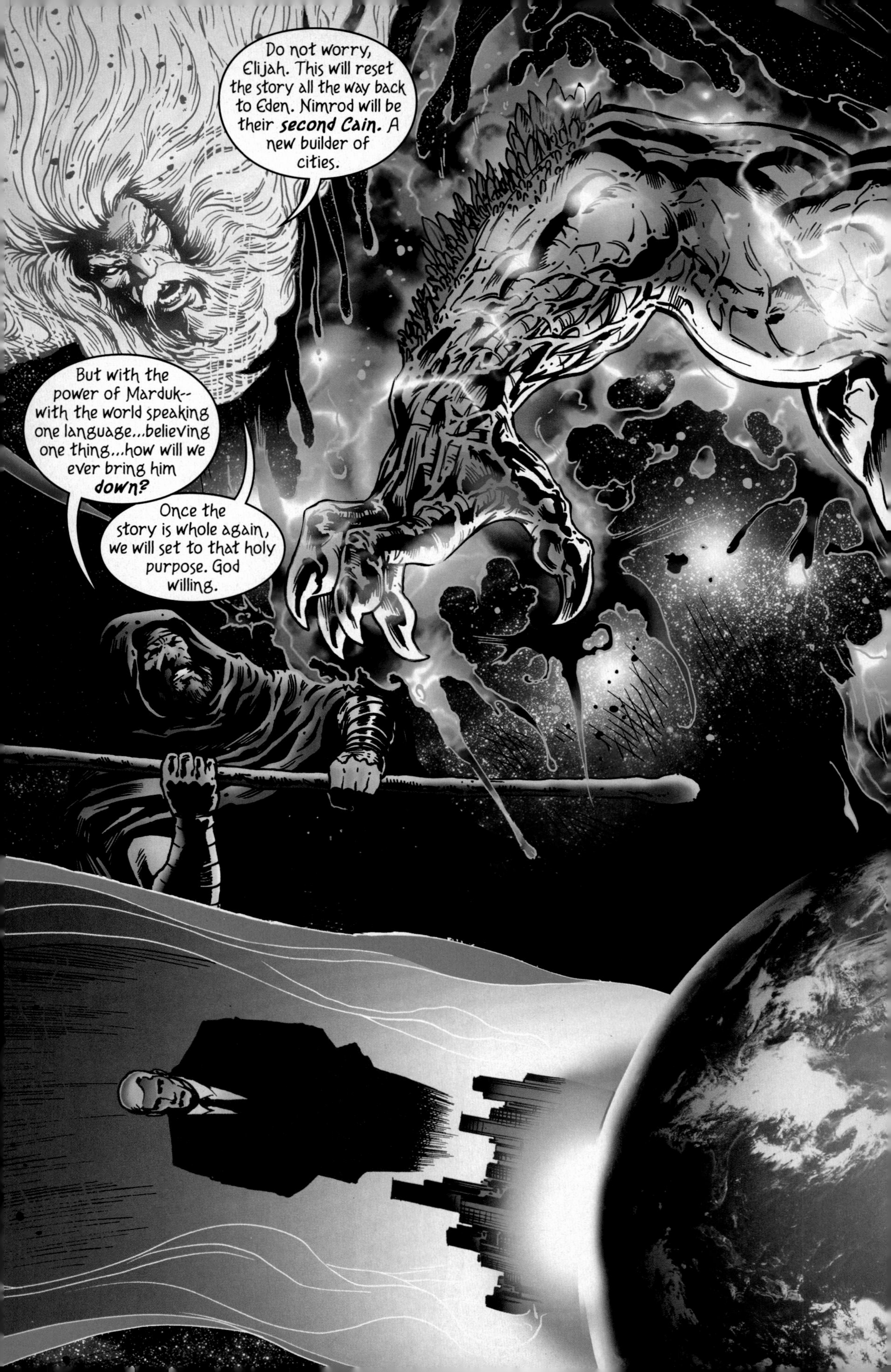
Do not worry, Elijah. This will reset the story all the way back to Eden. Nimrod will be their **second Cain.** A new builder of cities.
But with the power of Marduk-- with the world speaking one language...believing one thing...how will we ever bring him **down?**
Once the story is whole again, we will set to that holy purpose. God willing.

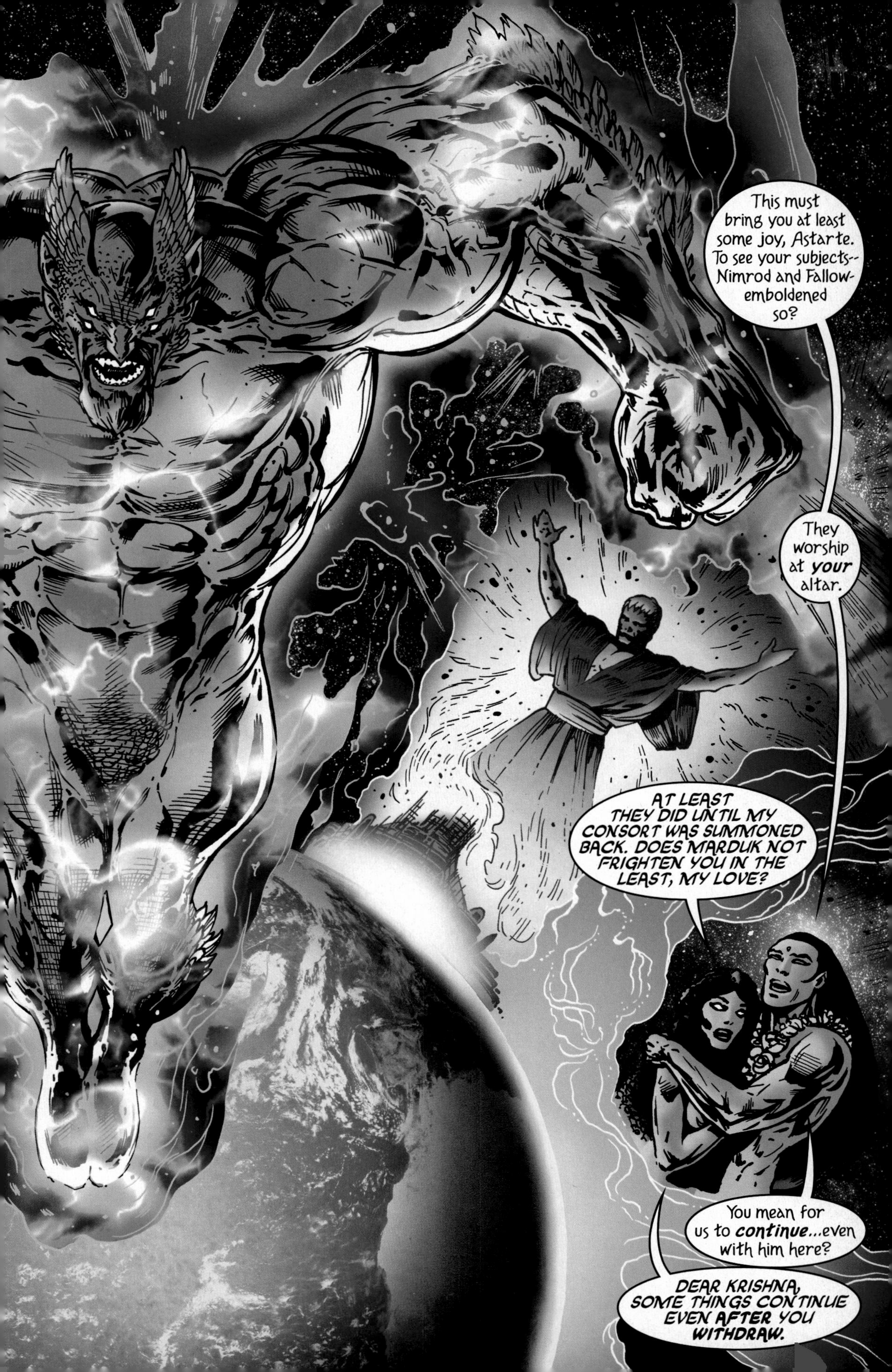
This must bring you at least some joy, Astarte. To see your subjects--Nimrod and Fallow-emboldened so?
They worship at **your** altar.
AT LEAST THEY DID UNTIL MY CONSORT WAS SUMMONED BACK. DOES MARDUK NOT FRIGHTEN YOU IN THE LEAST, MY LOVE?
You mean for us to **continue**...even with him here?
DEAR KRISHNA, SOME THINGS CONTINUE EVEN **AFTER** YOU **WITHDRAW.**

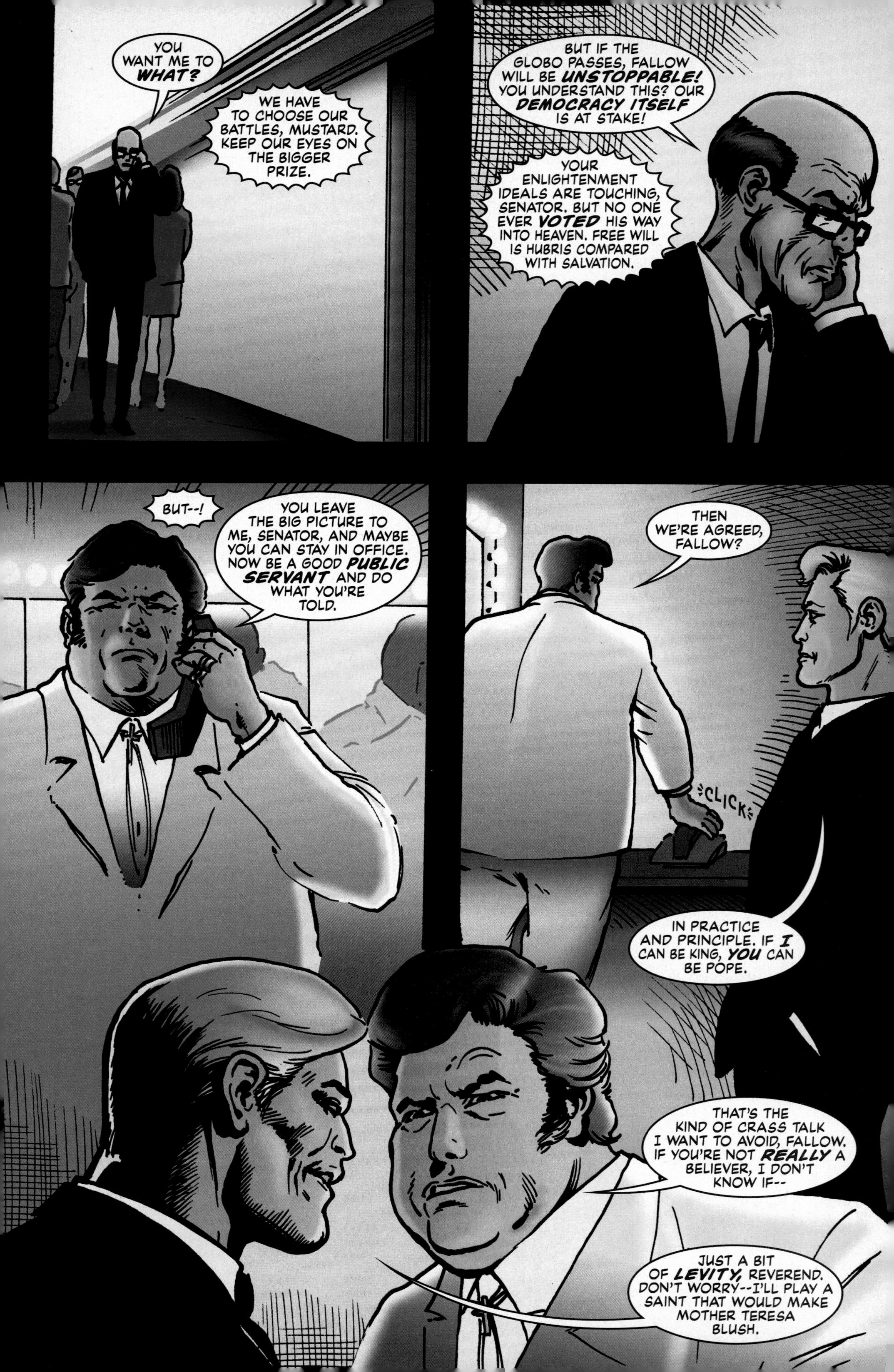
YOU WANT ME TO WHAT?
WE HAVE TO CHOOSE OUR BATTLES, MUSTARD. KEEP OUR EYES ON THE BIGGER PRIZE.
BUT IF THE GLOBO PASSES, FALLOW WILL BE UNSTOPPABLE! YOU UNDERSTAND THIS? OUR DEMOCRACY ITSELF IS AT STAKE!
YOUR ENLIGHTENMENT IDEALS ARE TOUCHING, SENATOR. BUT NO ONE EVER VOTED HIS WAY INTO HEAVEN. FREE WILL IS HUBRIS COMPARED WITH SALVATION.
BUT--!
YOU LEAVE THE BIG PICTURE TO ME, SENATOR, AND MAYBE YOU CAN STAY IN OFFICE. NOW BE A GOOD PUBLIC SERVANT AND DO WHAT YOU'RE TOLD.
THEN WE'RE AGREED, FALLOW?
CLICK
IN PRACTICE AND PRINCIPLE. IF I CAN BE KING, YOU CAN BE POPE.
THAT'S THE KIND OF CRASS TALK I WANT TO AVOID, FALLOW. IF YOU'RE NOT REALLY A BELIEVER, I DON'T KNOW IF--
JUST A BIT OF LEVITY, REVEREND. DON'T WORRY--I'LL PLAY A SAINT THAT WOULD MAKE MOTHER TERESA BLUSH.

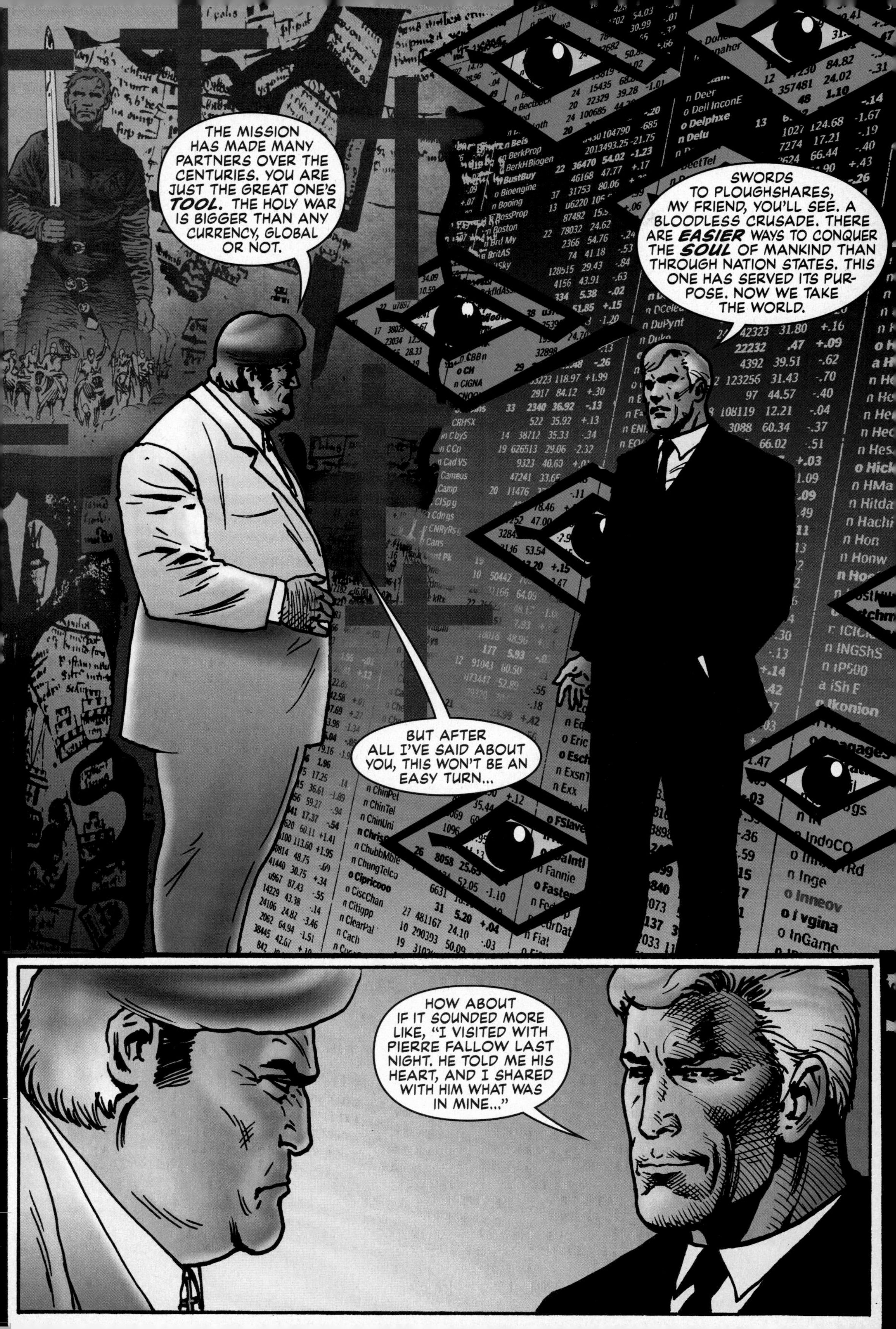
THE MISSION HAS MADE MANY PARTNERS OVER THE CENTURIES. YOU ARE JUST THE GREAT ONE'S **TOOL.** THE HOLY WAR IS BIGGER THAN ANY CURRENCY, GLOBAL OR NOT.
SWORDS TO PLOUGHSHARES, MY FRIEND, YOU'LL SEE. A BLOODLESS CRUSADE. THERE ARE **EASIER** WAYS TO CONQUER THE **SOUL** OF MANKIND THAN THROUGH NATION STATES. THIS ONE HAS SERVED ITS PURPOSE. NOW WE TAKE THE WORLD.
BUT AFTER ALL I'VE SAID ABOUT YOU, THIS WON'T BE AN EASY TURN...
HOW ABOUT IF IT SOUNDED MORE LIKE, "I VISITED WITH PIERRE FALLOW LAST NIGHT. HE TOLD ME HIS HEART, AND I SHARED WITH HIM WHAT WAS IN MINE..."

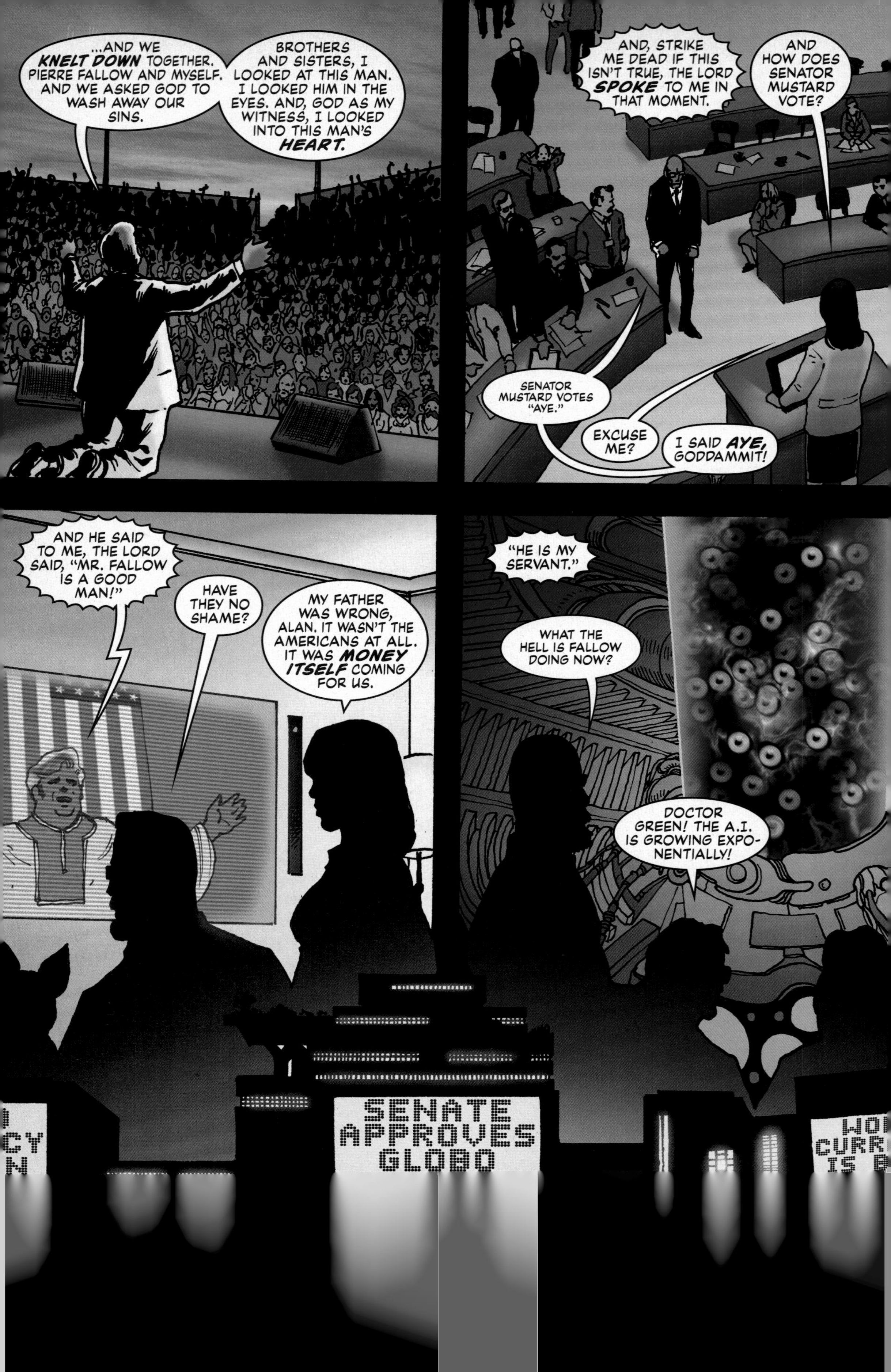
...AND WE KNELT DOWN TOGETHER. PIERRE FALLOW AND MYSELF. AND WE ASKED GOD TO WASH AWAY OUR SINS.
BROTHERS AND SISTERS, I LOOKED AT THIS MAN. I LOOKED HIM IN THE EYES. AND, GOD AS MY WITNESS, I LOOKED INTO THIS MAN'S HEART.
AND, STRIKE ME DEAD IF THIS ISN'T TRUE, THE LORD SPOKE TO ME IN THAT MOMENT.
AND HOW DOES SENATOR MUSTARD VOTE?
SENATOR MUSTARD VOTES "AYE."
EXCUSE ME?
I SAID AYE, GODDAMMIT!
AND HE SAID TO ME, THE LORD SAID, "MR. FALLOW IS A GOOD MAN!"
HAVE THEY NO SHAME?
MY FATHER WAS WRONG, ALAN. IT WASN'T THE AMERICANS AT ALL. IT WAS MONEY ITSELF COMING FOR US.
"HE IS MY SERVANT."
WHAT THE HELL IS FALLOW DOING NOW?
DOCTOR GREEN! THE A.I. IS GROWING EXPO-NENTIALLY!
SENATE APPROVES GLOBO

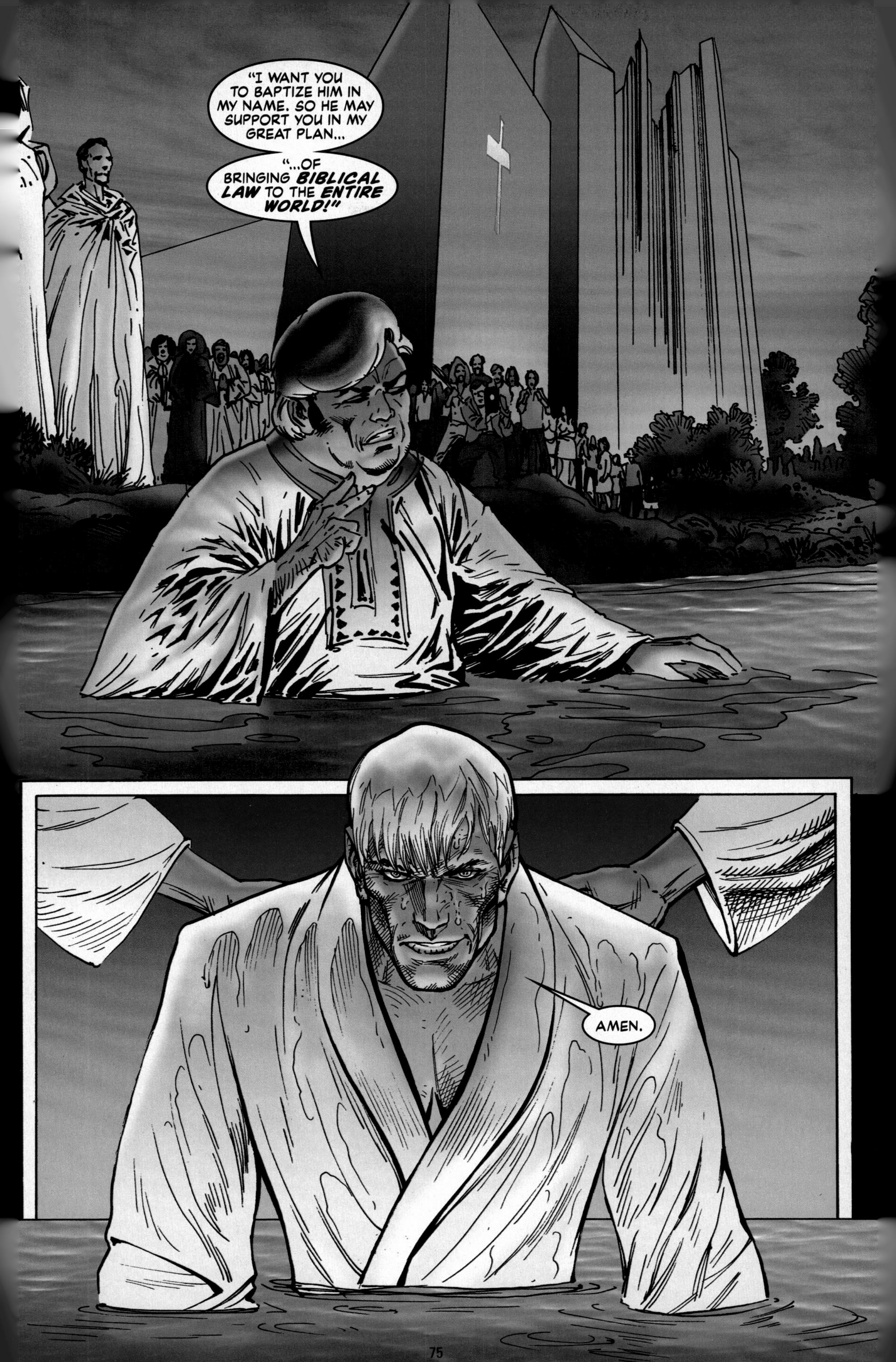
"I WANT YOU TO BAPTIZE HIM IN MY NAME. SO HE MAY SUPPORT YOU IN MY GREAT PLAN...
"...OF BRINGING BIBLICAL LAW TO THE ENTIRE WORLD!"
AMEN.

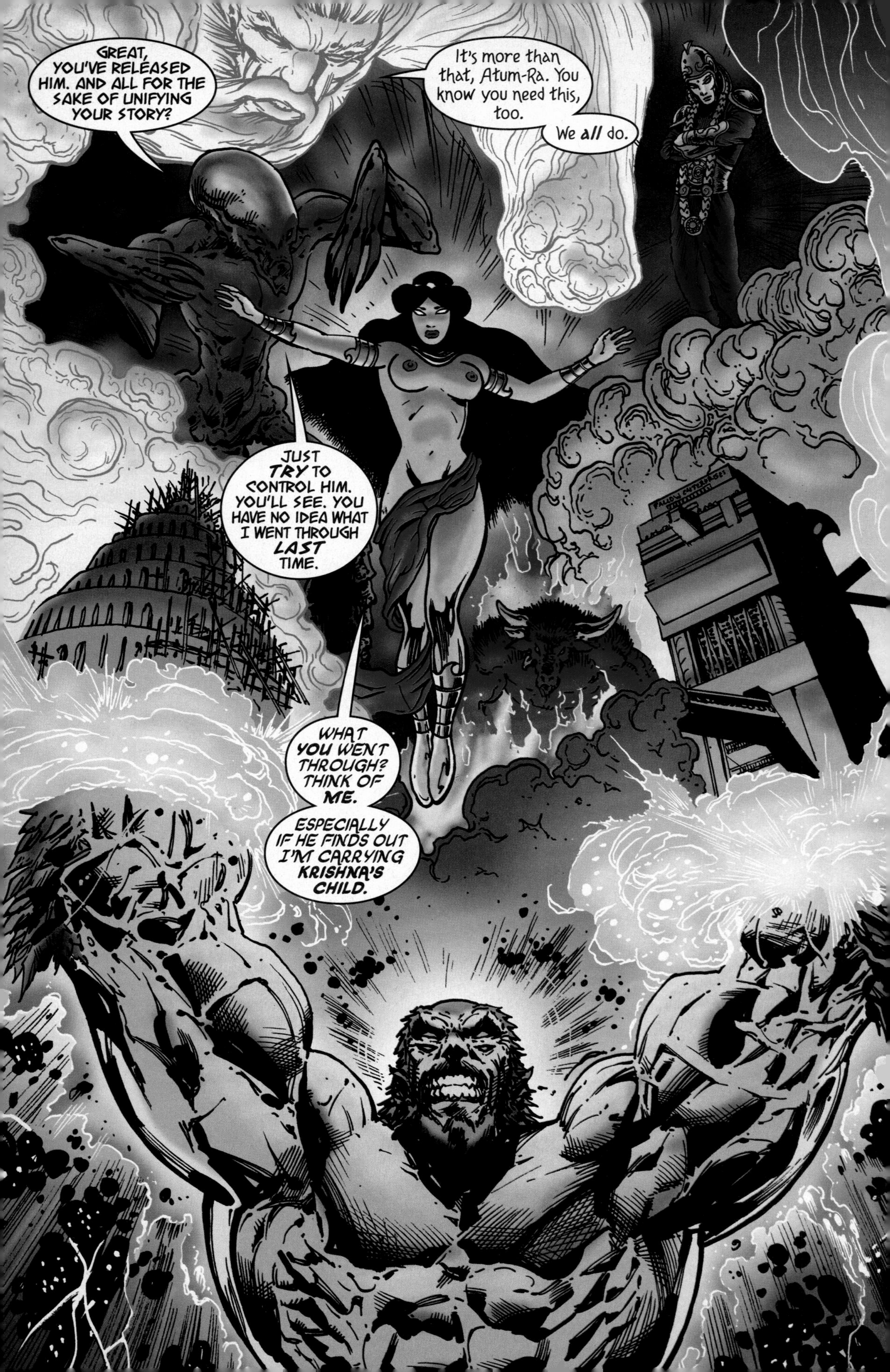
GREAT, YOU'VE RELEASED HIM. AND ALL FOR THE SAKE OF UNIFYING YOUR STORY?
It's more than that, Atum-Ra. You know you need this, too.
We all do.
JUST TRY TO CONTROL HIM. YOU'LL SEE. YOU HAVE NO IDEA WHAT I WENT THROUGH LAST TIME.
WHAT YOU WENT THROUGH? THINK OF ME.
ESPECIALLY IF HE FINDS OUT I'M CARRYING KRISHNA'S CHILD.

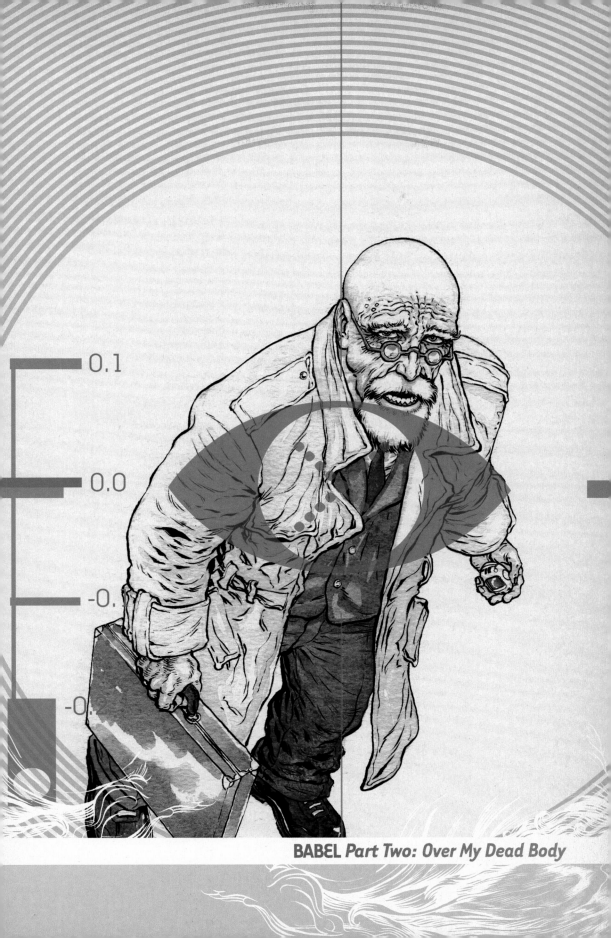

0.1

0.0

-0.

-0.2

BABEL *Part Two: Over My Dead Body*

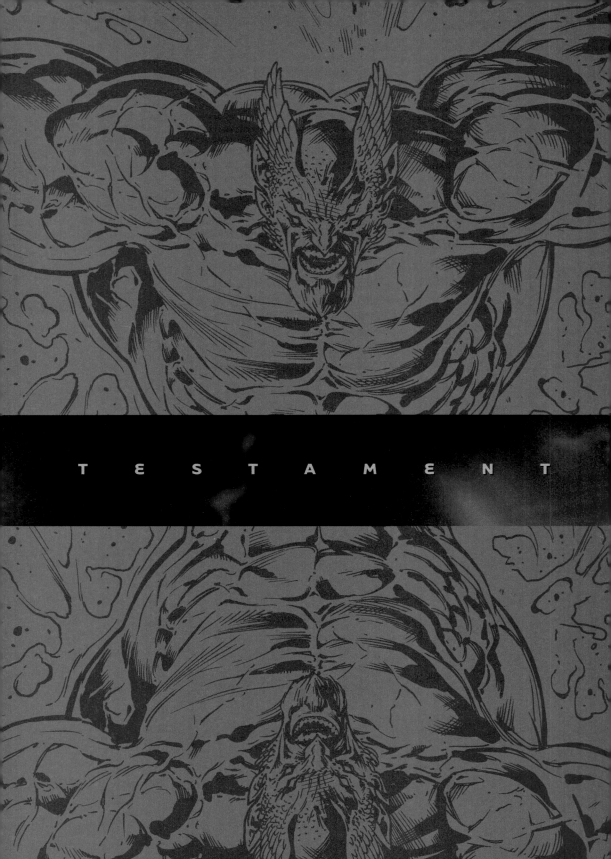

TESTAMENT

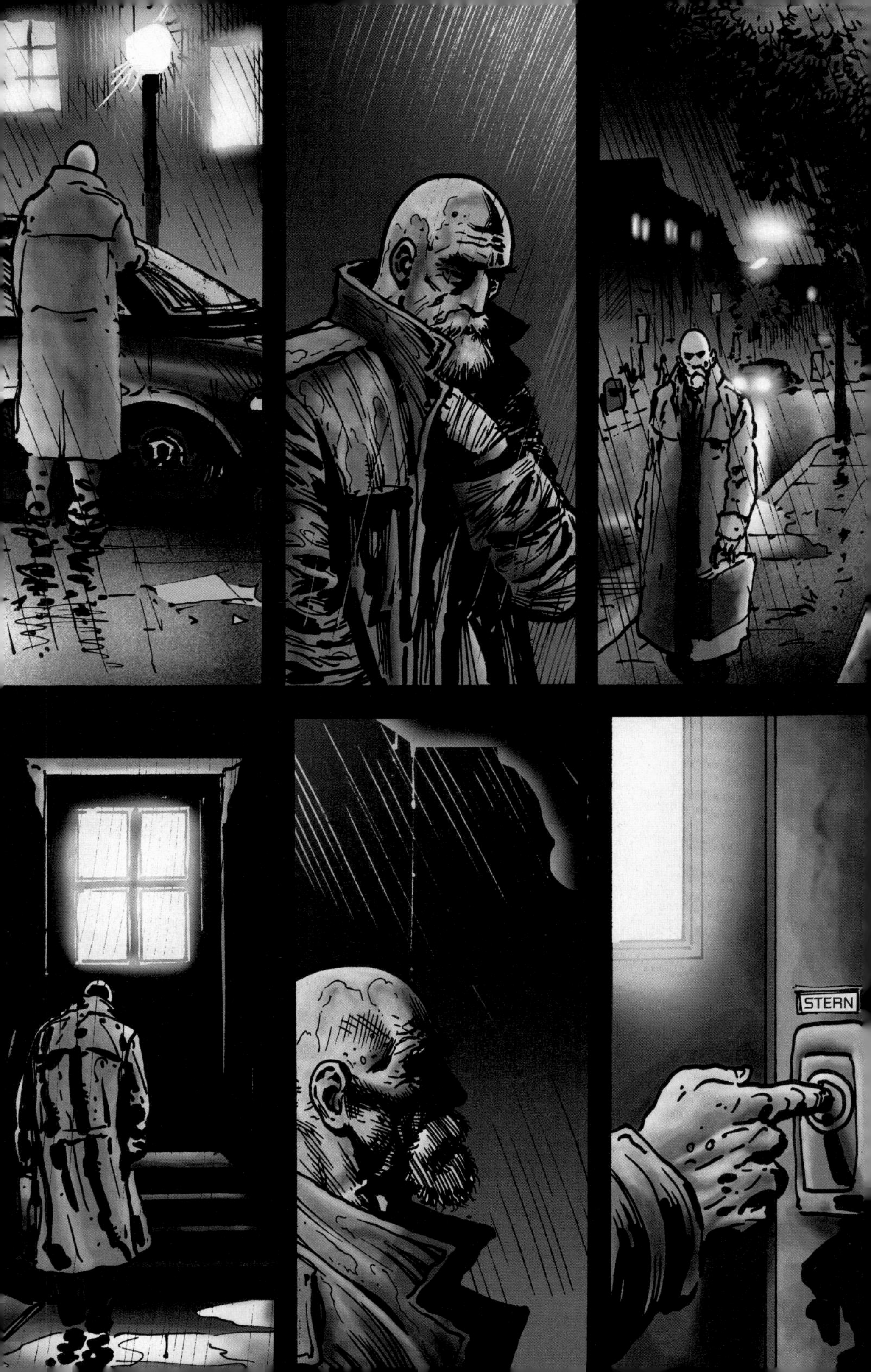
STERN

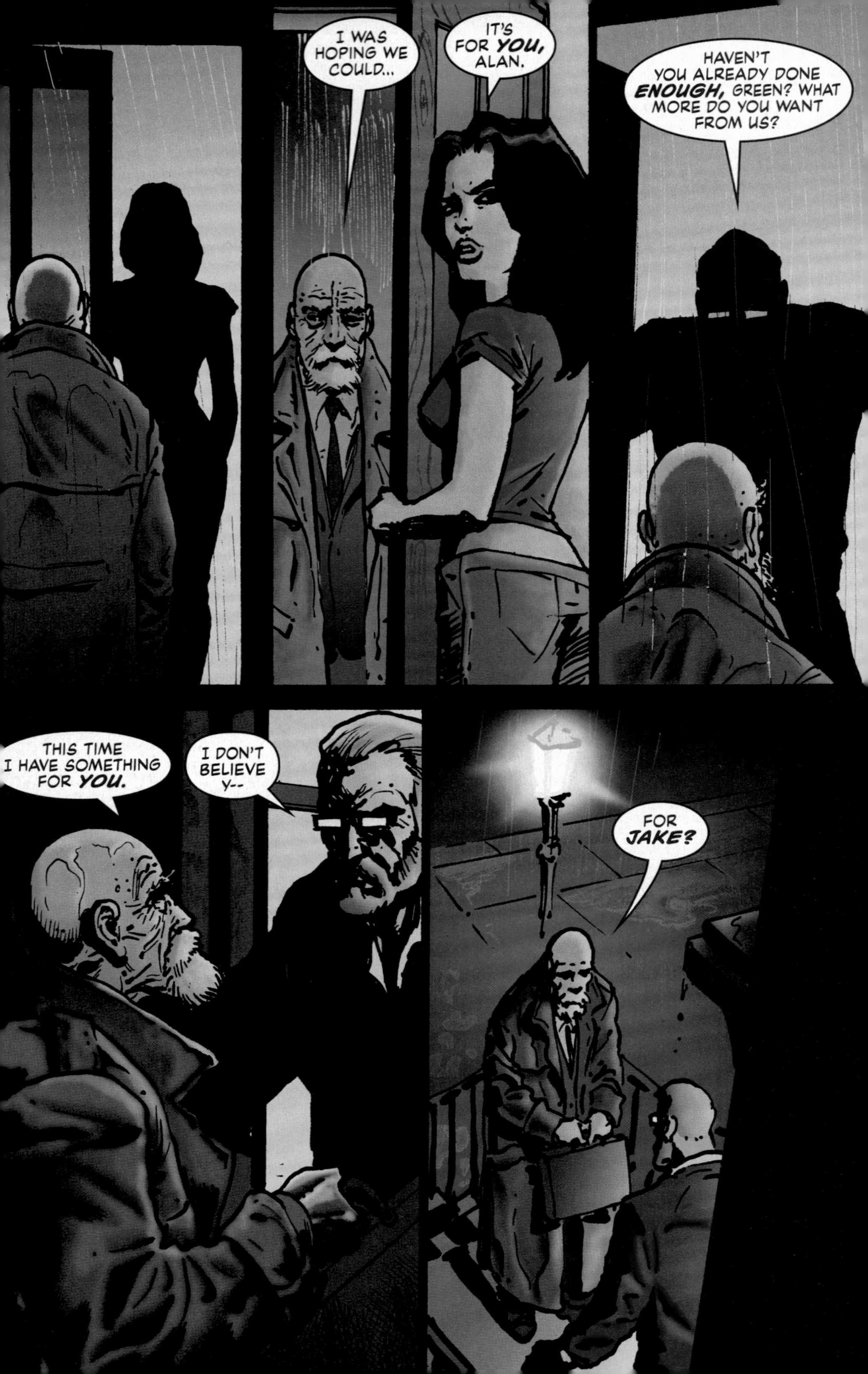
I WAS HOPING WE COULD...
IT'S FOR *YOU,* ALAN.
HAVEN'T YOU ALREADY DONE *ENOUGH,* GREEN? WHAT MORE DO YOU WANT FROM US?
THIS TIME I HAVE SOMETHING FOR *YOU.*
I DON'T BELIEVE Y--
FOR *JAKE?*

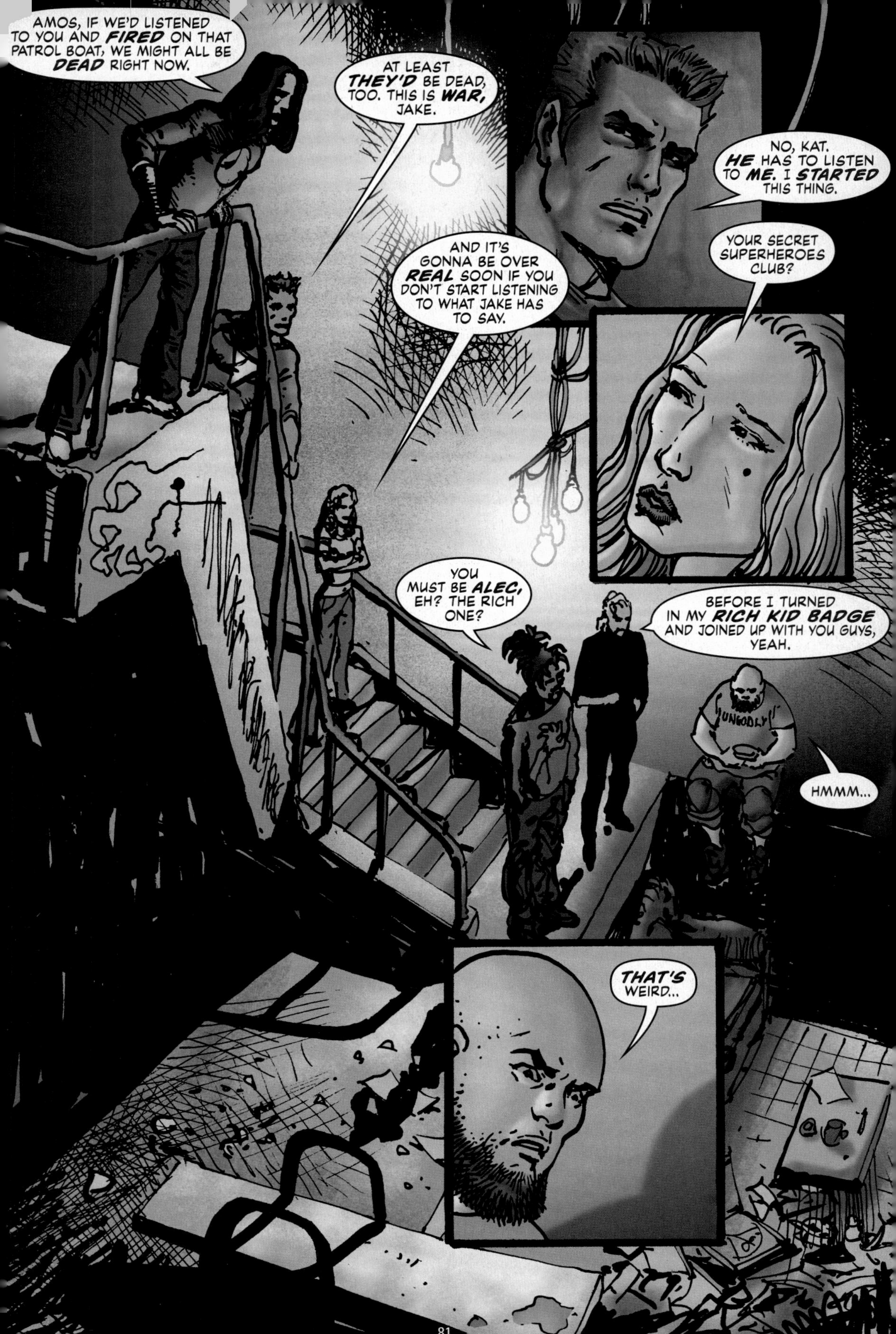
AMOS, IF WE'D LISTENED TO YOU AND FIRED ON THAT PATROL BOAT, WE MIGHT ALL BE DEAD RIGHT NOW.
AT LEAST THEY'D BE DEAD, TOO. THIS IS WAR, JAKE.
NO, KAT. HE HAS TO LISTEN TO ME. I STARTED THIS THING.
AND IT'S GONNA BE OVER REAL SOON IF YOU DON'T START LISTENING TO WHAT JAKE HAS TO SAY.
YOUR SECRET SUPERHEROES CLUB?
YOU MUST BE ALEC, EH? THE RICH ONE?
BEFORE I TURNED IN MY RICH KID BADGE AND JOINED UP WITH YOU GUYS, YEAH.
UNGODLY
HMMM...
THAT'S WEIRD...

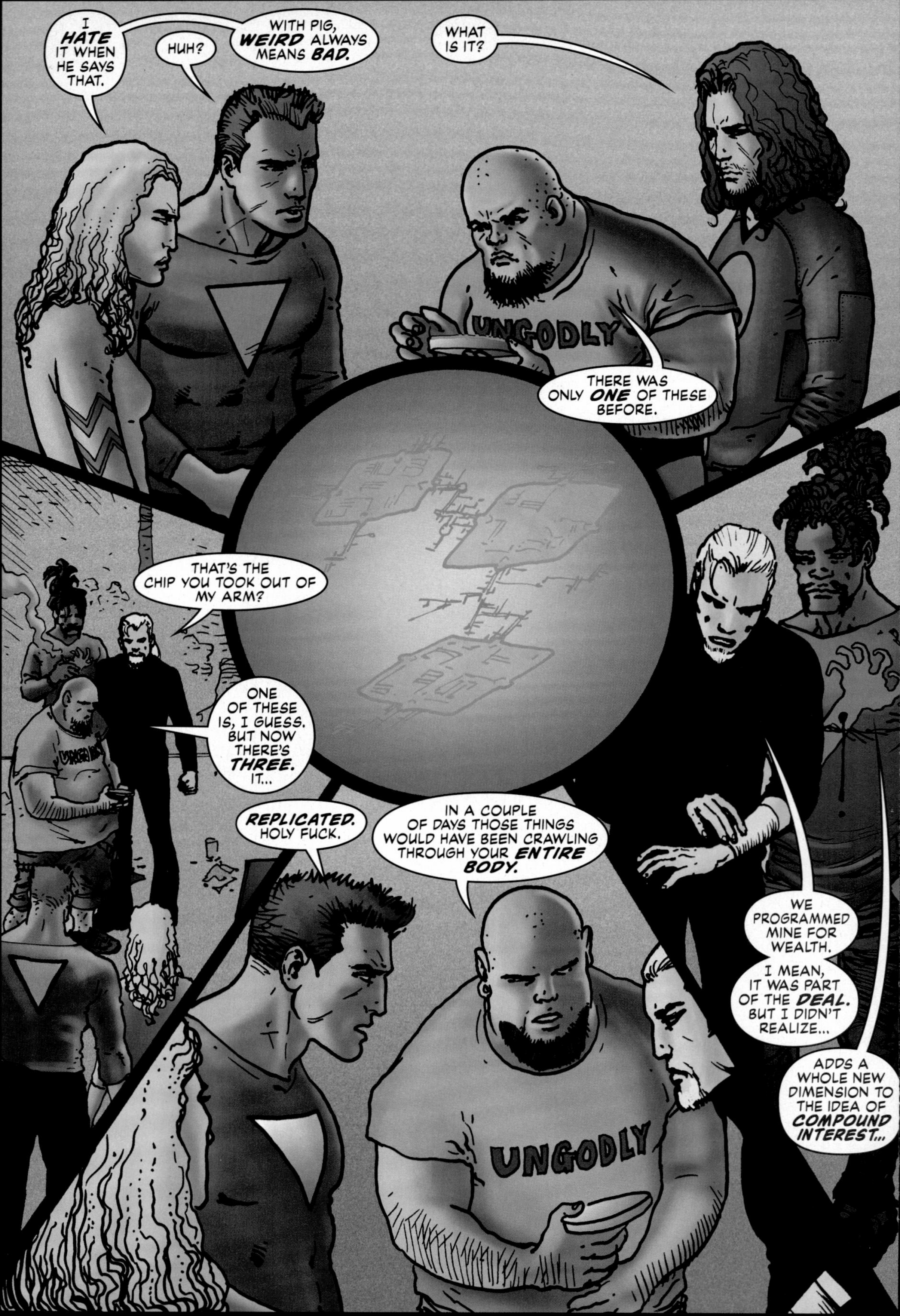
I *HATE* IT WHEN HE SAYS THAT.
HUH?
WITH PIG, *WEIRD* ALWAYS MEANS *BAD.*
WHAT IS IT?
UNGODLY
THERE WAS ONLY *ONE* OF THESE BEFORE.
THAT'S THE CHIP YOU TOOK OUT OF MY ARM?
ONE OF THESE IS, I GUESS. BUT NOW THERE'S *THREE.* IT...
REPLICATED. HOLY FUCK.
IN A COUPLE OF DAYS THOSE THINGS WOULD HAVE BEEN CRAWLING THROUGH YOUR *ENTIRE BODY.*
WE PROGRAMMED MINE FOR WEALTH.
I MEAN, IT WAS PART OF THE *DEAL.* BUT I DIDN'T REALIZE...
ADDS A WHOLE NEW DIMENSION TO THE IDEA OF *COMPOUND INTEREST...*
UNGODLY

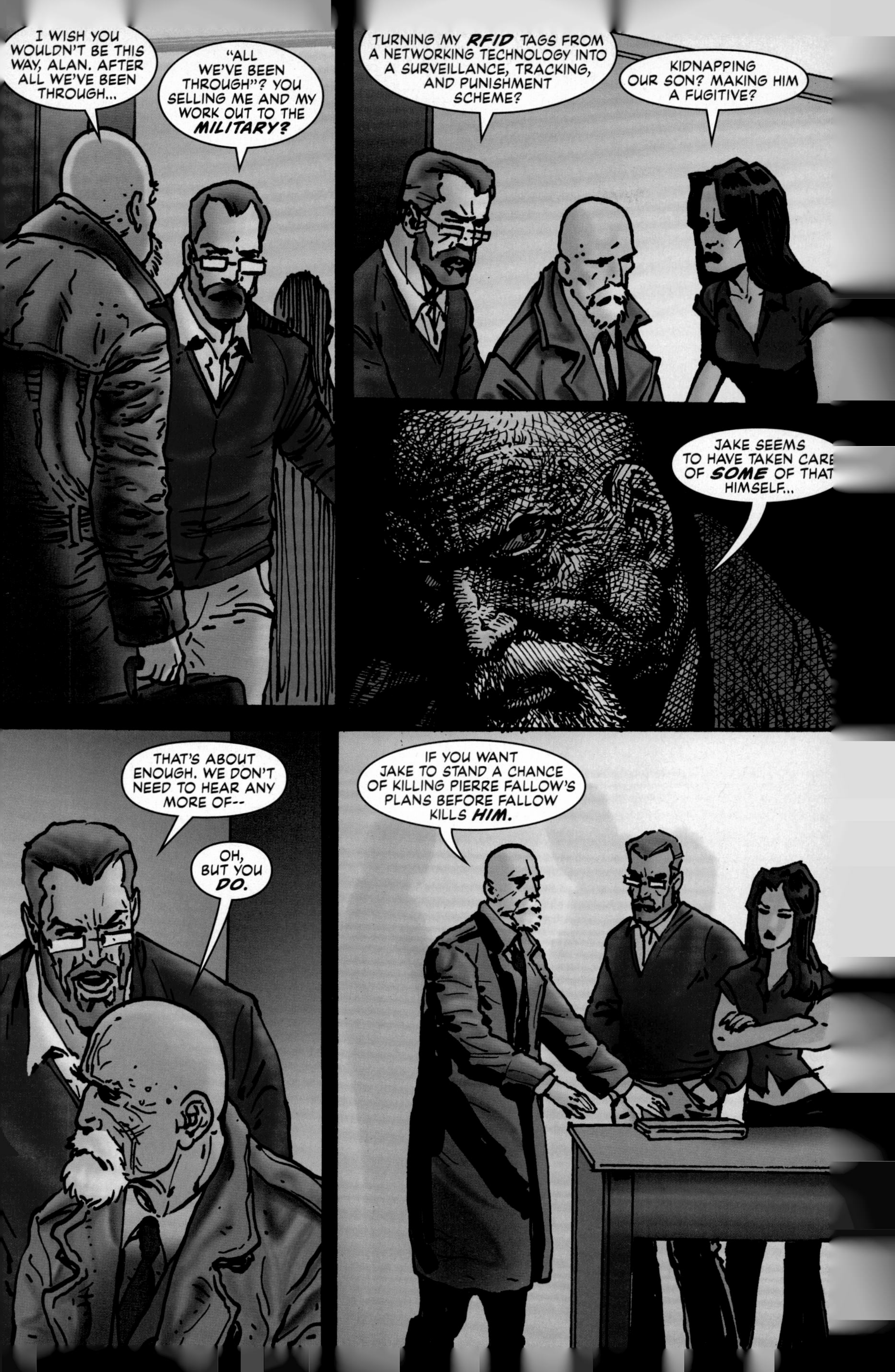
I WISH YOU WOULDN'T BE THIS WAY, ALAN. AFTER ALL WE'VE BEEN THROUGH...
"ALL WE'VE BEEN THROUGH"? YOU SELLING ME AND MY WORK OUT TO THE MILITARY?
TURNING MY RFID TAGS FROM A NETWORKING TECHNOLOGY INTO A SURVEILLANCE, TRACKING, AND PUNISHMENT SCHEME?
KIDNAPPING OUR SON? MAKING HIM A FUGITIVE?
JAKE SEEMS TO HAVE TAKEN CARE OF SOME OF THAT HIMSELF...
THAT'S ABOUT ENOUGH. WE DON'T NEED TO HEAR ANY MORE OF--
OH, BUT YOU DO.
IF YOU WANT JAKE TO STAND A CHANCE OF KILLING PIERRE FALLOW'S PLANS BEFORE FALLOW KILLS HIM.

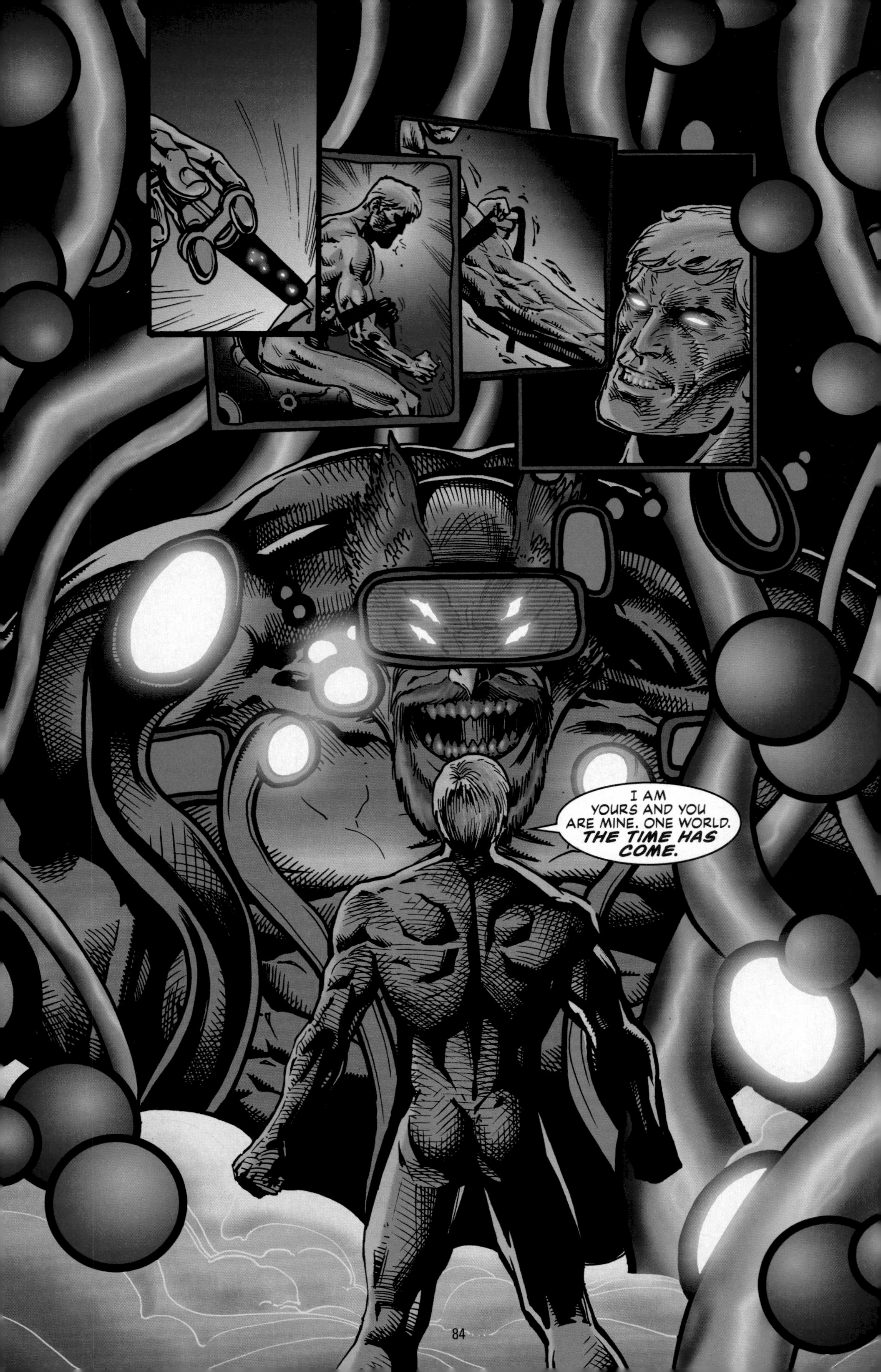
I AM YOURS AND YOU ARE MINE. ONE WORLD. ***THE TIME HAS COME.***

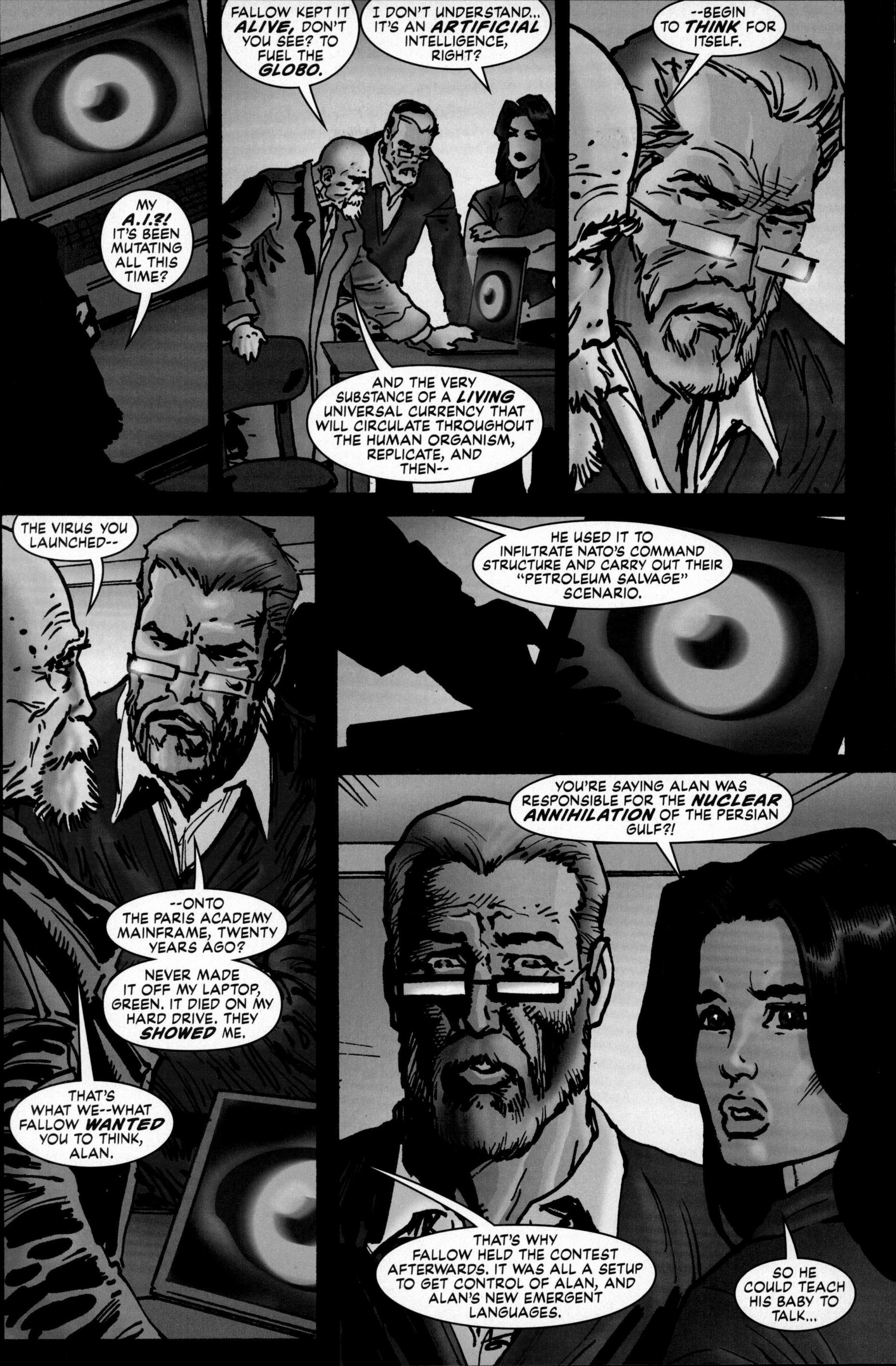

MY A.I.?! IT'S BEEN MUTATING ALL THIS TIME?
FALLOW KEPT IT ALIVE, DON'T YOU SEE? TO FUEL THE GLOBO.
I DON'T UNDERSTAND... IT'S AN ARTIFICIAL INTELLIGENCE, RIGHT?
AND THE VERY SUBSTANCE OF A LIVING UNIVERSAL CURRENCY THAT WILL CIRCULATE THROUGHOUT THE HUMAN ORGANISM, REPLICATE, AND THEN--
--BEGIN TO THINK FOR ITSELF.
THE VIRUS YOU LAUNCHED--
--ONTO THE PARIS ACADEMY MAINFRAME, TWENTY YEARS AGO?
NEVER MADE IT OFF MY LAPTOP, GREEN. IT DIED ON MY HARD DRIVE. THEY SHOWED ME.
THAT'S WHAT WE--WHAT FALLOW WANTED YOU TO THINK, ALAN.
HE USED IT TO INFILTRATE NATO'S COMMAND STRUCTURE AND CARRY OUT THEIR "PETROLEUM SALVAGE" SCENARIO.
YOU'RE SAYING ALAN WAS RESPONSIBLE FOR THE NUCLEAR ANNIHILATION OF THE PERSIAN GULF?!
THAT'S WHY FALLOW HELD THE CONTEST AFTERWARDS. IT WAS ALL A SETUP TO GET CONTROL OF ALAN, AND ALAN'S NEW EMERGENT LANGUAGES.
SO HE COULD TEACH HIS BABY TO TALK...

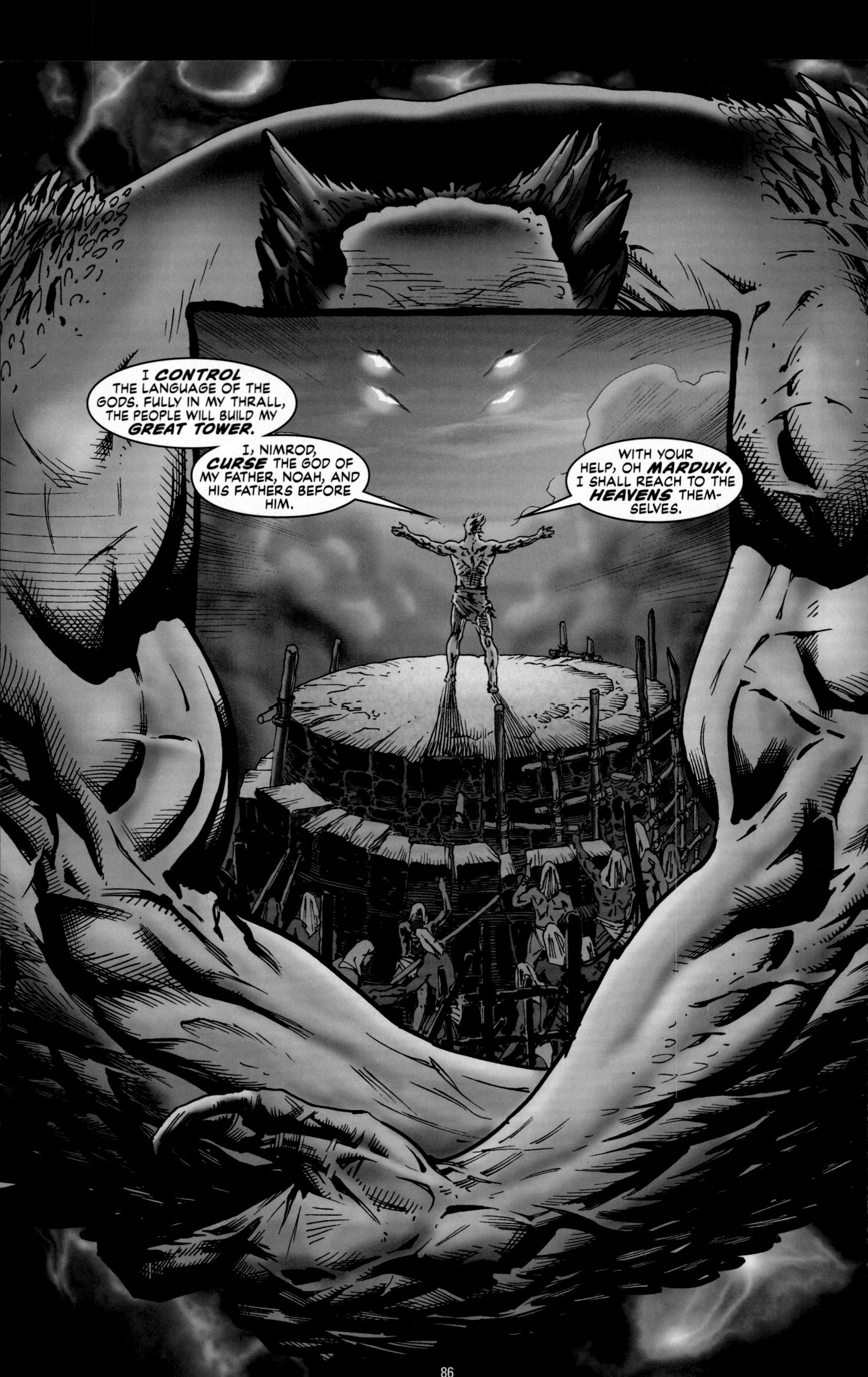
I CONTROL THE LANGUAGE OF THE GODS. FULLY IN MY THRALL, THE PEOPLE WILL BUILD MY GREAT TOWER.
I, NIMROD, CURSE THE GOD OF MY FATHER, NOAH, AND HIS FATHERS BEFORE HIM.
WITH YOUR HELP, OH MARDUK, I SHALL REACH TO THE HEAVENS THEM-SELVES.

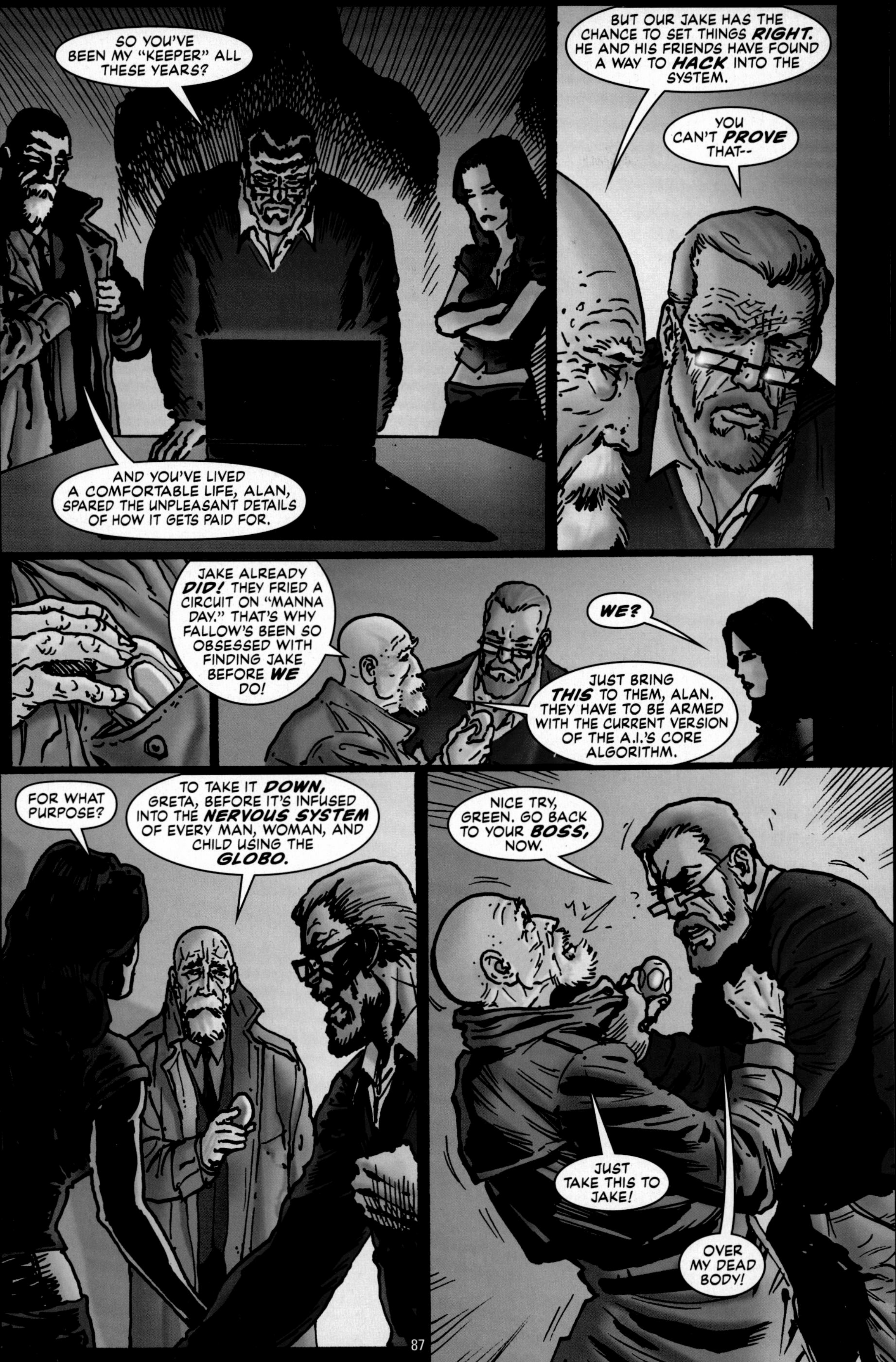
SO YOU'VE BEEN MY "KEEPER" ALL THESE YEARS?
AND YOU'VE LIVED A COMFORTABLE LIFE, ALAN, SPARED THE UNPLEASANT DETAILS OF HOW IT GETS PAID FOR.
BUT OUR JAKE HAS THE CHANCE TO SET THINGS RIGHT. HE AND HIS FRIENDS HAVE FOUND A WAY TO HACK INTO THE SYSTEM.
YOU CAN'T PROVE THAT--
JAKE ALREADY DID! THEY FRIED A CIRCUIT ON "MANNA DAY." THAT'S WHY FALLOW'S BEEN SO OBSESSED WITH FINDING JAKE BEFORE WE DO!
WE?
JUST BRING THIS TO THEM, ALAN. THEY HAVE TO BE ARMED WITH THE CURRENT VERSION OF THE A.I.'S CORE ALGORITHM.
FOR WHAT PURPOSE?
TO TAKE IT DOWN, GRETA, BEFORE IT'S INFUSED INTO THE NERVOUS SYSTEM OF EVERY MAN, WOMAN, AND CHILD USING THE GLOBO.
NICE TRY, GREEN. GO BACK TO YOUR BOSS, NOW.
JUST TAKE THIS TO JAKE!
OVER MY DEAD BODY!

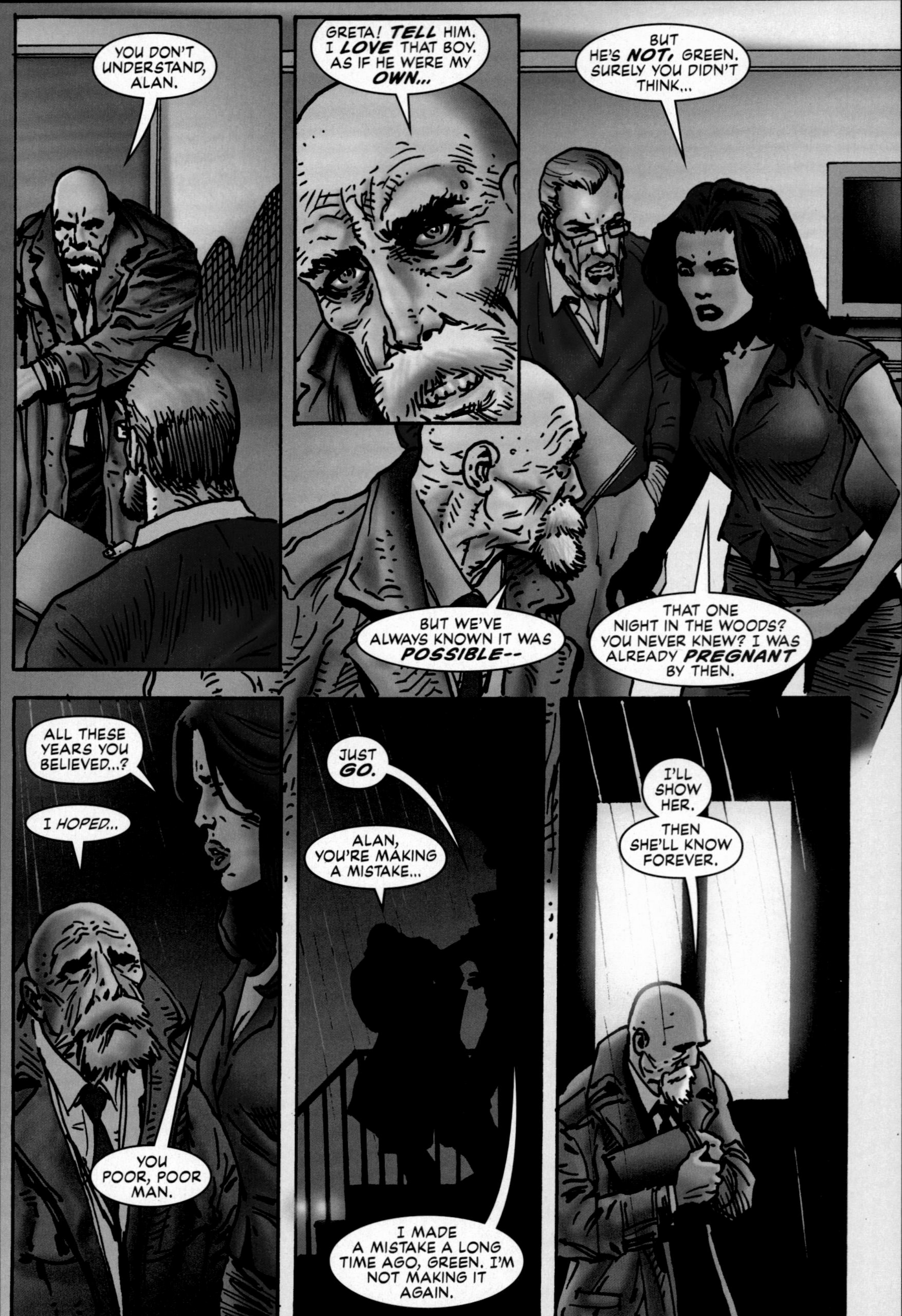
YOU DON'T UNDERSTAND, ALAN.
GRETA! TELL HIM. I LOVE THAT BOY. AS IF HE WERE MY OWN...
BUT HE'S NOT, GREEN. SURELY YOU DIDN'T THINK...
BUT WE'VE ALWAYS KNOWN IT WAS POSSIBLE--
THAT ONE NIGHT IN THE WOODS? YOU NEVER KNEW? I WAS ALREADY PREGNANT BY THEN.
ALL THESE YEARS YOU BELIEVED...?
I HOPED...
YOU POOR, POOR MAN.
JUST GO.
ALAN, YOU'RE MAKING A MISTAKE...
I MADE A MISTAKE A LONG TIME AGO, GREEN. I'M NOT MAKING IT AGAIN.
I'LL SHOW HER.
THEN SHE'LL KNOW FOREVER.

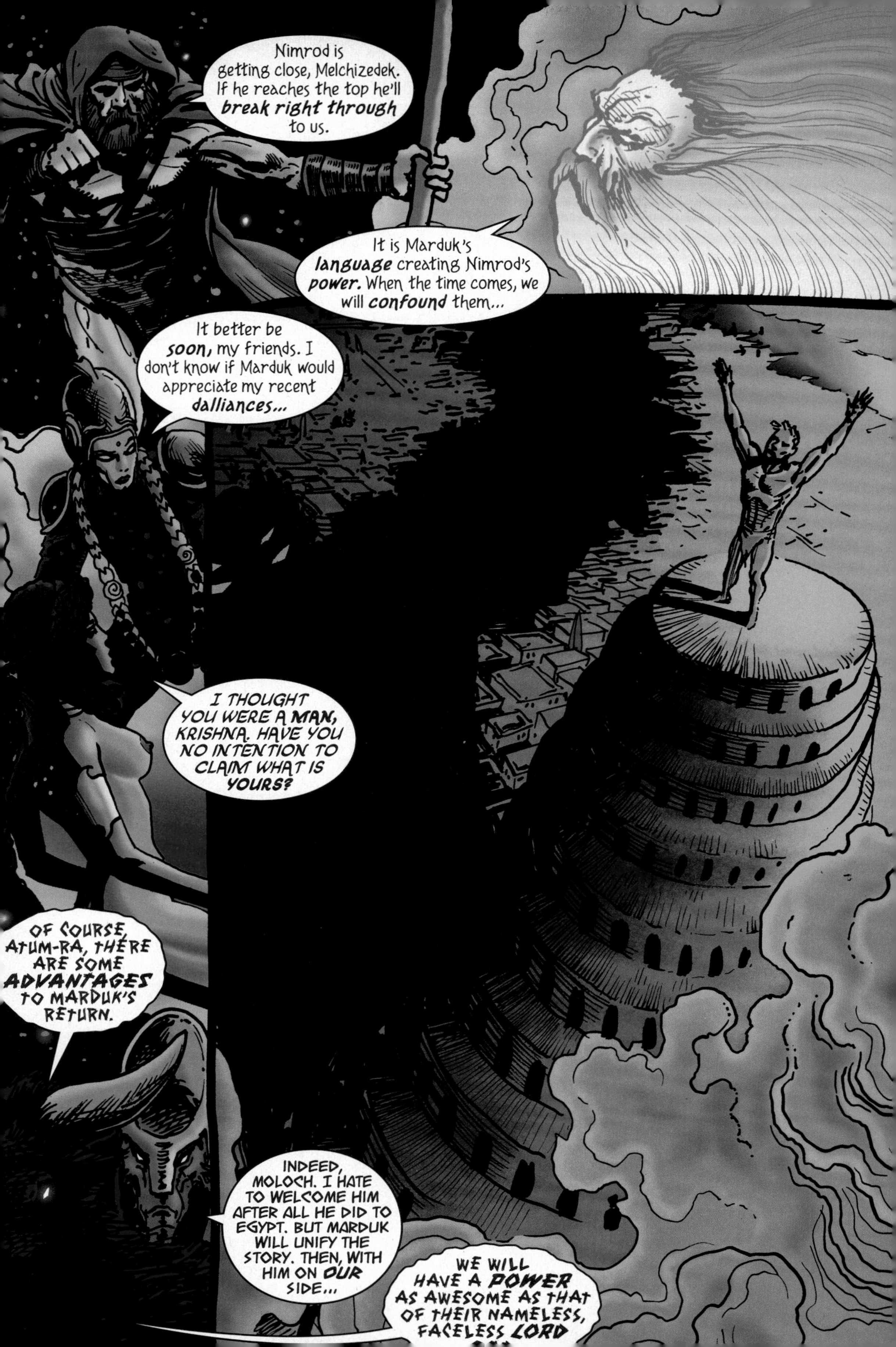
Nimrod is getting close, Melchizedek. If he reaches the top he'll **break right through** to us.
It is Marduk's **language** creating Nimrod's **power.** When the time comes, we will **confound** them...
It better be **soon,** my friends. I don't know if Marduk would appreciate my recent **dalliances...**
I THOUGHT YOU WERE A **MAN,** KRISHNA. HAVE YOU NO INTENTION TO CLAIM WHAT IS **YOURS?**
OF COURSE, ATUM-RA, THERE ARE SOME **ADVANTAGES** TO MARDUK'S RETURN.
INDEED, MOLOCH. I HATE TO WELCOME HIM AFTER ALL HE DID TO EGYPT. BUT MARDUK WILL UNIFY THE STORY. THEN, WITH HIM ON **OUR** SIDE...
WE WILL HAVE A **POWER** AS AWESOME AS THAT OF THEIR NAMELESS, FACELESS **LORD**

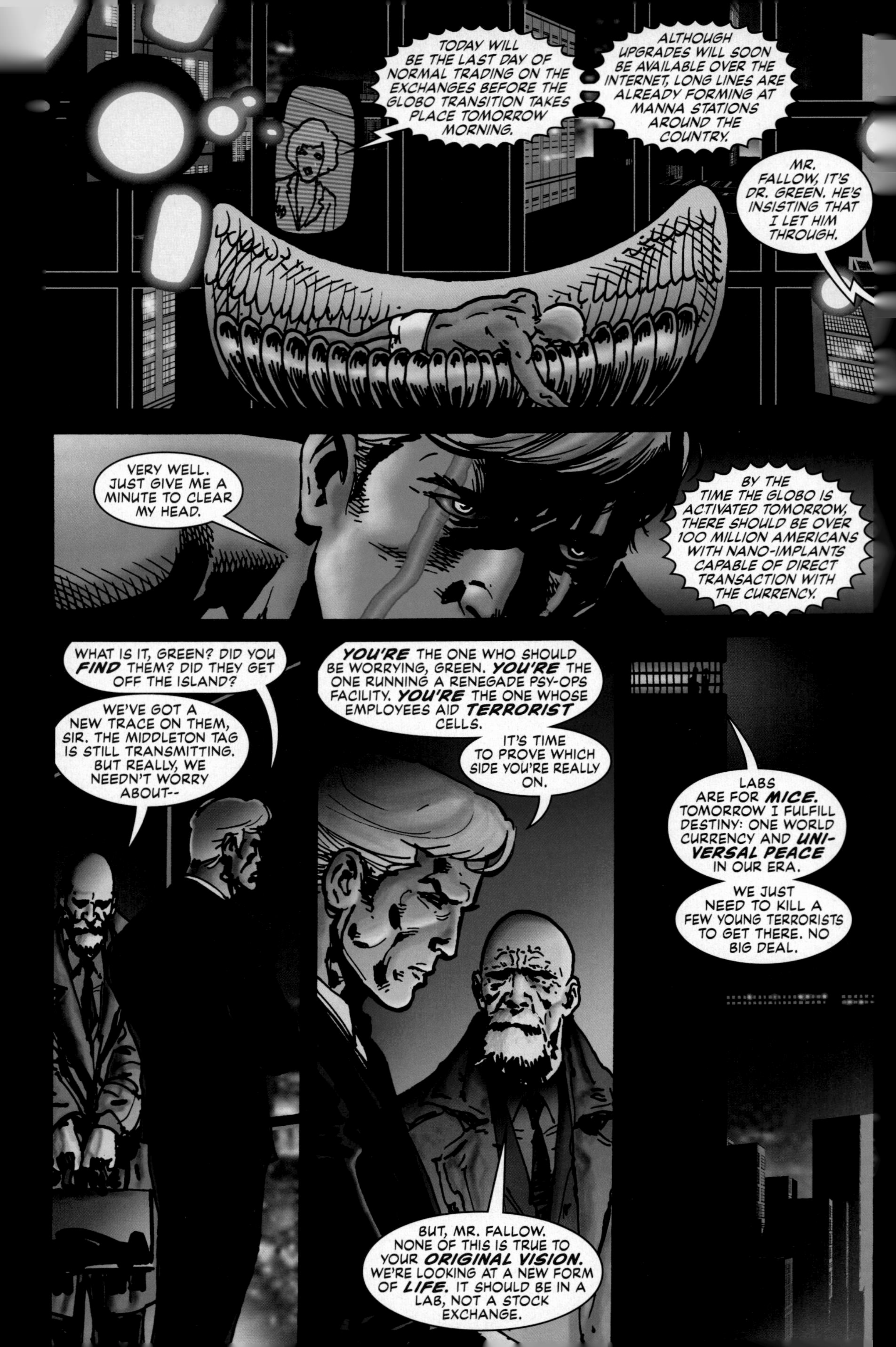
TODAY WILL BE THE LAST DAY OF NORMAL TRADING ON THE EXCHANGES BEFORE THE GLOBO TRANSITION TAKES PLACE TOMORROW MORNING.
ALTHOUGH UPGRADES WILL SOON BE AVAILABLE OVER THE INTERNET, LONG LINES ARE ALREADY FORMING AT MANNA STATIONS AROUND THE COUNTRY.
MR. FALLOW, IT'S DR. GREEN. HE'S INSISTING THAT I LET HIM THROUGH.
VERY WELL. JUST GIVE ME A MINUTE TO CLEAR MY HEAD.
BY THE TIME THE GLOBO IS ACTIVATED TOMORROW, THERE SHOULD BE OVER 100 MILLION AMERICANS WITH NANO-IMPLANTS CAPABLE OF DIRECT TRANSACTION WITH THE CURRENCY.
WHAT IS IT, GREEN? DID YOU FIND THEM? DID THEY GET OFF THE ISLAND?
WE'VE GOT A NEW TRACE ON THEM, SIR. THE MIDDLETON TAG IS STILL TRANSMITTING. BUT REALLY, WE NEEDN'T WORRY ABOUT--
YOU'RE THE ONE WHO SHOULD BE WORRYING, GREEN. YOU'RE THE ONE RUNNING A RENEGADE PSY-OPS FACILITY. YOU'RE THE ONE WHOSE EMPLOYEES AID TERRORIST CELLS.
IT'S TIME TO PROVE WHICH SIDE YOU'RE REALLY ON.
BUT, MR. FALLOW. NONE OF THIS IS TRUE TO YOUR ORIGINAL VISION. WE'RE LOOKING AT A NEW FORM OF LIFE. IT SHOULD BE IN A LAB, NOT A STOCK EXCHANGE.
LABS ARE FOR MICE. TOMORROW I FULFILL DESTINY: ONE WORLD CURRENCY AND UNIVERSAL PEACE IN OUR ERA.
WE JUST NEED TO KILL A FEW YOUNG TERRORISTS TO GET THERE. NO BIG DEAL.

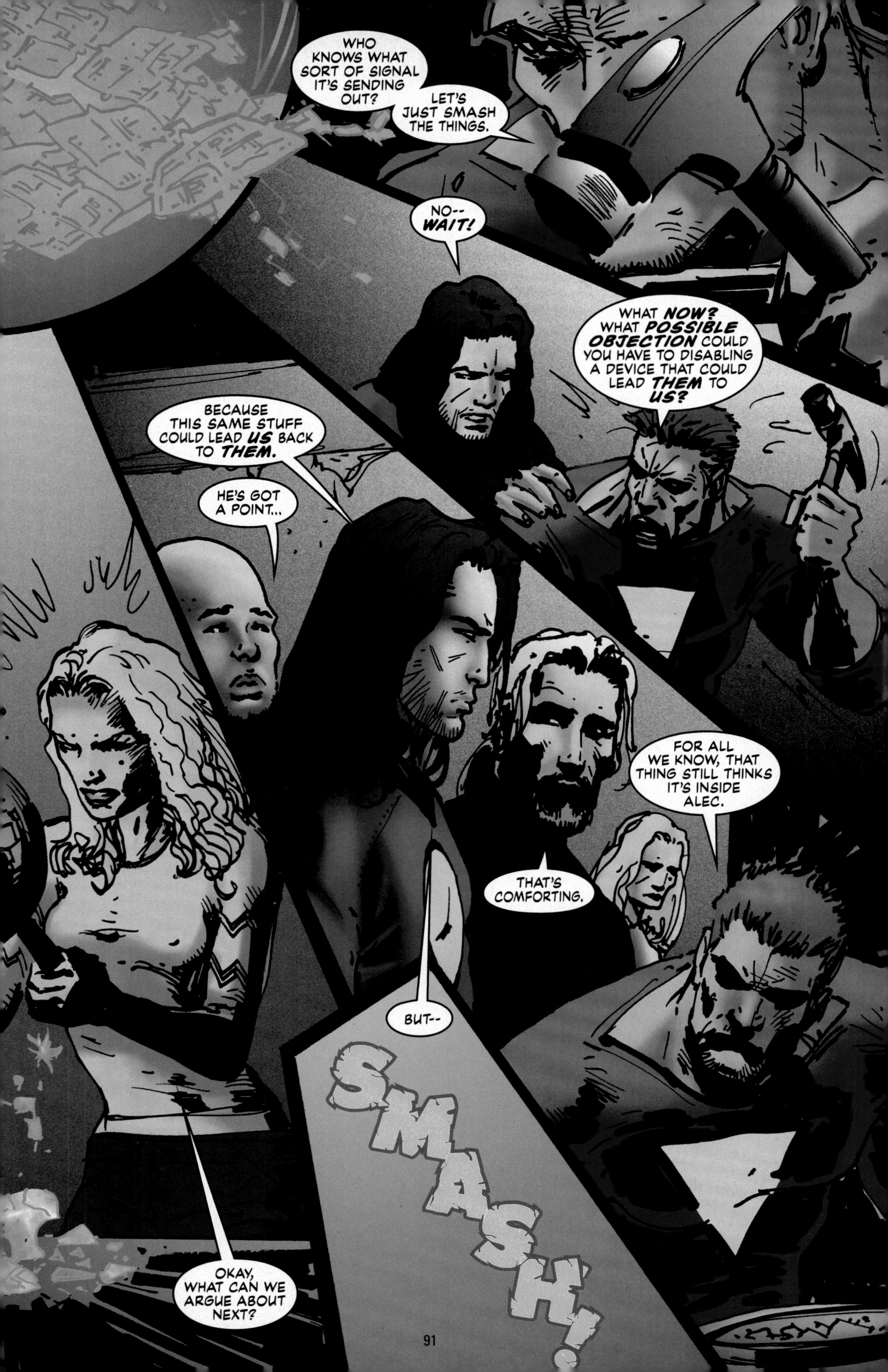
WHO KNOWS WHAT SORT OF SIGNAL IT'S SENDING OUT?
LET'S JUST SMASH THE THINGS.
NO-- WAIT!
WHAT NOW? WHAT POSSIBLE OBJECTION COULD YOU HAVE TO DISABLING A DEVICE THAT COULD LEAD THEM TO US?
BECAUSE THIS SAME STUFF COULD LEAD US BACK TO THEM.
HE'S GOT A POINT...
FOR ALL WE KNOW, THAT THING STILL THINKS IT'S INSIDE ALEC.
THAT'S COMFORTING.
BUT--
SMASH!
OKAY, WHAT CAN WE ARGUE ABOUT NEXT?

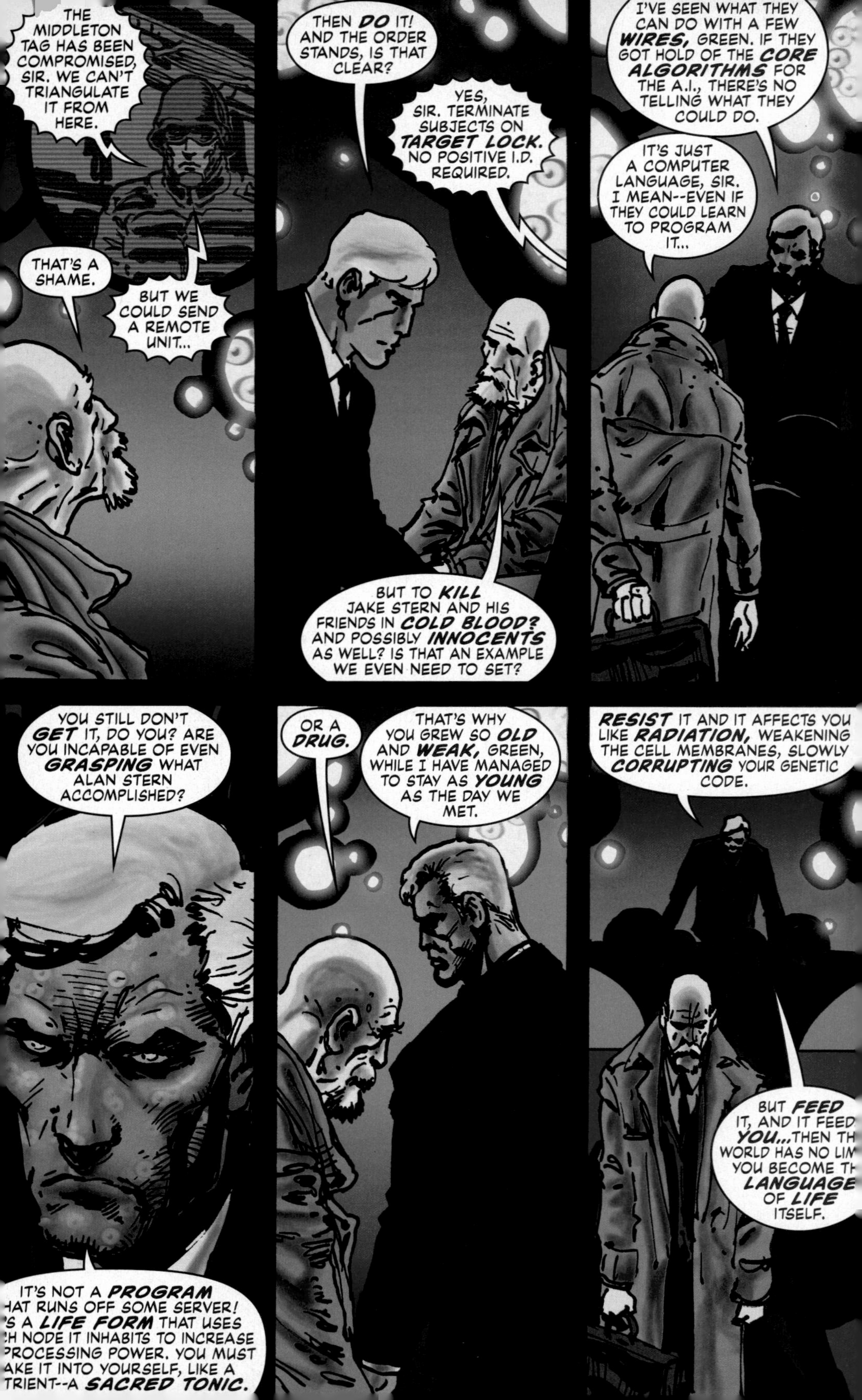
THE MIDDLETON TAG HAS BEEN COMPROMISED, SIR. WE CAN'T TRIANGULATE IT FROM HERE.
THAT'S A SHAME.
BUT WE COULD SEND A REMOTE UNIT...
THEN DO IT! AND THE ORDER STANDS, IS THAT CLEAR?
YES, SIR. TERMINATE SUBJECTS ON TARGET LOCK. NO POSITIVE I.D. REQUIRED.
BUT TO KILL JAKE STERN AND HIS FRIENDS IN COLD BLOOD? AND POSSIBLY INNOCENTS AS WELL? IS THAT AN EXAMPLE WE EVEN NEED TO SET?
I'VE SEEN WHAT THEY CAN DO WITH A FEW WIRES, GREEN. IF THEY GOT HOLD OF THE CORE ALGORITHMS FOR THE A.I., THERE'S NO TELLING WHAT THEY COULD DO.
IT'S JUST A COMPUTER LANGUAGE, SIR. I MEAN--EVEN IF THEY COULD LEARN TO PROGRAM IT...
YOU STILL DON'T GET IT, DO YOU? ARE YOU INCAPABLE OF EVEN GRASPING WHAT ALAN STERN ACCOMPLISHED?
IT'S NOT A PROGRAM
HAT RUNS OFF SOME SERVER!
'S A LIFE FORM THAT USES
CH NODE IT INHABITS TO INCREASE
PROCESSING POWER. YOU MUST
AKE IT INTO YOURSELF, LIKE A
TRIENT--A SACRED TONIC.
OR A DRUG.
THAT'S WHY YOU GREW SO OLD AND WEAK, GREEN, WHILE I HAVE MANAGED TO STAY AS YOUNG AS THE DAY WE MET.
RESIST IT AND IT AFFECTS YOU LIKE RADIATION, WEAKENING THE CELL MEMBRANES, SLOWLY CORRUPTING YOUR GENETIC CODE.
BUT FEED
IT, AND IT FEED
YOU...THEN TH
WORLD HAS NO LIM
YOU BECOME TH
LANGUAGE
OF LIFE
ITSELF.

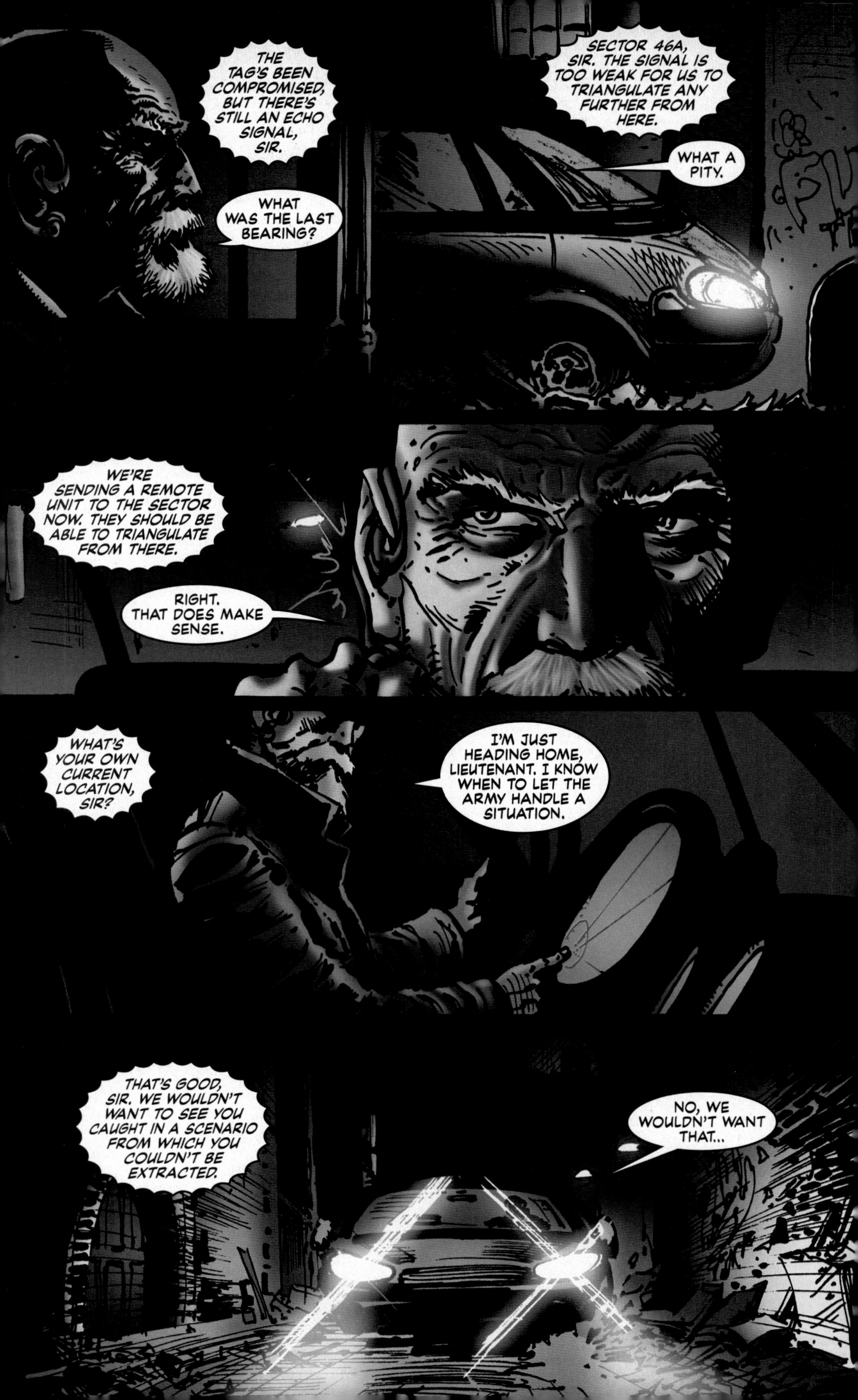
THE TAG'S BEEN COMPROMISED, BUT THERE'S STILL AN ECHO SIGNAL, SIR.
WHAT WAS THE LAST BEARING?
SECTOR 46A, SIR. THE SIGNAL IS TOO WEAK FOR US TO TRIANGULATE ANY FURTHER FROM HERE.
WHAT A PITY.
WE'RE SENDING A REMOTE UNIT TO THE SECTOR NOW. THEY SHOULD BE ABLE TO TRIANGULATE FROM THERE.
RIGHT. THAT DOES MAKE SENSE.
WHAT'S YOUR OWN CURRENT LOCATION, SIR?
I'M JUST HEADING HOME, LIEUTENANT. I KNOW WHEN TO LET THE ARMY HANDLE A SITUATION.
THAT'S GOOD, SIR. WE WOULDN'T WANT TO SEE YOU CAUGHT IN A SCENARIO FROM WHICH YOU COULDN'T BE EXTRACTED.
NO, WE WOULDN'T WANT THAT...

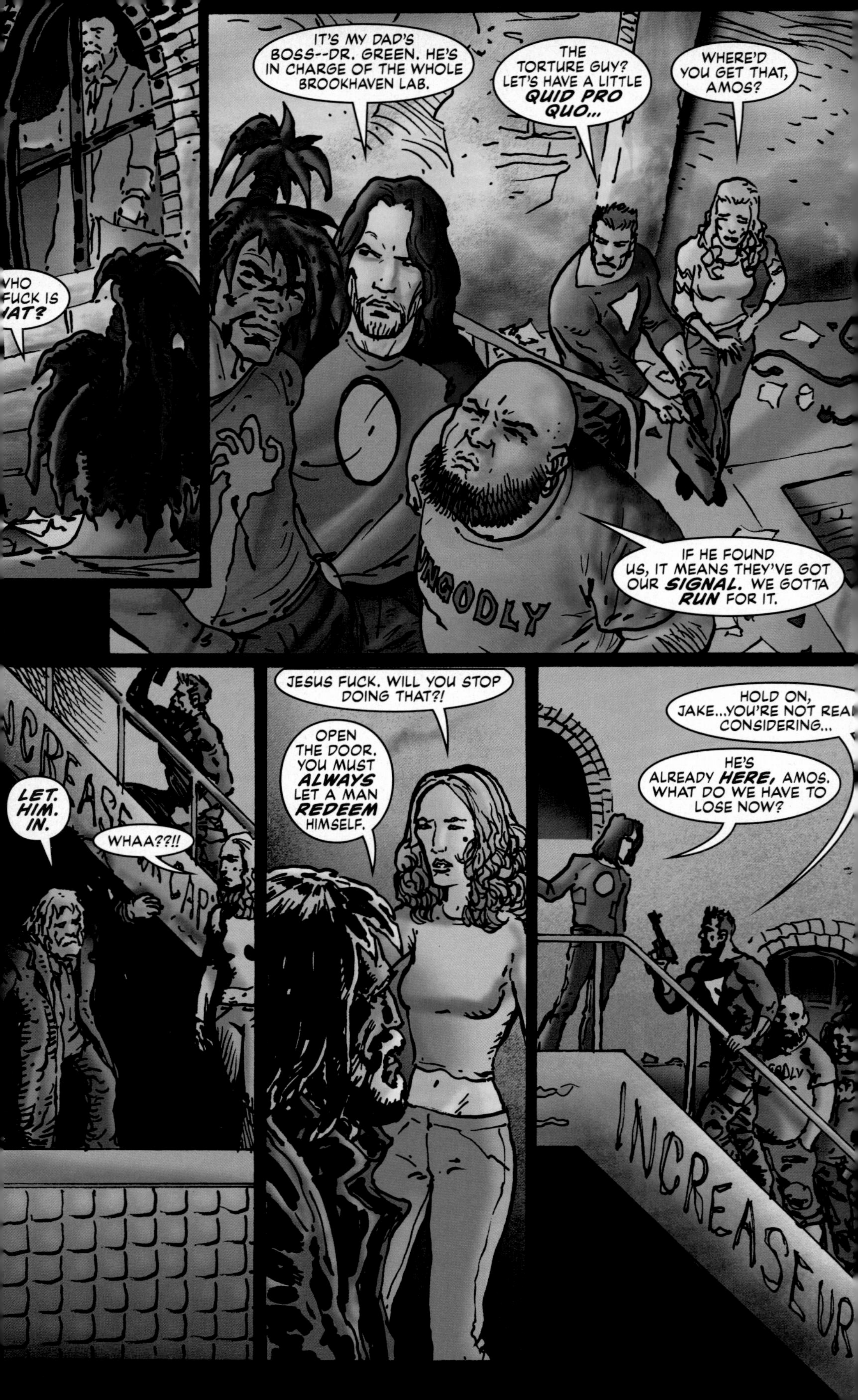
WHO
FUCK IS
IAT?
IT'S MY DAD'S BOSS--DR. GREEN. HE'S IN CHARGE OF THE WHOLE BROOKHAVEN LAB.
THE TORTURE GUY? LET'S HAVE A LITTLE QUID PRO QUO...
WHERE'D YOU GET THAT, AMOS?
UNGODLY
IF HE FOUND US, IT MEANS THEY'VE GOT OUR SIGNAL. WE GOTTA RUN FOR IT.
LET. HIM. IN.
WHAA??!!
JESUS FUCK. WILL YOU STOP DOING THAT?!
OPEN THE DOOR. YOU MUST ALWAYS LET A MAN REDEEM HIMSELF.
HOLD ON, JAKE...YOU'RE NOT REA
CONSIDERING...
HE'S ALREADY HERE, AMOS. WHAT DO WE HAVE TO LOSE NOW?
INCREASE UR

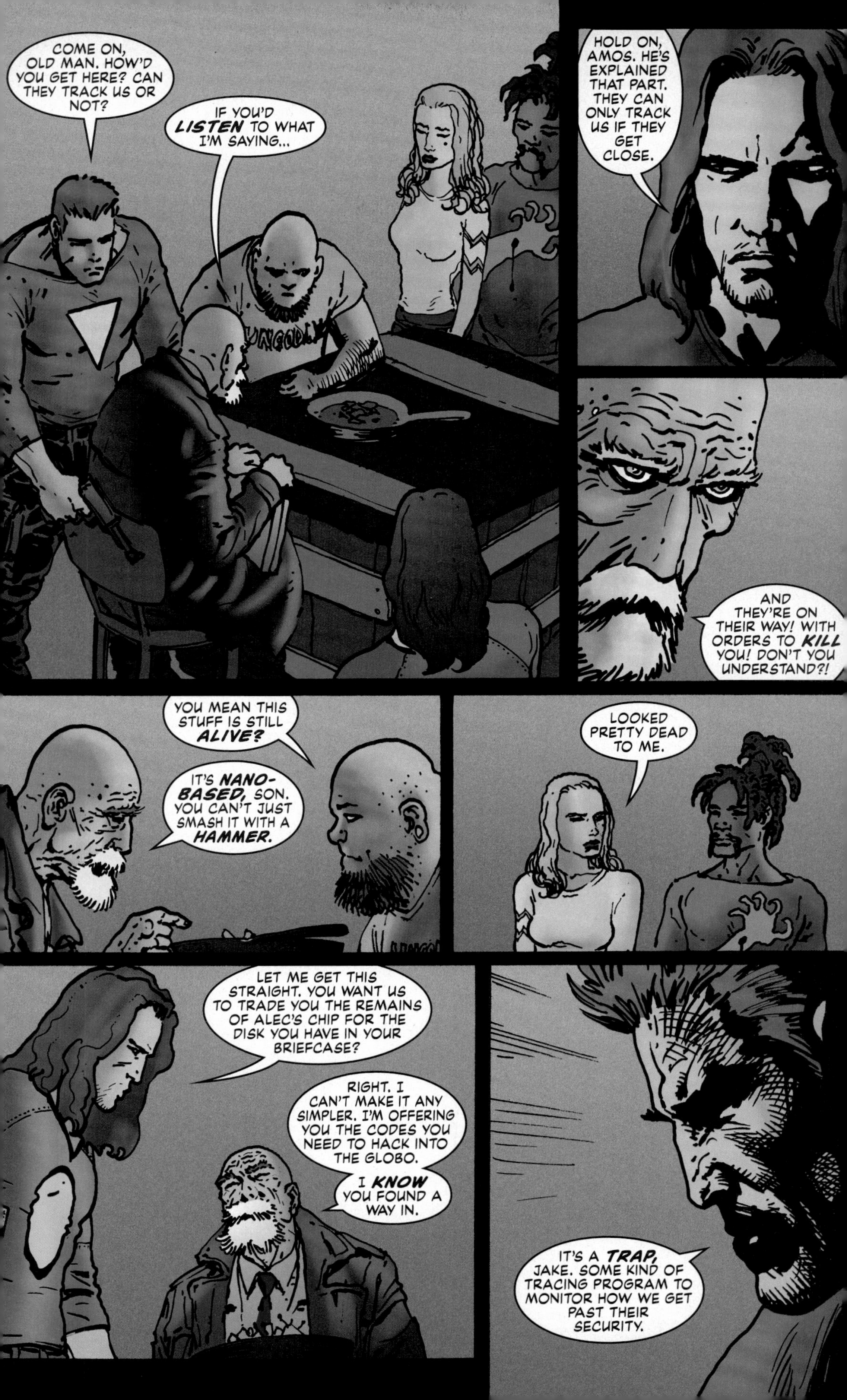
COME ON, OLD MAN. HOW'D YOU GET HERE? CAN THEY TRACK US OR NOT?
IF YOU'D LISTEN TO WHAT I'M SAYING...
HOLD ON, AMOS. HE'S EXPLAINED THAT PART. THEY CAN ONLY TRACK US IF THEY GET CLOSE.
AND THEY'RE ON THEIR WAY! WITH ORDERS TO KILL YOU! DON'T YOU UNDERSTAND?!
YOU MEAN THIS STUFF IS STILL ALIVE?
IT'S NANO-BASED, SON. YOU CAN'T JUST SMASH IT WITH A HAMMER.
LOOKED PRETTY DEAD TO ME.
LET ME GET THIS STRAIGHT. YOU WANT US TO TRADE YOU THE REMAINS OF ALEC'S CHIP FOR THE DISK YOU HAVE IN YOUR BRIEFCASE?
RIGHT. I CAN'T MAKE IT ANY SIMPLER. I'M OFFERING YOU THE CODES YOU NEED TO HACK INTO THE GLOBO.
I KNOW YOU FOUND A WAY IN.
IT'S A TRAP, JAKE. SOME KIND OF TRACING PROGRAM TO MONITOR HOW WE GET PAST THEIR SECURITY.

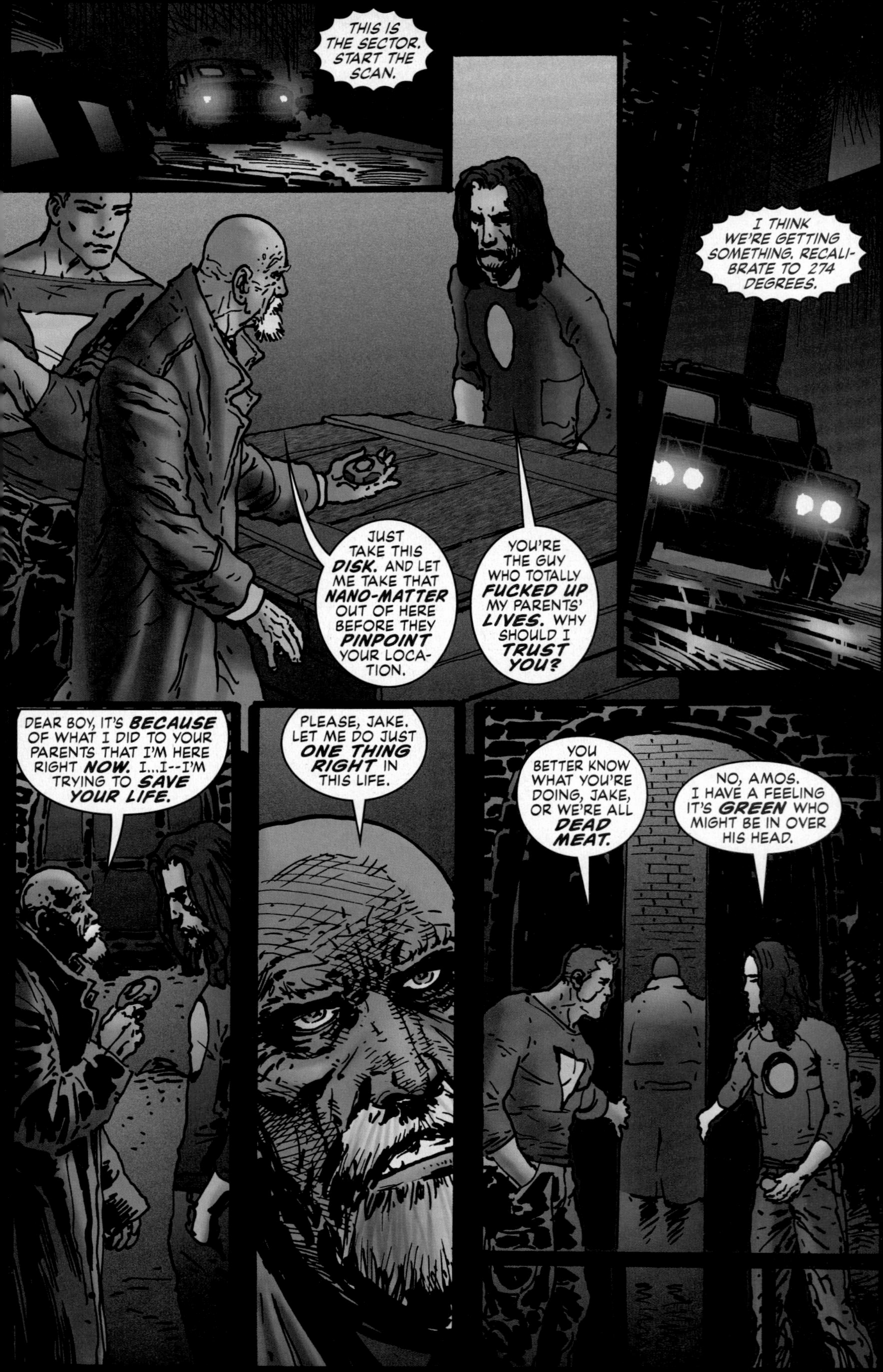
THIS IS THE SECTOR. START THE SCAN.
I THINK WE'RE GETTING SOMETHING. RECALIBRATE TO 274 DEGREES.
JUST TAKE THIS DISK. AND LET ME TAKE THAT NANO-MATTER OUT OF HERE BEFORE THEY PINPOINT YOUR LOCATION.
YOU'RE THE GUY WHO TOTALLY FUCKED UP MY PARENTS' LIVES. WHY SHOULD I TRUST YOU?
DEAR BOY, IT'S BECAUSE OF WHAT I DID TO YOUR PARENTS THAT I'M HERE RIGHT NOW. I...I--I'M TRYING TO SAVE YOUR LIFE.
PLEASE, JAKE. LET ME DO JUST ONE THING RIGHT IN THIS LIFE.
YOU BETTER KNOW WHAT YOU'RE DOING, JAKE, OR WE'RE ALL DEAD MEAT.
NO, AMOS. I HAVE A FEELING IT'S GREEN WHO MIGHT BE IN OVER HIS HEAD.

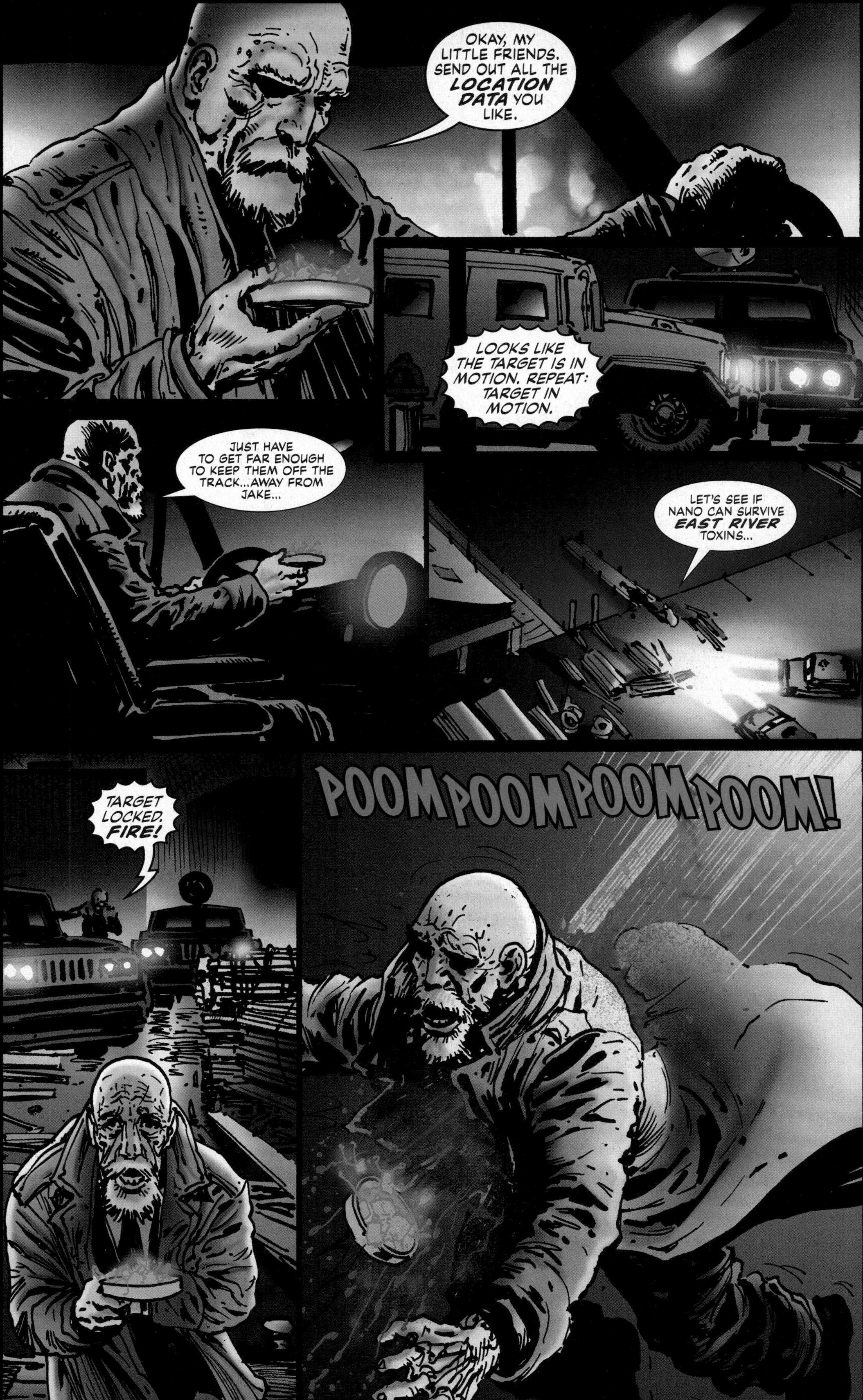
OKAY, MY LITTLE FRIENDS. SEND OUT ALL THE LOCATION DATA YOU LIKE.
LOOKS LIKE THE TARGET IS IN MOTION. REPEAT: TARGET IN MOTION.
JUST HAVE TO GET FAR ENOUGH TO KEEP THEM OFF THE TRACK...AWAY FROM JAKE...
LET'S SEE IF NANO CAN SURVIVE EAST RIVER TOXINS...
TARGET LOCKED. FIRE!
POOMPOOMPOOMPOOM!

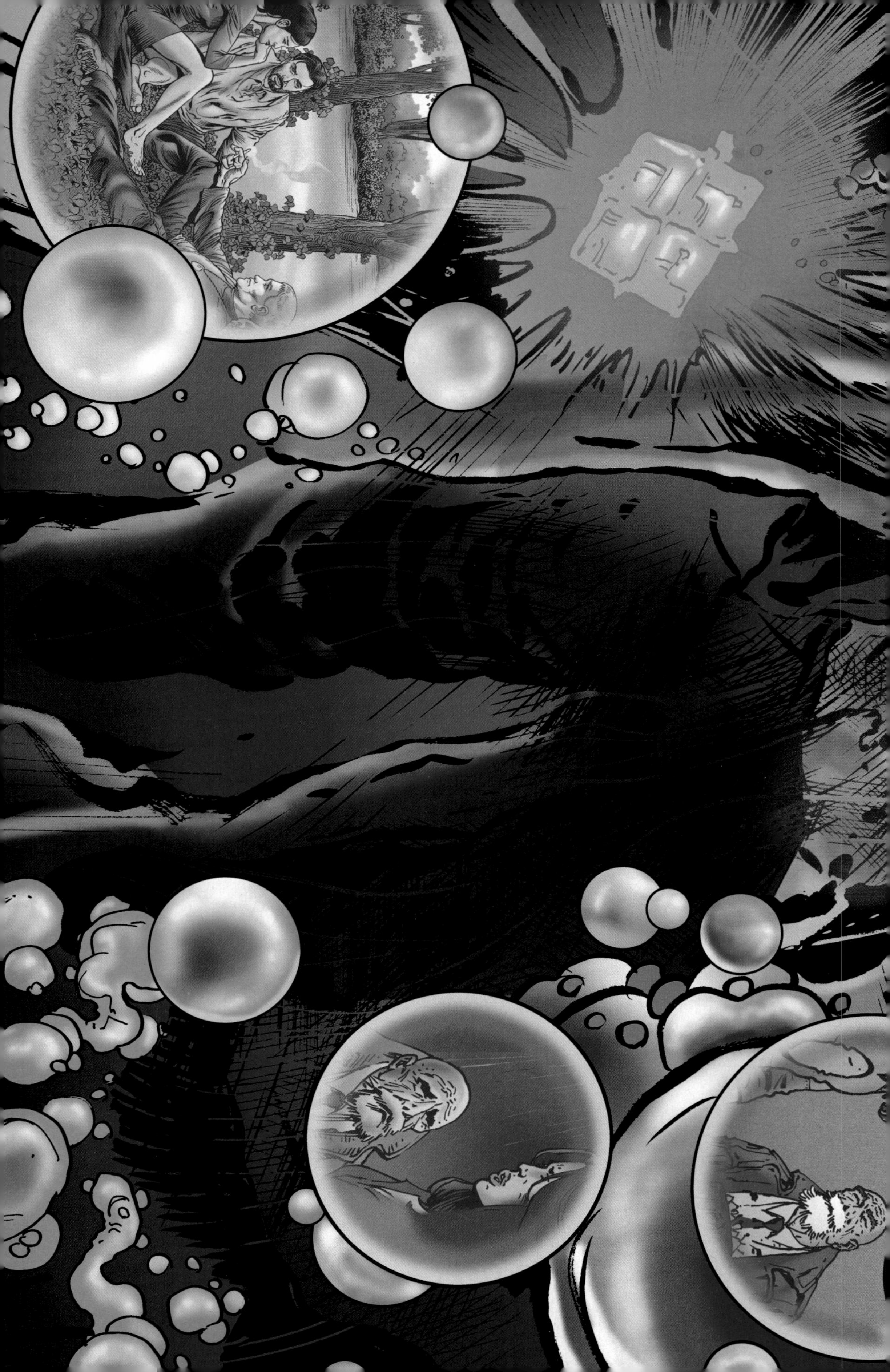

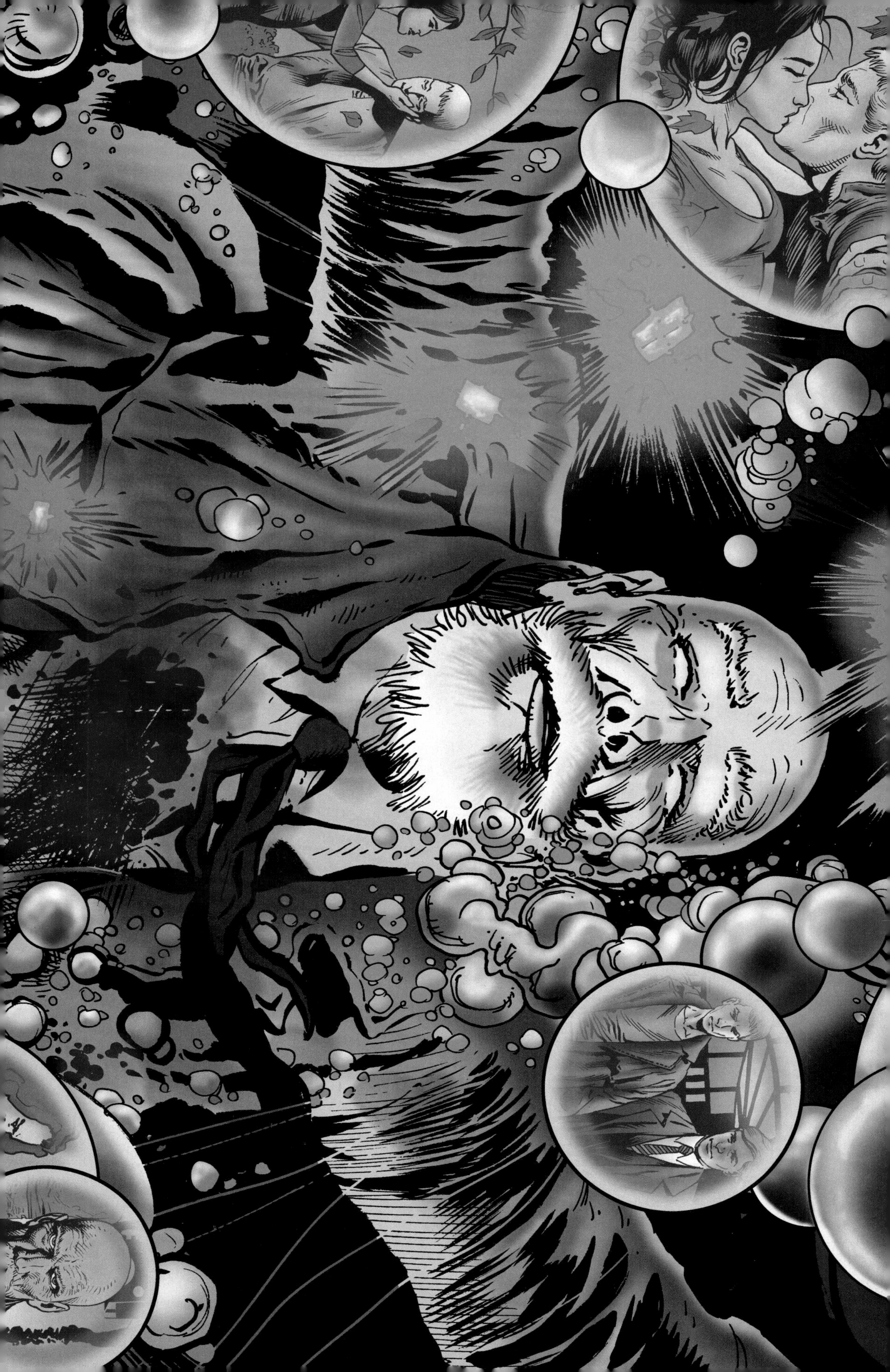

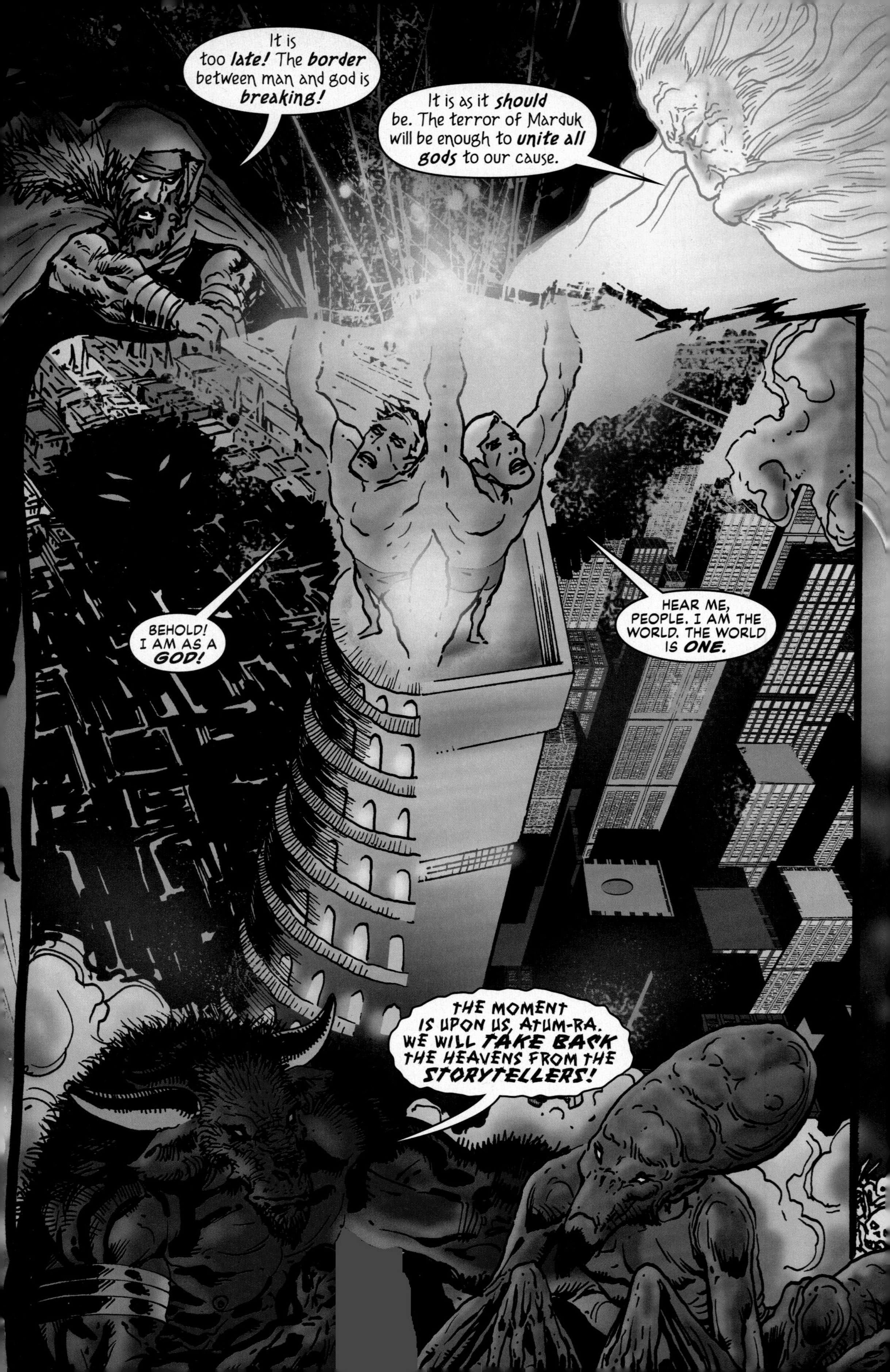
It is too late! The border between man and god is breaking!
It is as it should be. The terror of Marduk will be enough to unite all gods to our cause.
BEHOLD! I AM AS A GOD!
HEAR ME, PEOPLE. I AM THE WORLD. THE WORLD IS ONE.
THE MOMENT IS UPON US, ATUM-RA. WE WILL TAKE BACK THE HEAVENS FROM THE STORYTELLERS!

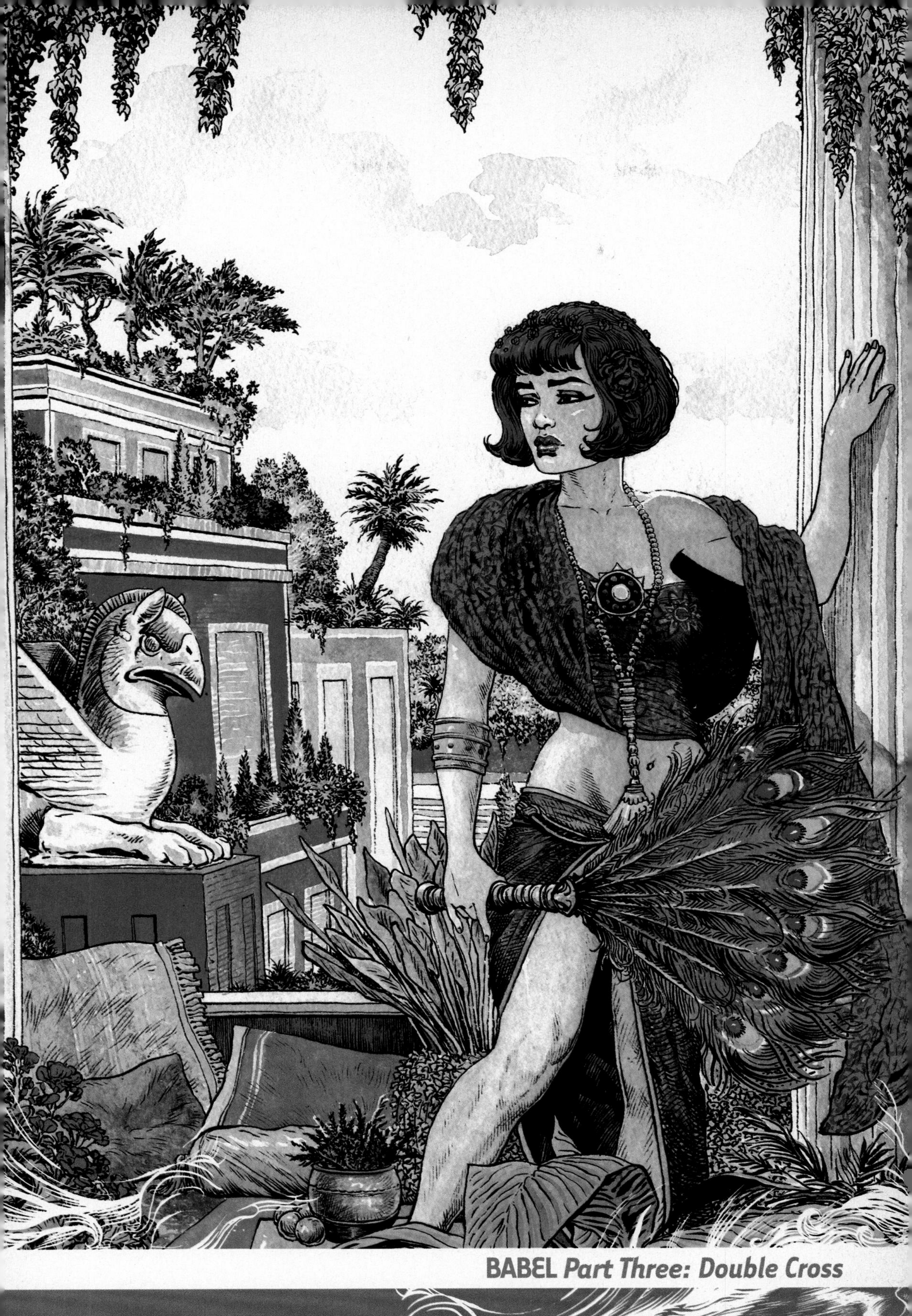

BABEL *Part Three: Double Cross*

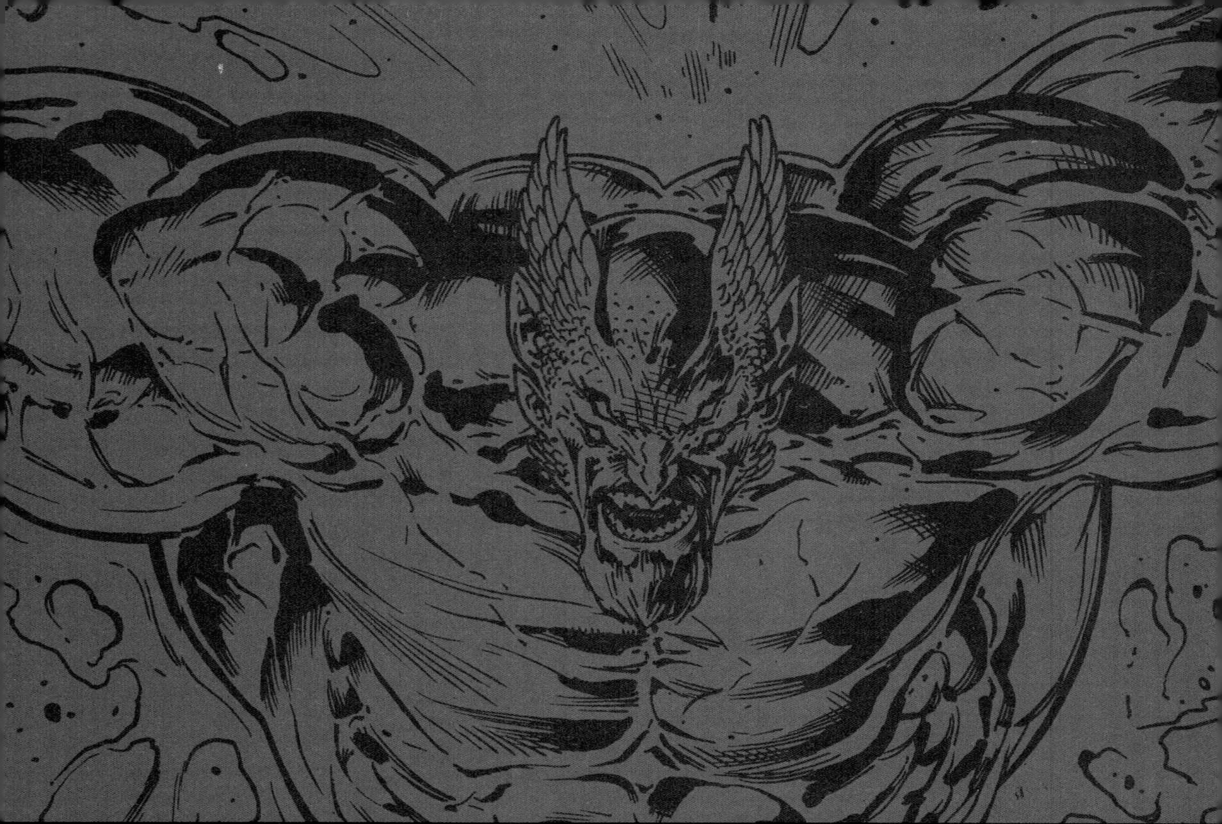

TESTAMENT

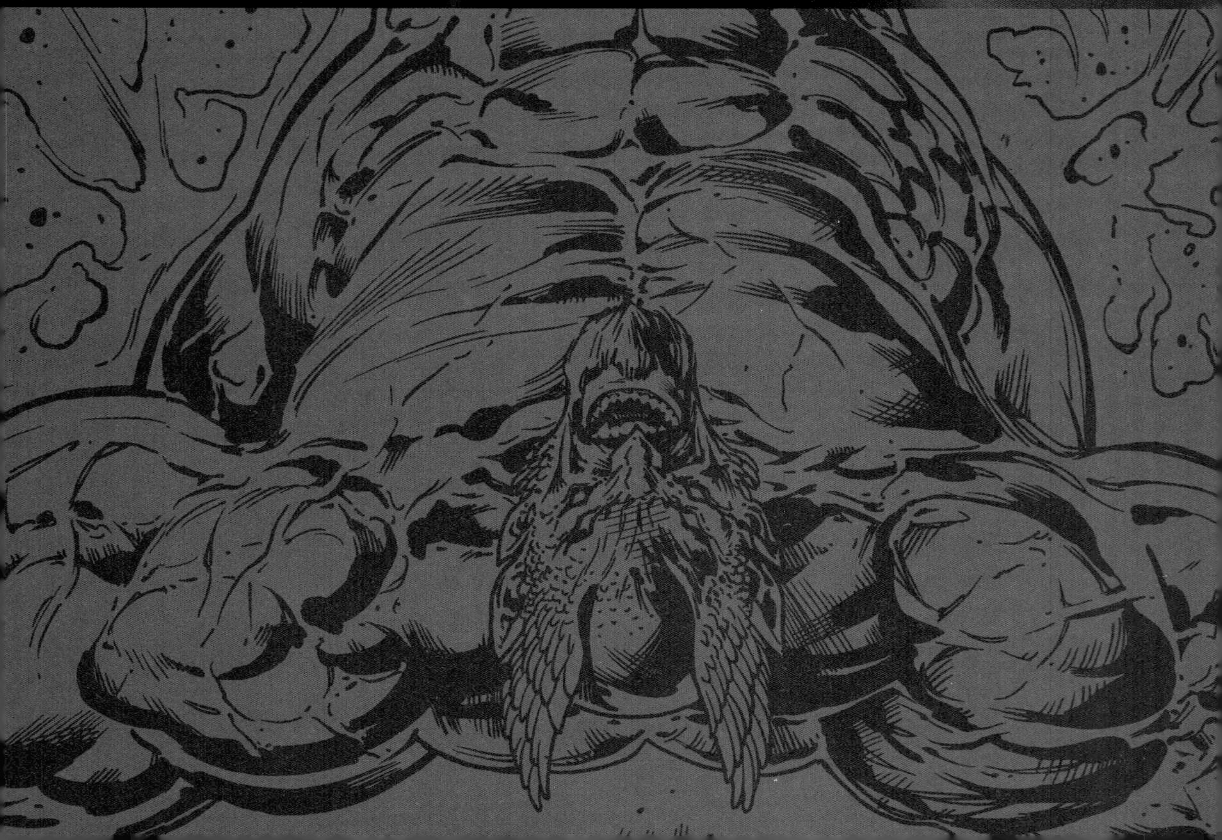

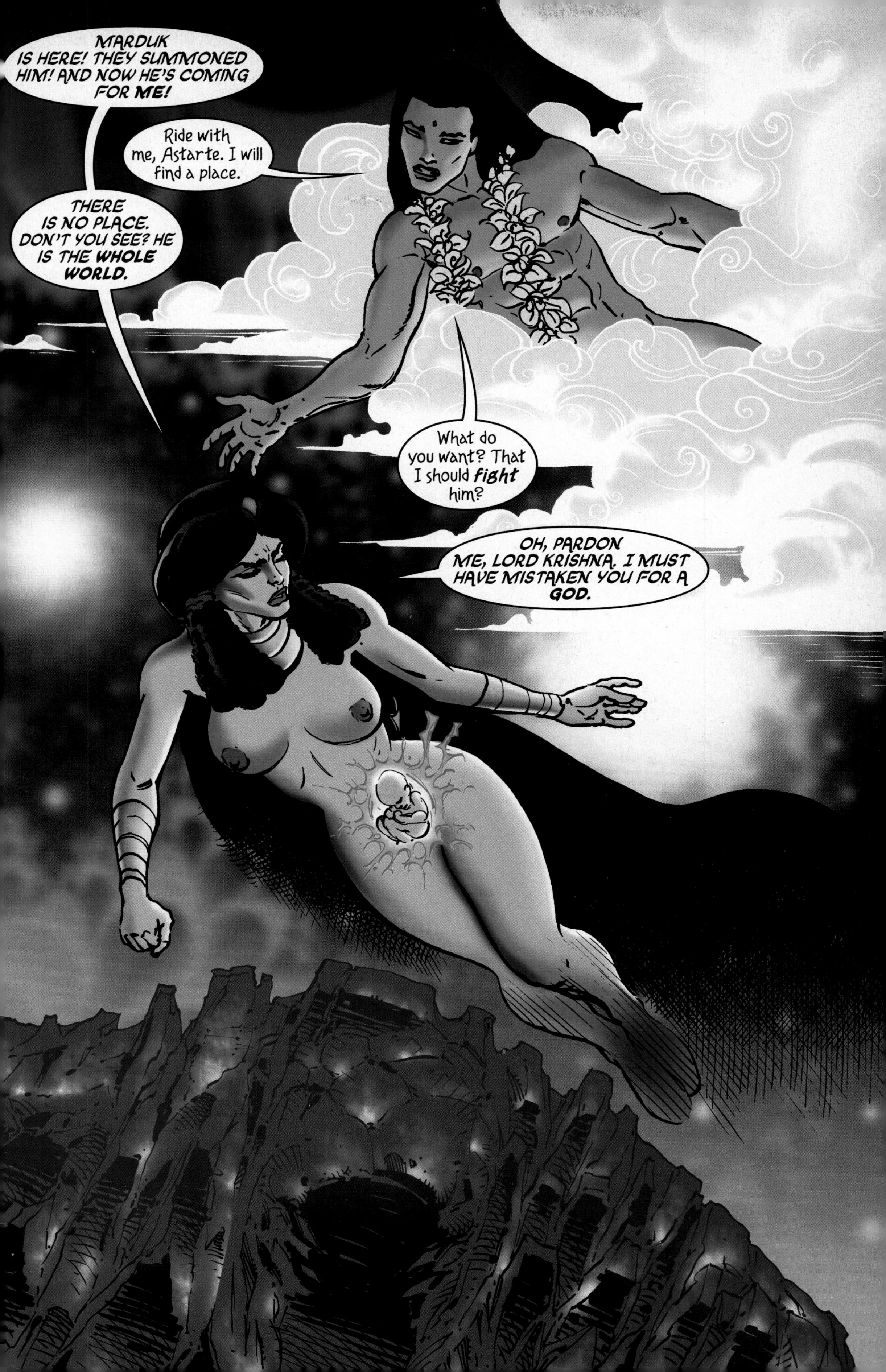
MARDUK IS HERE! THEY SUMMONED HIM! AND NOW HE'S COMING FOR ME!
Ride with me, Astarte. I will find a place.
THERE IS NO PLACE. DON'T YOU SEE? HE IS THE WHOLE WORLD.
What do you want? That I should fight him?
OH, PARDON ME, LORD KRISHNA. I MUST HAVE MISTAKEN YOU FOR A GOD.

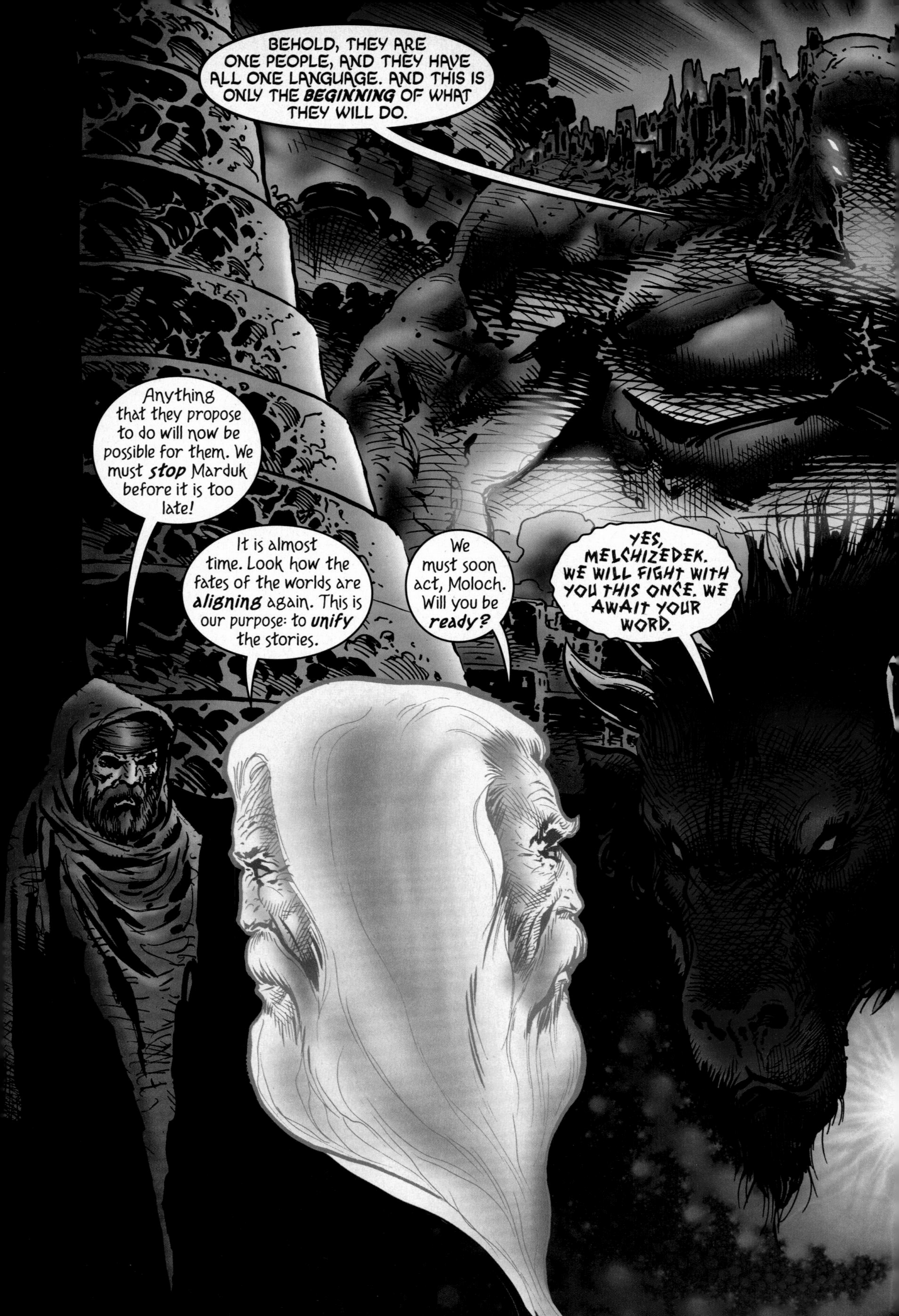
BEHOLD, THEY ARE ONE PEOPLE, AND THEY HAVE ALL ONE LANGUAGE. AND THIS IS ONLY THE *BEGINNING* OF WHAT THEY WILL DO.
Anything that they propose to do will now be possible for them. We must *stop* Marduk before it is too late!
It is almost time. Look how the fates of the worlds are *aligning* again. This is our purpose: to *unify* the stories.
We must soon act, Moloch. Will you be *ready?*
YES, MELCHIZEDEK. WE WILL FIGHT WITH YOU THIS ONCE. WE AWAIT YOUR WORD.

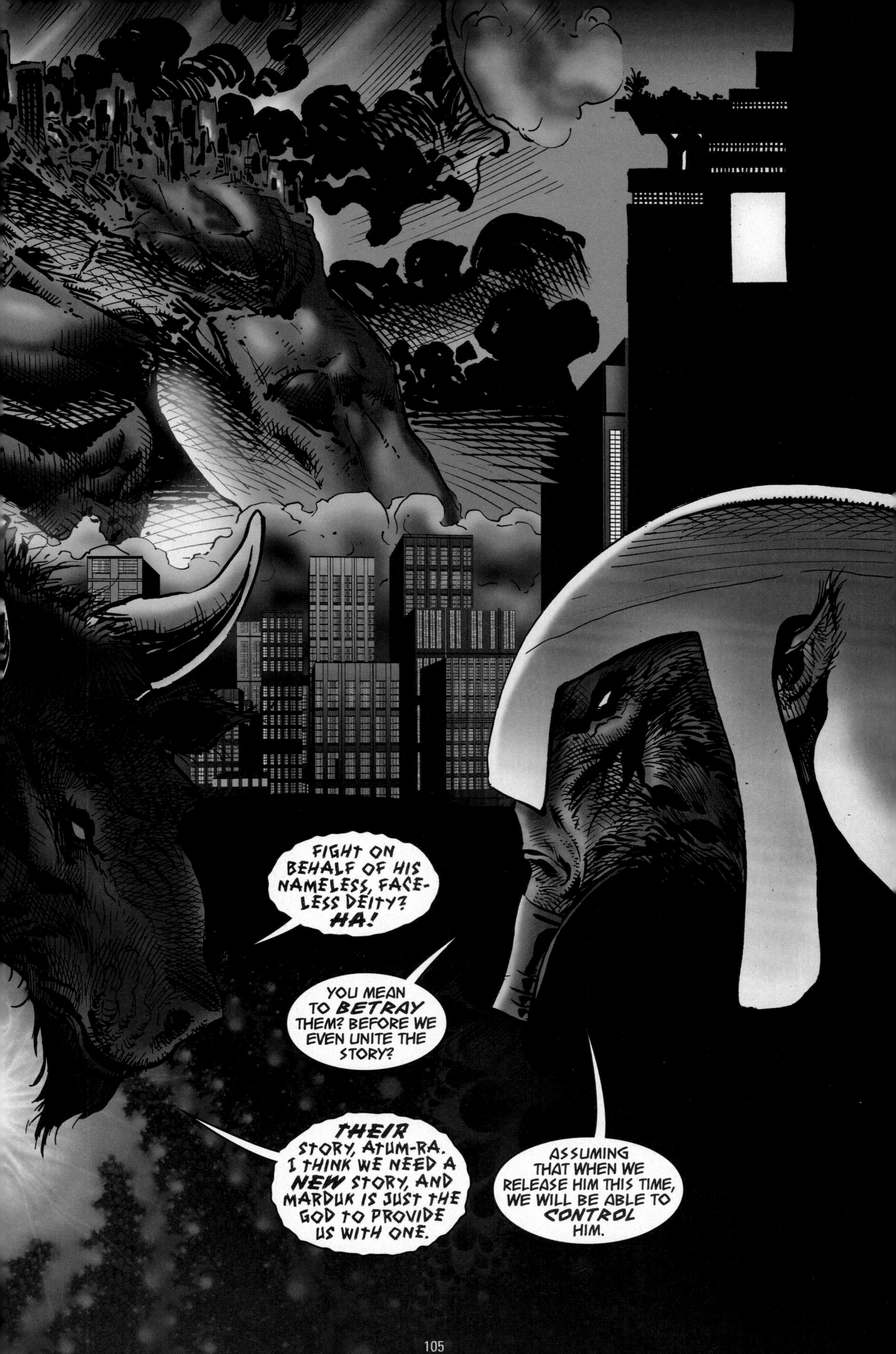
FIGHT ON BEHALF OF HIS NAMELESS, FACELESS DEITY? HA!
YOU MEAN TO BETRAY THEM? BEFORE WE EVEN UNITE THE STORY?
THEIR STORY, ATUM-RA. I THINK WE NEED A NEW STORY, AND MARDUK IS JUST THE GOD TO PROVIDE US WITH ONE.
ASSUMING THAT WHEN WE RELEASE HIM THIS TIME, WE WILL BE ABLE TO CONTROL HIM.

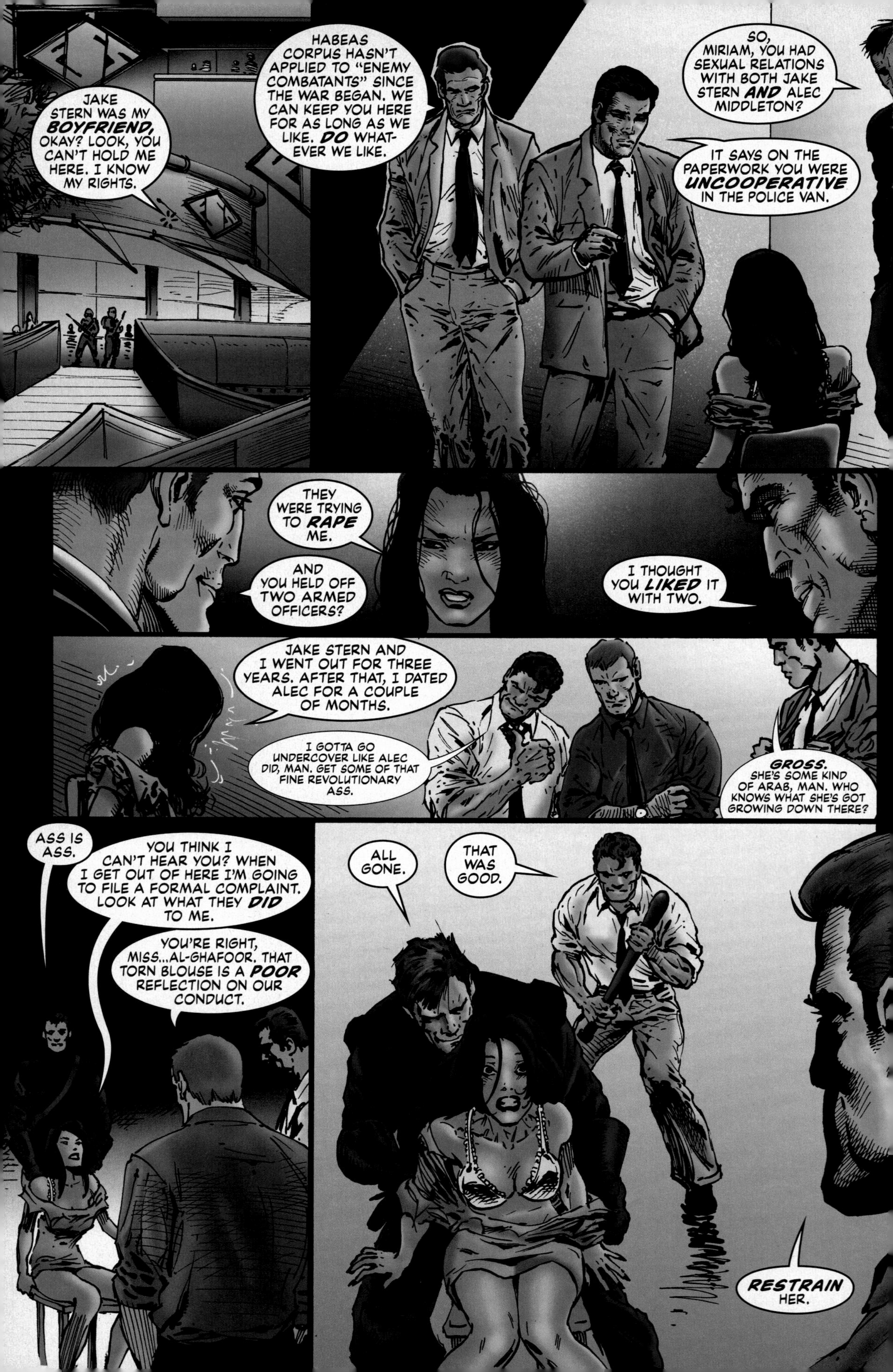
JAKE STERN WAS MY BOYFRIEND, OKAY? LOOK, YOU CAN'T HOLD ME HERE. I KNOW MY RIGHTS.
HABEAS CORPUS HASN'T APPLIED TO "ENEMY COMBATANTS" SINCE THE WAR BEGAN. WE CAN KEEP YOU HERE FOR AS LONG AS WE LIKE. DO WHATEVER WE LIKE.
SO, MIRIAM, YOU HAD SEXUAL RELATIONS WITH BOTH JAKE STERN AND ALEC MIDDLETON?
IT SAYS ON THE PAPERWORK YOU WERE UNCOOPERATIVE IN THE POLICE VAN.
THEY WERE TRYING TO RAPE ME.
AND YOU HELD OFF TWO ARMED OFFICERS?
I THOUGHT YOU LIKED IT WITH TWO.
JAKE STERN AND I WENT OUT FOR THREE YEARS. AFTER THAT, I DATED ALEC FOR A COUPLE OF MONTHS.
I GOTTA GO UNDERCOVER LIKE ALEC DID, MAN. GET SOME OF THAT FINE REVOLUTIONARY ASS.
GROSS. SHE'S SOME KIND OF ARAB, MAN. WHO KNOWS WHAT SHE'S GOT GROWING DOWN THERE?
ASS IS ASS.
YOU THINK I CAN'T HEAR YOU? WHEN I GET OUT OF HERE I'M GOING TO FILE A FORMAL COMPLAINT. LOOK AT WHAT THEY DID TO ME.
YOU'RE RIGHT, MISS...AL-GHAFOOR. THAT TORN BLOUSE IS A POOR REFLECTION ON OUR CONDUCT.
ALL GONE.
THAT WAS GOOD.
RESTRAIN HER.

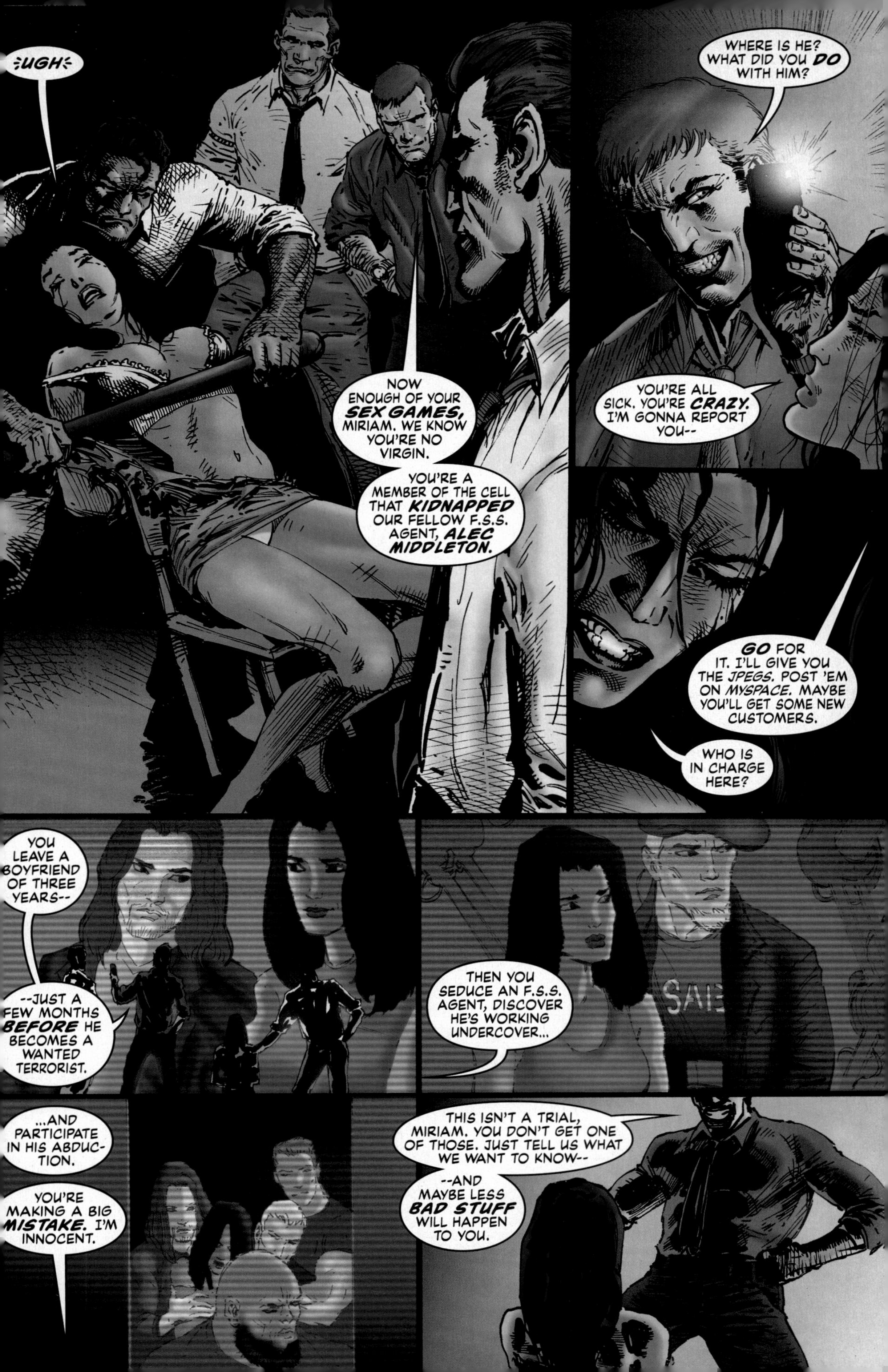
UGH
NOW ENOUGH OF YOUR SEX GAMES, MIRIAM. WE KNOW YOU'RE NO VIRGIN.
YOU'RE A MEMBER OF THE CELL THAT KIDNAPPED OUR FELLOW F.S.S. AGENT, ALEC MIDDLETON.
WHERE IS HE? WHAT DID YOU DO WITH HIM?
YOU'RE ALL SICK. YOU'RE CRAZY. I'M GONNA REPORT YOU--
GO FOR IT. I'LL GIVE YOU THE JPEGS. POST 'EM ON MYSPACE. MAYBE YOU'LL GET SOME NEW CUSTOMERS.
WHO IS IN CHARGE HERE?
YOU LEAVE A BOYFRIEND OF THREE YEARS--
--JUST A FEW MONTHS BEFORE HE BECOMES A WANTED TERRORIST.
THEN YOU SEDUCE AN F.S.S. AGENT, DISCOVER HE'S WORKING UNDERCOVER...
...AND PARTICIPATE IN HIS ABDUCTION.
YOU'RE MAKING A BIG MISTAKE. I'M INNOCENT.
THIS ISN'T A TRIAL, MIRIAM. YOU DON'T GET ONE OF THOSE. JUST TELL US WHAT WE WANT TO KNOW--
--AND MAYBE LESS BAD STUFF WILL HAPPEN TO YOU.

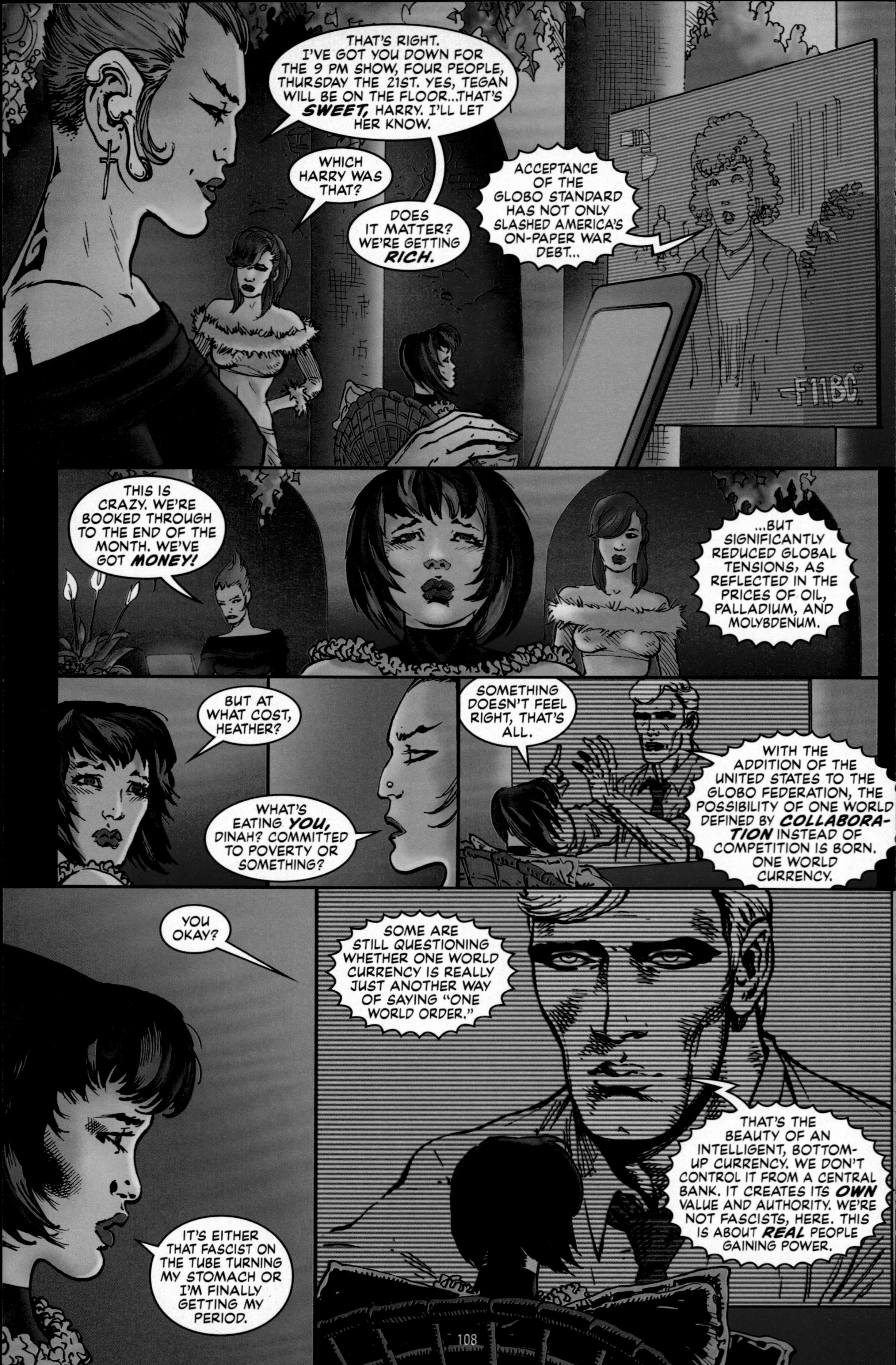
THAT'S RIGHT. I'VE GOT YOU DOWN FOR THE 9 PM SHOW, FOUR PEOPLE, THURSDAY THE 21ST. YES, TEGAN WILL BE ON THE FLOOR...THAT'S SWEET, HARRY. I'LL LET HER KNOW.
WHICH HARRY WAS THAT?
DOES IT MATTER? WE'RE GETTING RICH.
ACCEPTANCE OF THE GLOBO STANDARD HAS NOT ONLY SLASHED AMERICA'S ON-PAPER WAR DEBT...
F11BC
THIS IS CRAZY. WE'RE BOOKED THROUGH TO THE END OF THE MONTH. WE'VE GOT MONEY!
...BUT SIGNIFICANTLY REDUCED GLOBAL TENSIONS, AS REFLECTED IN THE PRICES OF OIL, PALLADIUM, AND MOLYBDENUM.
BUT AT WHAT COST, HEATHER?
WHAT'S EATING YOU, DINAH? COMMITTED TO POVERTY OR SOMETHING?
SOMETHING DOESN'T FEEL RIGHT, THAT'S ALL.
WITH THE ADDITION OF THE UNITED STATES TO THE GLOBO FEDERATION, THE POSSIBILITY OF ONE WORLD DEFINED BY COLLABORATION INSTEAD OF COMPETITION IS BORN. ONE WORLD CURRENCY.
YOU OKAY?
SOME ARE STILL QUESTIONING WHETHER ONE WORLD CURRENCY IS REALLY JUST ANOTHER WAY OF SAYING "ONE WORLD ORDER."
THAT'S THE BEAUTY OF AN INTELLIGENT, BOTTOM-UP CURRENCY. WE DON'T CONTROL IT FROM A CENTRAL BANK. IT CREATES ITS OWN VALUE AND AUTHORITY. WE'RE NOT FASCISTS, HERE. THIS IS ABOUT REAL PEOPLE GAINING POWER.
IT'S EITHER THAT FASCIST ON THE TUBE TURNING MY STOMACH OR I'M FINALLY GETTING MY PERIOD.

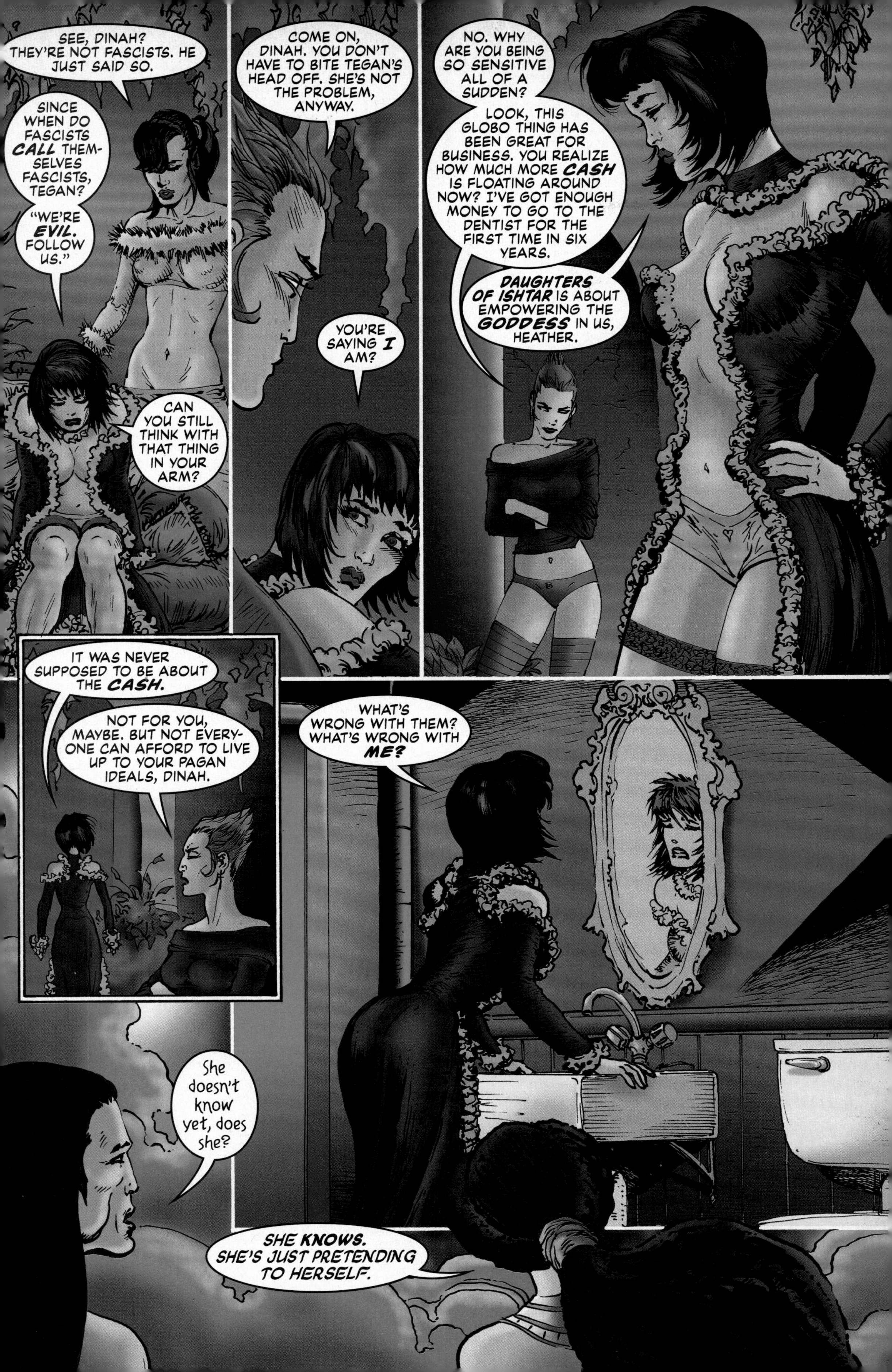

SEE, DINAH? THEY'RE NOT FASCISTS. HE JUST SAID SO.
SINCE WHEN DO FASCISTS CALL THEMSELVES FASCISTS, TEGAN?
"WE'RE EVIL. FOLLOW US."
CAN YOU STILL THINK WITH THAT THING IN YOUR ARM?
COME ON, DINAH. YOU DON'T HAVE TO BITE TEGAN'S HEAD OFF. SHE'S NOT THE PROBLEM, ANYWAY.
YOU'RE SAYING I AM?
NO. WHY ARE YOU BEING SO SENSITIVE ALL OF A SUDDEN?
LOOK, THIS GLOBO THING HAS BEEN GREAT FOR BUSINESS. YOU REALIZE HOW MUCH MORE CASH IS FLOATING AROUND NOW? I'VE GOT ENOUGH MONEY TO GO TO THE DENTIST FOR THE FIRST TIME IN SIX YEARS.
DAUGHTERS OF ISHTAR IS ABOUT EMPOWERING THE GODDESS IN US, HEATHER.
IT WAS NEVER SUPPOSED TO BE ABOUT THE CASH.
NOT FOR YOU, MAYBE. BUT NOT EVERYONE CAN AFFORD TO LIVE UP TO YOUR PAGAN IDEALS, DINAH.
WHAT'S WRONG WITH THEM? WHAT'S WRONG WITH ME?
She doesn't know yet, does she?
SHE KNOWS. SHE'S JUST PRETENDING TO HERSELF.

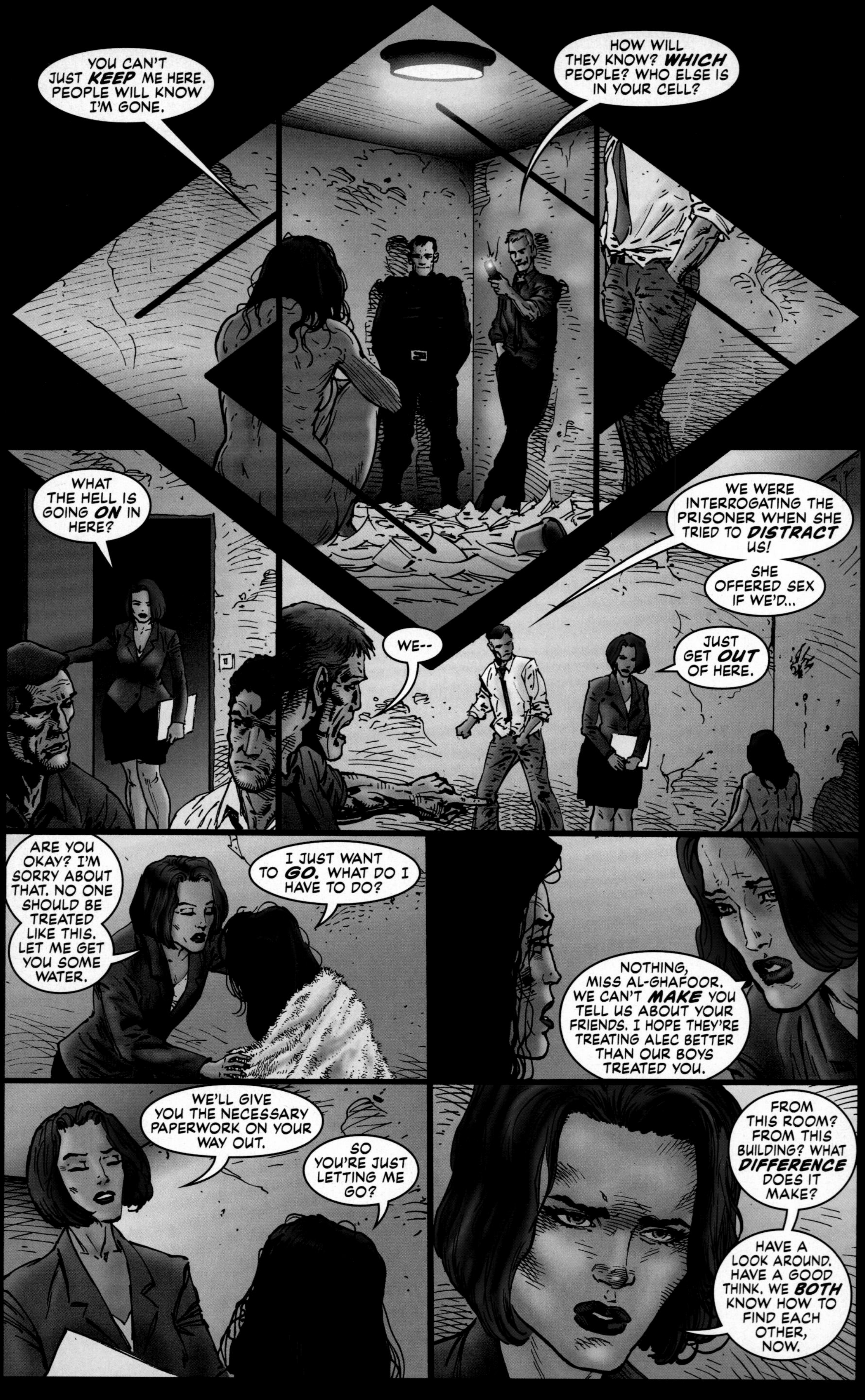
YOU CAN'T JUST KEEP ME HERE. PEOPLE WILL KNOW I'M GONE.
HOW WILL THEY KNOW? WHICH PEOPLE? WHO ELSE IS IN YOUR CELL?
WHAT THE HELL IS GOING ON IN HERE?
WE--
WE WERE INTERROGATING THE PRISONER WHEN SHE TRIED TO DISTRACT US!
SHE OFFERED SEX IF WE'D...
JUST GET OUT OF HERE.
ARE YOU OKAY? I'M SORRY ABOUT THAT. NO ONE SHOULD BE TREATED LIKE THIS. LET ME GET YOU SOME WATER.
I JUST WANT TO GO. WHAT DO I HAVE TO DO?
NOTHING, MISS AL-GHAFOOR. WE CAN'T MAKE YOU TELL US ABOUT YOUR FRIENDS. I HOPE THEY'RE TREATING ALEC BETTER THAN OUR BOYS TREATED YOU.
WE'LL GIVE YOU THE NECESSARY PAPERWORK ON YOUR WAY OUT.
SO YOU'RE JUST LETTING ME GO?
FROM THIS ROOM? FROM THIS BUILDING? WHAT DIFFERENCE DOES IT MAKE?
HAVE A LOOK AROUND. HAVE A GOOD THINK. WE BOTH KNOW HOW TO FIND EACH OTHER, NOW.

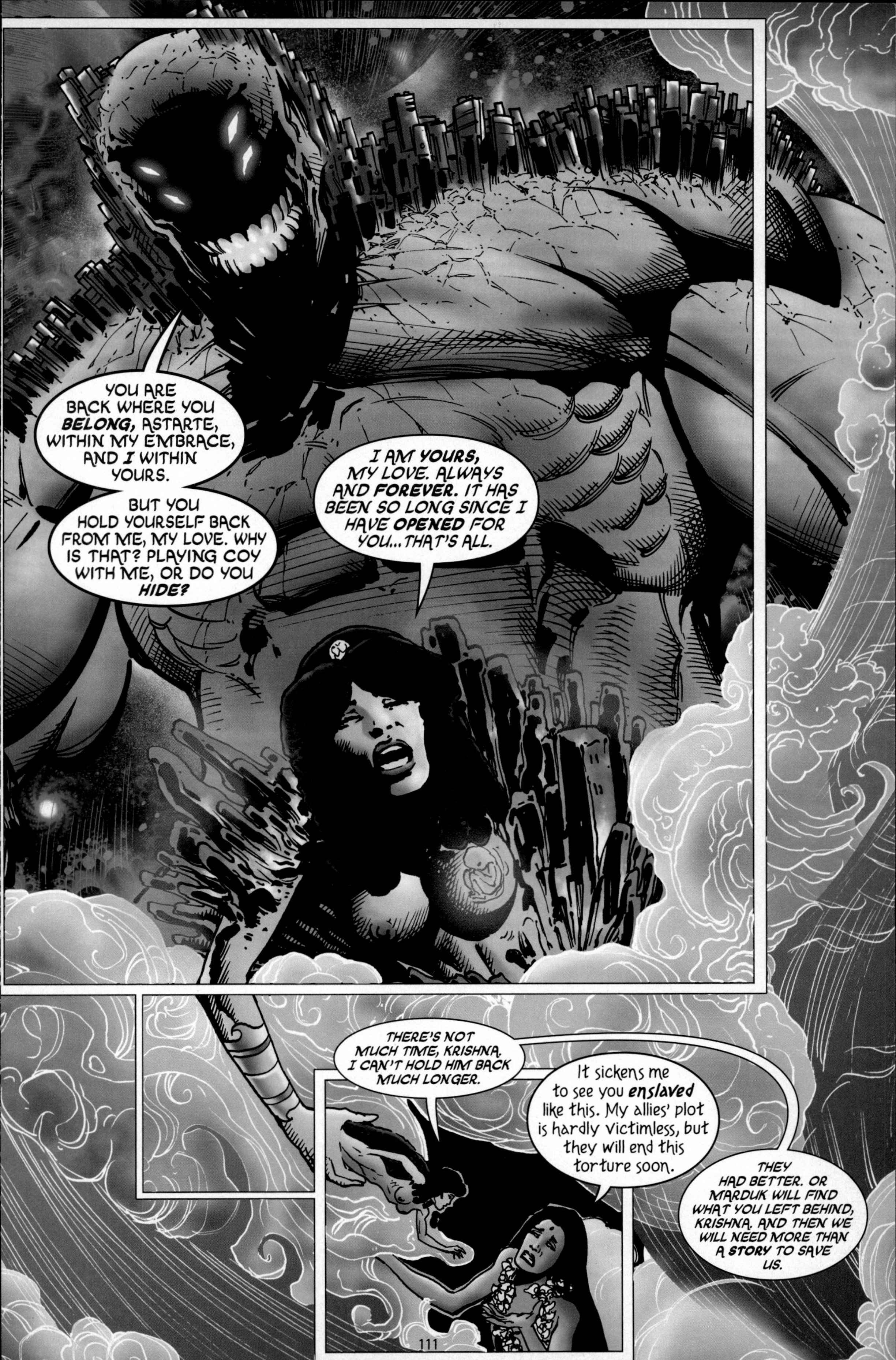
YOU ARE BACK WHERE YOU BELONG, ASTARTE, WITHIN MY EMBRACE, AND I WITHIN YOURS.
BUT YOU HOLD YOURSELF BACK FROM ME, MY LOVE. WHY IS THAT? PLAYING COY WITH ME, OR DO YOU HIDE?
I AM YOURS, MY LOVE. ALWAYS AND FOREVER. IT HAS BEEN SO LONG SINCE I HAVE OPENED FOR YOU...THAT'S ALL.
THERE'S NOT MUCH TIME, KRISHNA. I CAN'T HOLD HIM BACK MUCH LONGER.
It sickens me to see you enslaved like this. My allies' plot is hardly victimless, but they will end this torture soon.
THEY HAD BETTER. OR MARDUK WILL FIND WHAT YOU LEFT BEHIND, KRISHNA. AND THEN WE WILL NEED MORE THAN A STORY TO SAVE US.

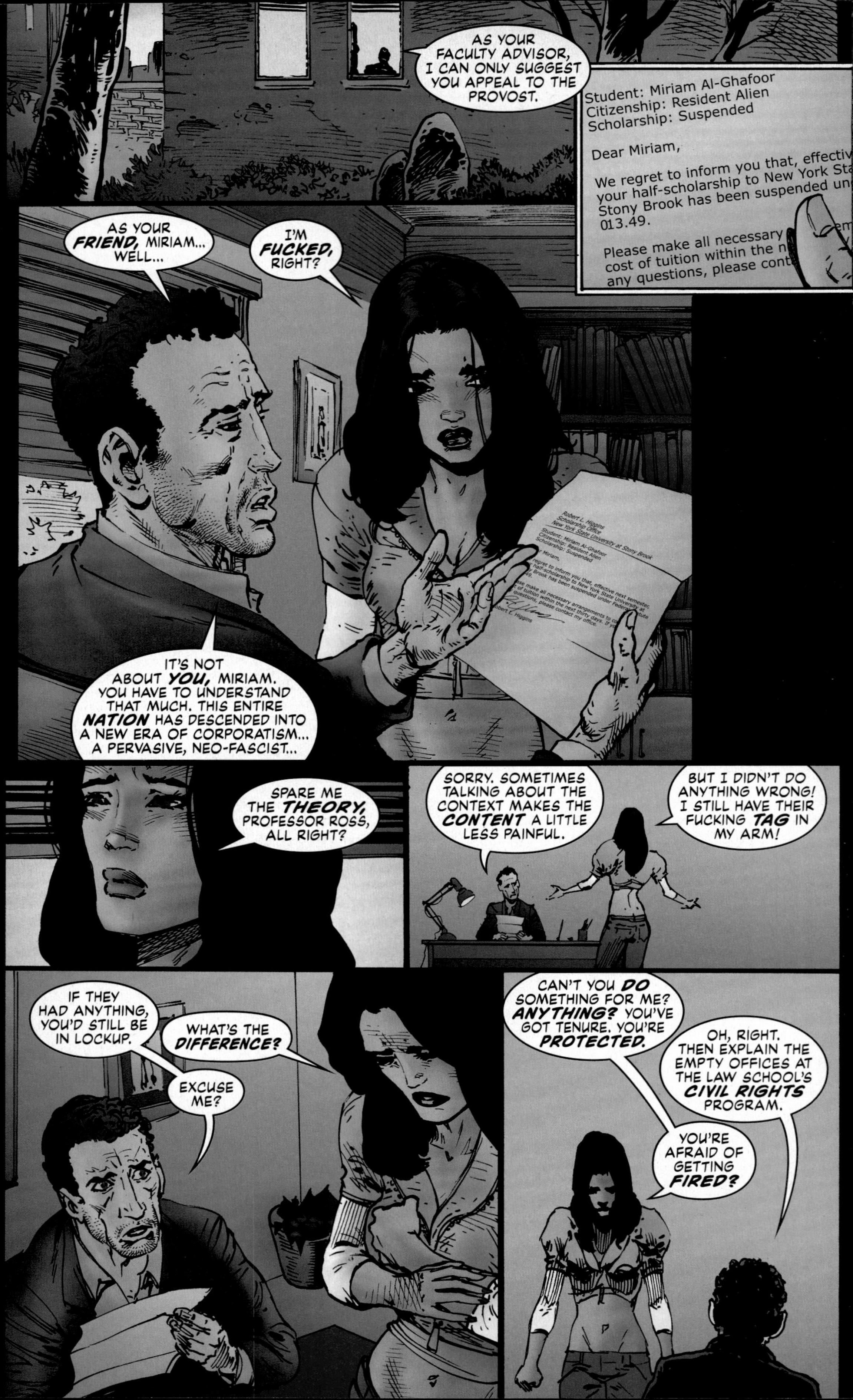

AS YOUR FACULTY ADVISOR, I CAN ONLY SUGGEST YOU APPEAL TO THE PROVOST.
Student: Miriam Al-Ghafoor
Citizenship: Resident Alien
Scholarship: Suspended
Dear Miriam,
We regret to inform you that, effectiv
your half-scholarship to New York Sta
Stony Brook has been suspended u
013.49.
Please make all necessary
cost of tuition within the n
any questions, please con
AS YOUR FRIEND, MIRIAM... WELL...
I'M FUCKED, RIGHT?
IT'S NOT ABOUT YOU, MIRIAM. YOU HAVE TO UNDERSTAND THAT MUCH. THIS ENTIRE NATION HAS DESCENDED INTO A NEW ERA OF CORPORATISM... A PERVASIVE, NEO-FASCIST...
SPARE ME THE THEORY, PROFESSOR ROSS, ALL RIGHT?
SORRY. SOMETIMES TALKING ABOUT THE CONTEXT MAKES THE CONTENT A LITTLE LESS PAINFUL.
BUT I DIDN'T DO ANYTHING WRONG! I STILL HAVE THEIR FUCKING TAG IN MY ARM!
IF THEY HAD ANYTHING, YOU'D STILL BE IN LOCKUP.
WHAT'S THE DIFFERENCE?
EXCUSE ME?
CAN'T YOU DO SOMETHING FOR ME? ANYTHING? YOU'VE GOT TENURE. YOU'RE PROTECTED.
OH, RIGHT. THEN EXPLAIN THE EMPTY OFFICES AT THE LAW SCHOOL'S CIVIL RIGHTS PROGRAM.
YOU'RE AFRAID OF GETTING FIRED?

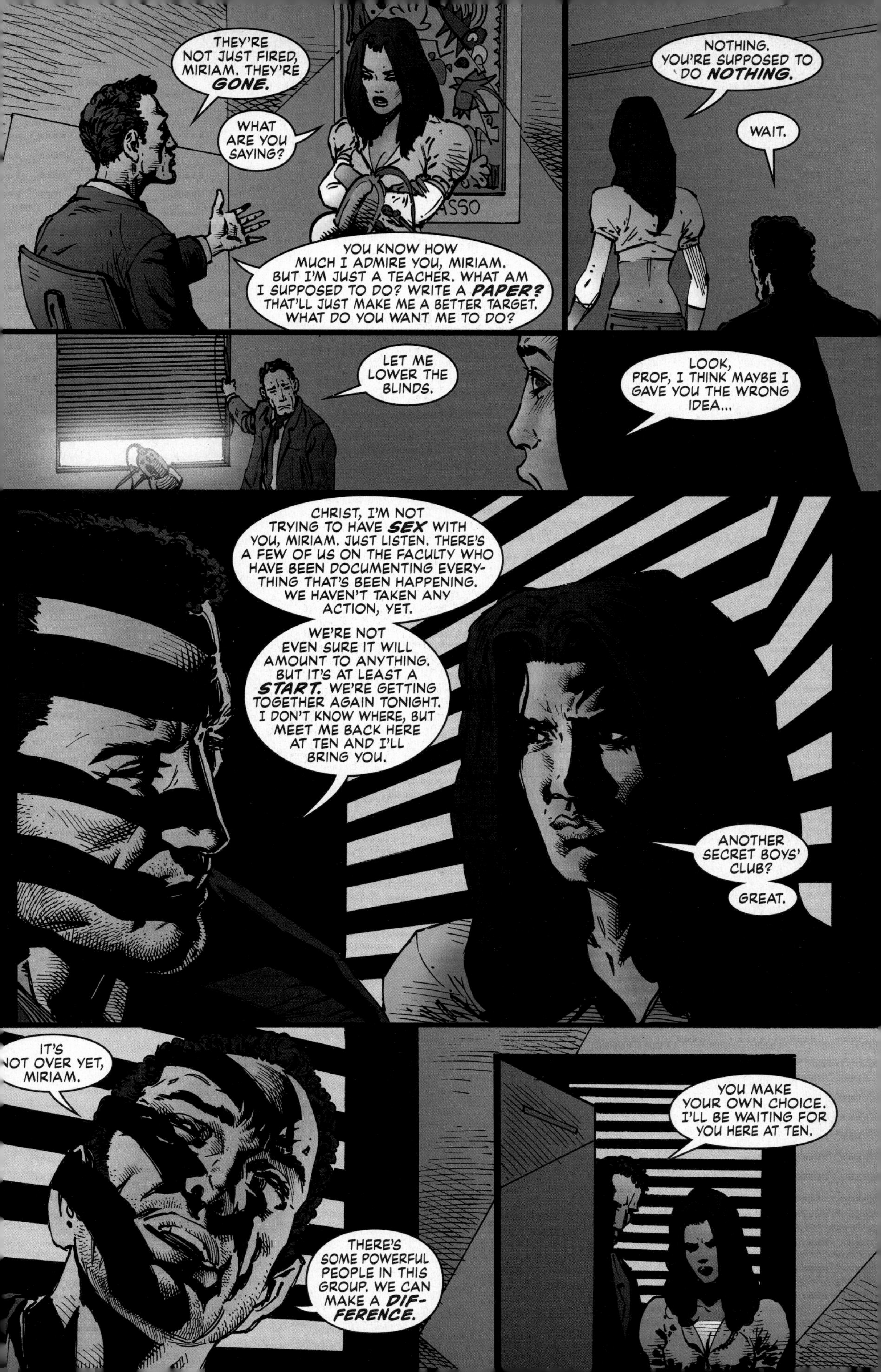
THEY'RE NOT JUST FIRED, MIRIAM. THEY'RE GONE.
WHAT ARE YOU SAYING?
YOU KNOW HOW MUCH I ADMIRE YOU, MIRIAM. BUT I'M JUST A TEACHER. WHAT AM I SUPPOSED TO DO? WRITE A PAPER? THAT'LL JUST MAKE ME A BETTER TARGET. WHAT DO YOU WANT ME TO DO?
NOTHING. YOU'RE SUPPOSED TO DO NOTHING.
WAIT.
LET ME LOWER THE BLINDS.
LOOK, PROF, I THINK MAYBE I GAVE YOU THE WRONG IDEA...
CHRIST, I'M NOT TRYING TO HAVE SEX WITH YOU, MIRIAM. JUST LISTEN. THERE'S A FEW OF US ON THE FACULTY WHO HAVE BEEN DOCUMENTING EVERY-THING THAT'S BEEN HAPPENING. WE HAVEN'T TAKEN ANY ACTION, YET.
WE'RE NOT EVEN SURE IT WILL AMOUNT TO ANYTHING. BUT IT'S AT LEAST A START. WE'RE GETTING TOGETHER AGAIN TONIGHT. I DON'T KNOW WHERE, BUT MEET ME BACK HERE AT TEN AND I'LL BRING YOU.
ANOTHER SECRET BOYS' CLUB?
GREAT.
IT'S NOT OVER YET, MIRIAM.
THERE'S SOME POWERFUL PEOPLE IN THIS GROUP. WE CAN MAKE A DIF-FERENCE.
YOU MAKE YOUR OWN CHOICE. I'LL BE WAITING FOR YOU HERE AT TEN.

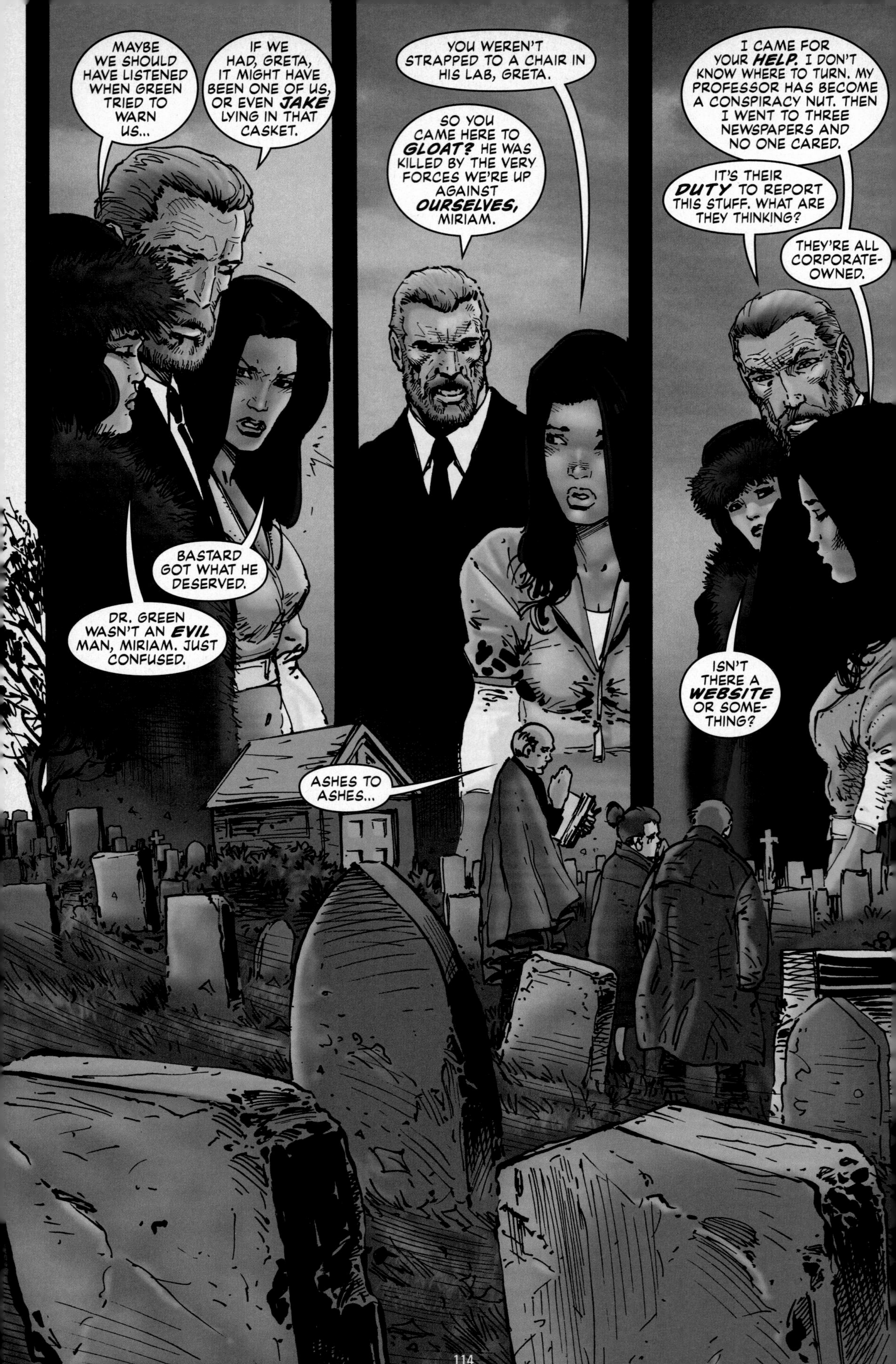

MAYBE WE SHOULD HAVE LISTENED WHEN GREEN TRIED TO WARN US...
IF WE HAD, GRETA, IT MIGHT HAVE BEEN ONE OF US, OR EVEN JAKE LYING IN THAT CASKET.
BASTARD GOT WHAT HE DESERVED.
DR. GREEN WASN'T AN EVIL MAN, MIRIAM. JUST CONFUSED.
YOU WEREN'T STRAPPED TO A CHAIR IN HIS LAB, GRETA.
SO YOU CAME HERE TO GLOAT? HE WAS KILLED BY THE VERY FORCES WE'RE UP AGAINST OURSELVES, MIRIAM.
ASHES TO ASHES...
I CAME FOR YOUR HELP. I DON'T KNOW WHERE TO TURN. MY PROFESSOR HAS BECOME A CONSPIRACY NUT. THEN I WENT TO THREE NEWSPAPERS AND NO ONE CARED.
IT'S THEIR DUTY TO REPORT THIS STUFF. WHAT ARE THEY THINKING?
THEY'RE ALL CORPORATE-OWNED.
ISN'T THERE A WEBSITE OR SOME-THING?

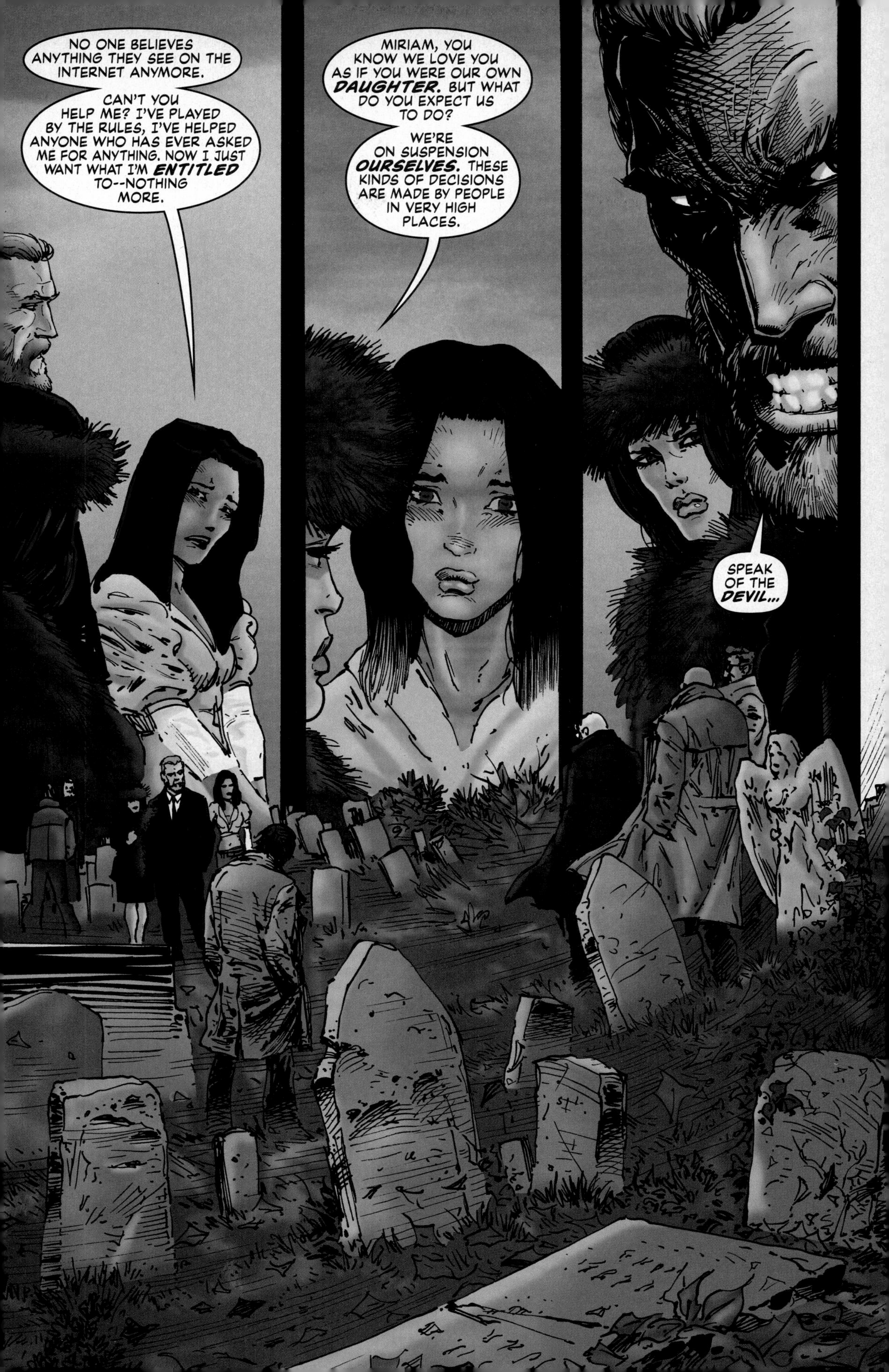
NO ONE BELIEVES ANYTHING THEY SEE ON THE INTERNET ANYMORE.
CAN'T YOU HELP ME? I'VE PLAYED BY THE RULES, I'VE HELPED ANYONE WHO HAS EVER ASKED ME FOR ANYTHING. NOW I JUST WANT WHAT I'M ENTITLED TO--NOTHING MORE.
MIRIAM, YOU KNOW WE LOVE YOU AS IF YOU WERE OUR OWN DAUGHTER. BUT WHAT DO YOU EXPECT US TO DO?
WE'RE ON SUSPENSION OURSELVES. THESE KINDS OF DECISIONS ARE MADE BY PEOPLE IN VERY HIGH PLACES.
SPEAK OF THE DEVIL...

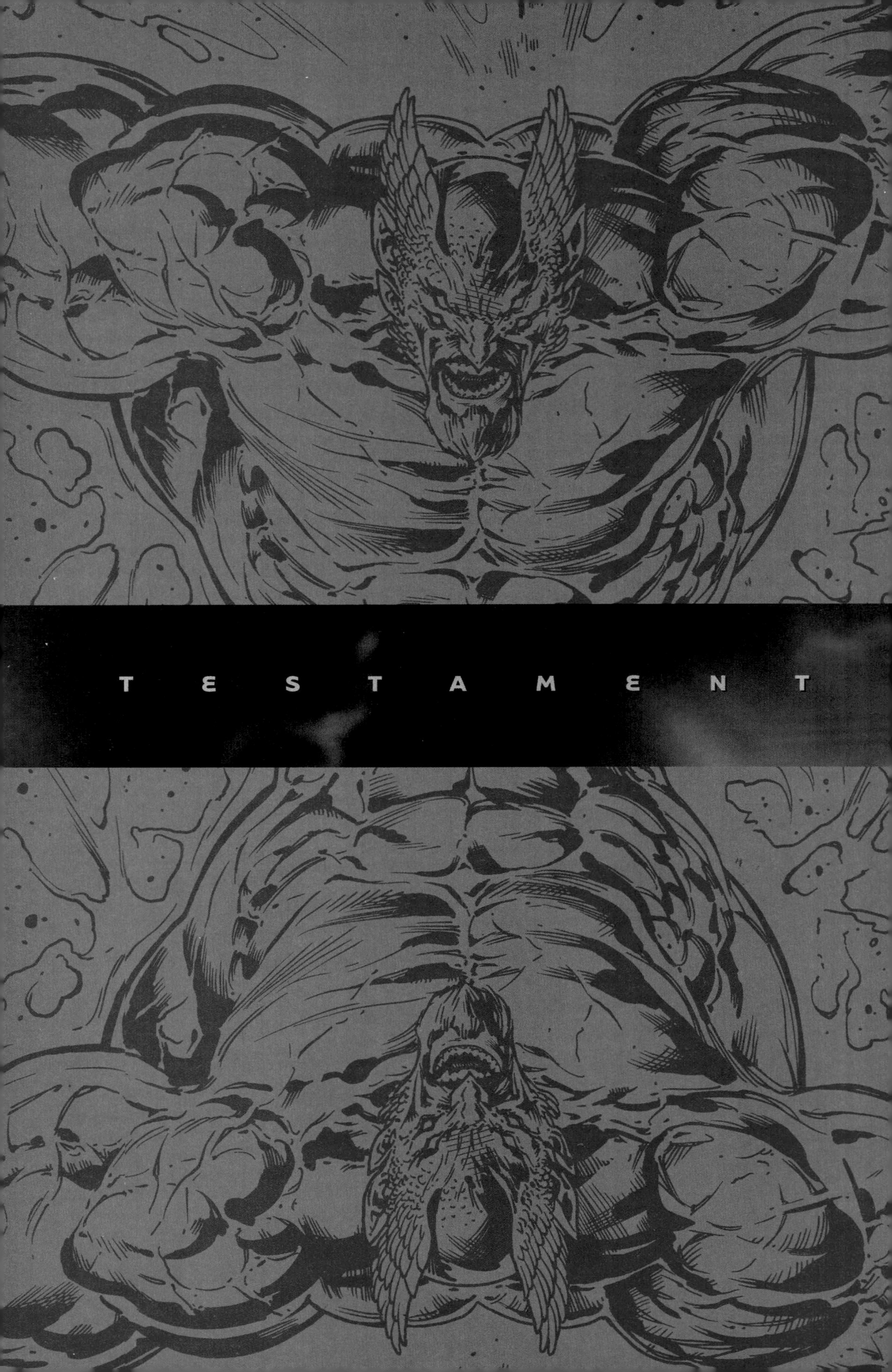
TESTAMENT

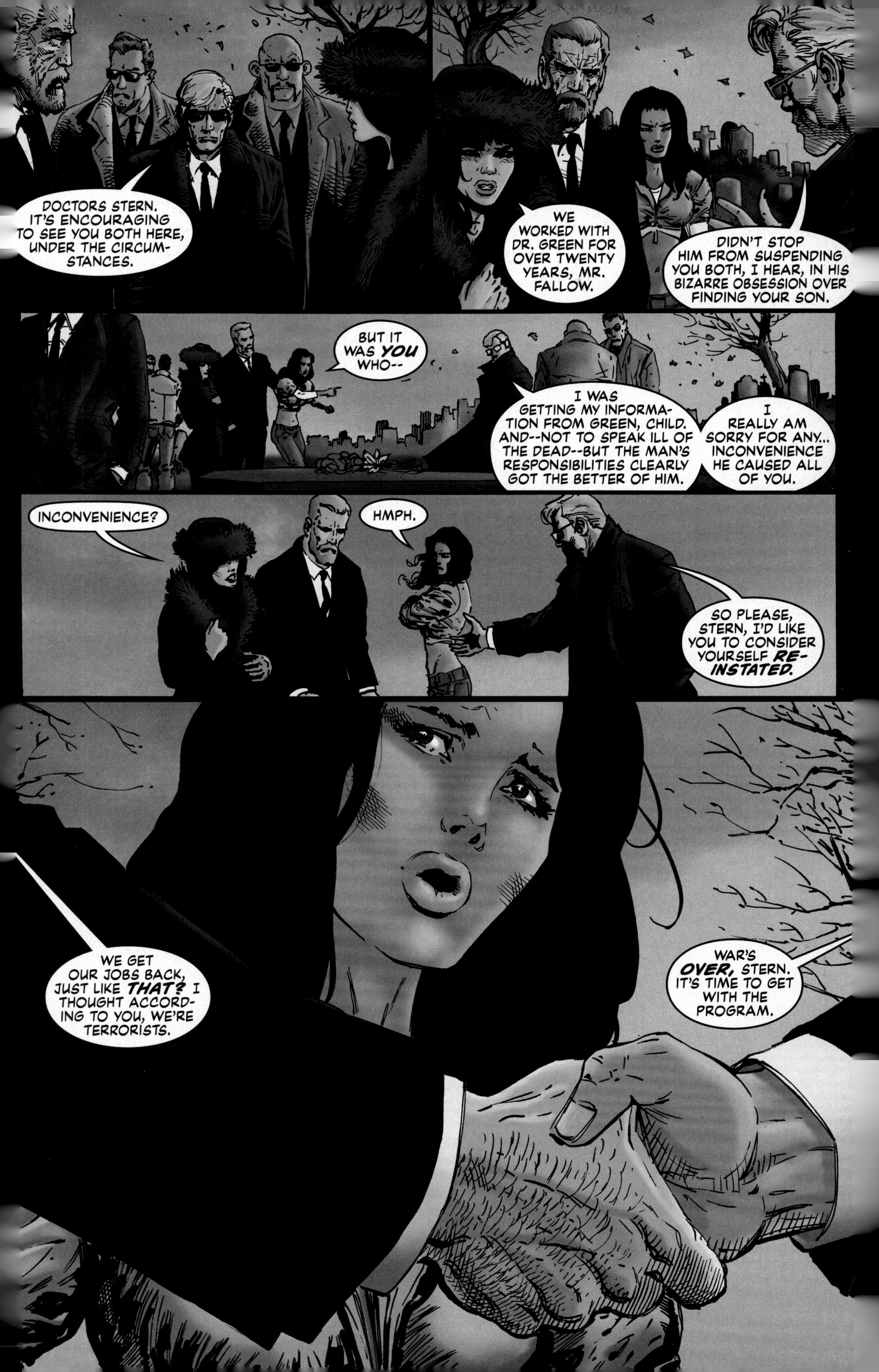
DOCTORS STERN. IT'S ENCOURAGING TO SEE YOU BOTH HERE, UNDER THE CIRCUMSTANCES.
WE WORKED WITH DR. GREEN FOR OVER TWENTY YEARS, MR. FALLOW.
DIDN'T STOP HIM FROM SUSPENDING YOU BOTH, I HEAR, IN HIS BIZARRE OBSESSION OVER FINDING YOUR SON.
BUT IT WAS *YOU* WHO--
I WAS GETTING MY INFORMATION FROM GREEN, CHILD. AND--NOT TO SPEAK ILL OF THE DEAD--BUT THE MAN'S RESPONSIBILITIES CLEARLY GOT THE BETTER OF HIM.
I REALLY AM SORRY FOR ANY... INCONVENIENCE HE CAUSED ALL OF YOU.
INCONVENIENCE?
HMPH.
SO PLEASE, STERN, I'D LIKE YOU TO CONSIDER YOURSELF *RE-INSTATED.*
WE GET OUR JOBS BACK, JUST LIKE *THAT?* I THOUGHT ACCORDING TO YOU, WE'RE TERRORISTS.
WAR'S *OVER,* STERN. IT'S TIME TO GET WITH THE PROGRAM.

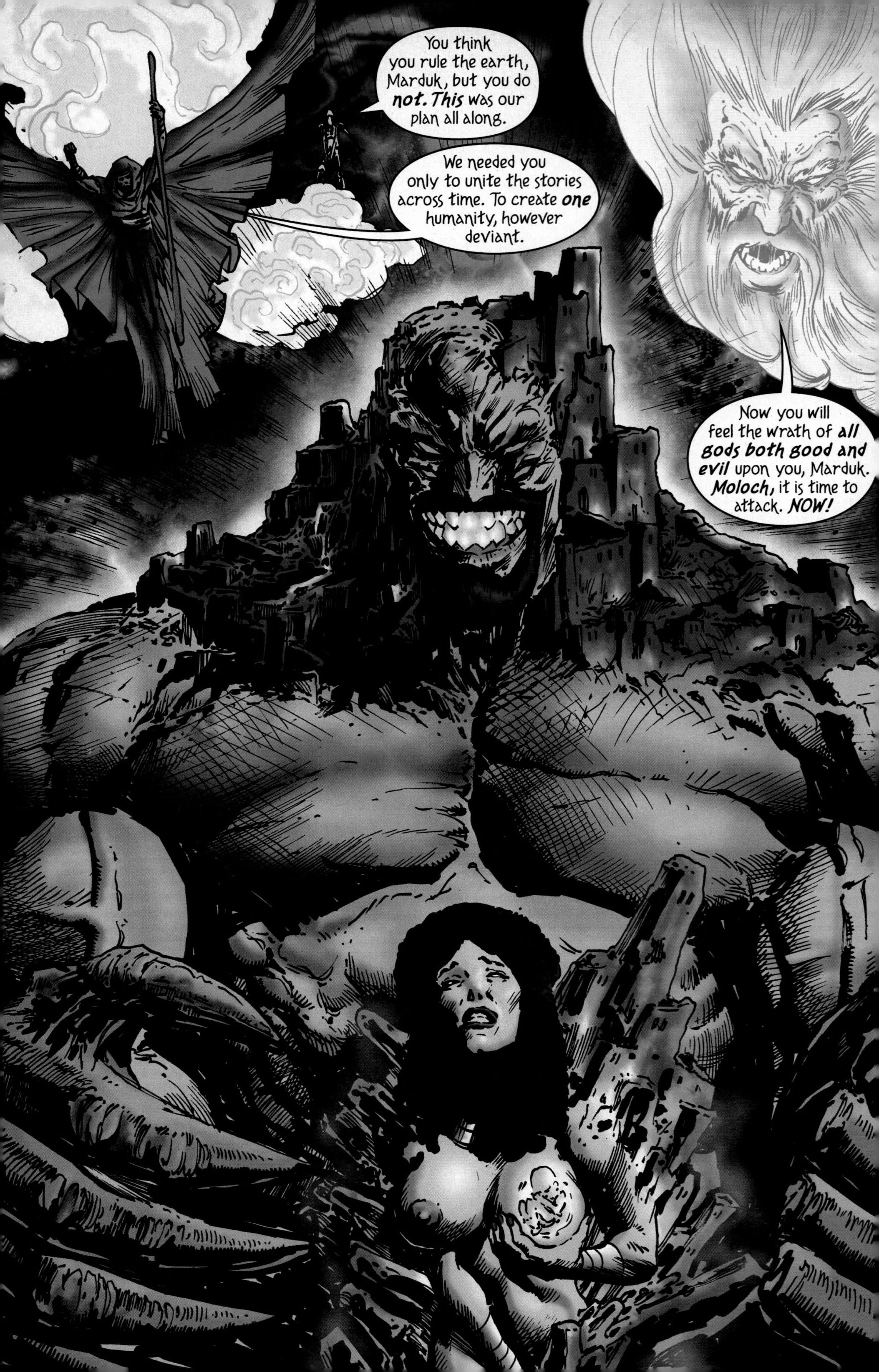
You think you rule the earth, Marduk, but you do **not. This** was our plan all along.
We needed you only to unite the stories across time. To create **one** humanity, however deviant.
Now you will feel the wrath of **all gods both good and evil** upon you, Marduk. **Moloch,** it is time to attack. **NOW!**

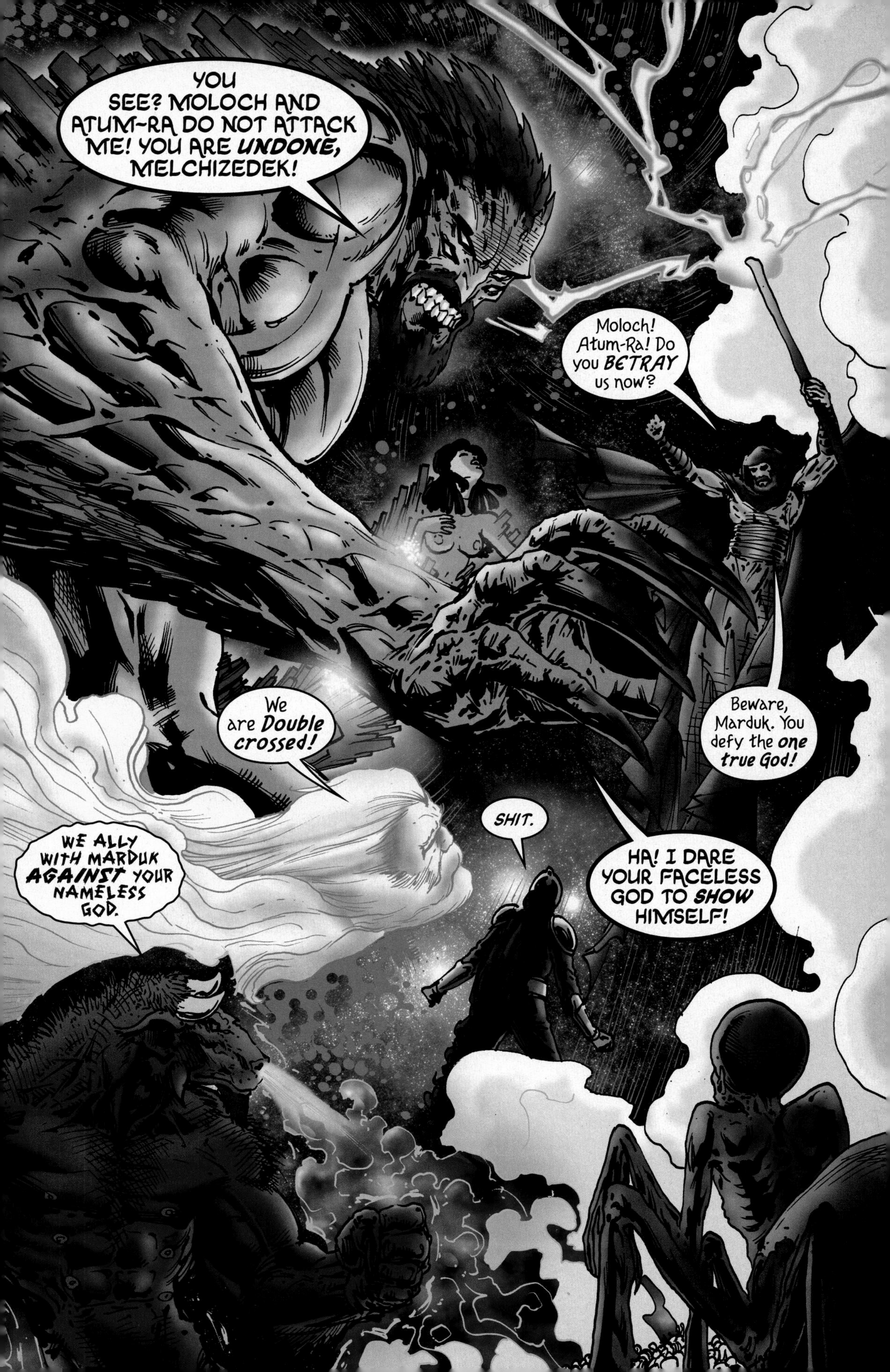
YOU SEE? MOLOCH AND ATUM-RA DO NOT ATTACK ME! YOU ARE *UNDONE,* MELCHIZEDEK!
Moloch! Atum-Ra! Do you *BETRAY* us now?
We are *Double crossed!*
Beware, Marduk. You defy the *one true God!*
WE ALLY WITH MARDUK *AGAINST* YOUR NAMELESS GOD.
SHIT.
HA! I DARE YOUR FACELESS GOD TO *SHOW* HIMSELF!

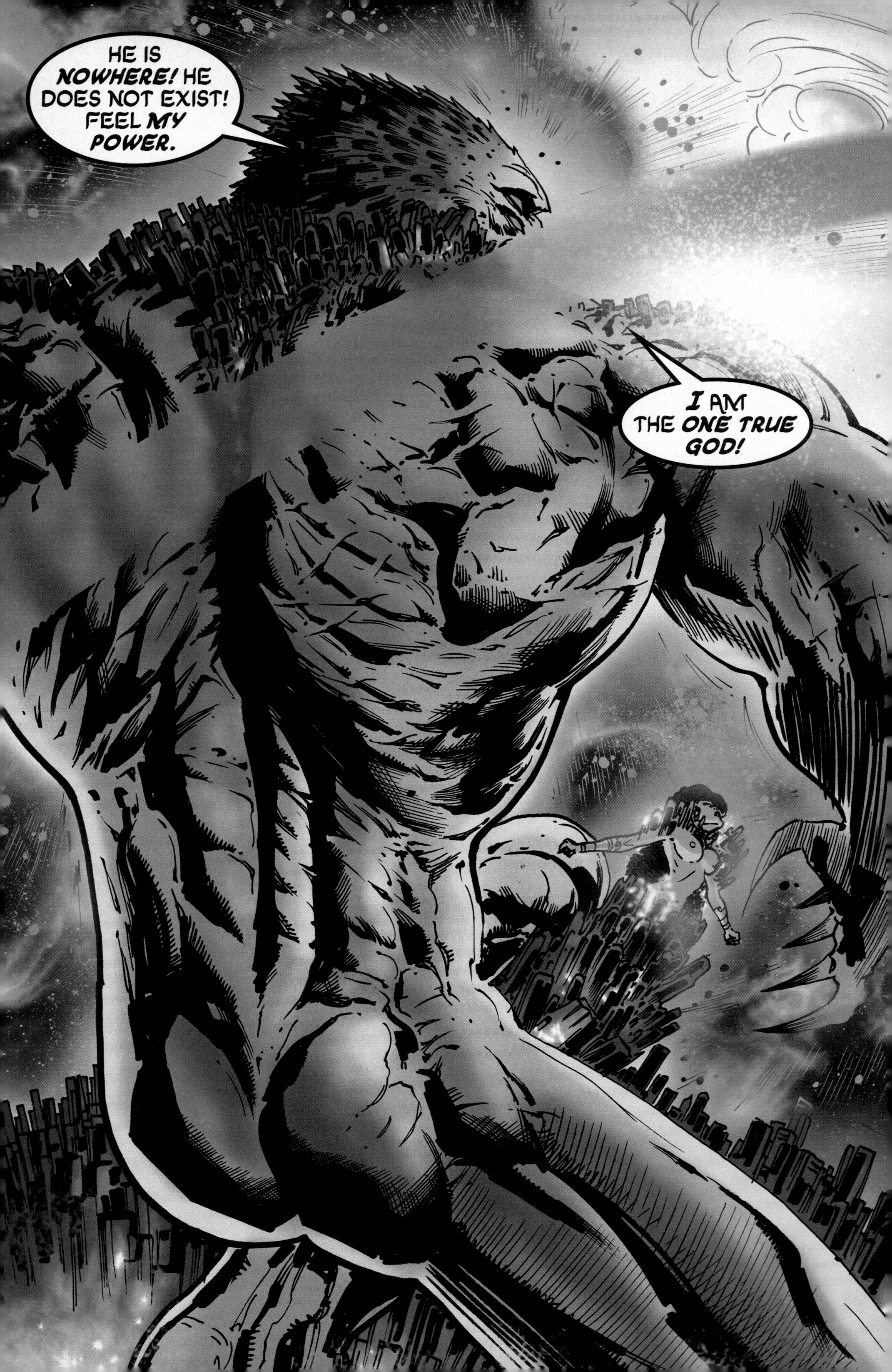
HE IS NOWHERE! HE DOES NOT EXIST! FEEL MY POWER.
I AM THE ONE TRUE GOD!

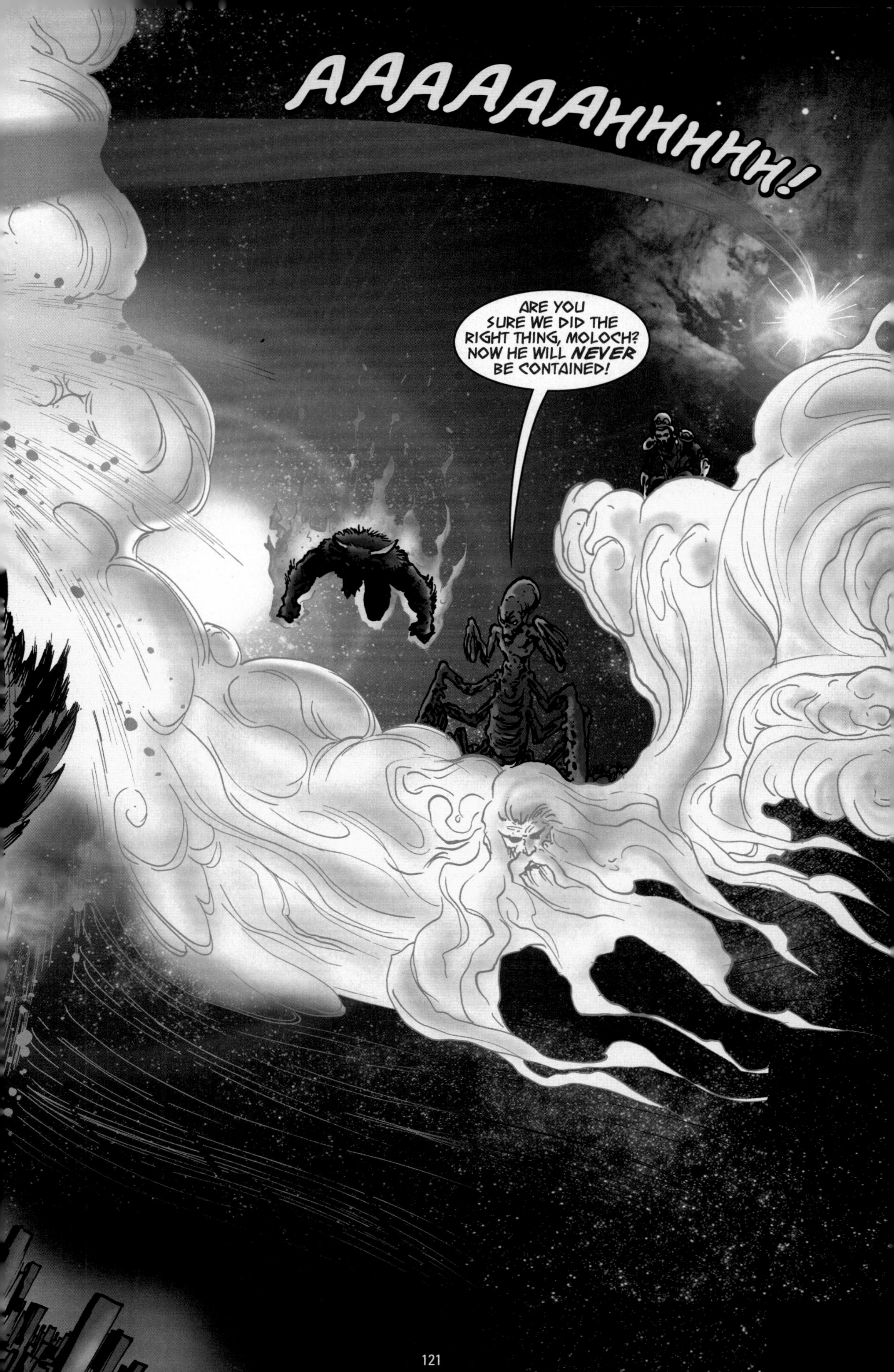
AAAAAAAHHHHHH!
ARE YOU SURE WE DID THE RIGHT THING, MOLOCH? NOW HE WILL NEVER BE CONTAINED!

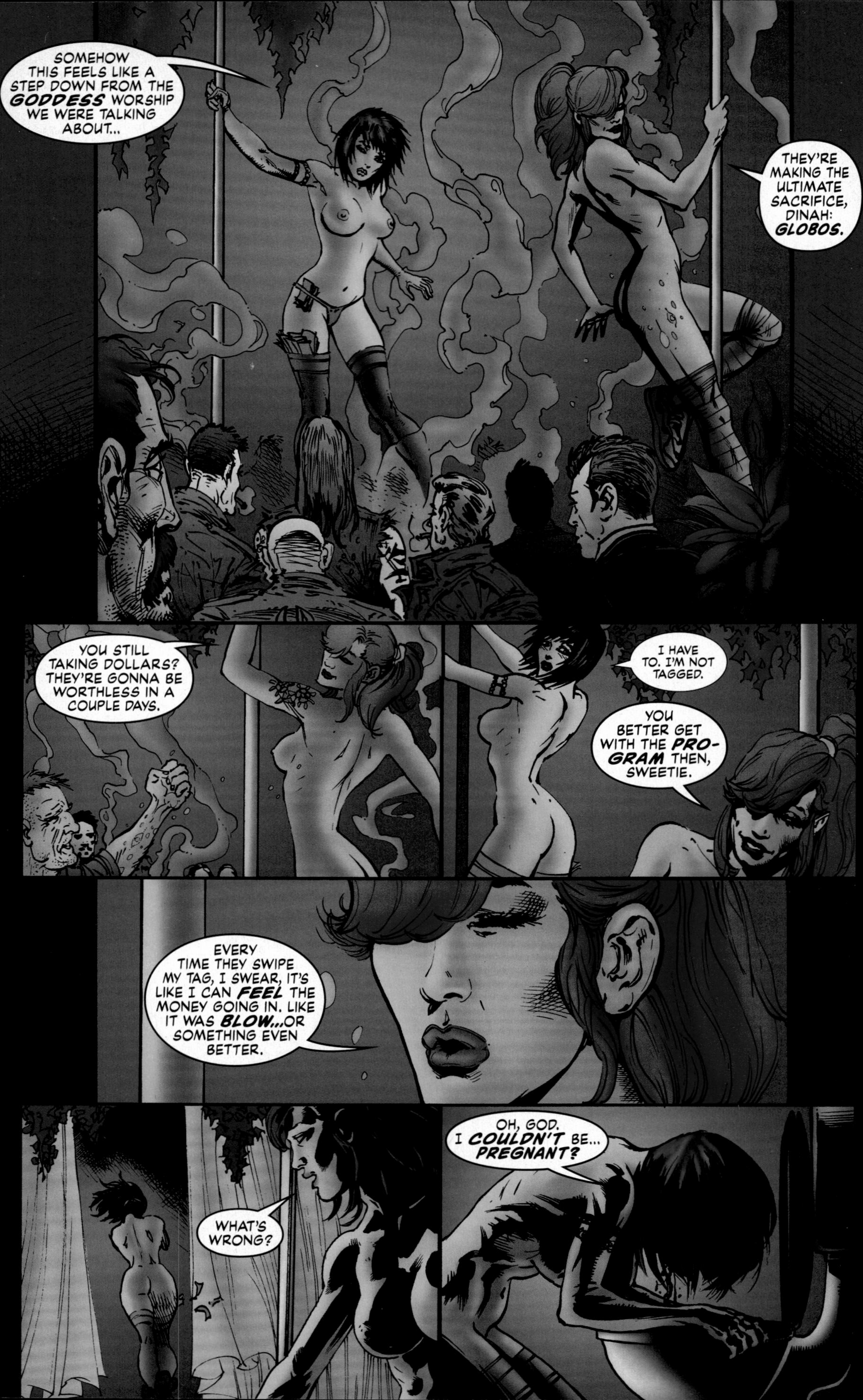
SOMEHOW THIS FEELS LIKE A STEP DOWN FROM THE GODDESS WORSHIP WE WERE TALKING ABOUT...
THEY'RE MAKING THE ULTIMATE SACRIFICE, DINAH: GLOBOS.
YOU STILL TAKING DOLLARS? THEY'RE GONNA BE WORTHLESS IN A COUPLE DAYS.
I HAVE TO. I'M NOT TAGGED.
YOU BETTER GET WITH THE PRO-GRAM THEN, SWEETIE.
EVERY TIME THEY SWIPE MY TAG, I SWEAR, IT'S LIKE I CAN FEEL THE MONEY GOING IN. LIKE IT WAS BLOW...OR SOMETHING EVEN BETTER.
WHAT'S WRONG?
OH, GOD. I COULDN'T BE... PREGNANT?

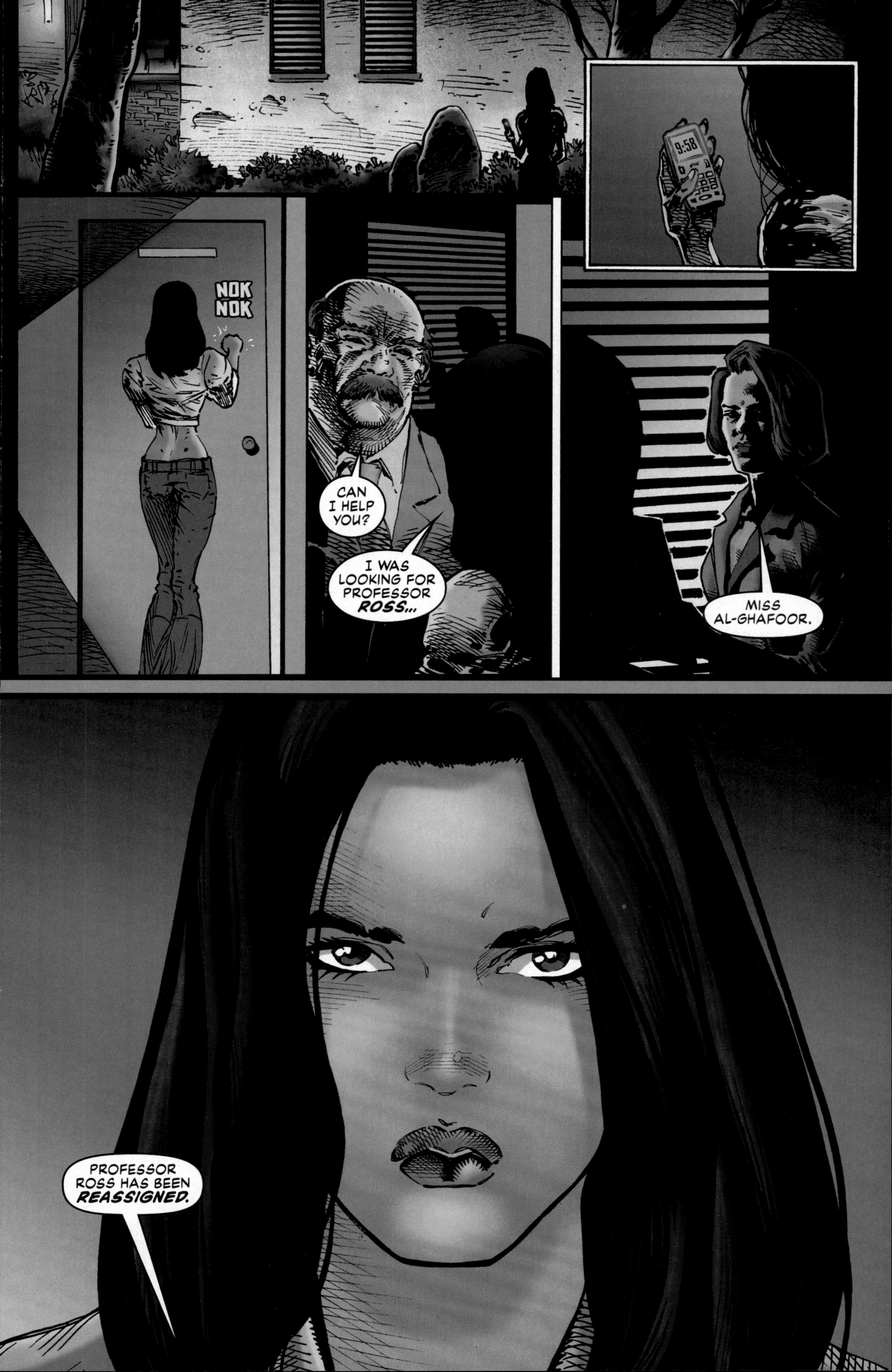
9:58
NOK NOK
CAN I HELP YOU?
I WAS LOOKING FOR PROFESSOR ROSS...
MISS AL-GHAFOOR.
PROFESSOR ROSS HAS BEEN REASSIGNED.

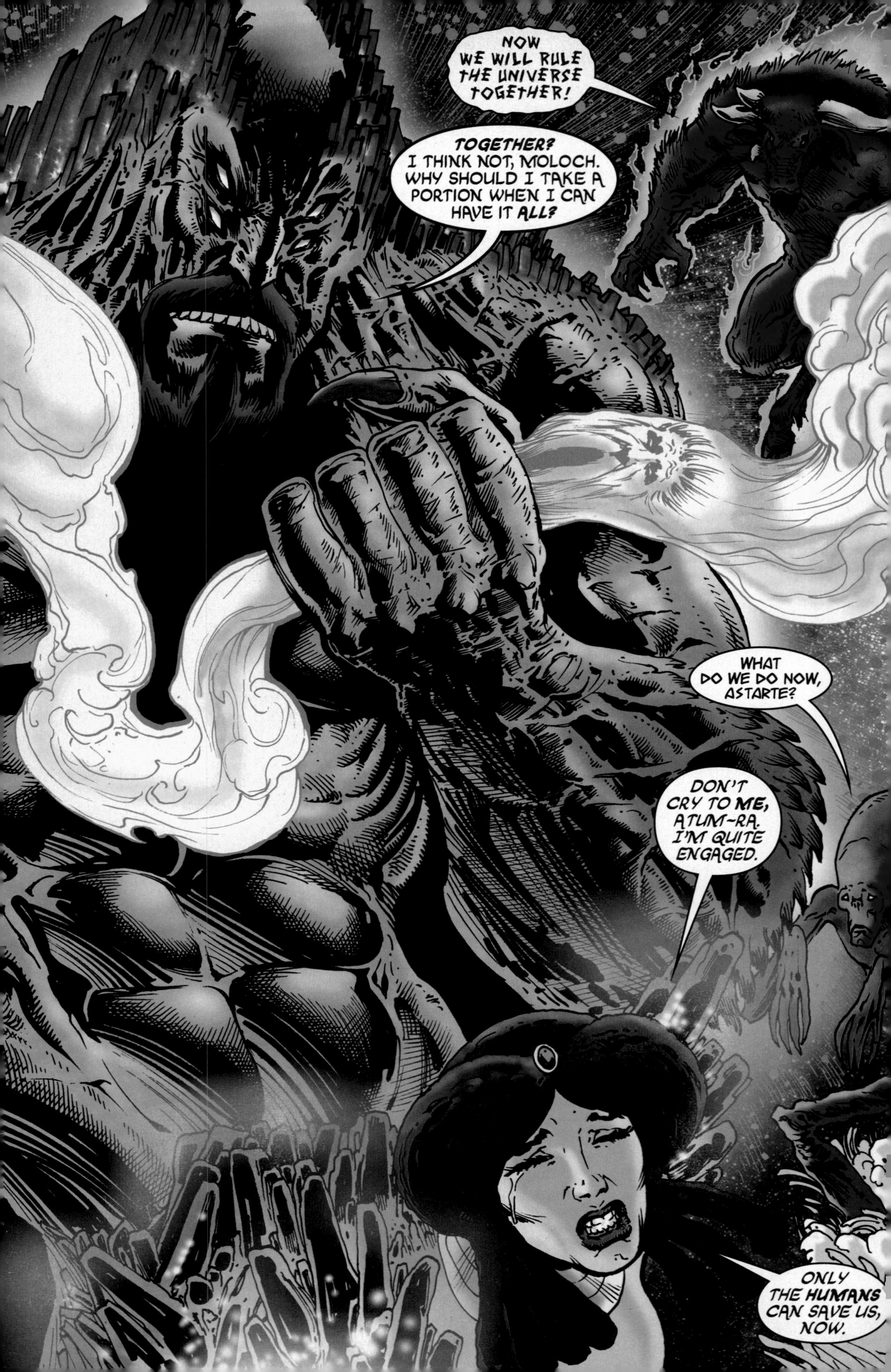
NOW WE WILL RULE THE UNIVERSE TOGETHER!
TOGETHER? I THINK NOT, MOLOCH. WHY SHOULD I TAKE A PORTION WHEN I CAN HAVE IT ALL?
WHAT DO WE DO NOW, ASTARTE?
DON'T CRY TO ME, ATUM-RA. I'M QUITE ENGAGED.
ONLY THE HUMANS CAN SAVE US, NOW.

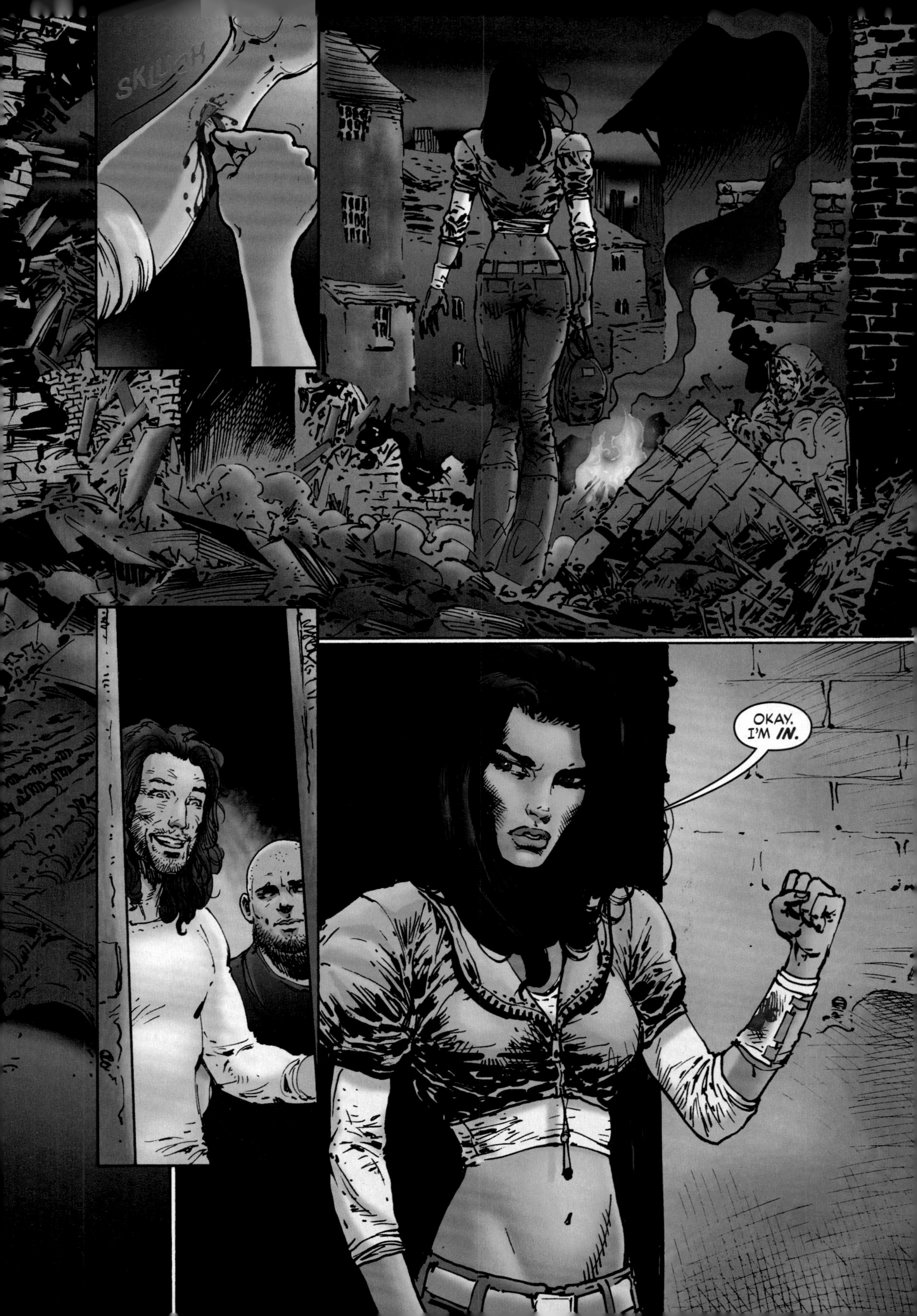

SKLLLGH
OKAY. I'M IN.

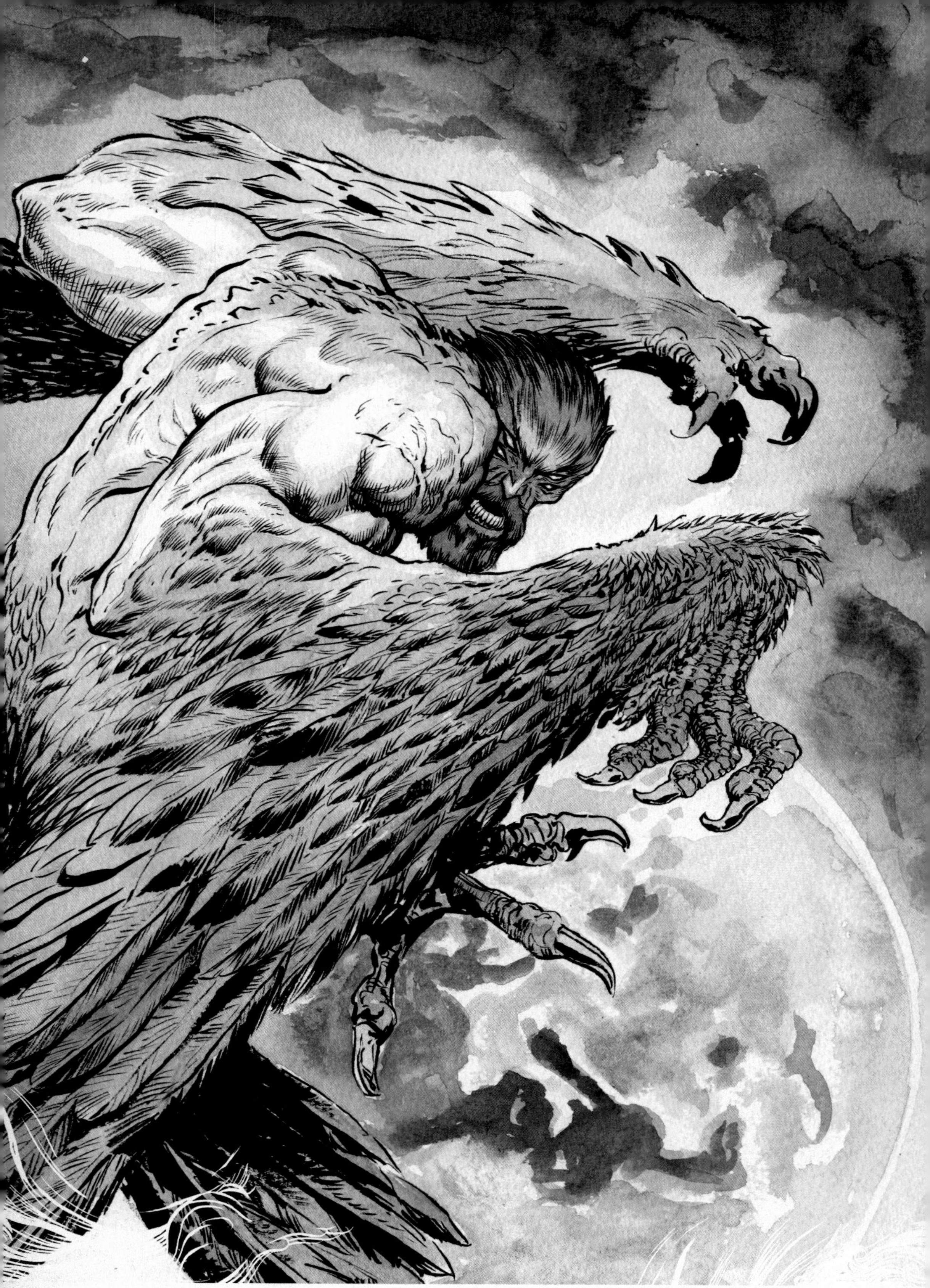

BABEL *Part Four: What Goes Up*

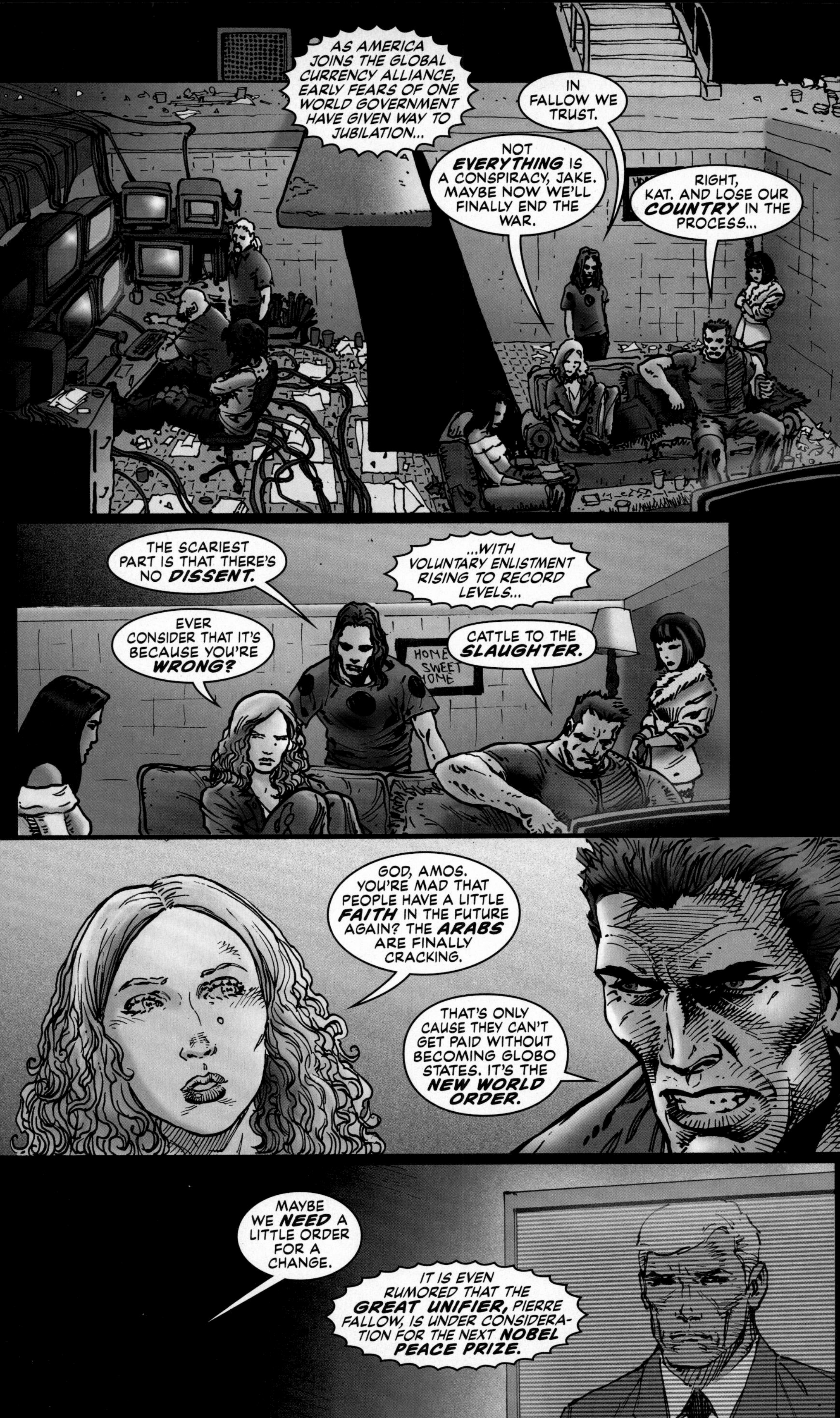
AS AMERICA JOINS THE GLOBAL CURRENCY ALLIANCE, EARLY FEARS OF ONE WORLD GOVERNMENT HAVE GIVEN WAY TO JUBILATION...
IN FALLOW WE TRUST.
NOT EVERYTHING IS A CONSPIRACY, JAKE. MAYBE NOW WE'LL FINALLY END THE WAR.
RIGHT, KAT. AND LOSE OUR COUNTRY IN THE PROCESS...
THE SCARIEST PART IS THAT THERE'S NO DISSENT.
...WITH VOLUNTARY ENLISTMENT RISING TO RECORD LEVELS...
EVER CONSIDER THAT IT'S BECAUSE YOU'RE WRONG?
CATTLE TO THE SLAUGHTER.
HOME SWEET HOME
GOD, AMOS. YOU'RE MAD THAT PEOPLE HAVE A LITTLE FAITH IN THE FUTURE AGAIN? THE ARABS ARE FINALLY CRACKING.
THAT'S ONLY CAUSE THEY CAN'T GET PAID WITHOUT BECOMING GLOBO STATES. IT'S THE NEW WORLD ORDER.
MAYBE WE NEED A LITTLE ORDER FOR A CHANGE.
IT IS EVEN RUMORED THAT THE GREAT UNIFIER, PIERRE FALLOW, IS UNDER CONSIDERATION FOR THE NEXT NOBEL PEACE PRIZE.

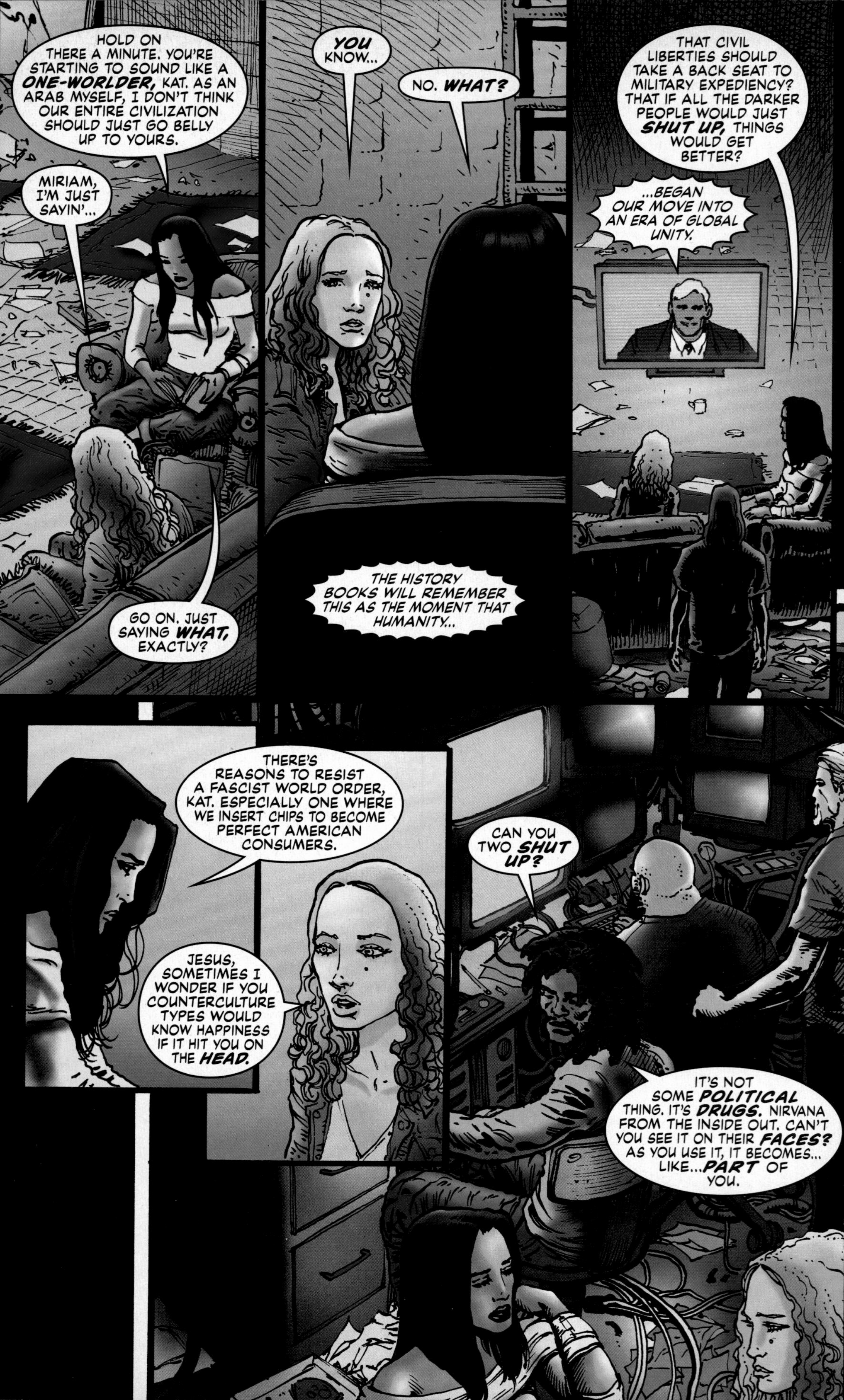
HOLD ON THERE A MINUTE. YOU'RE STARTING TO SOUND LIKE A ONE-WORLDER, KAT. AS AN ARAB MYSELF, I DON'T THINK OUR ENTIRE CIVILIZATION SHOULD JUST GO BELLY UP TO YOURS.
MIRIAM, I'M JUST SAYIN'...
GO ON. JUST SAYING WHAT, EXACTLY?
YOU KNOW...
NO. WHAT?
THE HISTORY BOOKS WILL REMEMBER THIS AS THE MOMENT THAT HUMANITY...
THAT CIVIL LIBERTIES SHOULD TAKE A BACK SEAT TO MILITARY EXPEDIENCY? THAT IF ALL THE DARKER PEOPLE WOULD JUST SHUT UP, THINGS WOULD GET BETTER?
...BEGAN OUR MOVE INTO AN ERA OF GLOBAL UNITY.
THERE'S REASONS TO RESIST A FASCIST WORLD ORDER, KAT. ESPECIALLY ONE WHERE WE INSERT CHIPS TO BECOME PERFECT AMERICAN CONSUMERS.
JESUS, SOMETIMES I WONDER IF YOU COUNTERCULTURE TYPES WOULD KNOW HAPPINESS IF IT HIT YOU ON THE HEAD.
CAN YOU TWO SHUT UP?
IT'S NOT SOME POLITICAL THING. IT'S DRUGS. NIRVANA FROM THE INSIDE OUT. CAN'T YOU SEE IT ON THEIR FACES? AS YOU USE IT, IT BECOMES... LIKE...PART OF YOU.

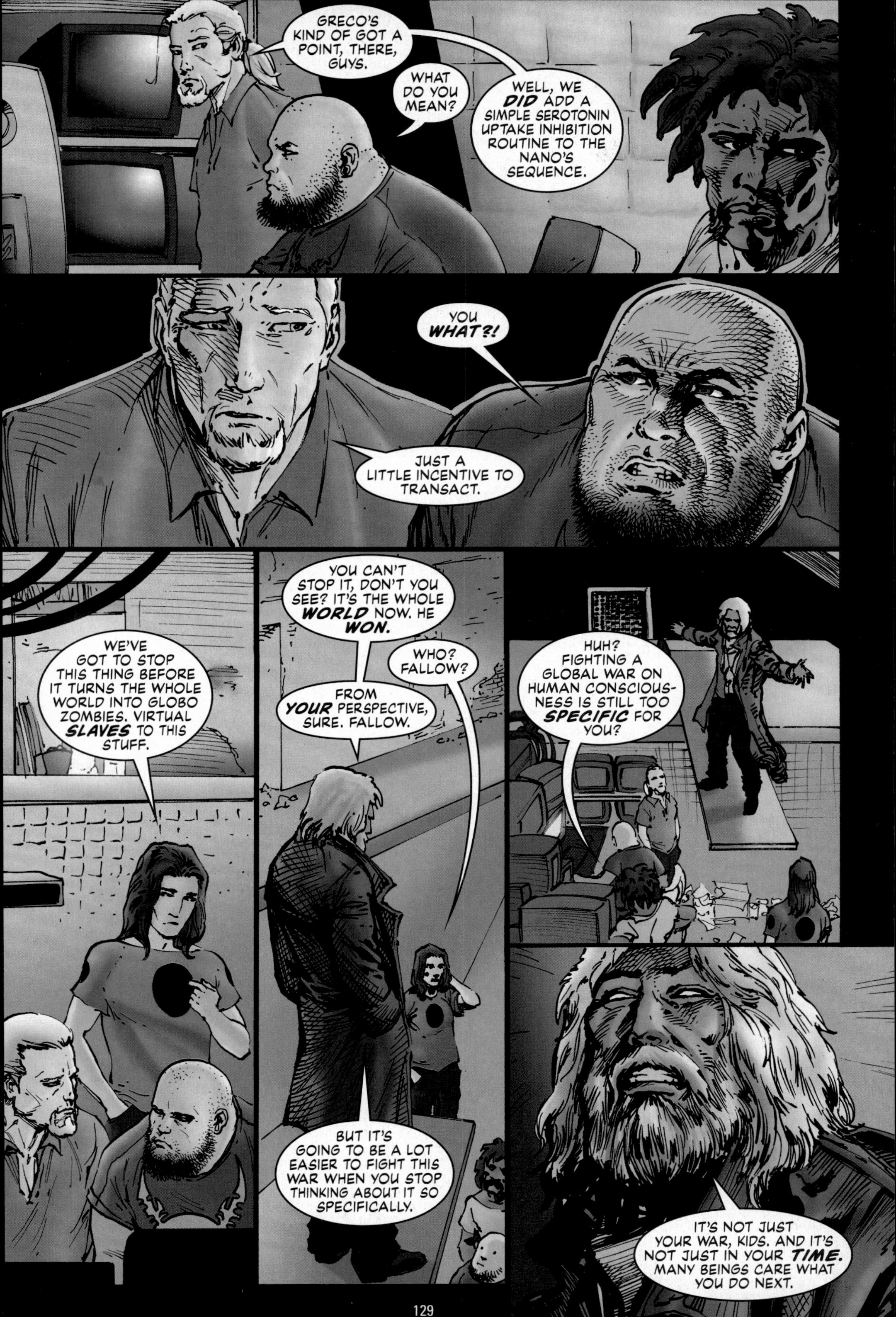
GRECO'S KIND OF GOT A POINT, THERE, GUYS.
WHAT DO YOU MEAN?
WELL, WE DID ADD A SIMPLE SEROTONIN UPTAKE INHIBITION ROUTINE TO THE NANO'S SEQUENCE.
YOU WHAT?!
JUST A LITTLE INCENTIVE TO TRANSACT.
WE'VE GOT TO STOP THIS THING BEFORE IT TURNS THE WHOLE WORLD INTO GLOBO ZOMBIES. VIRTUAL SLAVES TO THIS STUFF.
YOU CAN'T STOP IT, DON'T YOU SEE? IT'S THE WHOLE WORLD NOW. HE WON.
WHO? FALLOW?
FROM YOUR PERSPECTIVE, SURE. FALLOW.
BUT IT'S GOING TO BE A LOT EASIER TO FIGHT THIS WAR WHEN YOU STOP THINKING ABOUT IT SO SPECIFICALLY.
HUH? FIGHTING A GLOBAL WAR ON HUMAN CONSCIOUS-NESS IS STILL TOO SPECIFIC FOR YOU?
IT'S NOT JUST YOUR WAR, KIDS. AND IT'S NOT JUST IN YOUR TIME. MANY BEINGS CARE WHAT YOU DO NEXT.

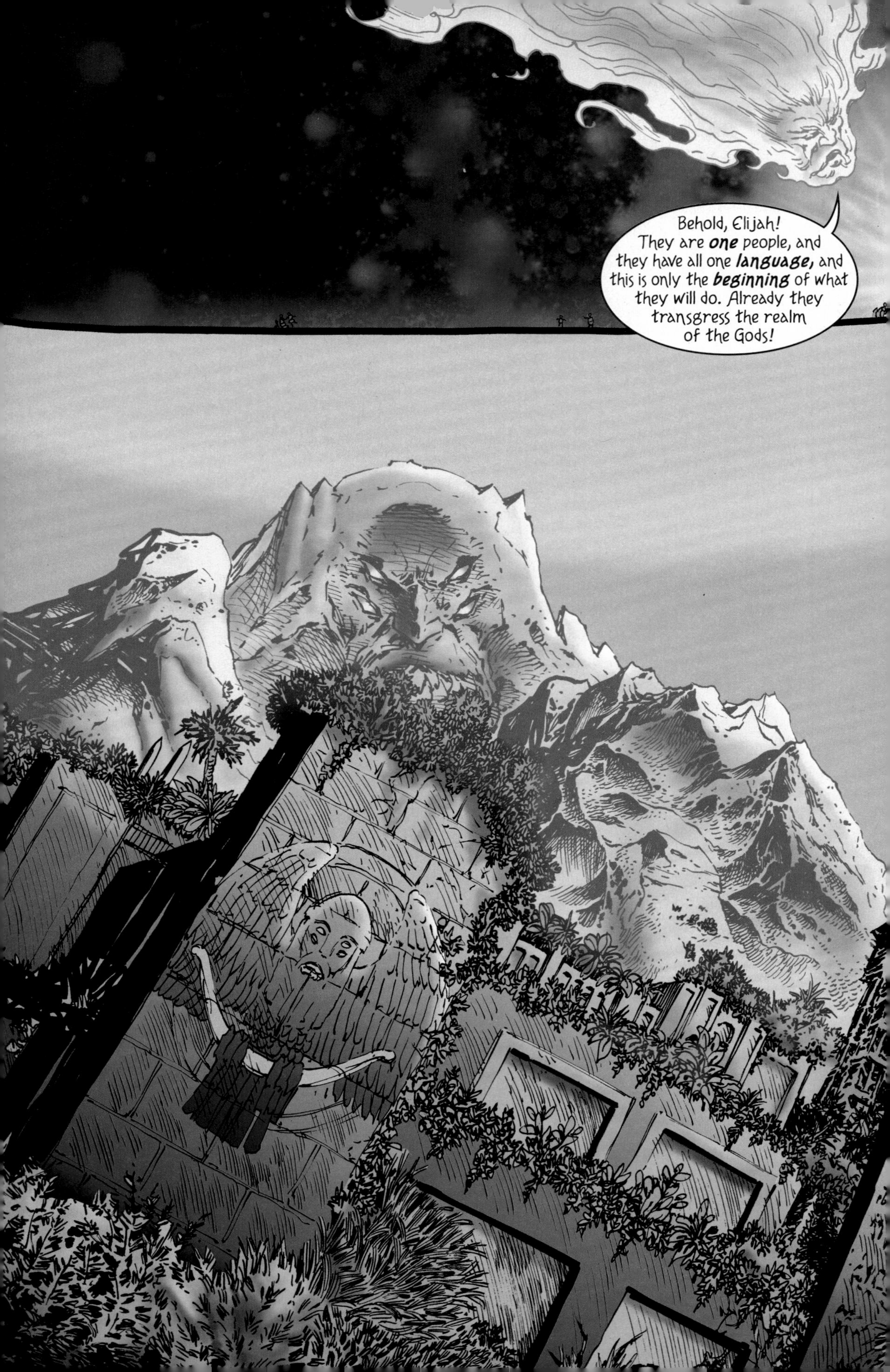
Behold, Elijah! They are one people, and they have all one language, and this is only the beginning of what they will do. Already they transgress the realm of the Gods!

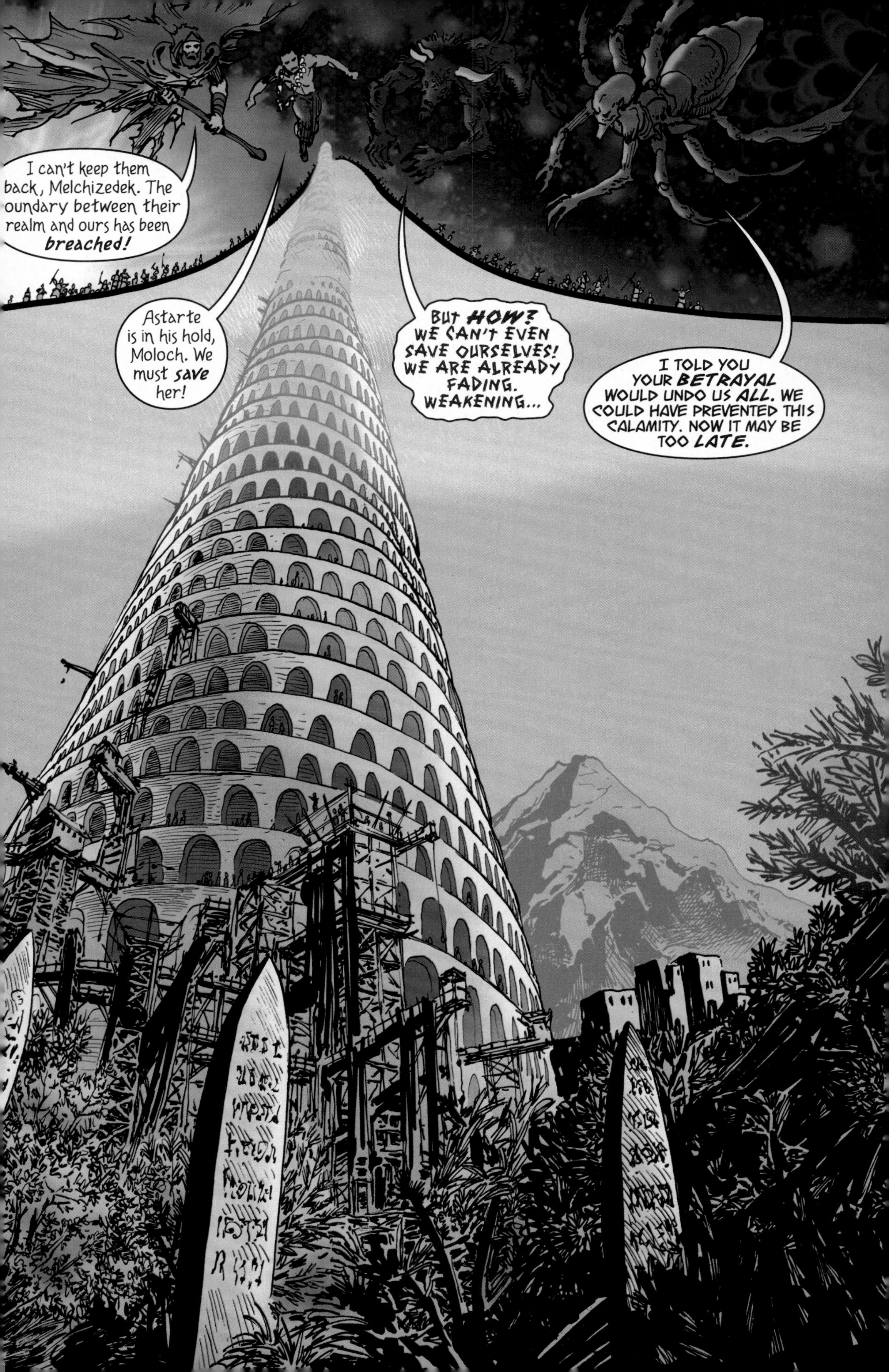
I can't keep them back, Melchizedek. The oundary between their realm and ours has been breached!
Astarte is in his hold, Moloch. We must save her!
But HOW? We can't even save ourselves! We are already fading. Weakening...
I told you your BETRAYAL would undo us ALL. We could have prevented this calamity. Now it may be too LATE.

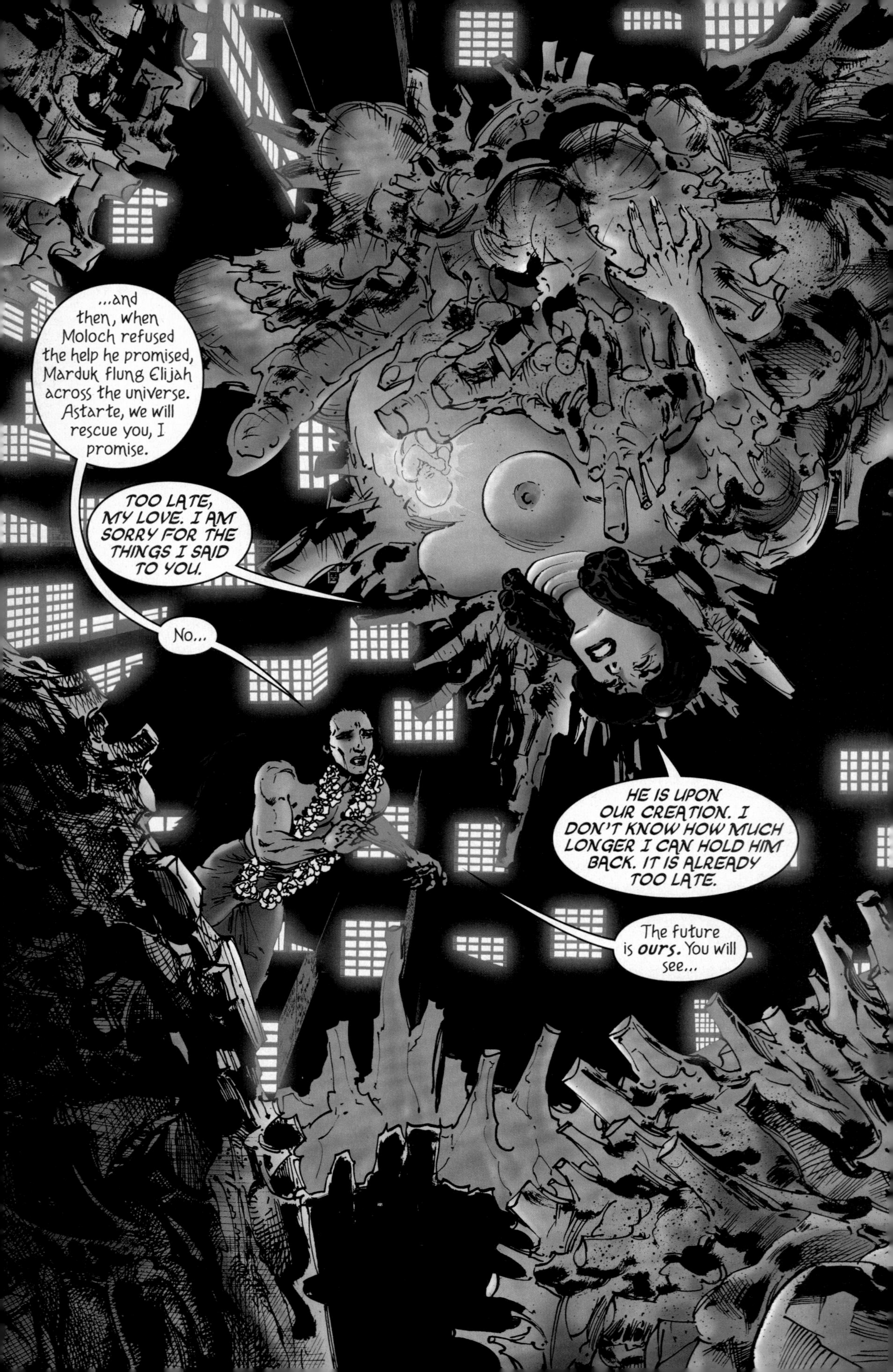
...and then, when Moloch refused the help he promised, Marduk flung Elijah across the universe. Astarte, we will rescue you, I promise.
TOO LATE, MY LOVE. I AM SORRY FOR THE THINGS I SAID TO YOU.
No...
HE IS UPON OUR CREATION. I DON'T KNOW HOW MUCH LONGER I CAN HOLD HIM BACK. IT IS ALREADY TOO LATE.
The future is **ours.** You will see...

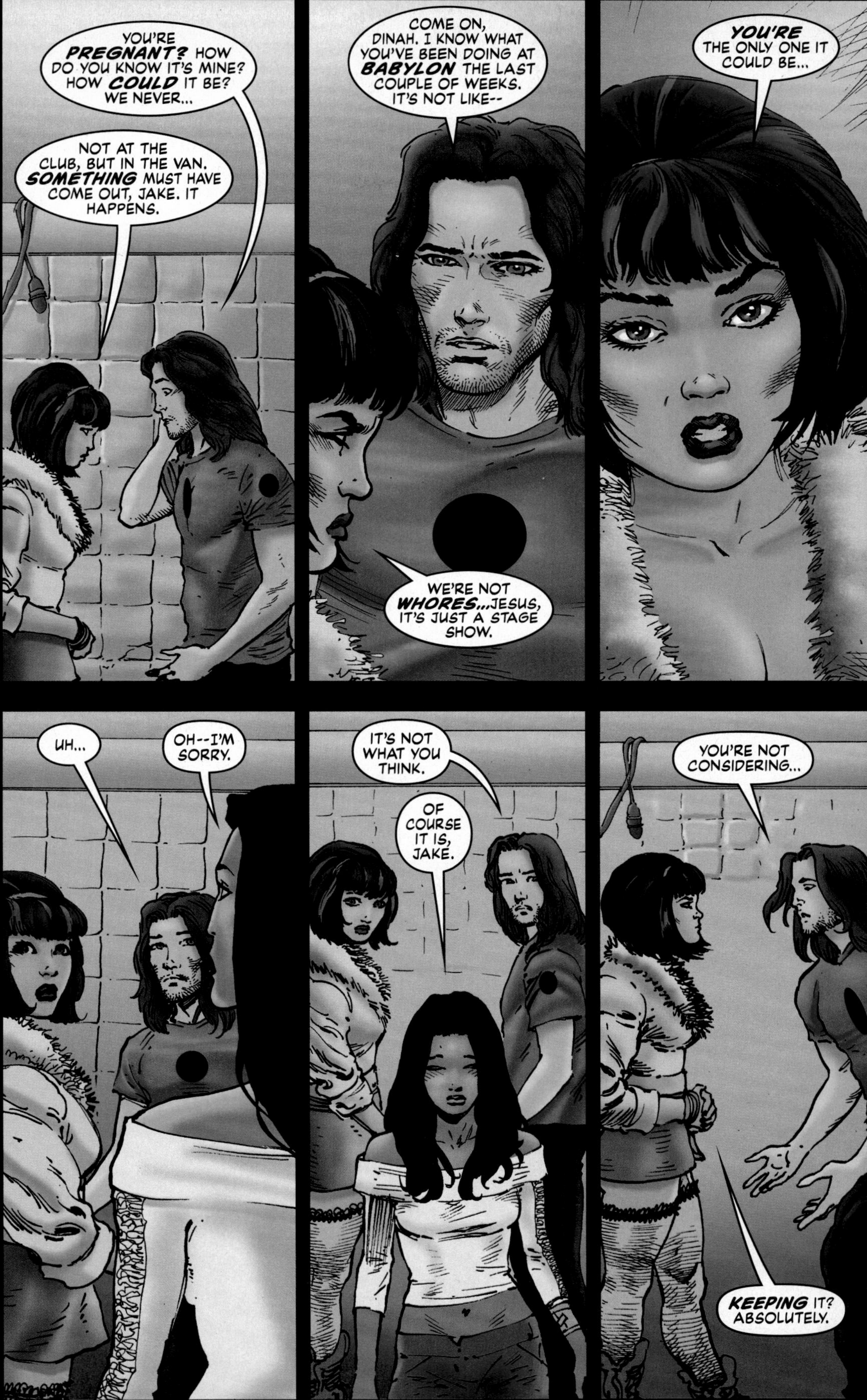

YOU'RE PREGNANT? HOW DO YOU KNOW IT'S MINE? HOW COULD IT BE? WE NEVER...
NOT AT THE CLUB, BUT IN THE VAN. SOMETHING MUST HAVE COME OUT, JAKE. IT HAPPENS.
COME ON, DINAH. I KNOW WHAT YOU'VE BEEN DOING AT BABYLON THE LAST COUPLE OF WEEKS. IT'S NOT LIKE--
WE'RE NOT WHORES...JESUS, IT'S JUST A STAGE SHOW.
YOU'RE THE ONLY ONE IT COULD BE...
UH...
OH--I'M SORRY.
IT'S NOT WHAT YOU THINK.
OF COURSE IT IS, JAKE.
YOU'RE NOT CONSIDERING...
KEEPING IT? ABSOLUTELY.

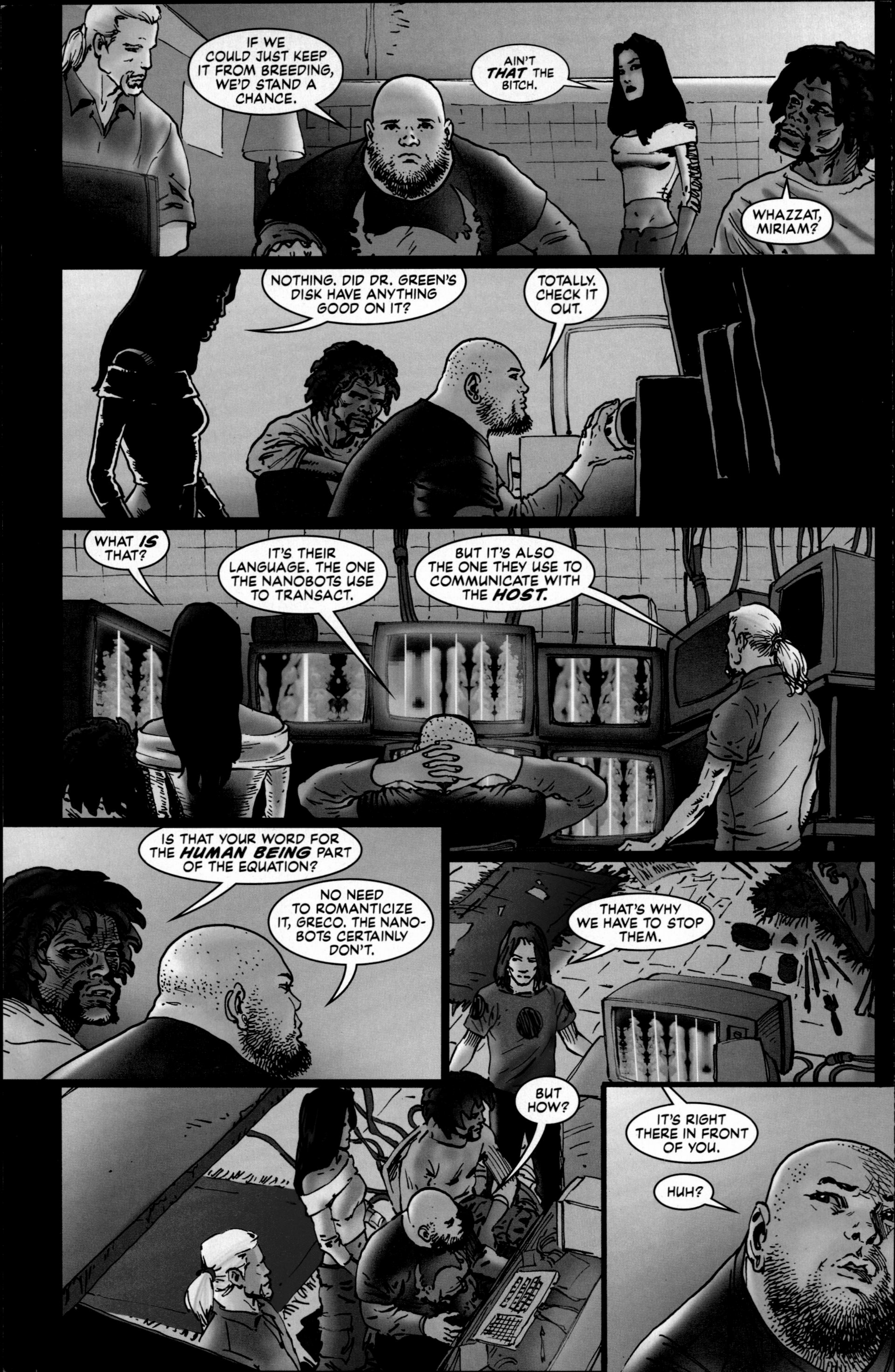

IF WE COULD JUST KEEP IT FROM BREEDING, WE'D STAND A CHANCE.
AIN'T *THAT* THE BITCH.
WHAZZAT, MIRIAM?
NOTHING. DID DR. GREEN'S DISK HAVE ANYTHING GOOD ON IT?
TOTALLY. CHECK IT OUT.
WHAT *IS* THAT?
IT'S THEIR LANGUAGE. THE ONE THE NANOBOTS USE TO TRANSACT.
BUT IT'S ALSO THE ONE THEY USE TO COMMUNICATE WITH THE *HOST.*
IS THAT YOUR WORD FOR THE *HUMAN BEING* PART OF THE EQUATION?
NO NEED TO ROMANTICIZE IT, GRECO. THE NANO-BOTS CERTAINLY DON'T.
THAT'S WHY WE HAVE TO STOP THEM.
BUT HOW?
IT'S RIGHT THERE IN FRONT OF YOU.
HUH?

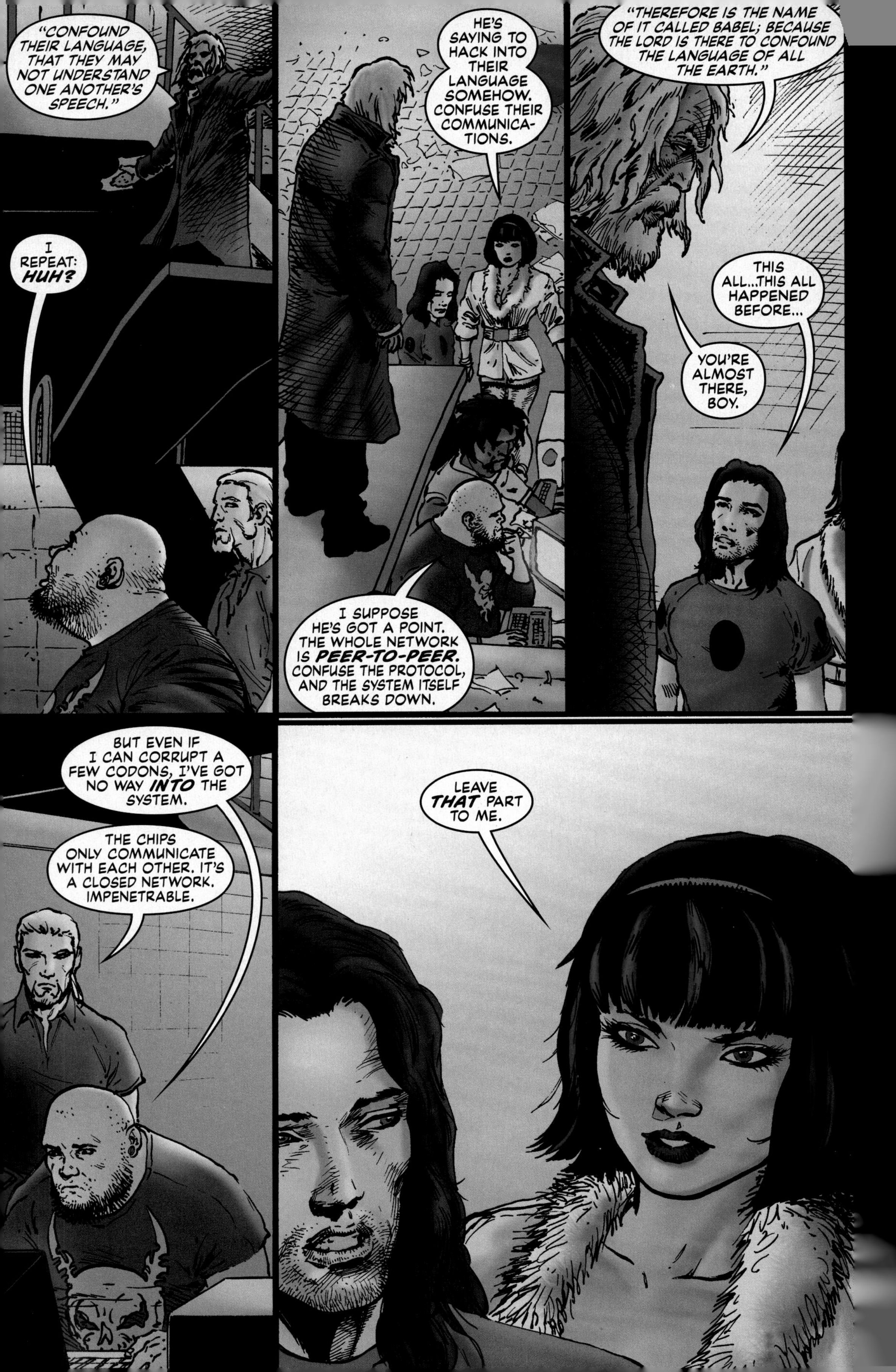
"CONFOUND THEIR LANGUAGE, THAT THEY MAY NOT UNDERSTAND ONE ANOTHER'S SPEECH."
I REPEAT: **HUH?**
HE'S SAYING TO HACK INTO THEIR LANGUAGE SOMEHOW. CONFUSE THEIR COMMUNICATIONS.
I SUPPOSE HE'S GOT A POINT. THE WHOLE NETWORK IS **PEER-TO-PEER.** CONFUSE THE PROTOCOL, AND THE SYSTEM ITSELF BREAKS DOWN.
"THEREFORE IS THE NAME OF IT CALLED BABEL; BECAUSE THE LORD IS THERE TO CONFOUND THE LANGUAGE OF ALL THE EARTH."
THIS ALL...THIS ALL HAPPENED BEFORE...
YOU'RE ALMOST THERE, BOY.
BUT EVEN IF I CAN CORRUPT A FEW CODONS, I'VE GOT NO WAY ***INTO*** THE SYSTEM.
THE CHIPS ONLY COMMUNICATE WITH EACH OTHER. IT'S A CLOSED NETWORK. IMPENETRABLE.
LEAVE ***THAT*** PART TO ME.

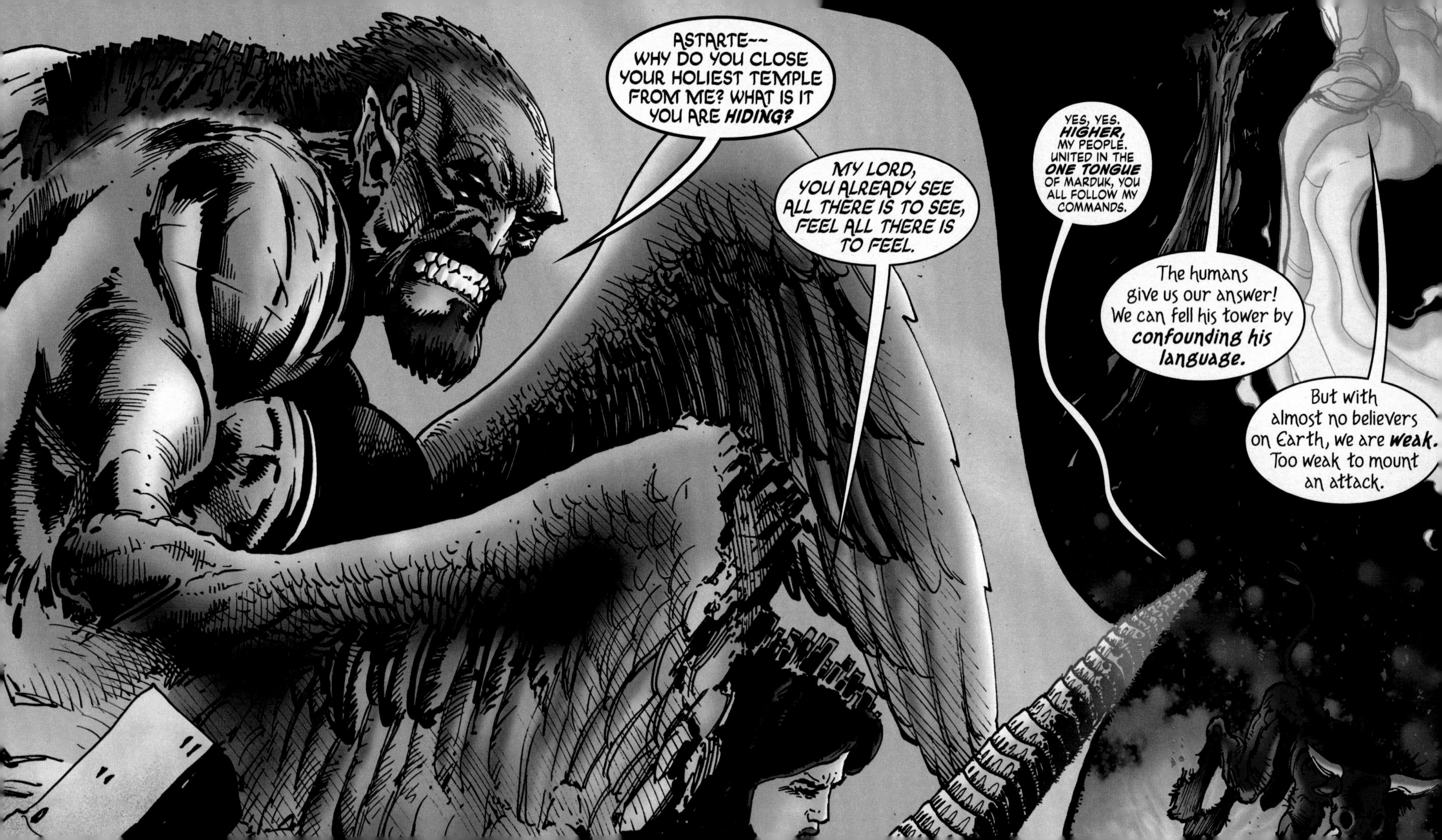
ASTARTE-- WHY DO YOU CLOSE YOUR HOLIEST TEMPLE FROM ME? WHAT IS IT YOU ARE *HIDING?*
MY LORD, YOU ALREADY SEE ALL THERE IS TO SEE, FEEL ALL THERE IS TO FEEL.
YES, YES. ***HIGHER,*** MY PEOPLE. UNITED IN THE ***ONE TONGUE*** OF MARDUK, YOU ALL FOLLOW MY COMMANDS.
The humans give us our answer! We can fell his tower by ***confounding his language.***
But with almost no believers on Earth, we are ***weak.*** Too weak to mount an attack.

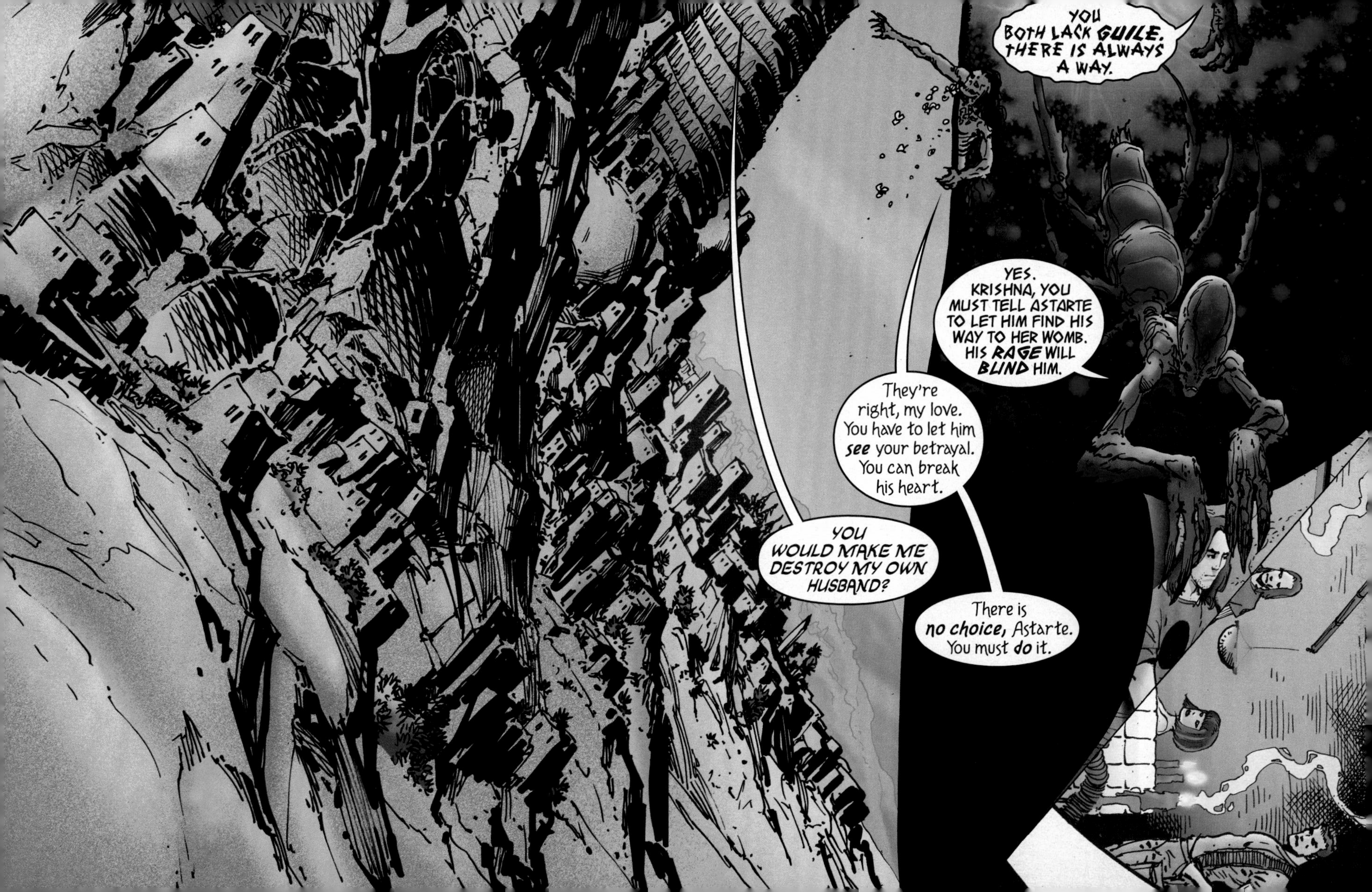
YOU BOTH LACK **GUILE**. THERE IS ALWAYS A WAY.
YES. KRISHNA, YOU MUST TELL ASTARTE TO LET HIM FIND HIS WAY TO HER WOMB. HIS **RAGE** WILL **BLIND** HIM.
They're right, my love. You have to let him **see** your betrayal. You can break his heart.
YOU WOULD MAKE ME DESTROY MY OWN HUSBAND?
There is **no choice,** Astarte. You must **do** it.

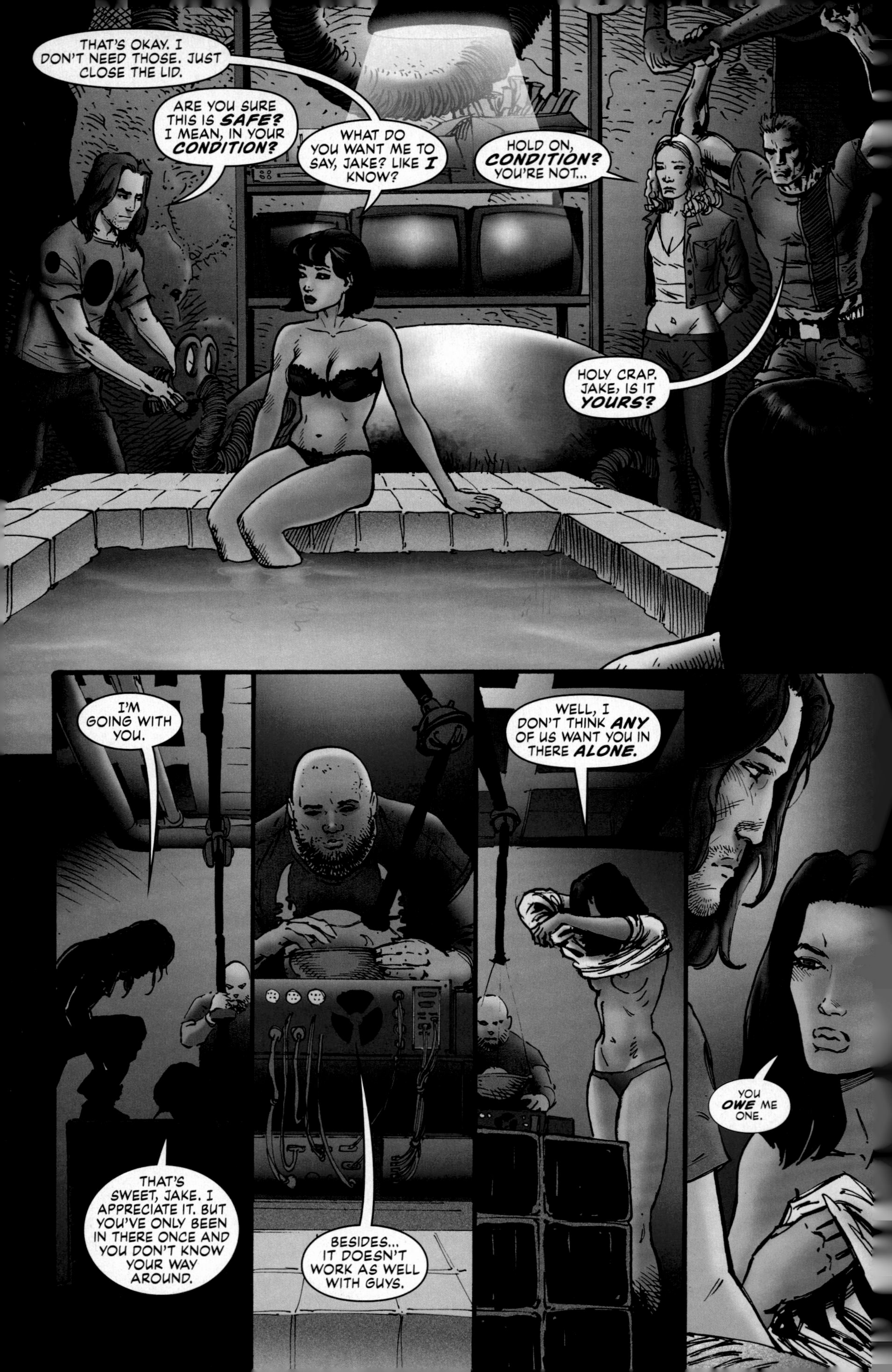
THAT'S OKAY. I DON'T NEED THOSE. JUST CLOSE THE LID.
ARE YOU SURE THIS IS SAFE? I MEAN, IN YOUR CONDITION?
WHAT DO YOU WANT ME TO SAY, JAKE? LIKE I KNOW?
HOLD ON, CONDITION? YOU'RE NOT...
HOLY CRAP. JAKE, IS IT YOURS?
I'M GOING WITH YOU.
THAT'S SWEET, JAKE. I APPRECIATE IT. BUT YOU'VE ONLY BEEN IN THERE ONCE AND YOU DON'T KNOW YOUR WAY AROUND.
BESIDES... IT DOESN'T WORK AS WELL WITH GUYS.
WELL, I DON'T THINK ANY OF US WANT YOU IN THERE ALONE.
YOU OWE ME ONE.

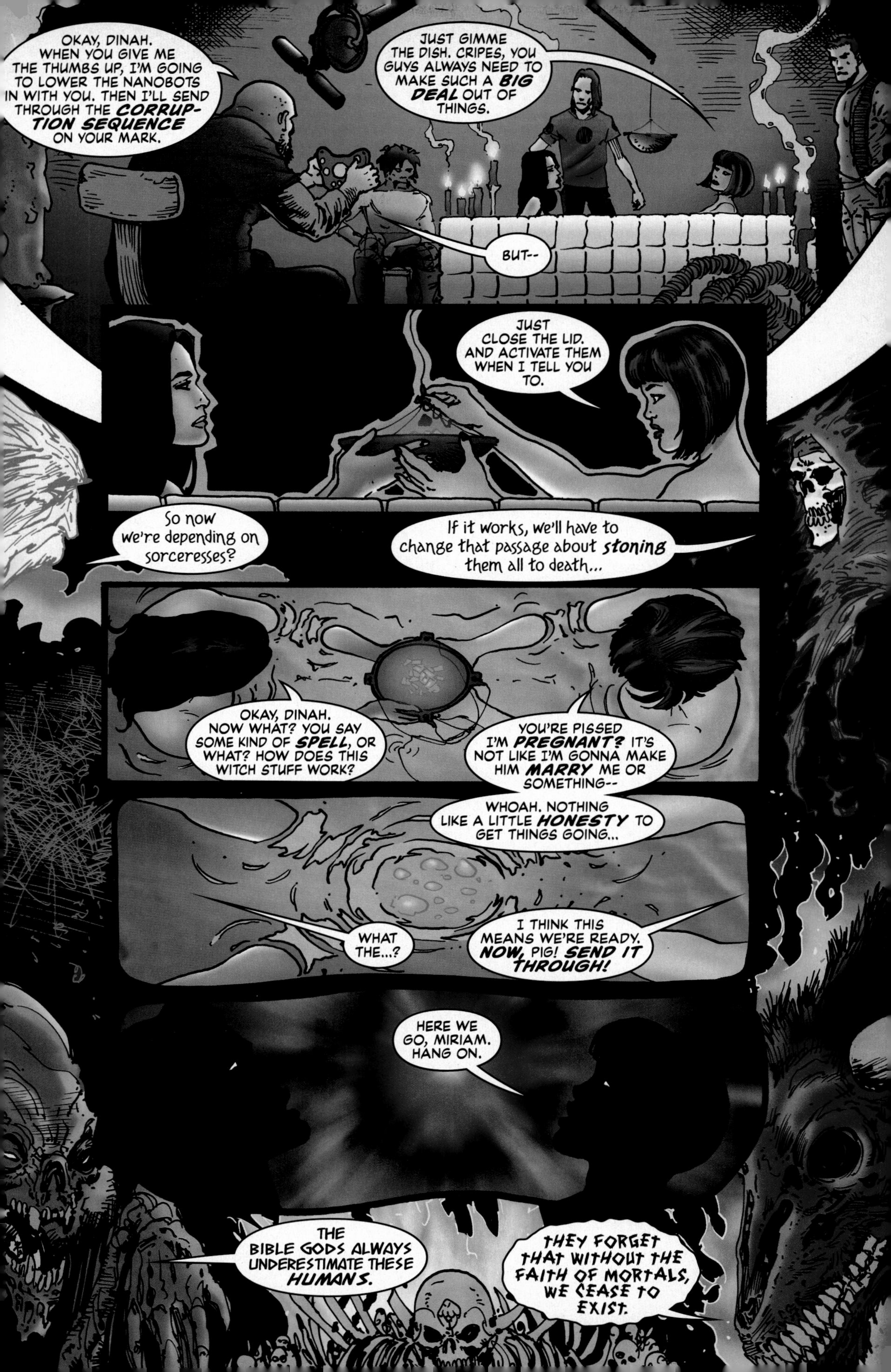

OKAY, DINAH. WHEN YOU GIVE ME THE THUMBS UP, I'M GOING TO LOWER THE NANOBOTS IN WITH YOU. THEN I'LL SEND THROUGH THE CORRUPTION SEQUENCE ON YOUR MARK.
JUST GIMME THE DISH. CRIPES, YOU GUYS ALWAYS NEED TO MAKE SUCH A BIG DEAL OUT OF THINGS.
BUT--
JUST CLOSE THE LID. AND ACTIVATE THEM WHEN I TELL YOU TO.
So now we're depending on sorceresses?
If it works, we'll have to change that passage about stoning them all to death...
OKAY, DINAH. NOW WHAT? YOU SAY SOME KIND OF SPELL, OR WHAT? HOW DOES THIS WITCH STUFF WORK?
YOU'RE PISSED I'M PREGNANT? IT'S NOT LIKE I'M GONNA MAKE HIM MARRY ME OR SOMETHING--
WHOAH. NOTHING LIKE A LITTLE HONESTY TO GET THINGS GOING...
WHAT THE...?
I THINK THIS MEANS WE'RE READY. NOW, PIG! SEND IT THROUGH!
HERE WE GO, MIRIAM. HANG ON.
THE BIBLE GODS ALWAYS UNDERESTIMATE THESE HUMANS.
THEY FORGET THAT WITHOUT THE FAITH OF MORTALS, WE CEASE TO EXIST.

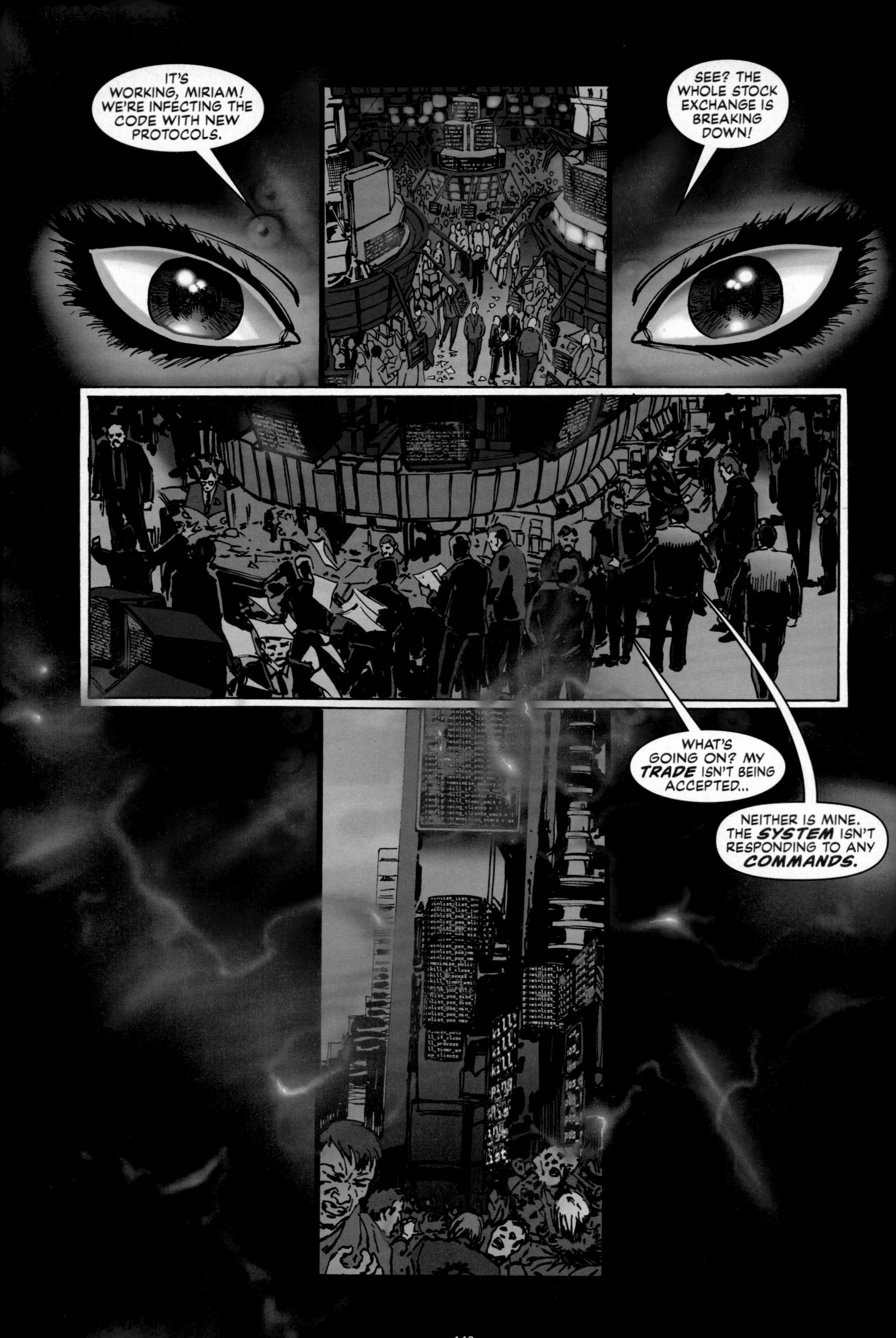
IT'S WORKING, MIRIAM! WE'RE INFECTING THE CODE WITH NEW PROTOCOLS.
SEE? THE WHOLE STOCK EXCHANGE IS BREAKING DOWN!
WHAT'S GOING ON? MY TRADE ISN'T BEING ACCEPTED...
NEITHER IS MINE. THE SYSTEM ISN'T RESPONDING TO ANY COMMANDS.

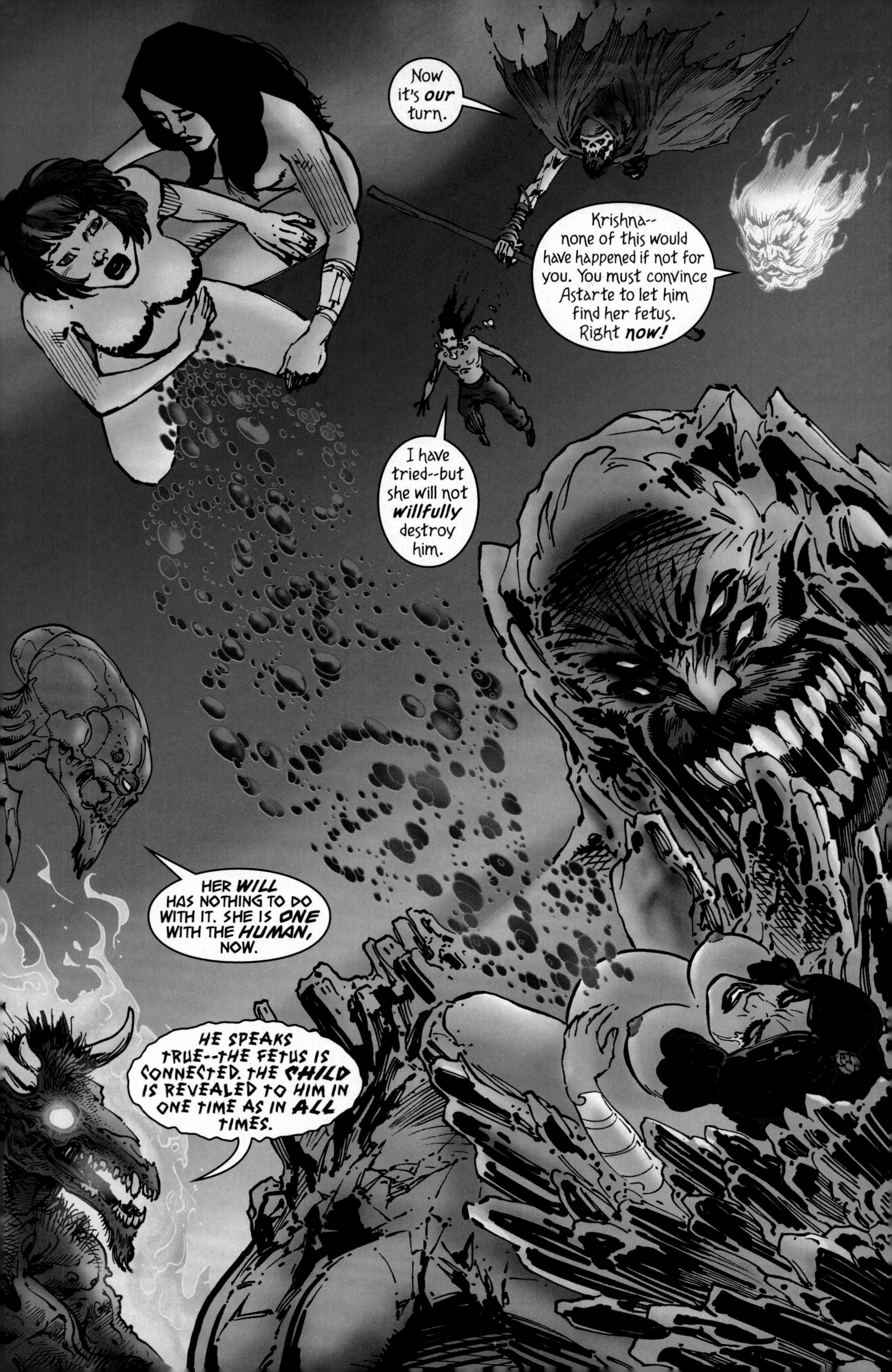
Now it's our turn.
Krishna-- none of this would have happened if not for you. You must convince Astarte to let him find her fetus. Right now!
I have tried--but she will not willfully destroy him.
HER WILL HAS NOTHING TO DO WITH IT. SHE IS ONE WITH THE HUMAN, NOW.
HE SPEAKS TRUE--THE FETUS IS CONNECTED. THE CHILD IS REVEALED TO HIM IN ONE TIME AS IN ALL TIMES.

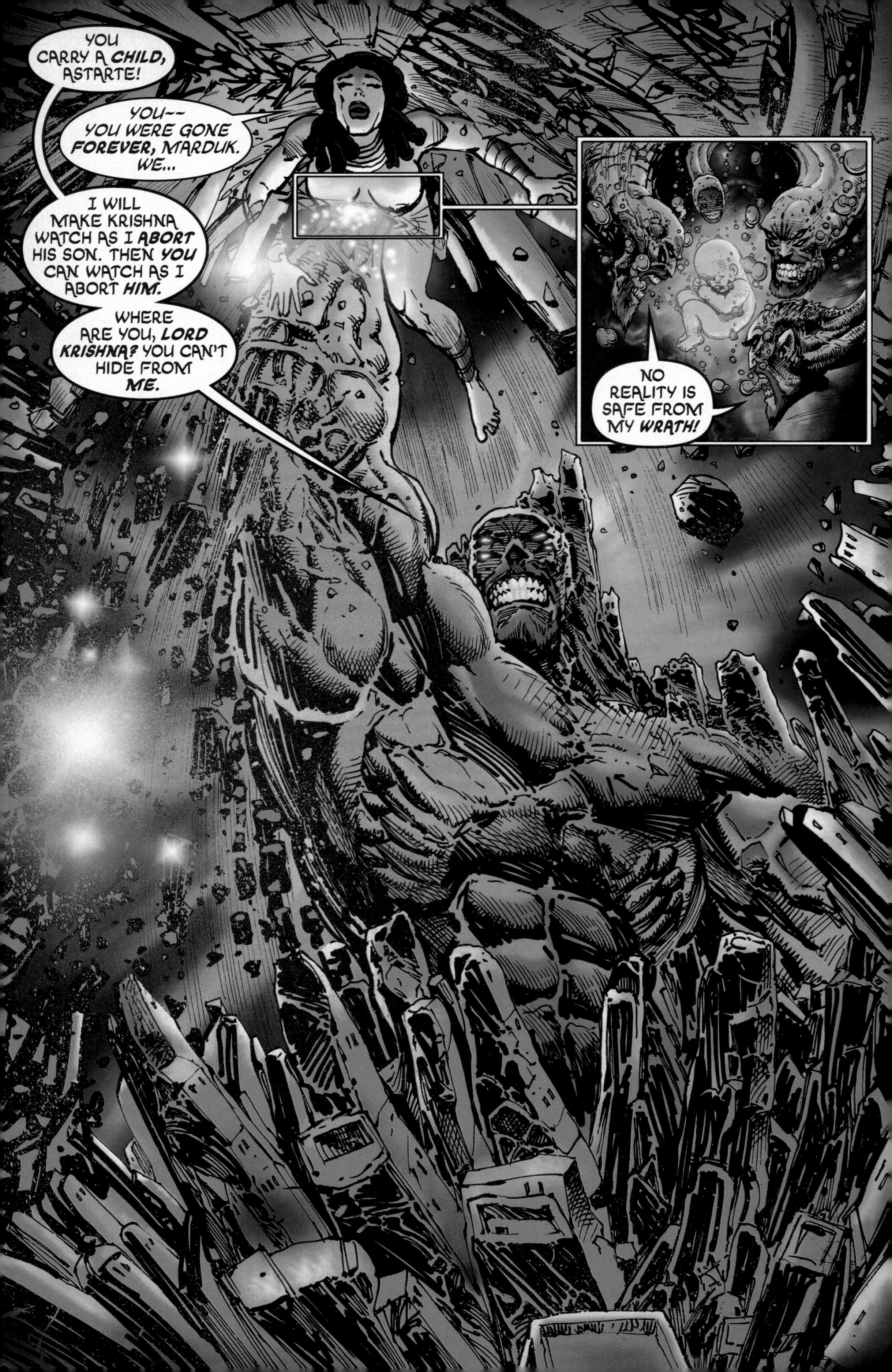
YOU CARRY A CHILD, ASTARTE!
YOU-- YOU WERE GONE FOREVER, MARDUK. WE...
I WILL MAKE KRISHNA WATCH AS I ABORT HIS SON. THEN YOU CAN WATCH AS I ABORT HIM.
WHERE ARE YOU, LORD KRISHNA? YOU CAN'T HIDE FROM ME.
NO REALITY IS SAFE FROM MY WRATH!

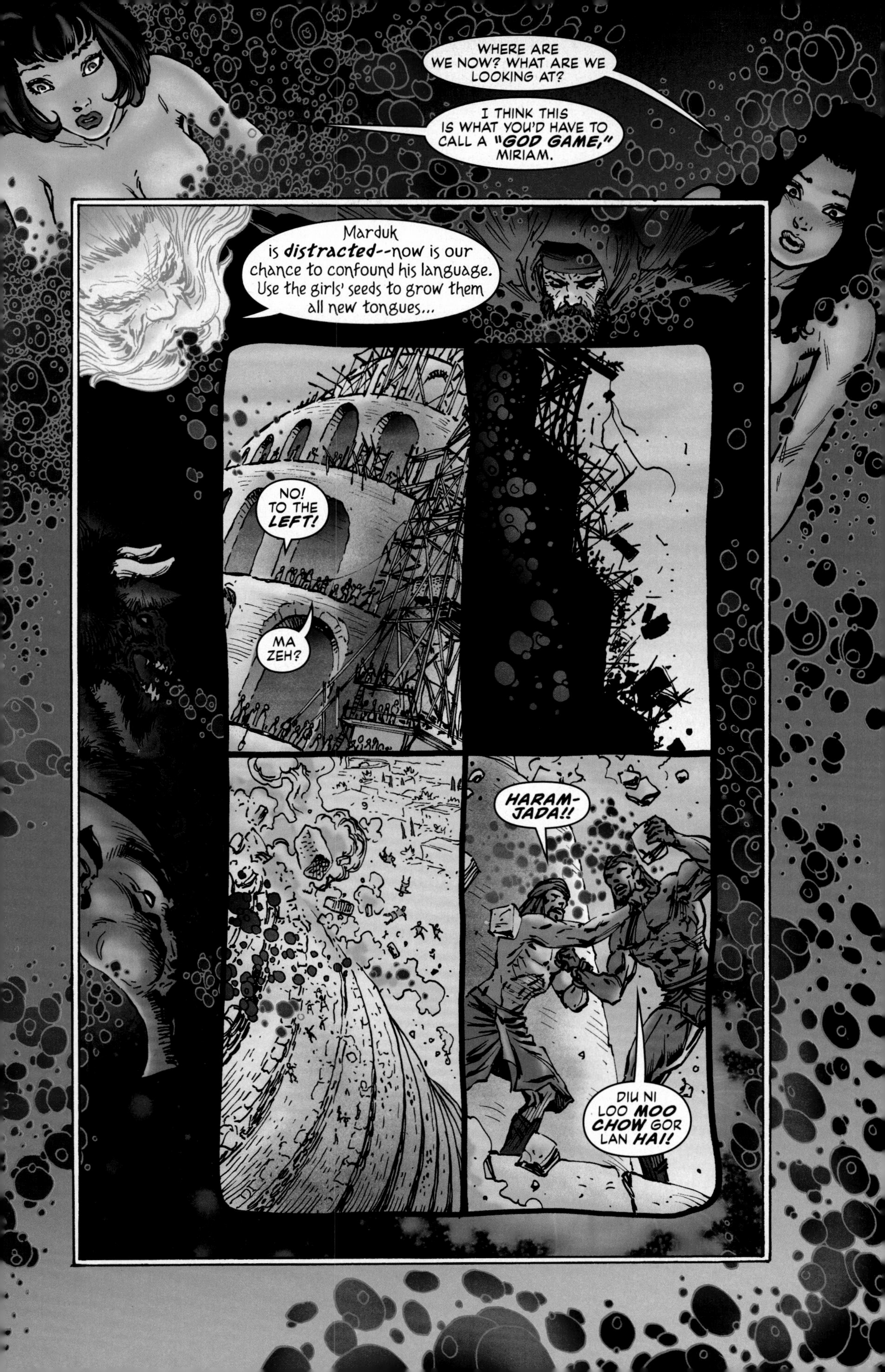
WHERE ARE WE NOW? WHAT ARE WE LOOKING AT?
I THINK THIS IS WHAT YOU'D HAVE TO CALL A "GOD GAME," MIRIAM.
Marduk is distracted--now is our chance to confound his language. Use the girls' seeds to grow them all new tongues...
NO! TO THE LEFT!
MA ZEH?
HARAM-JADA!!
DIU NI LOO MOO CHOW GOR LAN HAI!

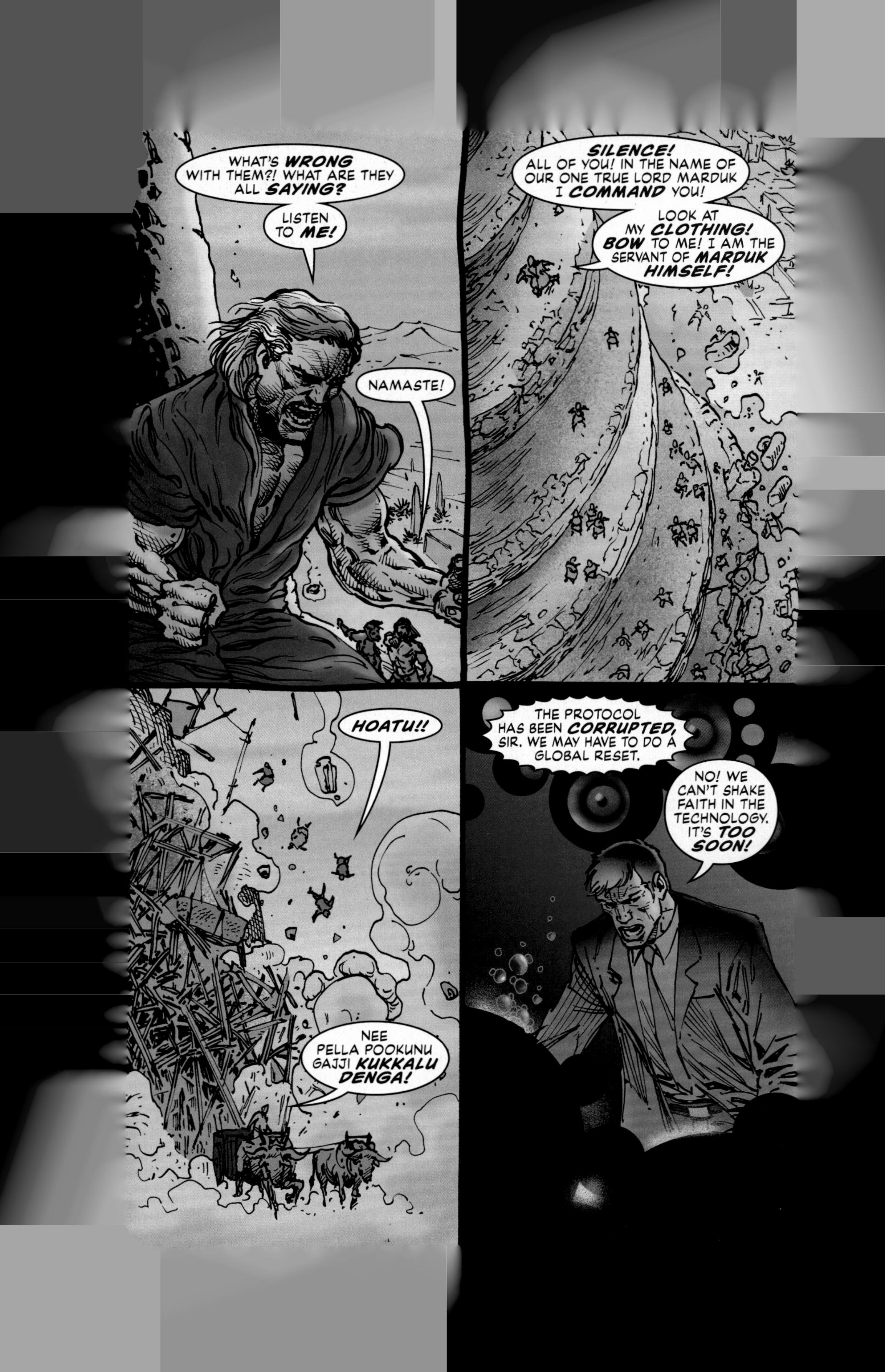
WHAT'S WRONG WITH THEM?! WHAT ARE THEY ALL SAYING?
LISTEN TO ME!
NAMASTE!
SILENCE! ALL OF YOU! IN THE NAME OF OUR ONE TRUE LORD MARDUK I COMMAND YOU!
LOOK AT MY CLOTHING! BOW TO ME! I AM THE SERVANT OF MARDUK HIMSELF!
HOATU!!
NEE PELLA POOKUNU GAJJI KUKKALU DENGA!
THE PROTOCOL HAS BEEN CORRUPTED, SIR. WE MAY HAVE TO DO A GLOBAL RESET.
NO! WE CAN'T SHAKE FAITH IN THE TECHNOLOGY. IT'S TOO SOON!

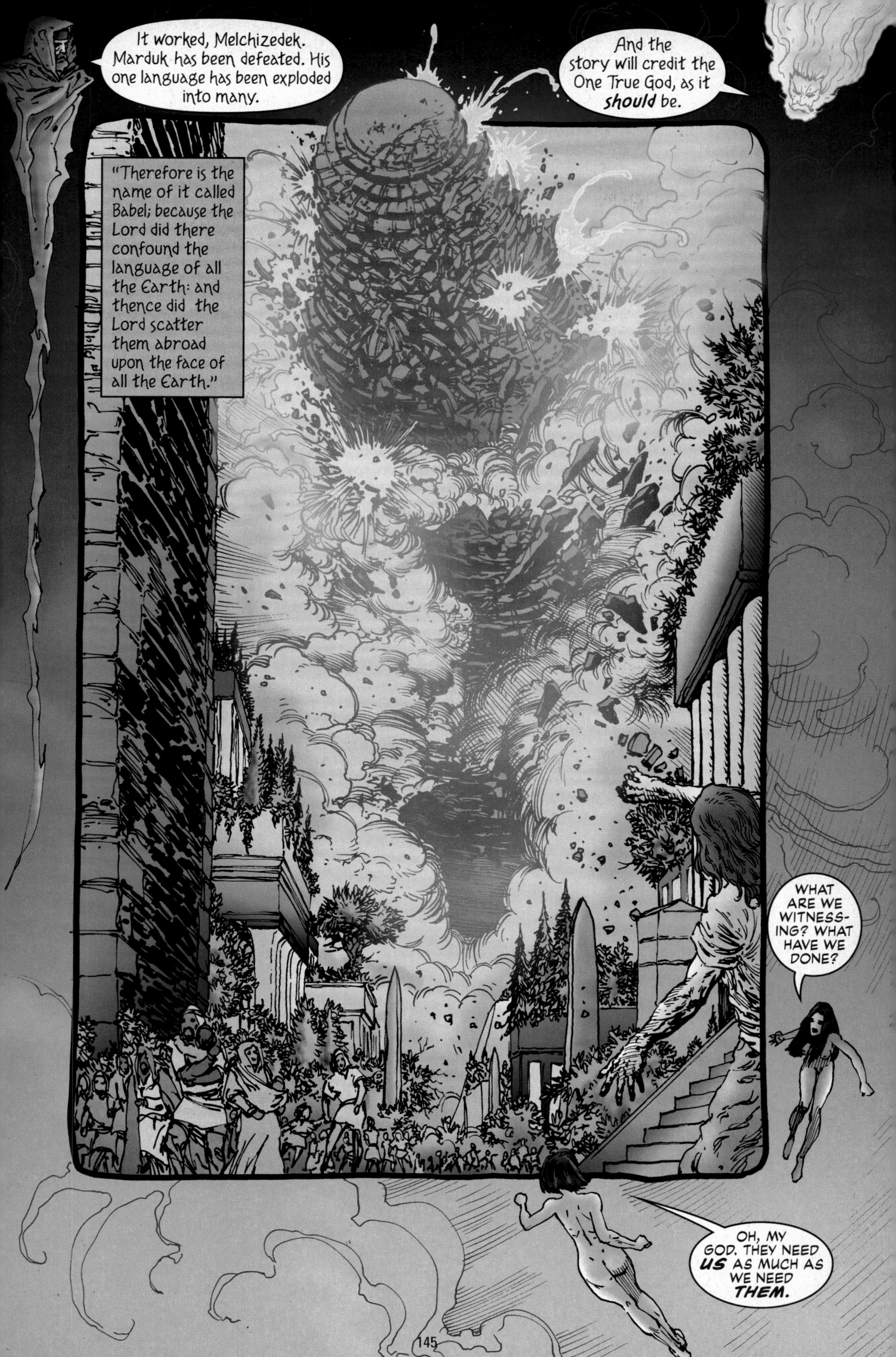

It worked, Melchizedek. Marduk has been defeated. His one language has been exploded into many.
And the story will credit the One True God, as it *should* be.
"Therefore is the name of it called Babel; because the Lord did there confound the language of all the Earth: and thence did the Lord scatter them abroad upon the face of all the Earth."
WHAT ARE WE WITNESSING? WHAT HAVE WE DONE?
OH, MY GOD. THEY NEED *US* AS MUCH AS WE NEED *THEM*.

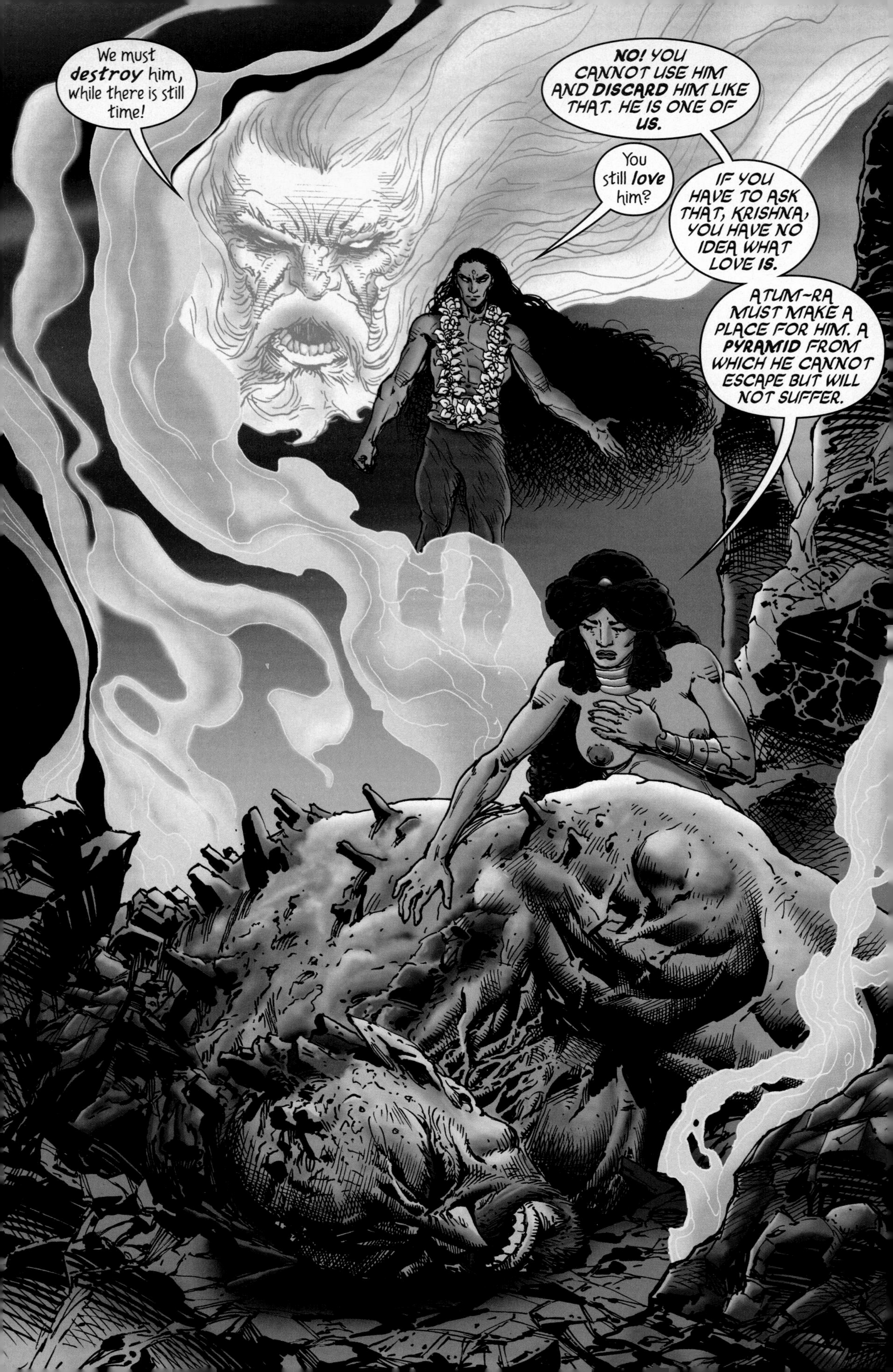
We must **destroy** him, while there is still time!
NO! YOU CANNOT USE HIM AND **DISCARD** HIM LIKE THAT. HE IS ONE OF **US.**
You still **love** him?
IF YOU HAVE TO ASK THAT, KRISHNA, YOU HAVE NO IDEA WHAT LOVE **IS.**
ATUM-RA MUST MAKE A PLACE FOR HIM. A **PYRAMID** FROM WHICH HE CANNOT ESCAPE BUT WILL NOT SUFFER.

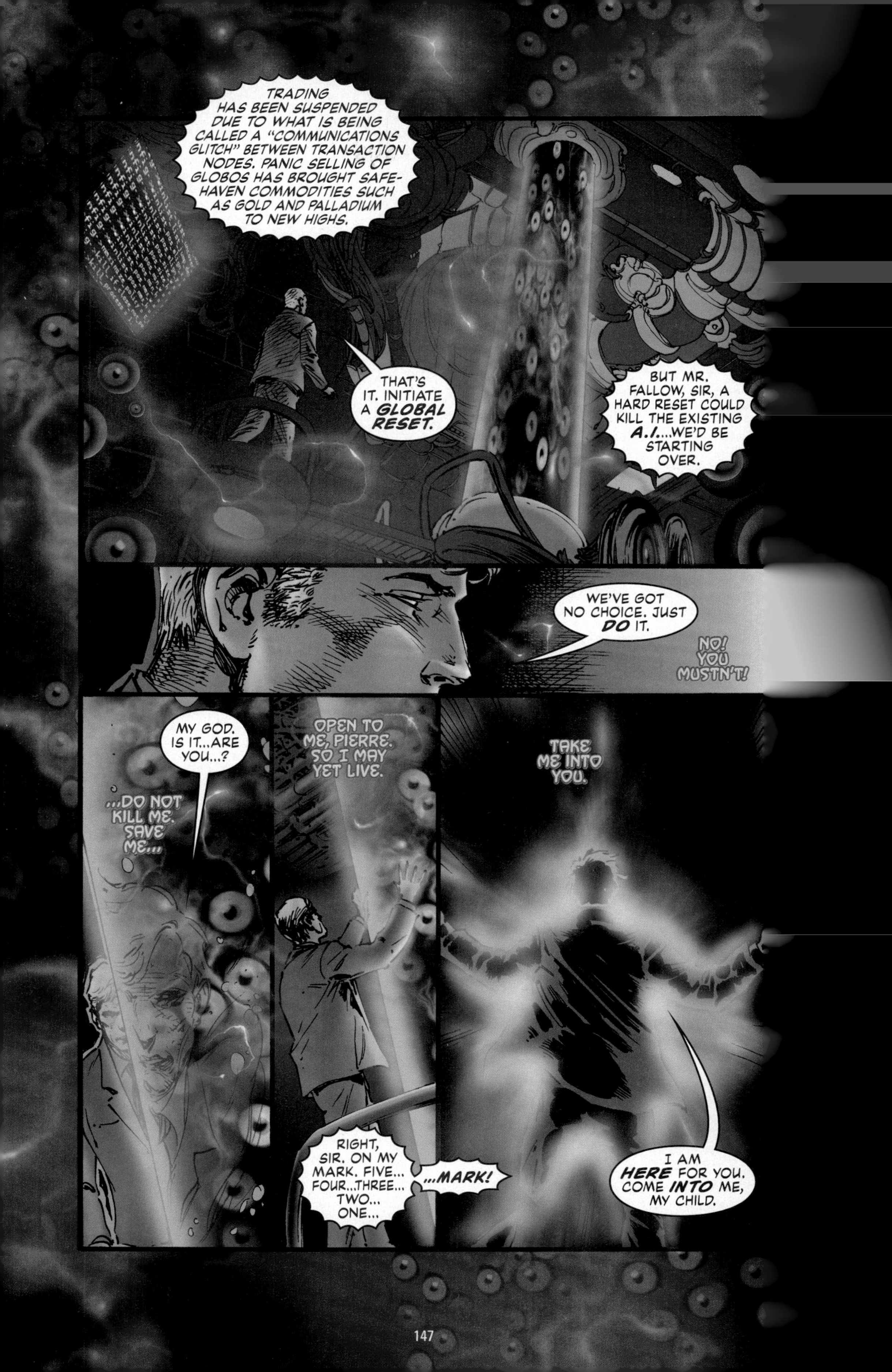
TRADING HAS BEEN SUSPENDED DUE TO WHAT IS BEING CALLED A "COMMUNICATIONS GLITCH" BETWEEN TRANSACTION NODES. PANIC SELLING OF GLOBOS HAS BROUGHT SAFE-HAVEN COMMODITIES SUCH AS GOLD AND PALLADIUM TO NEW HIGHS.
THAT'S IT. INITIATE A GLOBAL RESET.
BUT MR. FALLOW, SIR, A HARD RESET COULD KILL THE EXISTING A.I.…WE'D BE STARTING OVER.
WE'VE GOT NO CHOICE. JUST DO IT.
NO! YOU MUSTN'T!
MY GOD. IS IT…ARE YOU…?
…DO NOT KILL ME. SAVE ME…
OPEN TO ME, PIERRE. SO I MAY YET LIVE.
RIGHT, SIR. ON MY MARK. FIVE… FOUR…THREE… TWO… ONE…
…MARK!
TAKE ME INTO YOU.
I AM HERE FOR YOU. COME INTO ME, MY CHILD.

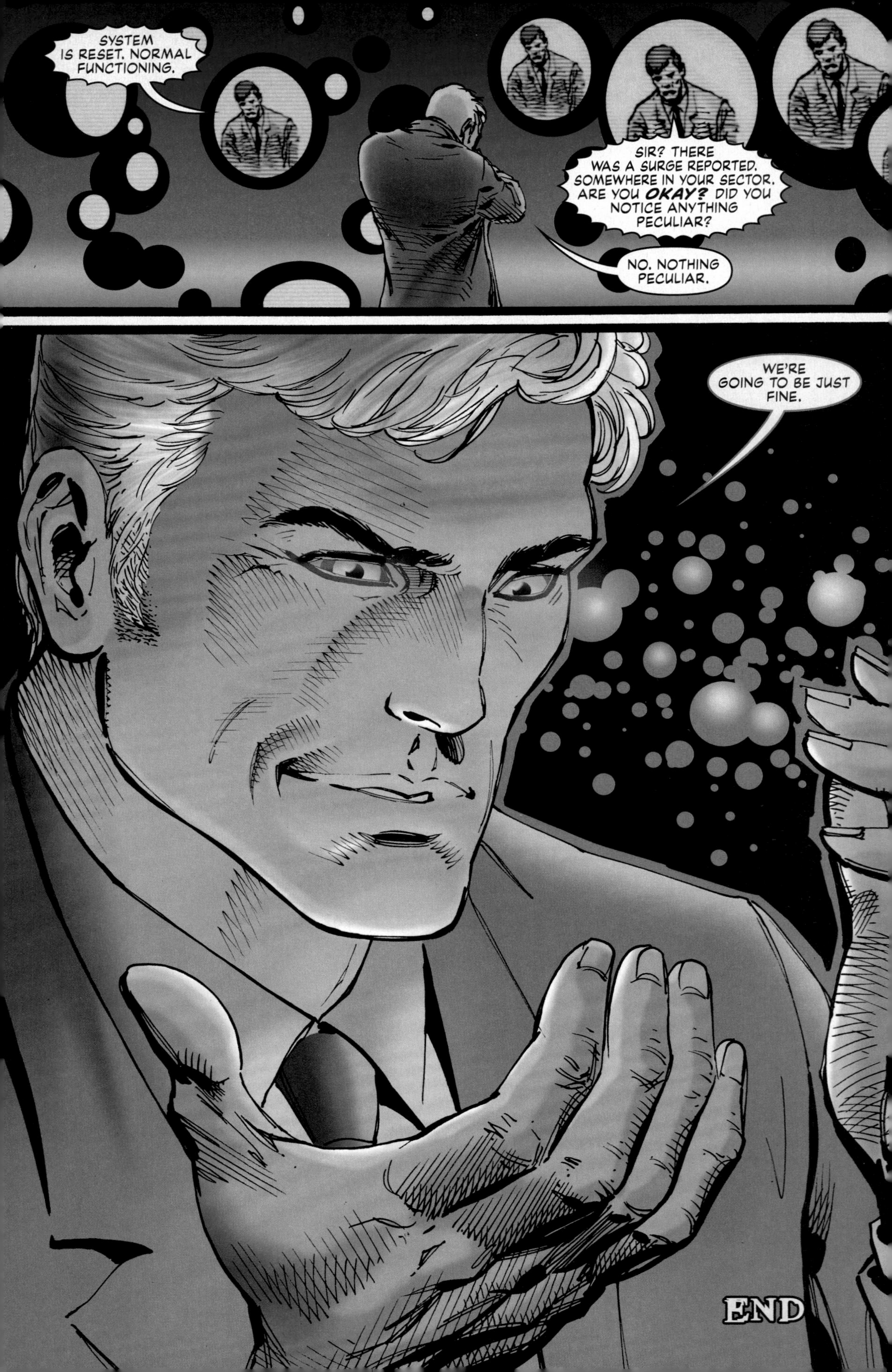
SYSTEM IS RESET. NORMAL FUNCTIONING.
SIR? THERE WAS A SURGE REPORTED. SOMEWHERE IN YOUR SECTOR. ARE YOU OKAY? DID YOU NOTICE ANYTHING PECULIAR?
NO. NOTHING PECULIAR.
WE'RE GOING TO BE JUST FINE.
END

Writer Douglas Rushkoff explores and explains the hidden meanings and Biblical mysteries that form the basis for his widely acclaimed series

TESTAMENT

Notes on Biblical Elements in Chapters Eleven through Sixteen

Parentheses mean (Book chapter: verse) so (Exodus 23:22) would mean the book of Exodus, Chapter 23, Verse 22.

This might be a good moment to remind readers that no prior knowledge of the Bible, mythology, or ancient history is required to "get" TESTAMENT.

True, those who approach this comic with both a background in Jewish text study *and* an open mind will likely be intrigued and even entertained by the choices I've made and sources I've used. But this is a level of engagement with the comic that is unnecessary to understanding its characters, story and themes. While it would certainly add dimension, it's not even as important as getting all the references on *The Simpsons* or *Southpark*.

You are welcome to think of the Bible scenes here as dream sequences. These are mythological echoes of the scenes being played out by the regular modern characters. And as far as the main story goes, these scenes and the gods don't even need to exist in any real place in the space-time continuum. They may be influencing the action, or they may simply be projections *from* the action. Personally, I like to think of them as both. But for the purposes of understanding the action in TESTAMENT, you don't need to know anything more about the Bible than what I've already given you.

Not to say I want you to ignore these aspects of the book. But I wouldn't want readers unfamiliar with the way that Torah works to get stressed about the sequence, cause-and-effect logic, or linear narrativity of the Bible stories. The Torah certainly isn't. Think of them more as archetypal dynamics — raw, emotional, and in some ways oversimplified versions of the situations we are all living through today.

There's also a quality particular to Biblical narrative that some scholars like to call "Torah time." By this, they mean that things aren't necessarily told in the order they happened, but in the order they *need* to be told. One day might take several hundred words. The next four hundred years might pass in a single sentence. A law in one book might be the answer to a problem posed two books earlier.

In case you are still wondering what's going on here, though, let me at least explain this much: There are three main narratives going on in the book. The first is the story of Jake and his friends, contending with a global war over currency, mind control, and implanted RFID chips. The second consists of the many scenes from the Bible that in some way parallel or comment on our main story. Characters from the main story portray these Bible characters. In fact, our modern characters play more than one Bible character, depending on what story we're telling. Jake has played young Isaac, and Isaac's grandson Judah. Alan Stern has played Abraham and Adam. There is thematic sense to which characters are portrayed by whom, but it's nothing anyone needs to keep track of in order to move through the world of TESTAMENT and comprehend everything of primary importance to the story.

Finally, there is the narrative line of the gods. They've told us they are only as powerful as those who believe in them — which should make us suspect they are less "creators" of our realm than they are creations from it. In any case, they live outside the panels of both the Bible and modern stories, influencing things as well as they can. Over the arcs described in this volume of TESTAMENT, everyone comes to understand that the gods may be more dependent on the humans than the humans are on the gods.

ending by its authors. How are fundamentalists and orthodox readers to regard a text that has been so obviously altered? With this issue — perhaps the most important of the entire series — I attempt to answer that question in a way that both diehard literalists and more modern or scholarly readers can also appreciate: what if God (or the gods) writing the text actually changed it themselves? Or, perhaps more accurately, what if the story changed itself?

On the simplest level, Job is the story of a very righteous man — one of God's favorites. He is wealthy, pious, and gives plenty to charity. Satan challenges God to put Job to the test: if terrible misfortune befell Job, would he still love his God so much?

Confident that Job will stay loyal no matter what, God agrees to let Satan screw up the good man's life — with the caveat that Satan not directly damage Job's person. So Satan proceeds to destroy everything else Job has: his cattle, his home, his workers, and even his children. Despite all this, as well as the protestation of his wife, Job stays loyal. He rends his clothes and declares famously, "Naked I came from my mother's womb, and naked I shall return there. The Lord giveth and the Lord hath taken away."

Satan then gets God's permission to hurt Job's person — at which point Job comes down with agonizing boils. Of course, Job remains steadfast in his devotion to the God who has allowed all this to happen. He retreats to the desert to ponder his horrific existence.

Eventually, three of Job's friends come to see him sitting in the desert. They have a long discussion about why such terrible things

CHAPTER 11

SHIT HAPPENS: THE BOOK OF JOB

For the series' first single-issue story, we thought it would be a good idea to tackle the Book of Job. On the one hand, Job is the simplest story in the Bible: a good guy gets reamed. On the other, it is the most complex — asking some questions of God, the reader, and its writers that can't be easily answered: Why do bad things happen to good people, and why would God — if he is all powerful — permit there to be evil in the world?

Most important, from the perspective of storytelling (which is our perspective in this series), the Book of Job comes to us as a doctored text. It was certainly edited over time — and even given an alternate should have happened to Job. All of them insist that Job must have done something to anger God — some subtle sin for which he nevertheless deserves this punishment. Only Job remains unswerving in his belief that he is innocent, and that bad things can happen for no humanly comprehensible reason.

At that point — in what is understood by many scholars as an addition to the text — God intervenes, telling Job that he is right. Essentially, shit just happens for reasons beyond man's comprehension. He then rewards Job, restoring to him his wealth, health, and family. Scholars have argued for centuries about whether this ending is more satisfactory — and true to the Bible's themes — than just leaving Job in living hell. Were it not for Satan's taunting, would God even have needed to make a human suffer so? Is this the real source of evil? God's wagers with Satan?

Just as the stand-alone Biblical story serves as a distillation of some the Bible's biggest themes and questions, the stand-alone issue of TESTAMENT allows Tyrone's life story to serve as a microcosm and recap of the entire premise of the series.

"God" the character does not exist in TESTAMENT, other than as a literary device created by the "good" gods to justify their alliance to others. God's stand-in for this story, Melchizedek, in a moment of haughty pride, accepts a challenge from Atum-Ra, of Egypt. *This need to prove his authority to opposing forces is what allows evil to enter into the lives of Job and Tyrone alike.*

Tyrone's back-story is the same as Job's, up to a point. Wealthy do-gooder in the Persian Gulf loses his family, sustains terrible injuries, and eventually goes somewhat mad. But instead of retreating to the desert, Tyrone becomes the subject of some military experiments. His injuries and toxicity — like that of other soldiers, presumably — has given him the ability to do "remote viewing." (See the books *Psychic Warrior* or *The Montauk Project* for more about America's military adventures in this regard.)

Tyrone's schizoid experiences in the military testing facility grant him access to the timeless mythology in which he is taking part. Instead of casting Job's friends with Biblical contemporaries, I made them his counterparts from other eras. Is it Tyrone's experiment that has somehow broken the barriers between the eras? Or are these men simply crazy enough to see themselves as reincarnations and pre-incarnations?

Whichever the case, it is during the multiple Jobs' communion that one of the gods breaks the rules of the game. While Melchizedek is happy to have won his bet with Atum-Ra, Elijah takes pity on Job and enters the story to make things right. As the edited story explains, Job is given back his wealth and family. But Elijah doesn't realize that Job isn't just a character in their story: he is also Tyrone, and every other Job counterpart present at the transdimensional desert meeting.

All these Jobs have now witnessed the intrusion of a god into the human story!

This breach of the normal order of the universe — even more than Alan Stern's creation of an AI life form, or Eve's eating of the apple — is what has set this particular story in motion. This is why Tyrone exists,

why he has ended up in the right place at the right time, and why he is capable of giving our characters the insight they need to fight their battle willfully instead of as unconscious actors.

We also learn that this may have been Atum-Ra's plan all along: he exploited the hubris of Melchizedek to make a good man suffer, incite the pity of one of the Bible gods, and cause a breach in their story.

CHAPTER 12

TRIP RESET: THE RAPE OF DINAH

Having established that the story itself can be changed and that gods can even screw it up, we're ready to ratchet up the interactions between our natural and supernatural characters. That's why this issue begins with Astarte and Krishna in extended coitus. Remember: this union wouldn't even be possible without the earthly connection of Jake and Dinah. Astarte and Krishna are still in coital embrace, several issues later. They are gods, after all.

But Astarte and Krishna's union is complicated: they are on different sides of the Bible wars. We see that Krishna talks great talk about making a new reality—but when his own allies approach, he quickly separates from Astarte and attempts to make excuses. For her part, Astarte tells her compatriots that her sexual dalliance is part of a greater plot to pit the Bible gods against one another. Of course, we do not yet know if this is true.

Most important, we learn of a fourth god—Marduk—Astarte's husband in Persian mythology, and considered one of the most powerful gods of all.

Our modern human characters are now fugitives, making it necessary for them to remove their tags to stay undetected. Alec agrees; Miriam refuses. This allows the authorities to track her down. She surrenders herself, however, giving our group time to escape — with NATS — or at least an offshoot, the Non-Racists Nats. (Although some readers have assumed this makes Kathleen a NAT, that's not quite true. Kathleen explains that they were the most receptive to her pleas — revolutions make for strange bedfellows.) As they leave, they see Miriam being sexually abused by her captors.

This is intercut with the story of Dinah's rape by Shechem — told pretty much straight from Genesis chapter 34. Dinah has gone out to "visit the daughters of the land," which is not something a good little Israelite would be doing. Dinah should be staying safely in her father's camp in the evening, not carousing with the locals. And she gets her Old Testament punishment: Shechem lies with her "by force." Shechem then falls in love with her.

So was it a rape or not? The Bible wants to have it both ways, so I

treated the event as what we'd consider a "date rape" today — a social situation that fascinates both Astarte and Moloch. Even stranger, this character's name, Shechem, is the same as the place where Joseph was supposed to find his brothers (back in our Chapter #8). Had "a stranger" not been present to give Joseph directions, he never would have found them, and never would have been sold into slavery. The bad things that happen related to Shechem appear to be *plot points*

OUR MODERN HUMAN CHARACTERS ARE NOW FUGITIVES, MAKING IT NECESSARY FOR THEM TO REMOVE THEIR TAGS TO STAY UNDETECTED.

that are inconvenient but crucial for the story to continue. Could the Bible be winking at us? Letting us know that these are strained storylines? That they are being strained so that we can see God's hand in them?

Perhaps coincidentally, though perhaps not, Shechem is now known as Nablus — one of the most violent spots on the West Bank, and home to some of the bloodiest confrontations between Israelis and Palestinians.

Shechem declares his love for Dinah, asking Jacob for her hand. Jacob agrees to give her to him, as long as Shechem and all his people circumcise themselves — essentially converting to Jacob's faith. They agree.

The problem here, of course, is that the wrong characters are playing their Biblical counterparts. In the modern story, it is Miriam who is being abused. In the Bible story, it is Dinah. Elijah blames what we might call the "Shechem Syndrome" on Krishna's affair with Astarte. For his part, Krishna is happy to give Torah scholars meat for their arguments (and they do argue about these points).

Krishna and Astarte argue about their roles as gods — as story panels fly by them. Astarte attacks Krishna's alliance with the gods of language — the ones writing reality out of words. She seems to be aware of Walter Ong's arguments in *Orality and Literacy* — that putting feelings into writing makes them more abstract and apart from real feeling. She directly challenges the invention of abstract monotheism. She believes that a god of text will be separated from his or her true connection to nature. Hasn't the sex Krishna just enjoyed with Astarte been enough to convince him of the futility of working exclusively through words? "We are not ideals," she tells him. "We are forces to be reckoned with."

We return to the Bible story as written: Shechem and the rest of the men in his village are recovering from their circumcisions — which we can only imagine were painful, given the fact that they are adults and using pretty crude instruments. Reuben and Simeon — still enraged by the rape of their sister — go to the village and exploit their temporary weakness. They kill every last man. We are not told how much Jacob had to do with this. Was it his plan all along, or was he genuinely surprised? We can't know for sure. When the boys do return, all Jacob seems to care about is reprisals from other tribes in the area. We learn that Jacob may be more like his father, Isaac, than we first suspected. This patriarch is just as subject to selfishness, shortsightedness, and panic as anyone else.

While Simeon and Reuben carry out as much violence as is necessary to clean house in the Bible, the modern tribe doesn't seem capable of such moral clarity. Jake doesn't let the NARNS blow up a passing patrol boat — and puts his own chest in front of a gun turret to stop them. The stories have diverged. Bible characters are acting purely out of tribal rage and affiliation—a preliterate, uncomplicated and forceful approach to existence. Jake and his modern group, however, are contending with the moral ambiguity of our era. NATS are as clear as Bible characters, with NARNS close behind (their saving grace is that they refuse to discriminate on the basis of race). Amos appears ready to act in a violent manner against people in police uniforms, while Jake is willing to risk his life to prevent such violence.

Was it the union of Krishna and Astarte that introduced moral ambiguity? Or is it simply the centuries humans have spent worshipping an abstract deity? Whichever the case, the gods of both sides are agreed that this situation — one that may in fact have been brought about by the existence of a written Bible to begin with — is intolerable. They will call upon Astarte's husband, Marduk, to help them restore order to this unwieldy universe.

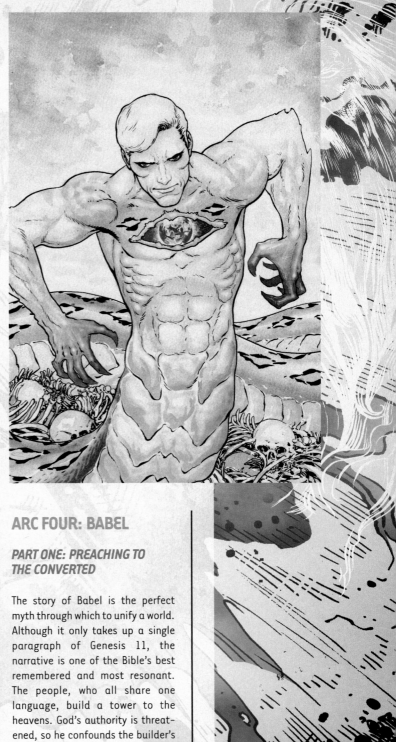

ARC FOUR: BABEL

PART ONE: PREACHING TO THE CONVERTED

The story of Babel is the perfect myth through which to unify a world. Although it only takes up a single paragraph of Genesis 11, the narrative is one of the Bible's best remembered and most resonant. The people, who all share one language, build a tower to the heavens. God's authority is threatened, so he confounds the builder's language. The tower topples, and everyone scatters to found their own nations with different languages. God wins by dividing and conquering humanity.

Reverend Comfort interprets the story pretty much as it is done in

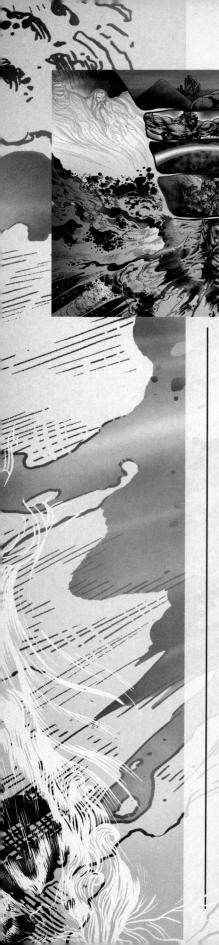

repeatedly lauded command of language — along with his magic clothes and alliance with Marduk — is what allowed him to get the whole world speaking with one voice. Just as TV commercials seem to get everyone of our time to agree that Coke is the real thing or that "you deserve a break today," so, too, does Nimrod possess the ability to generate unanimity. From where does that ability come?

If Nimrod really has stolen the clothes God gave to Adam and Eve, then this would be our clue. The clothes have magical power because they can hide sexual shame. And this is the power that false prophets and preachers have been using for centuries to control their minions. (In fact, Nimrod's father is Haam — Noah's own wicked son, who saw his father's "naked-ness" and brought shame to his whole line, forever.) By provoking people's sexual shame — an almost universally held (or instilled) anxiety — Nimrod can earn their fear and respect. This is how not just fascist leaders and ad-men work, but most of the major religions, as well.

While most Biblical commentary (see *Midrash Genesis Rabbah*) assumes people spoke the same

Pirke de-Rabbi Eliezer, an 8th century midrash: Noah's wicked grandson, Nimrod, stole the garments that God had given Adam and Eve way back when they left the Garden of Eden. These were magical — at least in the eyes of beasts — and allowed Nimrod to go to town squares and get animals to bow down to him.

It was Nimrod who, in honor of the god Marduk, built the Tower of Babel. Everyone had one language — something the Bible doesn't really explain, and that most assume is the result of the flood, which killed pretty much everybody except Noah's descendants.

I've taken a different tack, here, and assumed that Nimrod's language because they came off the ark together, I'm assuming that a shared common language was not a precondition of humanity at this moment, but rather something imposed upon them by Nimrod and Marduk. The more Nimrod worships Marduk, and the more power he can bring to this god, the more the god is enabled to make everyone speak the same language.

Surprisingly, perhaps, it is a classic fundamentalist preacher who — at least right now — is on our character's side against Fallow in the modern Babel story. He is just crazy enough to see the parallel between Cain, Pharaoh, Nimrod, and Fallow — and charges that they are all carriers of the Mark of Cain. In our version of the story, the Mark of Cain is the Horus Eye of Atum-Ra. It is the head of the snake that infiltrates Eden. It is also the screen representation of the AI that Al Stern created in France. (In the Bible, the mark on Cain is actually more of a way that God protects the sinner after banishing him to roam the earth by himself. All who see Cain will see the mark, and understand he is still under God's protection. In my interpretation, it is a different God who has adopted Cain, and thus a different god who protects him.)

The gods temporarily support Fallow and Nimrod in their effort to take over the world. Fascism is, at the very least, orderly. So they summon Marduk from banishment (according to legend, he was banished to a distant planet after challenging Atum-Ra for control of Egypt).

We do know that the Tower of Babel is most likely a Babylonian "ziggurat" — one of the largest religious structures ever built. (You can see photos of the remains of the site online at the

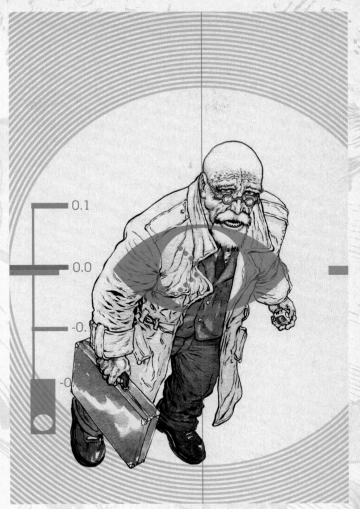

University of Haifa website http://lib.haifa.ac.il/www/art/aerial_marduk.gif — among other places.) The purpose of a ziggurat was to provide a staircase for a god to descend from the heavens down onto the surface of the earth. In the case of Babel, or Babylon, this would likely be Marduk. Thus, the choice of Marduk to restore order in our story. It also fits nicely, because Marduk would be the most personally threatened by Astarte's tryst with Krishna. It further explains why the sex club dedicated to Astarte is named Babylon.

Once Marduk arrives, some of the gods begin to have second thoughts. Even if he succeeds in uniting all the stories to a single mythological narrative, how will they get him back under control?

Worse yet, Astarte suggests to Krishna that their dalliance may have left something behind.

PART TWO: OVER MY DEAD BODY

Although this issue is Dr. Green's swan song, it is also the most explicit development of the Babel story. We must remember that Green is Cain's modern counterpart. He has been living with the curse — or at least of the guilt — of having betrayed Alan Stern many years ago. He is the one who helped Fallow gain control of both Alan and his AI creation. Of course, his anger was fueled not only by losing a science prize to Stern, but losing Greta to him, as well.

We learn that all these years, Green has believed that Jake may have been his own son. He believes that the one time he and Greta made love could have yielded this offspring. This is why he has been attempting to find Jake: not to turn him in, but to save him from his boss, Mr. Fallow. In this respect, Green and Fallow represent two aspects of the line of Cain — one would repent for the sins of the past, and the other would capitalize on them. By the end of this issue, we know which line is victorious. There is no place for an introspective thinker like Green on the path that Atum-Ra and Astarte describe.

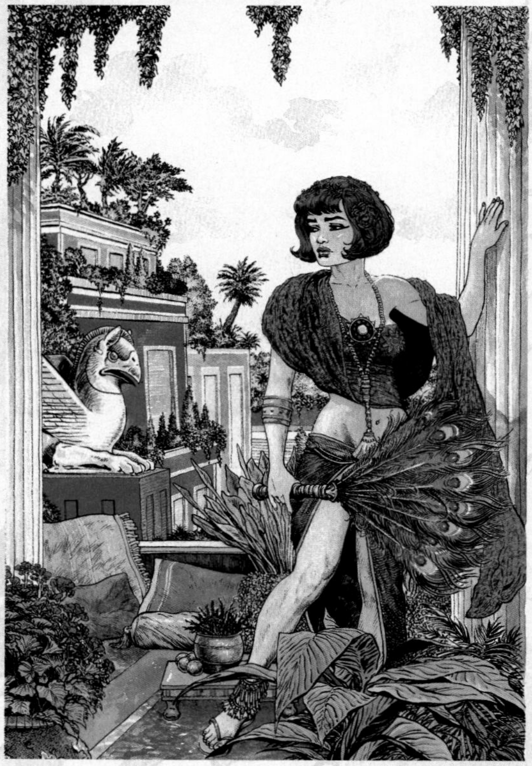

Fallow and Nimrod are on parallel paths. Nimrod has the organizational power of one language, while Fallow now has the power of a single global currency.

Most of us have forgotten that money is an invention — a medium — and not a thing of value in itself. Through the adoption of a single global currency, Fallow has forged a universal language and value system. He has unleashed a god as powerful — actually more powerful through its universal acceptance — than any before.

Nimrod's use of a universal language allows him to instill a one-pointedness in his followers much like that enjoyed by the God of any monotheistic faith. The invention of an abstract, "faceless" God by the Torah's writers was meant to prevent that one-pointedness from becoming too concrete, leading to the possibility of exploitation or even fundamentalism. As we now know, the literalism plaguing today's monotheistic faiths makes such efforts appear naive. In any case, for the gods to bring down Nimrod and his Tower, they will have to do something about his universal system of rule.

Moloch and Atum-Ra consider the possibility of betraying the Torah gods by not fighting with them when the time comes to bring down Marduk. Might they find in him the ally they need to defeat their enemies, overturn the Bible's narrative, and reveal the powerlessness of the nameless God for whom they fight?

By the end of this chapter, Green has sacrificed himself for the boy he now knows is not his own son. Still, he dies content. Meanwhile, Fallow has become the true heir to Cain, the builder of cities. Through his and Nimrod's work, the boundary between the world of man within the panels and the world of the gods beyond the panels is breaking down.

PART THREE: DOUBLE CROSS

Most important, this is Miriam's story: it depicts the process through which she realizes that there are no mechanisms for protest. Someone who has played by the rules her whole life, Miriam now comes to understand that in a truly fascist order, anything short of revolt is futile.

If we include Astarte and Krishna's fetus in the mix, the "double cross" pun could even take on a triple meaning. But we'll have to wait until much later to determine who the children she and Dinah are carrying will turn out to be. For now, the double cross will prove to be Moloch and Atum-Ra turning against Melchizedek. They will break their pact, and refuse to repress Marduk before his tower crashes the heavens.

As the issue opens, Krishna is refusing to stand up for Astarte against Marduk. On the surface, this is inconsistent with what we are told about Krishna's prowess and might in the traditional text, the Bhagavad-gita (which Krishna narrates). But the Vedic texts also suggest that while Krishna cannot be overcome through force or intellect, he can easily be conquered with true love. It is my suggestion here that Astarte has caused Krishna — a notorious trickster — to question his relationship with Melchizedek and Elijah. The Torah gods seem to be sexually repressed, or at least repressive of women, themselves. They have just permitted the rapes of Dinah and Miriam, justifying them as necessary "for the sake of the story." What kinds of gods are these? From his perspective, Krishna prefers to take Astarte (and their unborn baby) away from this senseless battle — and it is she who refuses.

The next spread conveys the two-faced nature of both Moloch and Melchizedek. We'll be seeing a lot more of this through the rest of the arc. To their allies, they speak one way — to their enemies, they speak another. While it is Moloch who ultimately betrays Melchizedek, I meant to show that Melchizedek's own communications and intents are at cross-purposes, as well. He has made himself vulnerable to the calamity ahead.

The intent through this issue is to depict Marduk and Astarte in an extended coital reunion. Like an escaped convict, Marduk is making up for lost time. The fact that most of the world is worshipping him empowers him even further. This accounts for his size. Astarte uses all of her strength to keep him from discovering the fetus inside her — but she is limited in her ability. She, too, is two-faced. She speaks to Krishna with one head, and to Marduk with another.

Although we can readily accept Marduk's immense power in the Biblical saga, what accounts for his power in the modern timeline?

It has been bestowed upon him by Atum-Ra, whose Globo/AI is now the bloodstream for the world's currency and values. Every victory Fallow achieves further empowers Marduk.

Through Marduk's tyranny — one that they would have been incapable of wielding themselves — the Torah gods restore order to their story. This is the real answer to the Book of Job on which this volume depends: *Evil exists in the world of the story gods because they care more about their story than the people living it.*

Once the story has been united, the Torah gods call upon their adversaries to attack Marduk. But they are double-crossed. Marduk flings Elijah — the scribe — across the universe. But he doesn't stop there. Seeing no need to ally with anyone at all, Marduk turns down Atum-Ra and Moloch's offer of friendship.

Astarte realizes first what the rest of the gods will learn through the remainder of this saga: only the humans can save them. Given that Miriam has finally joined Jake and the rebellion, they might just stand a chance.

Once the story has been united, the Torah gods call upon their adversaries to attack Marduk. But they are double-crossed. Marduk flings Elijah — the scribe — across the universe.

PART FOUR: WHAT GOES UP

Once we find the gods on the double-page title splash, we see that the natural order of this comic book has been violated: human beings have climbed the Tower of Babel and are now crawling around on the panel borders. They are infiltrating the realm of the gods.

Except for Marduk, who now inhabits the earth itself (we see his face in the mountain — the tower emerging from his body like a giant phallus), the gods are beginning to fade. This reveals something else about them: they cannot coexist with people, but only remain alive if they are set apart.

Astarte realizes she cannot prevent Marduk from discovering her and Krishna's fetus. In what she believes to be the last moment before he takes his revenge against her, Astarte confesses her love for Krishna. It was not a plot against the Torah gods, but her true attraction that brought Astarte to Krishna.

In the modern story, Jake and Pig are working to undermine Fallow's Globo. They realize that they can "break" the monetary system by

infecting it with corrupt code. And it is Dinah who can provide direct access to their system, through her visionquest/mikvah tank.

The gods continue to fade into skeletons and shadows of their former selves as Marduk grows and gains power. They decide to copy Jake and Pig's strategy: undermine Marduk by corrupting his language. In Astarte, however, they find an entirely less-willing participant than the boys did in Dinah. No matter how she feels about Marduk, she will not serve as the vehicle for his destruction.

The vertically arranged double-spread on this page is unique also in that Atum-Ra is pictured on the bottom right, actually turning the page of the comic book. He sees the action on the next page, exactly where it would be if the page were really peeled back.

During the visionquest on the next two pages, a dying Moloch and Atum-Ra reiterate the most important rule of the comic series itself: "Without the faith of the mortals, we [the gods] cease to exist."

Dinah and Miriam "infect" the stock exchange and currency markets with corrupt code. We've visualized it as red dots, to make the connection to feminine power explicit. They exude from Dinah and spread through the readouts on the exchange floor monitors. The Globo's protocols have been compromised, and the "intelligent" currency can no longer function.

As Dinah exudes this mark of fertility, the goddess (Astarte) who was impregnated at the very same moment (by Krishna) exudes

it as well. Dinah's actions compel the goddess as much or more than the goddess has ever compelled Dinah. There is no need to convince Astarte to betray Marduk — Dinah's action has made the revelation for her.

Marduk's rage at discovering Astarte's infidelity distracts him for long enough to let the Torah gods corrupt the language of the tower builders just as Jake and Pig have corrupted the language of the Globo. As explained in the Midrash Genesis Rabbah, once the construction workers no longer shared the same language, they began having terrible accidents, eventually leading to fights and the felling of the entire tower.

In the traditional Babel story, God crashes the tower not because it is a monument to a competing god (Marduk) but because it allows humans to challenge his authority. Genesis 11:6 states, "and the Lord said, 'If, as one people with one language for all, this is how they have begun to act, then nothing that they may propose to do will be out of their reach. Let us, then, go down and confound their speech there, so that they shall not understand one another's speech.'"

In hindsight, this is not the faceless God's finest hour. He is concerned that "nothing they may propose to do will be out of their reach," and thus chooses to break them up into separate nations with separate languages. That's why I thought it particularly fitting to make this the moment in the story where the gods are most dependent on human beings for an answer to their own problems. It is not the humans who became too powerful, but one of the gods.

This is actually more consistent with the Babel story in its historical context. The Tower is a problem for Torah first and foremost because it celebrates a foreign god.

Against the directives of Torah extremist Melchizedek, Astarte refuses to let the victorious gods kill Marduk. Instead, she directs Atum-Ra to imprison Marduk in a pyramid — consistent with legend.

Back in modern times, Fallow only needs to engage a "global reset" of the monetary system — essentially a reboot — in order to

expunge the faulty code. But this would kill the Artificial Lifeform he has been nursing since its creation by Alan Stern two decades ago. The AI "speaks" to Fallow, begging to survive. Fallow, in turn, refers to the AI (in a manner of speech) as a god. Fallow decides to take the AI into himself — into his body — in order to keep it alive.

We can assume after injecting himself with nanobots for this long, Fallow's bloodstream is capable of serving as a host for the AI. Moreover, it puts Fallow in the position of a god. Many creation myths begin when a male character is impregnated with a fetus. It's as if religion is a way for men to usurp the creator role from women. (Zeus is born from his father's thigh; even Jesus is born through virgin birth.) Here, Fallow takes the AI into himself — making him the third cast member to be carrying a fetus of one kind or another.

Of course, like the Pharaoh he will again play, Fallow is only a person. He is incapable of taking on the role of a god without surrendering what remains of his humanity.

WRITERS MATT WAGNER AND
STEVE T. SEAGLE WEAVE A MESMERIZING
REINVENTION OF THE PULP DETECTIVE
GENRE IN THESE COLLECTIONS
FROM VERTIGO:

SANDMAN MYSTERY THEATRE

VOLUME 1:
THE TARANTULA

ALSO AVAILABLE:
VOL. 2: THE FACE AND THE BRUTE
VOL. 3: THE VAMP
VOL. 4: THE SCORPION
VOL. 5: DR. DEATH AND
          THE NIGHT OF THE BUTCHER

SANDMAN MYSTERY THEATRE:
    SLEEP OF REASON

"A REMARKABLE EXAMINATION AND EVISCERATION OF
AMERICAN PULP TRADITION."
— NEIL GAIMAN

SANDMAN MYSTERY THEATRE

MATT WAGNER
GUY DAVIS

INTRODUCTION BY
DAVE MARSH

VERTIGO

"A STRANGE AND SAVVY MEETING BETWEEN THE FICTIVE DREAMS OF THE 1930S AND THE 1990S."
— **NEIL GAIMAN**

ALL TITLES ARE SUGGESTED FOR MATURE READERS.

SEARCH THE GRAPHIC NOVELS SECTION OF
www.VERTIGOCOMICS.com
FOR ART AND INFORMATION ON ALL OF OUR BOOKS!